Packaging Girlhood

Packaging Girlhood

RESCUING OUR DAUGHTERS
FROM MARKETERS' SCHEMES

Sharon Lamb, Ed.D., and
Lyn Mikel Brown, Ed.D.

ST. MARTIN'S PRESS ✖ NEW YORK

Book design by Gretchen Achilles

www.stmartins.com

Library of Congress Cataloging-in-Publication Data

Lamb, Sharon.
Packaging girlhood : rescuing our daughters from marketers' schemes /
Sharon Lamb and Lyn Mikel Brown.—1st ed.
p.   cm.
ISBN-13: 978-0-312-35250-9
ISBN-10: 0-312-35250-6
1. Children's paraphernalia—Marketing—Social aspects—United States.
2. Girls—United States—Social conditions—21st century.   3. Child
consumers—United States.   I. Brown, Lyn Mikel, 1956–   II. Title.

HD9970.5.C483U655   2006
306.3—dc22

2006002304

FIRST EDITION: August 2006

10 9 8 7 6 5 4 3 2 1

To our students, who inspire and teach us,
and to our families for their love and support

Contents

Preface

We wrote this book not as academics but as women, moms, and teachers living in a world of reality TV, instant messaging, and preteen lingerie. We teach about girls' and women's development in our day jobs, and we've both written books about girls. We are considered experts and are called by journalists when they want a comment about a recent incident involving a girl or a new trend. We didn't take on this project as "experts," though, but as consumers of a culture we share and sometimes don't share with girls—culture as presented in stores such as Victoria's Secret and Hot Topic; kid cartoons such as *Kim Possible* and *SpongeBob SquarePants*; Mean Girl and Princess movies; magazines from *Teen Voices* to *Teen People*; books from Newbery winners to *Gossip Girls*; reality shows such as *America's Next Top Model* and *The Bachelorette*; and all the other things that capture girls' imaginations, time, and energy in the new millennium.

We've been told our world empowers girls by offering them anything they want, including infinite sights and endless ports of call. In reality, it's a world designed by media and marketing executives that targets children as consumers, channels girls' desires, and entices them into predictable types: "pretty pink dolls," "cute little shoppers," and "hott teens."

We did research to find out what girls are listening to, reading, and watching so that we could make sense of girl culture and think about what it means to our daughters and to us as parents and as muses to the next generation of girls. Beyond our own research we drew from the insights of scholars and popular culture gurus who have analyzed such products as magazines and lyrics, as well as from psychologists who have measured the influence of TV on the development of children, and more. What we would like to convey is something less particular and more systemic: a way of looking at the world that is both simple and revolutionary, a habit of seeing. We believe that parents can do what we've done without any particular training: They can analyze what their daughter sees, hears, wears, and reads in terms of how girlhood is packaged and sold to her.

This may sound like a cynical way to view the world, but once you see the insidious patterns and techniques of the media and marketers, you, too, will be suspicious. Just as you now read the nutrition content on the side of a cereal box before buying it for your child, you will be able to read the messages in the shows she watches, the stores she walks into, and the activities she engages in. It is our hope that moms and dads will be able to present the world to their daughters in such a way that she will have *real* choices in the world.

Researchers and educators in the 1970s began some important work when they analyzed how girls were represented in math story problems; they found that girls were less represented than boys and were shown doing traditionally feminine tasks such as cooking and sewing. These researchers and educators published studies which showed that both girls and boys pictured scientists as men in white lab coats; that few storybooks had female protagonists; and that to young children male pronouns are not gender neutral at all. They showed us that gender unfairness in school classrooms can be revealed by simply counting who gets called on and what kinds of feedback they receive from teachers. We all benefited from this foundational work that uncovered basic unfairness and its effects on children.

In today's world, where more young women than young men are going to college, where girls have opportunities to do so much more than ever before, the issue is not a simple one of who gets more or less. There are more women now on prime-time TV, but when they are competing in hot tubs for the attention of one man or undergoing radical surgery to compete in a beauty contest, we can see that simply being on TV isn't enough. The problem is one of image. What choices, what ways of being a girl are offered to our girls as they make their way in the world? We must look beyond the numbers at the kinds of girls presented and created as models for all girls. In our so-called girl power world, we can get fooled into thinking there is equity, but it's more complicated than counting up how many girls are on cereal boxes. If you do that counting (we did), you will find many more boys than girls. Depending on the TV season, you may find no leading girls or girl characters on the covers of these boxes. Turn them around, look on the backs, and zero in on the gender of the cartoon characters. You will also see that girls are wearing the bows and barrettes, and boys are wearing the binoculars; that girls are passengers, and boys are drivers; that girls are batting long eyelashes, and boys are batting baseballs.

We encourage parents to look beyond the particulars and start to see the big picture. Examine that cute pink purse attached to the brand-name jeans and see that same little purse and jeans on a popular doll, in a popular movie, in a popular magazine; see it talked about in a popular book series and worn by a popular artist on a popular Web site and on a popular book's cover. You will begin to appreciate the impact of marketing on your daughter. Her "choice" to buy that purse suddenly doesn't seem so free. Parents who look further and see that *all* the new jeans have little pink purses and make the connection to those other messages that encourage young girls to see themselves as "hott," cute little shoppers will appreciate the larger intent of marketers and understand that what first appears as a lot of disconnected items actually amounts to a hard sell and big money for companies—at your daughter's expense. Once your eyes have been opened, you might start looking for patterns and analyzing everything that has gone through the hands of marketers and the media. And once you start doing that, there is no going back. You've lost the mindless innocence that marketers hope you have. You will be harder to fool and a harder sell. Most important, you'll see that every new package a marketer creates is more of the same and hardly new at all. Score one for the parents and one for the daughters, too, because parents can help girls see what they're being sold about themselves.

Our focus is not just on the manipulation, however. There are wonderful books that warn parents about the cheesy and deceitful ways that marketers target our children. We also look at the message they're selling through their practice, a message about normal girlhood packaged in the form of that little pink purse, the sexy performer who wears it, the tight low-rider jeans it is attached to, and the pouty hot boy it is supposed to attract. The little purse connects girlhood with shopping, yes, but mostly it defines a *kind* of girl, whether she's shopping or not.

We are focusing on girls, but parents can apply this method of analyzing popular culture to the world of boys and see the kind of boy who is marketed through WWE (World Wrestling Entertainment), violent video games, and the proliferation of war toys. This marketing of boyhood is as pervasive as the marketing of girlhood, but we believe that the particular identities offered to girls today through this marketing are more problematic because they offer so much less real power in exchange for pseudo-powerful activities.

Parents have to compete with this bright and shiny world before it gobbles up their interesting, feisty daughters and spits them out in pink satin Wonderbras and panties. It's a world of spectacle and sensationalistic stories. Headlines scream: Young girls are having plastic surgery and taking steroids! Oral sex is rampant in middle schools! Sex bracelets! Pro-anorexia Web sites! Girls post sexy pictures on the Internet for money! Most girls don't, won't, and aren't, of course, but the stories keep us all on edge and worried about the possibilities. While any parent can look at these trends and say, "Well, *my* daughter doesn't do that. She's safe," or "I would never allow *my* daughter to do that," and feel safe, this *Fear Factor* world has become the red herring that drives parental concerns, distracting them from realizing their daughters' lives are filled with stereotypes and narrow images. The power of the everyday is more damaging than the occasional sensational story. Look at the TV shows she watches, hear the lyrics she listens to, and go into the stores she frequents. While most girls will never get breast implants, most *will* play with Barbie, see the new cleavage-creating bras at Victoria's Secret (the recent one has been patented), and watch *The Swan* or some other cosmetic surgery makeover show.

Our technique is not to keep girls away from the real world, but to join with them in understanding it, rising above it, detaching from it, and critiquing it. It is hard to do. But trust us: It is much harder to undo the damage of a pre-packaged image of girlhood than to learn this way of seeing.

Introduction

Isn't "girl power" great? Girls are getting so much more attention these days and are free to be whoever they choose. If you believe this, you're not to blame; that's what marketers have been selling you and your daughter ever since the invention of the phrase. We want to show you that the beginning of a genuine movement to give girls more power and more choice got co-opted and turned into a marketing scheme that reinforced age-old stereotypes. These stereotypes are everywhere, from Disney movies to hip-hop lyrics, Nickelodeon cartoons to *Seventeen* magazine.

Marketers, illustrators, authors, songwriters, TV producers, movie scriptwriters, journalists, buyers for mall stores, and more are currently competing with you for the right to teach your little girl what it means to be a girl. To all these people trying to shape your daughter and narrow her vision, girls are not much more than a string of stereotypes: Your littlest girls are "perfect little angels," sometimes with a sassy twist; your elementary school girls are boy-crazy tweens, ready to be sold a version of mini-teendom that eclipses the wonderful years of childhood which truly belong to them; your middle school girls are full-fledged teenagers or at least teenage wannabes eager to conform to that *CosmoGIRL!* lifestyle. Your high school girls are sold an identity story of the sexually free model-diva-rock star that the younger girls are supposed to look up to.

We are two moms and friends and also developmental psychologists. Lyn has a daughter, teaches girls' development to young women at Colby College, and helps to run Hardy Girls Healthy Women in Maine. Sharon has two sons and six nieces, teaches hundreds of young women at Saint Michael's College, and sees girls and teens in her therapy practice in Vermont. We have been studying girls for more than twenty years now and believe there needs to be a different message other than a warped version of "girl power." That message is now corrupt and used too frequently to sell your daughter an *image* of being powerful; this means tons of money spent every day to help girls look powerful and feel powerful by conforming to a stereotyped image of an independent, "hott," boy-obsessed, shopping teenager. Too little money is spent on developing the activities and programs and guidance that girls need to become truly powerful.

We want to take the pressure off girls to conform to this image of the powerful girl and put the power back in the hands of moms and dads who want to learn about their daughters' world and communicate directly with them about the things they wear, watch, hear, read, and play. In *Freaky Friday* fashion, we will help you feel what it's like to be in your daughter's skin. Each chapter will take you through the world of girls ages four to eighteen, a world that changes rapidly from Bratz dolls to sexy lingerie, from Saturday-morning cartoons to nighttime soap, from Raffi to rap videos. We will do more than show you what your daughter is being sold. We will help you to have the important conversations with her that *must* start at an early age.

Our advice is simple: Talk to her about what you see. We will not tell you to turn your TVs off or throw away her Polly Pocket dolls or forbid her to see certain movies or listen to certain rap songs. We cannot shut off the world. The images and stereotypes are everywhere and need to be addressed. Most important, you're the one who needs to address them, to bring them to your daughter's awareness and help her develop a critical sense of the world around her. You can start doing this when she is about four. Sure, from day one her grandparents might be pushing pink as if there were no other colors of the rainbow, but you're the one she most wants to hear from. Although she has sucked up a lot of visual images by three or four, the age when gender identification begins to settle in and gather some permanence, she will be listening more closely to *your* thinking about what it means to be a girl and the kind of choices you'd like her to have as she grows up.

We want to be clear about one thing before you take this journey with us. We're not writing about the inner girl. That discussion has run its course and, frankly, puts too much pressure on girls to conform and be perfect even when authors identify striving to be "good little girls" as one of the problems. Parents know that to "raise strong girls" they can try to get them to play more sports, talk to them about standing up to bullies, and tell them how wonderful girls are. But has all the talk about girls' psychology changed the culture? Watch the Discovery Channel, open an American Girl catalog, or take a walk through Limited Too, and you'll see stereotypes of girls with very limited choices about who they can be alongside continuous pleas for them to shop, primp, chat, and do the things girls are "supposed to do." In fact, be aware that every time the phrase "girl power" is used, it means the power to make choices *while shopping!*

This book isn't about self-esteem. We don't buy into the view that low self-esteem is the biggest problem for girls today. Girls get plenty of self-esteem whenever they can fit themselves into an image that marketers have created, and that's the way they're enticed to seek out confidence. Some have said that marketers create impossible ideals that girls cannot live up to; we think marketers are more clever than that. Even as they present an ideal girl, they make her appealingly vulnerable and offer aspects of her image to every girl with the purchase of an accessory or two for only a few dollars. Marketers know that girls do feel better when they shop, buy the newest lip gloss, and conform to current fashion trends by creating their own little makeovers. If they didn't, the industry would fail.

In the end, it's the market *and* it's the media. Some savvy parents try to counteract the draw of these two forces on their girls but find that they, too, are pulled in by the pink and pretty stuff for the young girl as well as the glamorous "hott" and fun-looking stuff for the middle schoolers. These things *are* pretty and they *are* cute even when we know we're being sold a narrow image of how a girl should dress, think, act, and *be*. But parents must learn to resist pop culture, too. You can resist without saying no, forbidding, and turning off the TV. We want parents to be confident critics of culture so that they can raise daughters who can resist what they are being sold.

We believe that parents can help their daughters read the culture, recognize bids to turn her into a "Stepford girl," and help her defy the marketers who are trying to sell her an identity story that they call "girl power" but that only makes girls feel powerful when they are conforming to the cute, sweet, hot, little shoppers they think girls should be. Parents can see when the world around their daughters is sucking up that lovely youthful energy and luring them to express it in ways that could box in their futures. Parents know that their girls are up for grabs, enticed into the commercial culture through more than advertisements. If parents are better informed, though, and learn how to talk with their daughters—to listen more closely to their views and to express more clearly their own thoughts and feelings—they can compete with the consumerism, the market, and the media.

Your Daughter's World

By the time your child is four years old, she has probably watched tens of thousands of advertisements, most of them designed to appeal to her little heart and mind. Marketers know how to reach young children because they employ developmental psychologists to conduct research on what kids desire and respond to. These psychologists don't care about your child's healthy development; their job is to help companies acquire cradle-to-grave brand loyalty so they can "own" your children. When Susan Linn, author of *Consuming Kids: The Hostile Takeover of Childhood*, went undercover at a marketing-to-kids conference, she didn't hear anyone at any level utter a single concern for kids' needs or discuss the ethics of marketing to children too young to tell the difference between fantasy and reality. Juliet Schor, author of *Born to Buy*, interviewed top executives at companies that sell products to children, only to find them shrugging their shoulders and saying that although they know what they sell isn't good for kids, it's up to parents to say no. Plain and simple, marketers study children to understand what will grab their attention and make it more difficult for parents to point their children in healthier directions. Psychology provides the research on the emotional hooks they use to get them to buy—humor, a visual delight, or a promise of happiness, friendship, competency, or power.

And girls? Well, of course it depends. For little girls it's an emporium of pink and pretty. Old messages about being soft, sweet, and lovely in pink have all but taken over consumer girl world. The sheer volume and uniformity of the pink-and-pretty message ensures that little girls are especially invited into this world. Just as more opportunities have opened up for little girls, they also are being presented with pre-makeup glitter and lip gloss, pre-perfume fragrances, spa treatments for their stuffed animals, room decor for their dolls, accessory-making craft kits, and pretend purses with credit cards. In this way marketers can channel her desires along familiar conventional routes of beauty, romance, homemaking, nurturing, and shopping, all the while telling her how fun, imaginative, powerful, creative, and free she'll be when she buys these products.

Imagine turning on the TV, flipping through a catalog, choosing a birthday card, or shopping in a grocery store and believing that every slogan you hear, every image you see, and every face that smiles back at you is absolutely real, good for you, trustworthy, and true. This is your young daughter's world. It is the world of someone unable to understand the intentions of advertisers and who believes that what she sees and hears is the way things are. Until about age six, children can't fully distinguish reality from fantasy, and children eight and younger lack the ability to appreciate the various tricks that advertisers and marketers use to grab their attention or persuade them. It is critical that parents realize how deliberate and pervasive the messages targeting their children are and how defenseless little ones are to the powerful effect of seeing their favorite TV character on cereal and juice boxes, fruit snacks, shampoos, yogurt, T-shirts, sleepwear, and toys. Children are also encouraged to nag and pester their parents for the products that showcase them. Every day on *Nick Jr.* kids are offered a variety of funny suggestions for politely pestering their parents for a magazine that is itself one big advertisement: "*Nickelodeon Magazine*, please!"

As girls grow older, the messages change in interesting ways. Little girls become "tweens" before you can blink an eye and corporations are delighted with the buying potential of girls as young as seven or eight. Tween—a combination of teen and between—is a marketing concept developed in the eighties to get kids, primarily girls, to continue buying toys. When the top age of toy users dropped from twelve to eight, toy stores started offering diva dolls, makeup, jewelry craft kits, and room decor to encourage girls to identify with issues and products older than they are. The common concern we hear from parents and school counselors—that girls are buying into a culture that has them growing up too fast—is the marketers' dream come true: a crossover market! Marketing publications are filled with gleeful stories about the spending power of this age group; strategies for capturing the tween doll, shoe, music, accessory, and clothing market; how to get girls' attention in new and more spectacular ways; how to own them and channel their desires while not alienating the parents. We can see the results of all this effort in the ways products are marketed to preteens, ingenious strategies that combine innocence and edge: childlike stories with teenage stars and romantic plotlines (for example, all those princess movies of the past few years), slogans like "cute angel" on Victoria's Secret–like undergarments, and dolls in bikinis mixing pretty drinks and lounging in hot tubs.

What's troubling about all this is the way "tween" has made its way smoothly into the psychological lexicon through newspapers, parent magazines, and books, giving us all the false notion that the tween years, like the adolescent years, are something more than pure marketing, something carefully thought through with our children's needs in mind, a discovery by developmental psychologists. The early marketing reference to tweens identified kids between the ages of eight and fifteen, which gives us an idea of just how out of touch with the development of real kids the marketers initially were. A parent of a girl in this age range knows what a ridiculously wide gap this is. What does a third grader have in common with an eighth grader other than being a potential target for the same products? As a psychological category tween falls short; as a marketing strategy it is brilliant.

While products aimed at tween girls promise perfect faces and bodies, friends, and boyfriends, the marketers and manufacturers don't have to confront the negative impact on girls: the confusion about sexuality and romantic relationships, the anxiety about weight and appearance, the struggle with popularity and fitting in. No, they leave that to you.

Another blink and your preteen has become a middle schooler. Parents are generally aware that this is a tough time for kids, a time of transition, a time when they anxiously struggle to fit in and appear normal, and when schools include in the curriculum sex education and drug education along with math, language arts, and social studies. Most parents are stunned at the world their middle school children confront every day thanks to media and marketing, some of it even in their classrooms! Middle schoolers are the "new teens." They are invited into a teen lifestyle, a teen existence actually, that used to be the stuff of high school. But are these sixth, seventh, and eighth graders really the new teens, or are they only so to the marketers who want to broaden their markets? Is the move to middle school such a very big leap, or are there ways for them to grow up a little bit at a time without checking into the Cosmo-Elle hotel?

Your middle school daughter is being sold a version of teen life that has her buying into and just plain buying stuff earlier than ever; she's being sold a way to be a teen *girl*. Middle schoolers are identity seekers, and they've been taught that identity is the same as image. And the image of teen girlhood sold is more limiting than parents could ever imagine. Instead of princesses and fairies, girls are told they can be special in new ways. At a time when daughters could be developing skills, talents, and interests that will serve them well their whole life, they are being enticed into a dream of specialness through pop stardom and sexual objectivity that will derail other opportunities. While fantasies of fame and fortune are typical and harmless at this age, the investment in a lifestyle that imitates and works toward getting attention and power through looking good and attracting boys can be harmful.

Another way of being special is, ironically, by fitting into some category. The teen magazines that middle school girls read, for example, constantly ask them to put themselves in a box. Are you this kind of girl or that kind of girl? Are you a Jessica or an Avril? Are you a girly girl or a tomboy? Are you a glam girl or a nerd? Playing on girls' worst fears that they will be labeled by someone else, magazine articles ask them to label themselves. Some of the categories are appealing, but they offer phony choices. They are phony because most girls are too complex to be categorized and because the choices don't offer alternative identities that show their individuality or interests. There is never a tuba- and soccer-playing girl who doesn't care that much about clothes but who works at the grocery store, babysits, and does well in school. It is hard to visualize that kind of girl. Marketers don't want her for the same reason that parents do: She is complex and not an easy sell.

We are aware that early adolescence is a time when girls begin to openly challenge their parents as well as tune them out, believing that older girls have much more to teach them. It is remarkable that girl power continues to be presented to them without any reference to women of power in their lives. In fact, the power to be like a teenager gets confused with the power to convince your mother that you're mature enough to do what older girls are doing. Girls also pick up on the power a girl can get from being a model, a pop star, or a diva on TV.

Parents can learn to combat this narrow view of the world that TV and movies promote to girls this age, a view that tells girls "separating" and "individuating" means leaving behind the love and support of family. We can respect the individuation process and our daughters' search for an identity via "style" while helping her be a true individual and not, as she would put it, a "poser" in a world of superteen, supermodel, super-"hott" older girls. Research tells us that middle school girls need and want good relationships with their moms and dads. That makes it all the more important for parents to be savvy about the world their daughters are living in. They can then be players in their world, not nerdy tagalongs.

Don't even *think* about tagging along with your teen. But the wonderful thing about talking to your older teenager is that she's really very capable of reading the culture, uncovering hypocrisy, detecting deception, and discovering manipulations—and she loves to do it. Why not do it with her? Showing that she can't be fooled makes her feel smart and savvy. We think teenage girls are ready and eager to do the kind of work we're suggesting in this book—making themselves more aware of the marketing schemes and fighting them heart and soul. Not all teenagers have been raised to resist, and not all want their parents to be the ones to point out that they are being manipulated, fooled, or made to conform. Above all, teens want to believe that every choice they make comes from their unique independent selves. They may very well be doing what they're doing to fit in with their friends, but they *feel* as if they've made decisions as independent actors. The best way to work with teen daughters is to be with them in their world, share observations, and point at the culture and not directly at her fishnets, her music, or her slang.

It's a new world for parents of girls. What used to be sexual innuendo and suggestive is now crass and direct and contains references to a variety of sex acts. There's been a shift in the selling of the teenage image from sweet and sexy to a growing interest in the out-there sexy, porn-influenced version of teen girlhood. We see this in the clothing marketed to them as well as the music they listen to. While their little sisters copy them and try to be like high school girls, high school girls are looking at the images of adult women on TV and in movies, magazines, and music videos; the overwhelming number of these images are supersexy, superhot.

What Happens to the Feisty Girls?

Each of the following chapters follows girls as they grow, and each shows how the media's choices of who and what they should become gets narrowed down to two: You're either for the boys or one of the boys. To be for the boys, you look good for them, you perform sex acts for them, and you support them as friends and girlfriends. To be one of the boys is to be an outspoken hard girl who doesn't take crap from anyone. Remember that feisty girl you knew in kindergarten? The one who was independent and could think for herself? A leader? Well, this image has been co-opted and sold to girls as a male image. The fact that it's a male image is betrayed in the way these power girls put down other girls, show shame about things that are associated with feminine things, and align themselves with boys. While the girls who are for the boys are given status and privilege for their looks and their sexiness, these girls are promised status and privilege by joining with guys to diss girls and all things female.

We don't blame the girls for their choices. These are the current avenues they are offered to self-esteem. That is why people have begun to take a second look at the whole concept of self-esteem. One mother wrote to us: "My daughter loves giving oral sex to boys. It makes her feel good about herself, and it gives her pleasure to do it." We discuss oral sex in Chapter 5; for now, let's just agree that there are ways to obtain self-esteem that are better than the ways the media are suggesting!

And there are alternatives to these two types of girls that your daughter can embrace. One alternative is the *observer*. The observer takes in the culture without wearing it. She learns to critique it and to notice when marketers are trying to hit her where she's vulnerable or anxious. She knows when what she is reading, watching, or hearing is trying to sell her an image that is narrow and incomplete. She may try out a few things, but she quickly learns to pick up on the oversell, the overhyped, and the over-glammed. Another alternative, and quite possibly an evolution from the first, is the *resister*. After many observations your daughter will begin to question and challenge the marketers' and the media's version of what is real. She'll begin to recognize her own reality, the one she has experienced and observed around her. In so doing she will make her reality the truth, not the glammed-up world bombarding her. She will also be more inclined to do something about it—not just for herself but for other girls.

By discussing the things that confront girls in stores, online, in magazines and books, on TV and the radio, at the movies, and so on, we will help you to help your daughter become more aware. We'll also help you identify sources of confusion so you can teach her how to become a resister.

WHAT TO DO ABOUT IT

If you let her find her own way, the media and commercialism will wrap itself around her, convincing her that she is independent and making her own choices, making her *believe* she is free by selling her an *image* of a free girl. (And this image depends on buying certain products.) You probably know already that if you lay down the law and keep saying "no," "bad," and "sexist," she could think you don't understand and rebel. We don't want her to believe that "freedom" is simply doing what you say not to.

Listen to her. She is right that her world is different from the one you grew up in, that it has different images, expectations, and pressures. That's why we surveyed more than six hundred girls to find out what is in their world. Our survey, in collaboration with www.girlzone.com, has reached girls from all walks of life, all over the country, and of varying races and ages. We also held focus groups with girls and talked with them in malls and in stores to ask their opinions. We talked to parents and surveyed school counselors, teachers, and coaches.

Knowledge is power, and knowledgeable parents have the power to influence their daughters. We want to help you read the material world. Most books, TV shows, movies, and lyrics foster the same old stereotypes. We hope to help you recognise the persuasiveness and enormity of their influence.

By showing you patterns, connecting those patterns to research, and labeling the strategies the commercial world uses to compel our daughters to want things that aren't good for them, we offer you openings for real and informed conversations. We show you ways to have discussions with your daughters that engage the culture. When you use the following prin-ciples, you will move into a different relationship with your daughter and help her make choices—good choices, real choices, not media-driven choices.

Principle 1: Do your own work.

Parents need to do their own work before approaching their daughter about a disturbing item such as a T-shirt or TV show. Parents must tune in and recognize their discomfort with the "little hottie" T-shirt, the FCUK clothing ads, the Dirty Girl products, and the slew of pink divas, pink Barbies, pink cheerleaders, and pink princesses. Taking the time to name and understand what is so unhealthy and constraining about the item may make you uncomfortable, but it is necessary before talking to your daugh-ter and opening a pathway for real conversation and influence.

Principle 2: Listen to what your daughter likes and why she likes it.

We teach the importance of seeing things from your daughter's per-spective. Parents need to understand their daughter's investment in what-ever issue is on the table. Girls are a part of the culture and play a role in creating that culture. There are good reasons for why they are pulled in certain directions. Parents who understand the appeal before reacting have an opportunity for genuine connection and conversation with their daughters. This requires active listening, a sense of humor, and an open-ness to fun, beauty, and even satire.

Principle 3: Bring your daughter the world on your terms,
through your broader view.

It is important not to bulldoze her with your views or shut her down; instead, you should bring her the world on your terms instead, as an informed, rational, compassionate adult in her life. She has lyrics, TV, friends, and the mall suggesting how to think, feel, and act. Now you get to be part of the conversation. Many parents of preteens and adolescents give up, but we will help you find a way to be in there, to be real, to be a player in your daughter's world.

This is *reality-based parenting*. We've found studies which point out the recurrent patterns and the marketing strategies that parents can refer to in order to make compelling arguments. Not everything we've found will stay current. Perhaps as you read this, it might be the case that Neopets are passé, Hilary Duff is a has-been, or YM magazine has gone out of business. Even when a product is packaged anew, the messages are the same. In fact, that's a principle of marketing: to keep creating the same old thing packaged differently and with a slightly new twist—Pepsi, Pepsi Light, Pepsi lime, Pepsi vanilla, old Coke, new Coke, red Coke, blue Coke. The conversations we've provided at the end of the book focus on recognizing these patterns and undermining the hold that marketers have on girls. They will be relevant to parents for years to come.

CHAPTER 1

Pretty in Pink: What Girls Wear

Girl or boy?" is almost always the first question people ask when they hear about the birth of a baby. They don't need to ask, however, when they see a newborn in her carriage on the street—the clothes and accessories provide the answer. Typically, a little girl will be dressed in pink and frills, and a boy in blue with a sporty theme. Lots of parents go to great lengths in this first year to distinguish gender for other people. They tie ribbons around bald heads and plant barrettes in bare wisps of hair; they put tough-looking Nikes or patent leather Mary Janes on little feet that don't yet walk. Clearly gender is a parents' issue long before it's a child's concern.

But there's a grace period—a timeout, if you will—between ages one and three when smart moms puts their children in comfy pants or overalls for the tumbling, crawling, and cruising that they do. Clothes and diapers may still be color coded, but styles match the developmental needs of little ones and provide optimal comfort and movement. Who would want to restrict a little girl from learning how to walk by putting her in slippery, too-tight shoes or in a dress that doesn't protect her knees from falls? But funnily enough, once toddlerhood is behind them, developmental needs seem less important and, alas, clothing for girls becomes "fashion." And that's the beginning of a lifelong lesson.

Who is pushing fashion to your preschooler? Little girls are likely to wear what their parents suggest or choose for them. Six- and seven-year-olds, even those with cool older sisters, are still more influenced by parents than are girls in the preteen or tween years. Knowing this, marketers have been much more interested in selling your young daughter toys and sugary cereal than a specific brand of jeans. But that's changing. It used to be that clothing for five-year-olds was different from clothing for ten- or twelve-year-olds. Not anymore. Many brands now market clothing in sizes 4 to 16, which means your little girl can be very much the big girl when it comes to that halter, camisole, or denim mini-skirt. She can go from diapers to the cute little briefs that have replaced thongs. They make them that small.

Dressing for fashion à la Barbie or Lil' Bratz dolls and dressing for physical play are completely different things. So what does that suggest to your daughter when you dress her in the latest fashions, such as low-rise jeans or belly shirts? It suggests that her play clothes no longer work for school as boys' play clothes do, that play is a circumscribed area of her life and no longer her raison d'être. It says school clothes need to impress, to say something about you. This differentiation between clothes and play clothes may be okay for older adolescents and adults (when school sports teams replace the free play of the younger years and exercise is something you buy clothes for and do at set periods of the day), but it is completely wrong for children.

Following a trend that researchers have observed, your daughter may be spending less time at play than girls of earlier decades. This is very unfortunate and unhealthy. Play is the substance, the foundation of childhood. Girls live and breathe active play for a reason. They need to be physical; they need to run and jump and test their limits. According to philosopher Iris Marion Young, this kind of physical testing is intimately connected to how girls grow up to approach and experience the world. She writes that girls need to feel their bodies as "strong, active subjects moving out to meet the world's risks." Physical challenges prepare them for both social and intellectual challenges to come. So those crop tops and tight low-rise jeans do more than discourage movement. They tell your daughter—at an age when she needs to feel big, try new things, and widen her reach—that how she looks is more important than what she can do and more important than racing to the corner or rolling down the grassy hill as fast as she can. She may look cute in the moment as a mini Barbie or a corseted Cinderella, but the hill she forgoes or the race she doesn't run will impact how she interacts with the world for a long time. It is a great loss to the preteen and the teen. What have they exchanged play for? A world of glamour, playing at dressing up, and doing makeovers?

We show how clothing for little girls, preteens, and teens announces the type of girl she can be and then extends this type into everything about her. Some of this dressing up is fun, but as we will say over and over, our problem is primarily with the lack of choice or, rather, the false idea that girls have lots of choices when these types are closing out other options. Parents can help create these options. Offering your daughter a wide-open view of the world and promising her she can be anything has to begin early and extend over time. One of the first way is to offer her all the colors of the rainbow and give her the clothes needed for full movement in play.

Pretty (Sexy) in Pink: Your Perfect Little Angels

P —perfect

O —off the hook

P —princess

S —stylin'

T —too cool for you

A —angel

R —rockin'

(Written on a bikini underwear set for sizes 4 and up)

Walk into J.C. Penney, Wal-Mart, Kmart, Old Navy, or any similar department or clothing store and try to find a regular T-shirt for your daughter. You remember the kind—no clingy, Lycra-enhanced material; no Bratz or Barbie or Disney faces; no rhinestones; no fashion accessories attached; no slogans or funny sayings that announce the particular tribe she identifies with, such as princesses, cuties, shoppers, cat or monkey lovers; no fake pink sports team logos. Just a basic brightly colored cotton T-shirt that she can wear with jeans. It's next to impossible. Once common, they're now specialty items found in expensive children's clothing stores, in sporting goods stores (although there's lots of pink there, too), and in L.L. Bean catalogs. When we asked for them in J.C. Penney, the helpful saleswoman pointed to a section and told us there might be a few left. Sure enough, tucked between racks of glittery fairies, rhinestone-emblazoned "Born to Shop" slogans, and pink "Angels Varsity Track Champs" shirts, we found one lone red T-shirt stylishly fitted in its own plain way. One left? If this is supply and demand, wouldn't it be the other way around?

The commercialization of girlhood hits hard. Sexy clothing for four- and five-year-olds is all the rage, and if you read T-shirt slogans, you know how girlhood is marketed. Your daughter can choose her identity, but the choices are frightfully limited: Professional Drama Queen, Paradise Princess, or Pretty Princess Beauty Queen. (That covers all the options!) There is also Extra Fancy & Delicious/Quality Guaranteed, Spoiled, Princess Soccer Club, 100% Angel, Hollywood Superstar Film Crew, and Cheer Bunny. These shirts are all in sizes 4 to 16. Isn't that an awfully broad age range? There used to be a distinction between little girl and pre-teen. No more.

In our review of clothing for younger girls, we were continuously surprised by the ways little girls are enticed to look older. A few stores sell sizes 4 to 6x, but even these had a much older look. Penney's Total Girl brand touted tight, hip-hugging, flair-legged jeans with little purses attached in red, pink, or a pink-and-black leopard pattern. (Purses for four-year-olds?) The little embroidered hearts, flowers, and butterflies on the legs suggested little girl, but the style said sassy teen. How do five-year-olds play in these pants? What do they put in the purses? Probably marbles, candy, or little plastic animals, unless they've been to Toys "R" Us and bought an Imaginarium Purse Play Set, complete with wallet, credit card, and makeup compact.

Most stores fill the racks with clothing geared to older girls but in little girl sizes. In the fall of 2004, Kmart sported biker chic that seemed racy for even preteens, much less the tiny bodies that would fit into size 4: faux black leather jackets with zippers and leather lacing up the sides; low-rise, flair-legged jeans with leather ties and little pewter hearts (a nod to younger girls perhaps), sleeveless jean jacket shirts, and shirts with sexy pink lace over black. Even Kmart's Tinker Bell nightgown had an edge: Pixie Chick.

When we wondered aloud in a store called Fashion Bug what girls from sizes 4 to 16 would have in common, a cheerfully defensive clerk attempted to explain. Walking to a rack of skirts, she told us there was something for everyone: the older girls would probably go for the low-rise denim miniskirt with chains, while the younger girls would prefer the low-rise gray stretchy miniskirts with the pink ruffle. The same goes for the little sweatshirts. "The girls do the distinguishing themselves," the clerk told us. "A twelve-year-old would not wear the guitar-playing monkey. She'd go for the 'My Favorite Subject Is Social Studies' T-shirt." So why make the monkeys in size 16 and the social studies T-shirts in size 4? Her answer sounded like an answer from a slippery marketer: "So everybody's happy." (And we find it interesting that a salesgirl getting paid $7.50 an hour can step right up and defend the multimillion-dollar corporation.)

Sure, there are also sweet little tops with animals on them for the younger girls, but the older styles are all available, too, so of course the younger girls want them. Procter & Gamble set up a sweepstakes with Limited Too clothing stores to advertise their Secret Sparkle Body Spray deodorant to girls as young as seven. They also placed ads in teen and tween magazines. Dave Knox, assistant brand manager at P&G overseeing the body-spray launch, explained the rationale: "If you don't target the consumer in her formative years, you're not going to be relevant through the rest of her life." The problem was that their warning label said, "Keep out of reach of children." Following an investigation by the Children's Advertising Review Unit (CARU), the children's advertising industry's self-regulatory forum, P&G stopped the sweepstakes and pulled the ads. But the point was made, show the girls the brand and style that older girls are wearing, and let them see it's possible to wear it, too. Not only does this make it hard for parents to say no, but it hooks girls really young on products they don't need and begins their dressing for fashion rather than for practicality—what they might, given their own devices, dress for versus how they should dress for good health and comfort. These older clothing styles show up on the girls in TV shows that kids are watching, they are strategically placed in doll sets, and they are choices in popular computer games. Reality and fantasy may be blended for young kids, but parents shouldn't fall for it. In the real world where child pornography on the Internet is a problem, there is something disturbing about little girls in leather, chains, and lace.

But what are the options? In spite of all the little Mia Hamm and Cheryl Swoopes sports fans, if you walk around the mall you will observe that wherever you find a mention of something sporty, it is balanced by some pink, some glitter, or some other indication of a girliness/fashion diva. Most girls' sports pants are not really for sports; they don't have the durable make, the loose fit, the breathable fabric, or the high waist of real sports pants. They're a fashion statement, a "sport princess" or "sport cutie" announcement. As with that cotton T-shirt, you have to go to high-priced specialty sports shops or buy from more expensive catalog stores such as Lands' End to find real sports pants in a range of colors for girls. Or you can go to the boys department because, of course, sports clothing of all kinds hangs in rack upon rack in the boys' section of any store. Even in those pricey catalogs from stores that seem to take active girls seriously, we find page after page of stereotypes. Girls' clothes are "so soft she won't want to give them up on laundry day," and "Quality never looked so cute." Boys' clothes are touted as "the coolest in class," or "Guy blows out knee in a week? Climber will cure the habit!" Whether it's T-shirts, pants, or sleepwear, according to marketers boys live for action and girls live to look cute.

As much as most stores subtly discourage girl athletes, they train girls to be *shoppers* as soon as they're old enough to voice their preferences. You find T-shirt slogans such as "Love Shoppin' and I'm Never Stoppin'" and "I'd Rather Be Shopping" and an overabundance of accessories available to them, such as those little purses attached to everything from jeans to sweaters to backpacks. "Shopping: the real exercise for girls"—while that's a slogan we've never seen, we think marketers would love it. In this regard, the influence of fashion dolls is everywhere. The wide-eyed, big-headed, sexy "passion for fashion" Bratz dolls or their wannabe look-alikes are on every form of clothing, starting at toddler age. You can fashion-train your little girls with images of purr-fect sleek cats with big doll-like eyes. They adorn sweaters, purses, and shirts, and often are featured holding a shopping bag.

Don't get us wrong: Most girls love this stuff. We know they do. In J.C. Penney we heard two girls about five or six years old begging their mom for "Pretty Princess Beauty Queen" T-shirts. And they know how to beg! They've had training from TV commercial girl models. "Come on, Mom," they plead. "It's on sale. Look, two for one. Pleeeease." But loving it isn't really the point. Girls love double-fudge-frosted brownies, too, but you wouldn't want them eating a steady diet of the stuff. The problem is not the single, silly T but the sheer quantity of products that offer so few options to girls and come with the marketing tentacles that seem to reach out, grab, create, or remake everything into a narrow sexy image. It is a very big problem.

Pink and Girly, Red and Feisty: Are They So Different?

Some girls seem to love everything pink and glittery while other girls want nothing to do with it. Why? There are lots of reasons, including what their parents are drawn to, what their friends like, and what shows and ads they're watching on TV. They may need to be different from an older sister who seems to have claimed a style for herself. But have you noticed that girls seem to choose either pink or anything but pink? This isn't by chance. Marketers are not only offering clothes, they're offering a kind or type of girl. This kind of girl is either really feminine, or she rejects the feminine for more masculine choices.

Feminine for the littlest girls is coded pink. Pink baby dolls line toy shelves, pink clothing dominates girls' departments in stores, pink bedding and room decor grace the pages of catalogs. Pink, usually accessorized with white and pastel colors such as lilac and yellow, symbolizes all that is sugar and spice. It announces sweetness, innocence, and security (in all those pink bedrooms). Wherever there is pink, there are angels, princesses, hearts, and flowers.

Angelina Ballerina is a great example of what pink represents for young girls. Made famous in a series of picture books and now a PBS cartoon and doll sold in American Girl catalogs, Angelina is a little white mouse in a pink tutu adorned with pink roses, pink-ribboned ballet slippers, and a glittery tiara. She is the embodiment of sweet, soft, pretty, and delicate. American Girl sells Angelina with loads of pink clothing (both for the dolls and real girls), accessories, room decor, purses, pajamas, and a sleeping bag. Parents can buy pink Angelina bedding so that little girls can "dream sweet dreams with Angelina!"

The choice for girls who are not into all that pink are the colors associated with boys: blue, red, green, and black. These colors convey action and aggressiveness. So it becomes more than a choice of frills or colors; it is a choice of characteristics, qualities, and labels—those associated with stereotypes of girls (girly, cute, sweet, innocent, soft) and stereotypes of boys (active, sporty, aggressive, strong, bold). Girls understand the difference and how it feels from a very early age.

But is pink the only girl color? Pretty in pink has lately been accompanied in the girls' department with sassy in red. Check out the packaging for toys and crafts with brave and independent girl characters. There's sassy Eloise ("I'm a nuisance in the lobby"), outspoken Madeline ("Bonjour! I'm Madeline. Tiny I may be, I'm a leader naturally"), and ever independent Dora the Explorer. A welcome alternative to pink, red is not coded sweet and soft but bold and assertive; not delicate and pretty but strong and feisty. The red girl is the girl who is not like the other girls, and not like the other girls can develop into not liking what makes those other girls who they are, putting them down for being too girly and weak. The girl wars mentality we see in the media is most often between girly girls and tomboys, between what we fear starts out as the pink girl and the red girl.

Pink, too, has undergone a fashion adjustment. There is innocent pink (pastel pink with lacy white), and there is pink with a sexy edge (hot pink with black—sometimes lace or leather). The pink wars. Will it lead to the girl wars? The innocent good girl and the sexy diva? We prepare girls for these choiceless choices by giving them an illusion of choice. You can see the types emerge already in the products available to young girls. If there are only two kinds of girls, the "black and hot pink" girl soon chooses glittery bikini panties over Hanes briefs, the "drama queen" T-shirt over the "little princess," Lil' Bratz and Bratz (in which pink with black is explicitly connected to sexualized clothes and animal prints) over the sweet pink baby doll, the devilish costume over the halo and wings. It is innocent enough when we're talking about five- and six-year-olds, but things get more difficult when boys enter the picture in middle school and girls struggle to find their place in the age-old good-versus-bad girl split.

DRESSING LIKE YOUR DOLL OR DRESSING TO PLAY

We also see this girl-typing in the latest move for younger girls: dressing like your dolls. Mattel's Barbie has entered the girls clothing business, but of course Barbie Fashion is so much more than clothes. It's a type of girl, an attitude, a toy, a lip gloss, a fragrance, a secret. All too often it is marketed as desire for what another girl has. A four-page spread in *Nickelodeon Magazine* in 2004 had the following:

Page 1: A girl dressed in hot pink: "The blue jeans. The cute tops. The lip gloss. Where'd you get that?"

Page 2: Barbie dressed in variations of hot pink and black; fashion shots of her hips, legs, shoes, and sunglasses: "Where'd you get that? Fashion Fever Dolls. Dolls with all the latest fashions available in the toy aisle. Collect all 21."

Page 3: Girls ranging in age from about five to twelve made up and dressed like Barbie in hot pink, black and red, black faux leather, a black boa, pink and black miniskirts. They are posing as they would at a photo shoot or at the end of a fashion show catwalk. "Dressing to impress. The gossip. The phone calls. The emails. Secrets to confess. Where'd you get that?"

Page 4: Close-up of one of the girls dressed in Barbie fashion in a black leather jacket with a pink rose on the front. A pink bottle of Barbie fragrance is in the corner. "Where'd you get that? Barbie Fragrance. Available at Macy's. Introducing Barbie: The Fashion."

It's the "total girl" that marketers are after, right? But "total girl" isn't what teachers mean when they say they're educating the whole child or what you and we mean when we say we support the total girl. "Total" to marketers means finding every inch of their body to adorn. Expanding one's market means not just reaching down to the lower ages for products introduced to the older ages but finding new parts of their bodies to colonize or own. The tiniest parts, the forgotten parts, such as nails, which should be dirty after a day of play. Unfortunately, there are kits for manicures and pedicures; there are spa-like kits and ones with makeup. They are meant to get little girls thinking about and investing in how they smell and how they appear to others. American Girl, now in cahoots with Bath & Body Works, has Truly Me, a line of body products that "celebrates the qualities that make you original—your hopes, your dreams, your inner star that shines so brightly," and a body consciousness that goes well beyond fashion. For a limited time little girls can receive a free compact, perfect for applying that pre-makeup glitter Bath & Body Works markets to ages three and up. Claire's has Snapple-brand lip glosses called apple lip juicer and strawberry lip yumms as well as candy versions called Junior Mints lip balm and Reese's Pieces lip gloss pot. Walgreens sells lip smackers and face glitter and a Rose Art Glamour Gear Glitter Magic Makeover for ages six and up. Think of the message: Boys can gorge themselves on candy; girls need to decorate themselves with it.

Then, of course, there are the accessories. On the displays overlooking the girls' section, Gap Kids tells girls their products are "so fresh. so fun. so sweet. Just like you." Here they sell that idea of fresh natural sweetness to six-year-olds with unnatural lip gloss, hula girl charm clips, pink sunglasses, necklaces, shimmer powder, bath fizzie, and a "charming" beauty set, complete with nail polish, lip gloss, and a star charm. They sell a "totally toes" pedicure set, and their signs tell girls to "keep it clean" with lots of hair and body wash, and body lotions. They can keep some of that stuff in one of the seventeen different bags or purses the Gap sells, or they can slip it into their three-ring binder. Gap Kids Pretty Pocket Kit in "old school pink" masks as a pencil case, but it really holds lip gloss, body glitter gel, and nail polish. So much for the three Rs.

Boys can keep it dirty at Gap Kids with accessories that suggest on-the-go action: visors, camo (camouflage) soccer balls, sneakers, goggles, backpacks, and a camo tent. (Girls wear sexy camisoles; boys get military camo? Pink and blue seem tame in comparison.) They have accessories, too, such as wallets and key chains, but none to make them look nicer or smell pretty. They have *no* personal hygiene worries. They can be naturally stinky and proud of it!

HALLOWEEN COSTUMES

Boys are dressing up as military personnel, policemen, and explorers. Girls dress up as hot little teenagers. This is no more apparent than on Halloween. Walk through Wal-Mart or look through any Halloween flyer or catalog, and you'll see pirates, firefighters, and superhero clothes offered to boys; princesses, cheerleaders, and sexy divas are offered to girls.

When we were kids, Halloween was a chance to dress up like someone you weren't. It was a time to be a little transgressive, to cross the usual boundaries set in place by social mores and convention. At Halloween's gloaming, the powerless became superheroes, the young became wrinkled and bent, the poor donned dazzling jewels, and people of the day became monsters of the night—vampires, witches, and all manner of ghastly ghouls. Sometimes girls became mustached men, and boys became big-breasted women, just for the absurdity and the fun of it! We raided our parents' closets and makeup supplies, tore up sheets for bandages, painted lipstick blood down our cheeks, or dug out Dad's big rubber boots to invent someone outlandish. The streets resembled something out of *Night of the Living Dead,* save for a few oddly bright Tweety Birds and Cinderellas.

Halloween is still a chance to be who you aren't, but anyone with kids can tell you that costumes have become something of an art form. No wonder all the kids want them; Mom's closet looks drab by comparison. They are elaborately accessorized affairs made of every fabric and material known to humankind. Costumes come with things like hats, boas, glasses, wands, microphones, wigs, swords, slippers, purses, pom-poms, wings, medallions, scarves, crowns, handcuffs, whistles, badges, and broomsticks. They have muscles sewn in, plush animal-like fur, foam chest armor, layers of chiffon, and fake leather or metal. Some are full-fledged fantasies that parents who can afford it pay $20 to $40 to see come alive on their child. (Sixty dollars will buy you a bride's costume, complete with "giant diamond ring." Alas, there is no groom's costume in sight.)

But there's one obvious way that Halloween costumes lack imagination.

Go ahead and pick out the boy and girl costumes from the following list of catalog descriptions:

"Pow! Bang! Batman to the rescue."

"Evening star enchants everyone."

"The Gladiators enter the arena, and the crowd goes wild!"

"Made in Heaven."

"Shadow Panther Cyber Ninja, protector of the galaxy!"

"Chic pink pussy cat is spotted at all the best soirees."

You get the idea. Halloween has become less about being who you aren't for a night and more about fantasizing that you are the ultra-girl or *uber-boy* the material world says you should want to be. Boys are tough, active superheroes, ninjas, and warriors, ready to save the empire, the world, and the universe, complete with fake muscles to prove their manhood. "Ask the incredible hulk over to your house—but don't get him angry," warns one catalog. "Bulging padded 'muscles' are stitched into torso, arms, and legs. . . . Transform your little hulk into the most powerful human-like creature." Little girls don't "take on evil" or have "bold adventures" or even "incredible fun." They don't save, capture, leap, strike fear, or stop enemies—they don't *do anything.* Even Wonder Woman, a rare exception, only "*encourages* fortitude and self-confidence." That she does so in a spaghetti-strapped leotard with beige stretch nylons and what resembles a bikini bottom suggests the only thing she's ready to battle are Halloween-night goose bumps.

According to these costumes sold in department and drugstores, in catalogs and online, girls get their power almost solely from their looks. They just *are*—"puuurfectly coordinated," "darling," full of "lightness and beauty." If they act at all, it's to "sizzle," "slither," "rock the stadium," or "stalk the stage in zebra stripes." They are lotus blossoms and beautiful princesses. (And have little to do and no sense of direction. "Which way to the castle?" asks one girl featured in a costume catalog.) They are danc-ing queens, pink cheerleaders, divas, fairies, and Barbies, Barbies, Barbies. Girls are beautiful to behold in their short skirts, full skirts, grass skirts, and even pirate skirts (something no self-respecting pirate—and there *were* real women pirates—would wear) and off-the-shoulder gowns and lace-up bodices, made of shimmering satin and pink sequins. Even the more traditional Halloween-type costumes speak to the ultrafeminine and increasingly sexy—pretty witches and gothic princess, sexy genies and hot devils who aren't scary but plan to "paint the town red in a stretch velvet leotard with fluffy marabou trim." As one of our surveyed girls told us, "I wore a devil outfit because it was simple and looked sexy."

Is it as limited and narrow as it seems at first glance?

Web sites sort their categories explicitly along gender lines, with categories like "Princesses and Barbie" and "Star Wars and Sci-Fi," or even more pointedly "Girl Costumes" and "Boy Costumes." When we checked a promisingly neutral "When I Grow Up" category on one site, we found the same gender divide. There parents can find fifty-five costumes for boys and only twenty-two for girls. Of these, fifteen are cheerleaders, divas, and rock stars. Included in this "when I grow up" section was our number one thumbs-down nomination. Don't all parents wish their daughter will grow up to be a "French maid"?

There is something especially pernicious about all this. Fantasy for children is about trying on new roles, about imagining the unusual or impossible, about wearing whatever wild and crazy identity suits their fancy or captivates them at the moment. Why would we want—and, indeed, pay good money—to limit kids in such stereotypical ways? (We're including the littlest kids here. Don't forget to dress your infant in a baby Hulk, Spiderman, or Superman costume.) And why especially on Halloween? After all, isn't Halloween the night when the veil between the worlds is thin, when the real and imagined come close to merging? It's the one magical night when we can expect imagination to wander far and wide, to let carnival and spectacle overtake convention.

Do your daughter a big favor and encourage her to see herself as something other than the pretty princess, the sexy diva, the veiled genie, or the glittery fairy. Help her imagine that she has power over more than how she looks, how well she serves her master, or what prince she attracts. This Halloween, go ahead and raid the closet with her. Imagine that anything is possible. If her heart is set on glitter, at least help her imagine a feisty fairy who takes on the magical realm's evil dragon, a butterfly that saves the insect world, or a princess who can use a map to find her own way to the ball.

Fit for a Princess: The So-called Tween Years

"They're smart, they're Web-savvy, and they're a retailer's dream," gushes a *Good Morning America* online chat. Today's tweens are the children or grandchildren of baby boomers. This means there are a lot of them, and that translates into lots and lots of buying potential. To grab these young consumers, a great deal of attention has been given to the consumer psychology of kids this age: what they desire, are attracted to, and are likely to buy. But little to no attention has been given to their psychological health and well-being. For $5,000 or more you can buy a report that tells you what these girls are "into."

Who are these tweens? Well, marketers believe they're any kid from six or seven to about twelve years of age, although the upper end blurs into the teen market. What a range! This means the same kinds of things being marketed to middle school girls are designed to entice six- and seven-year-olds. Juliet Schor, author of *Born to Buy*, discovered that marketers have a term for this: KAGOY (kids are getting older younger). Not all girls are buying. There are still many differences in this age group. You may know one nine-year-old who plays with her stuffed animals and another who seems prematurely into shopping and designer clothes. The challenge to marketers is changing the former child into the latter, or finding that special niche of clothing that speaks to the nine-year-old who loves her furry animals—by, say, putting a cute monkey on the front of a T-shirt.

Fortunately, one thing remains constant throughout these years (and given the intense targeting of our daughters by marketers, this is a huge advantage): Preteen girls remain close to and seek guidance from their parents and still see family as an integral part of their lives. This means parents can be wonderfully influential during these years. The social and material world may be confronting them with an array of choices too often out of synch with their psychological and emotional development, but girls whose parents are available, media savvy, and responsive have an enormous advantage.

We think "tweens" is a misnomer, which is why we differentiate preteens from middle school girls. Eight-, nine-, and most ten-year-olds are radically different developmentally from eleven-, twelve-, and thirteen-year-old girls who attend middle school. Preteens delight in variety and take pleasure in collecting things associated with the kind of girl they are;

they are also drawn toward that appealing teen outlook that floods their world. Marketers know this, so preteen girl culture is fun, busy, brightly colored, and all consuming (pun intended).

To capture the frenetic energy with which marketers go after your daughter at this age, we shift gears a bit in this section and create one of those *Freaky Friday* moments. Let's live and breathe preteen culture, starting with a walk through J. C. Penney (although it could have been a walk through any number of other department stores). We move on to Limited Too, which has its own designs on this age group and which is helping to sell a version of tween that lasts a full seven shopping years (ages seven to fourteen). Finally, we walk through Claire's because, as you'll see, accessorizing becomes a huge part of training girls to be shoppers.

First stop: J. C. Penney

We are immediately confronted with the following on a pink T-shirt:

Official Cheer Bunny
We're hip, we hop, we're always on top!

Clothes make the girl, or so girls are led to believe, especially as they move into their preteen years. Clothing stores play to any nascent insecurity a girl may have about herself. Will she be popular? Will she be invited somewhere? With what group does she belong? Before a girl has half a chance to reflect on issues of belonging and desirability she is being confronted with a market that tells her she *should* be concerned about this—even when she's as young as eight! On the T-shirt mentioned above there is a silhouette of a bunny jumping in the air with two pompoms. Although bunnies are a feminine symbol, the word *bunny* here stands for something else and is suggested by the sexy phrase that follows: "We're always on top." Does "Playboy bunny" come to mind? It needn't. It's in the collective unconscious of a culture that girls are cute and cuddly and rather quiet, like bunnies. On the other hand, manufacturers are buying the Playboy license and retailers are selling the products to kids. (Recently teen girls in Britain protested the WH Smith stationery store because they placed Playboy stationery next to Winnie the Pooh and Disney stationery.)

Next to the Official Cheer Bunny T-shirt there is a shirt that has "Girls Team" and "74" on the front. Inside the 74 are words in script that describe girls to girls: friend, life, cheerleader, yea team, we won, all-star champ, we are cool, rock, and shout. Champ is good, no? But rarely do you see a girl described as a "champ" without offering the alternative sports version of a "champ" right next to it: a cheerleader. The word *cheerleader* is all over girls' clothing. What about a shirt with "Pep Rally Rebel?" Those promising words are followed by "No fear all cheer." Well, of course. When girls rebel, we become anxious, so keep them all cheering and on the sidelines, and there will be no fear.

Girls sort through a heaping dose of stereotypes on this and any shopping excursion. There are

the Sassy Kitty—for the PUR-R-R-fect look

Spoil me . . . cause I'm worth it (flirty eye-lashed kitty)

Come to Cutie Summer Camp—Feel the Nature

Salon of the Stars—a Cut Above the Others

Recess Flirt—meet by the swings when the bell rings (lips in the background)

Recess stops around sixth grade; when does "flirting" start?

The fun doesn't stop there. They can mix and match those T's with fake sports pants that say things like "Varsity Fantasy League (it's only in her fantasy, we guess that she can make varsity!)" across her bottom. Speaking of sports, unlike boys who wear NFL, NBA, and NASCAR shirts, the logos that are given to girls aren't real. And this isn't because there aren't any girls' teams. Of course there are, but there are no Ts saying 2002 Women's World Cup Soccer Champs or Go, New York Stars! There is just generic stuff like Girls Varsity Tigers and Champions—Basketball All-Girls League. This is because marketers don't take girls' sports seriously.

One shirt quotes Gandhi: "You must be the change you want in the world." Okay, that's a nice sentiment. But it seems difficult for most girls to be the change they want to see in the world when they're wearing their "cheer bunny" and "prep school flirt" shirts.

Why do we moms buy girls these shirts? Because they seem harmless, it is what's out there, and girls want them. And we think that maybe if we buy girls shirts that label them as flirts, then they're not really sexy (like the teens they try to emulate), they're still our little angels.

We notice that angels have been highjacked by marketers, too, making their biggest appearance on preteen underwear—bras and panties for girls, mimicking the Victoria's Secret Angel Room and angel collection. In the little girl section, sizes 7 to 16, there is a bra and panty area that actually carries a size 4. The sign above the items shows two girls, one blond and one ethnic (as is common). One girl looks about ten, the other about seven. Both are so small and thin that surely neither is wearing a bra yet. They are both wearing lipstick, as if to say, "Mommy, I'm more grown up than you think I am. Buy me a bra!" An eight-year-old can wear bikini underpants that show the cartoon head of a woman asking, "Will I never be a princess?" Such slogans are preparation for the reverse message as the girls get older: The angel on the outside is harboring a little hottie underneath!

Limited Too

Our survey tells us that lots of preteen girls shop at stores like J. C. Penney primarily because Mom still has a big say in where and what clothes are bought. It is also confirmed by our survey that Limited Too is the place for cool girls who have their own money to shop for fashion. It also targets tweens exclusively.

Limited Too has a carnival atmosphere: bright colors, bright lights, and different sections of the store with carousels of accessories at every turn. Limited Too is the training ground for the middle school years; this is where a very specific notion of what it means to be a teenager gets marketed to seven-, eight-, and nine-year-olds. This is also where girls can experience what marketers believe is the "fun" of being a girl.

Part of the fun, according to the people who want to sell your daughter stuff, is accessorizing. How do accessories become so important to girls? Well, marketers make them cheap so girls can always buy a little something and parents can always give in to a little something extra after clothes shopping. Another reason is that it is part of the general adornment girls are taught from day one. (Remember those little ribbons on bald heads?) Every photo in a magazine, every girl on TV, every girl on a box of cereal or board game has some little extra something adorning her—a bow, a bracelet, earrings, a hair clip, a belt, a scrunchy. For boys it's simple—a baseball cap and *maybe* a pair of binoculars.

Limited Too's accessory carousels sell items that adorn more than just bodies. There are accessories for girls' rooms and for their lives: picture frames, games that involve collecting charms and thus buying different versions of the game to buy more charms, notebooks, pillows, posters, stuffed animals, mini-compact disc players, sunglasses, purses, buttons, and books. They're not just selling fashion, they're selling girl culture.

What's in this girl culture? A whole lot of boy worship. They have buttons, purses, pillows, and T-shirts that say "I love [*fill in latest pop star*]." Eleven- and twelve-year-olds sometimes get crushes on stars, yes, but pre-preteens and pre-pre-preteens? The eight- to ten-year-olds are given an important lesson that part of being a teen or preteen is developing a crush on one of these teen hunks and decorating yourself and your room with proclamations of love. At eight, nine, and ten, their rooms don't typically show this, but eventually they will. We wish that there were ways a girl could admire other girls through their room and clothing accessories— such as "Venus for President"—but that's not a part of girl culture to marketers.

Another message about what it means to be a girl happens through accessorizing, and that is the "rule" that even though girls must conform to the latest fashion trend, they must also be unique, special, and not like any other girl. Selling "special" to girls in very limited ways is like pretending they have choices within a very narrow box they must fit in. Take a look at the way the link bracelet that was popular in 2004 gave girls the "opportunity" to express what is special about them by inserting little sections or links (somewhat like charms) into a part of the bracelet made to receive those links. The choices are limited, too; we counted twenty-five different charms but only two about sports: "I love soccer" and a picture of a basketball. The rest were Lil Miss Attitude, Best Friends, Angel, Princess, Girls Rule (selling girl power again), Cutie Pie, and different designs of hearts.

Think of an eight- to ten-year-old you know and what these little symbols might represent to her at this point in her life. Would it be a piano for the piano lessons she loves? A goldfish for the fish in her room? A tae kwon do suit for the lessons she takes? A picture of a book because she loves to read? Or maybe a picture of Emma Watson because she loves the character Hermione Granger? You would then have a bracelet that represents something different, something that represents *your* girl rather than the generic "girl" with links of hearts, butterflies, and flowers. This selling of what marketers consider special is rampant and can make girls very anxious over time about the need to stand out and get attention without stepping over any lines.

A third message of girlhood is that girls of any age can have fun being sexy. Every season there is some item of clothing that is forbidden. Our survey tells us that the very clothing girls think is "cool" is also the item parents are forbidding their daughters to wear. We asked a salesclerk if there are items girls want to buy but moms object to, and she said, "not really." The main thing she hears is that girls are allowed to buy something but can't wear it to school. So are moms separating school clothes from fun clothes? But shouldn't fun clothes be play clothes when you're eight, nine, or ten? The kind of clothes you can get dirty or feel comfortable riding a bike in, not a cami-bra, string panties, and a drop-waist skort?

Every message to a preteen girl says that it's preferable to pose on the beach rather than surf, to shop rather than play, to decorate rather than invent. One company defined it all on a journal, supposedly a place for a girl to put down in writing her true feelings, and yet the cover states:

> Pink
> *You are sweet and loveable*
> *You love surprises, chasing butterflies,*
> *And sliding down rainbows*
> *Dressing up and making believe are your favorites*
> *Everyone thinks you're special*
> *If you like pink,*
> *You're a princess.*

Is a journal a place for prefabricated dreams and predetermined aspirations? This is much too limited a vision of what a girl can be.

Claire's—"Where Getting Ready Is Half the Fun"

Claire's is a wall-to-wall preteen visual delight. A dizzying smorgasbord of color—bright and glittery and busy. Every small square of space is crammed with possibilities. "Over 80 million ears pierced worldwide" reads the sign at the entrance, reminiscent of the billions served at McDonald's. And, indeed, this store feels like the fast food of accessorizing. Seas of pink and purple tags hang from earrings, bracelets, and necklaces of every kind—retro, glamorous, delicate, brassy. "Real body jewelry," "Add a charm," "Classic candy collection," and "It's all about Bling" announce the signs. Black and white feather boas with matching black, white, gold, or silver purses and elbow-length satin gloves hang on the walls. Girls pick their way through narrow aisles of diaries and notebooks, every color and design of flip-flops, peel-and-stick rhinestones, plush door hangers that announce "the Capricorn girl," rhinestone-lined "Spoiled" signs to hang on bedroom doors, body tattoos, glitter, "bling lip gloss," barrettes, hair ribbons, and fake hair extensions. Mirrors are everywhere to check out how the latest, coolest thing looks on you.

The magazines that girls read tell them they must have "the freedom" and "the power" to accessorize, so many of them choose to shop at stores like Claire's. The college-age salesclerk at Claire's tells us that girls ages three to twenty-one shop there. We didn't believe her at first; maybe the older girls, but that young? Soon after arriving, though, we overheard the following conversation between a mother and her three-year-old daughter, Emily. The mom's older daughter, about ten, was browsing nearby.

MOM: Oh, look, here are some magnet earrings. Do you want them?
THREE-YEAR-OLD: What for?
MOM: Well, they're magnets. They stay on your ears.
THREE-YEAR-OLD: Yes.

A few minutes later:

THREE-YEAR-OLD: Buy *me* something too, Momma. You gotta get jewelry for *me*.
MOM: We got you three things. We got you jewelry. We got you makeup. We got you earrings. Did you get enough, Emily? Oh, we got you four things . . . a pair of socks. No, five. There are two pairs here.
THREE-YEAR-OLD: Yeah.

So the clerk was right. Girls as young as three shop at Claire's, although with more help from their moms than the older girls we saw giggling together in the back of the store.

We don't relay this interaction to criticize the mom. She was gentle and sweet with her daughter; she sat on the floor with her, explained things, and took her time with her. To Emily this was fantasy play, not much different from playing dress-up. For all we know Emily goes home to play soccer with her mom and help her dad cook dinner.

The front part of the Claire's store clearly geared itself to the Limited Too crowd, the preteens and middle school girls looking for the coolest things—and also to the occasional mom who might briefly check out the store for any R-rated items before letting her preteen daughter loose. At the front was the "nice girl" stuff—the add-a-charm bracelets, bright lime green earrings, initial key chains, and colorful "jelly totes" with matching wallets.

Midway through the store, however, things took a slight turn. Along the walls were the edgy stuff that told another story of girlhood: funnier, irreverent, a bit nasty, sexy, and diva-like. Here was a line of lip jelly that said things like "Boys are smelly," "Trouble-maker," and "Drama Queen." Here were bright pink flip-flops that announced: "Hey, that butt needs kicking" and little boxes of cookies inscribed "Hey, you make me throw up" or labeled "Poison [playfully crossed out] cookies for a friend." A bright pink-and-orange plush baseball cap reads "Mrs. Timberlake," and address books and notebooks are covered with phrases like "You suck and must be punished," "Can't listen, you're dumb," and "It's all about me, deal with it." It is a diva's delight and a girl's version of Spencer's, a favorite store of boys that sells items that are rude, crude, and in your face.

Beyond the sale table, near the far back wall, are the products that little Emily was after—the pinkest, fluffiest, glitteriest Disney stuff imaginable: princess tiaras, Cinderella and Prince Charming purses, and Snow White makeup kits. Here are the dream net bed canopies, *Swan Lake* ballet slippers, and Dora the Explorer earrings and necklaces. Right next to all this is the boy-crazy stuff. Boyz File notebooks and other items say things like "Boys make great pets, every girl should have one." (Imagine selling something like that to a boy about a girl!) The Hottie Handbook announces: "Attention girls. . . . If you have a boyfriend don't bring him around me because you won't have a boyfriend anymore. . . . I sizzle. I scorch, hotter than any flame. Don't hate me because I'm beautiful. OK. Hate me if you want. . . ." Inside there's a Slam book–like system for rating boys on every page: "What makes him a hottie?" Is he "very hot, hot, medium, or mild?" Is he "so hot I'm on fire" or "warm enough to toast my buns." It's a good thing little Emily can't read yet!

What does Claire's sell besides accessories? It sells younger girls the ultimate fantasy of sweetness, innocence, Prince Charming, and winning Prince Charming by beating out other girls—in other words, competition over boys. Because she is probably not shopping alone, it sells her a closeness with her mother associated with consuming these things. And if you think of the store space as a metaphor for girlhood, it sells girls a stereotypical view—that girls should show their perfectly nice, sweet, innocent smiley sides in public (at the front of the store) and hide those irreverent, resistant, "bad girl" parts of themselves (at the back).

We think even this doesn't quite capture the crux of the issue. The real trouble with Claire's and other stores like it is that it sells every aspect of girlhood contained in that box we mentioned earlier: the good, the bad, the funny, the sexy—and now even the resistance, that edginess and irreverence that once gave girls a pathway out of the magic kingdom and the pressure to accessorize in the first place. Claire's sells girls a false sense of choice and possibility, a feeling that they can create a resistant girlhood by creatively matching the "friend" bracelet with the body tattoos and troublemaker lip jelly. But it's a closed circle or maybe a hall of mirrors. The resistance to gender stereotypes is now sold at the same store that perpetuates them. It is like the time when sixties tie-dyed shirts lost their roots in the counterculture and became available at Sears and Bloomingdale's. Don't think about what it really means to challenge or take a political stand. Just buy the appearance of taking a stand. And selling resistance means, of course, containing it, restricting it so that it is manageable and not really resistance at all.

Clothes Make the Girl: The New Teens

Junior high is a tough age by any standards. Middle school girls enter and participate in a world in which their bodies are up for constant comment: "My face is up guys," reads one shirt. "Objects under shirt may be larger than they appear," reads another. It's not just the boys that check out what the girls are wearing. Other girls are checking out where a girl shops and making comments. Dress codes tell them that they will be checked over by teachers and paraprofessionals in schools to determine how appropriate their choices are.

This new visibility (and constant monitoring) can be annoying or intoxicating. Girls want to stand out by fitting in. They want to say something about who they are, but they're not yet sure of who they are. Marketers love anxiety. They fill those uneasy spaces with products that girls can use to form a statement—bracelets, skirts, hair color, T-shirts.

Selling individuality really begins in middle school. Caught between a rock and a hard place, girls want to fit in and show that they are different and unique through the way they dress. Marketers tell them that the clothes they buy can help them create a special look. Middle school girls agree that they dress to appear unique. In response to a question about why they wear what they wear, they told us: "I'm the only one obsessed with making her own bracelets." "It shows I'm different." "[It indicates] I'm not so plain and boring; I have a style." "[It says] I look unique; that's how I want people to see me." "My clothes and styles say 'I'm me, not you.'" "I got purple highlights; I wanted to show that my personality was purple." "I want others to see me as an individual."

Some girls wrote more than a few words to explain that they saw the potential problems with trying to be different: "Yeah, I wear 'in-style' things to show I do fit in, but I don't always try to fit in. I want to be different." One twelve-year-old wrote that she changes her outfits to show "I'm a unique person. I wear all different kinds of styles. I just want people to know that I'm different, like I can be someone some day then I'm another person the next day." Thirteen-year-old Danielle's comment shows how manufacturers exploit this desire to be different: "I like underwear and thongs that have sayings on them that kinda tell who i am. Even though people don't see them, I still like them . . . they say stuff like 'tuff girl.'"

Middle schoolers also make negative statements through what they wear. Negative identities, though, are tricky. They can come from heartfelt rejection of the status quo, or they can be considered a style that embraces feelings of rejection for being too different. Stores such as Hot Topic create a goth or punk look for middle school girls. One girl told us, "I wear clothes that make people think I'm a goth, but I don't want them to think that." She wants to make a statement but doesn't want to be judged and labeled. Some girls wear clothes that say something about not caring what other people think or proudly proclaim that they wear what's comfortable. They wear clothes to show they're "not afraid of what you think." Some are intelligent about the fashion industry's attempts to shape them, so they dress "to show that I'm satisfied with the way I look" or "to show you can still be pretty without showing so much skin" or "I'm me and I like it." Still others struggle to find clothes that express their interests without becoming trendy. As one girl said: "I don't wear what everyone else is wearing, and if I do, it's because I like it and I had it first."

Maybe some girls are trendsetters. Statements about comfort might also be about not bending to pressure to wear trendy clothes: "I wear what's comfortable on me" and "I just wear stuff that's comfortable. If that's not a statement then . . ."

But there were also girls who admitted dressing to attract boys: "The way I dress says that I have a nice shape." "It says that I'm fine." "It says that I want guys' attention." One acknowledged, "I wear makeup so boys can see the good side of me." Another said she wore both "preppy and slutty clothes [which say that] I'm tough but still sexy and a girly girl." Girls know that looking sexy is cool: "It makes me look hot and cool." They also associate pink, sexy, girly, and cool: "I like to wear pink because it shows that I'm girly." "They say I'm a fashion princess, and I love to look good." "I wear sexy little shirts that say to everyone that I'm outgoing."

The relationship between clothing and behavior is not always so direct. Girls who dress to look different don't always misbehave. And girls who dress sexy don't always engage in sex. If a seventh grader wears a T-shirt that has a marijuana leaf or Bob Marley on the front because she thinks it's rebellious and funny, parents may wonder if she is likely to be or become a user. If she wears "camis," belly shirts, and micro-mini skirts in eighth grade and her dad thinks she looks like a hooker, is she already involved with sex or more likely to have sex early? There are no studies that link early identity choices through clothing with early commitment to questionable groups or behavior. Although her clothes may not reflect the girl inside, they do present a type of girl to the world, and this is the conversation you need to have with her. She may still decide to wear that edgy T-shirt, but she'll know her choice has consequences and that you're there to help her think through her response to others' assumptions.

In spite of all the different statements that girls think they are making at this age, our survey indicates that they shop at two types of stores. The first type sells "cute." Sometimes cute is girly, sometimes preppy, and sometimes sexy, but it is always trendy. Girls shop at Aeropostale, J. C. Penney, Pacsun, Forever 21, and stores like them to create this look. The other kind of store sells alternative styles and is represented by only one for this age group, Hot Topic, which now boasts more than one thousand stores in malls across the country.

LOOKING CUTE

Certain stores emphasize looking cute, and cute is, unfortunately, a lead-in to looking sexy. For middle schoolers cute isn't exactly like the "cute" that's painted all over Limited Too. It has a bit of a joke to it, an edge, a flaunt, a flirt. Lip gloss at the Body Shop called Born Lippy, which comes in fruity flavors, are for middle school girls. There are also versions for high schoolers that are plain and less cute, which tells us these older girls aren't playing at dressing up as teens. In the same vein, one clothing store has a carousel of clothing called dorm gear that has cute animals and slogans on colorful pajamas and slippers. Like lip gloss for middle school girls, dorm gear is about dressing up as college girls at a slumber party (a kind of twelve-year-old fantasy version of what a college dorm is like). These cute versions of presumed older-girl wear get them ready to be teenagers, just like Starbucks' frappuccinos get them ready for coffee. Transitional items such as fruity lip gloss and frappuccinos reflect the marketing departments' awareness that the middle school years are a crucial transitional time that calls for transitional products.

The "cute" that is sold in these stores can be spunky small-animal cute or I've-got-an-edge cute. This edge is either a little obnoxious or girly and sexy. Small-animal-cute has ducks, frogs, and monkeys. Cute with edge is on clothing that says "Royal Pain" (instead of princess) and "Once Upon a Time I Met a Boy and I Kicked His Butt." But for every edgy statement made against boys there are six or seven "cute" adoring ones such as "If It Weren't for Boys, I'd Never Go to School."

Marketers are well aware that middle schoolers are trying on identities, and it sometimes seems as if they are selling pretend-wear. The carousel labeled Active Wear appears to be pretend active wear, not at all fashioned for actual activity except maybe for actively looking cute. What passes for active is writing on shorts or T-shirts that says you are varsity this or that on a light cottony sweatshirt material. But how active can a girl be in shorts that promise to reveal half her butt or fall way below the navel even before the waistband is folded over? The boys' side of the shop doesn't have an Active Wear carousel. Again, boys are presumed to be always active but girls need to dress up as if they were active.

The sexy "outgoing" girl is also a part cast and costumed at stores such as Aeropostale. "Hello, My Name Is Hottie" is printed on one set of pajamas, and "Cuties vs. Hotties" is on a T (setting girls up for those catfights that get so much media attention). There are rows of camis (tiny strapped shirts that are imitations of camisoles) as well as regular shirts with bits of cami sticking out at the chest level. They are trimmed with lace, sequins, and embroidery, all to create a unique look. One can imagine that a girl feels special and original as she claims her "taste": "I like the ones with sequins."

Although these fashions will change through the years, the stores continue to sell the same old thing: "as if" personalities for girls. They are selling a type, and the type often expresses white, middle-class, or rich girl "style," à la Paris Hilton, luring girls with promises of being unique, being noticed, and fitting in.

HOT TOPIC

A different "as if" personality is for sale at Hot Topic, a store that may seem "out there" to parents at first glance. Given that this store can be found in practically every mall in every state, store buyers work very hard not to alienate parents who may wander in with their middle schoolers. Their buyers even respond to school dress code bans by changing their inventory accordingly.

Hot Topic may look a little scary to moms and dads who notice the multiply-pierced salespeople in black and red and metal-studded accessories. Like the pretend sexy of Aeropostale, Hot Topic provides a pretend alternative or a starter alternative style for middle schoolers who venture in, a sort of "goth girls gone mild."

There is, for example, a whole retro section that seems especially made for younger girls. Jason, a cute twenty-something clerk, tells us what appeals to the girls. They rarely buy the Ts with bands or band insignias on them but instead buy girl Ts, the ones especially shaped for a girl. They cling a little more tightly, and the sleeves are a little shorter. They also go for the "sweet Ts" and the retro ones with images of Strawberry Shortcake and the Last Unicorn, all from the eighties, before their time, but brought back for their consumption. (In 2005, Tinker Bell was given a new sexy twist on Ts for little girls.)

There is still a bit of a Limited Too emphasis on "boys to crush on." Girls aren't buying Ts with their favorite bands, but are buying Ts with photos of male stars on them. It was surprising that there weren't any with images of Avril Lavigne nor Eowyn, the princess who vanquishes the enemy in *Lord of the Rings*, truly a heroine to many girls according to our survey.

The salespeople say the middle school girls most frequently go for cutesy stuff; they want preppie with edge, but they're not all that daring. They prefer the cutesy earring collection, complete with guitars, brightly colored zippers, and rubber spike balls in hot pink, blue, and orange. The ubiquitous butterfly of the tween years reappears at Hot Topic as a black butterfly on a necklace.

Cute and edgy seems to be a way girls can shop if they aren't yet interested in identifying as goth and punk through their hair color or a brand of makeup called Morbid Makeup that includes liquid black eyeliner. Cute and edgy seems to be represented by a character called "Happy Bunny," an obnoxious pink bunny that says things like "You suck." It appears on a pair of finger cuffs (sort of sweat bands for fingers) with slogans like "Cute but psycho" and "Hi, Loser." The Happy Bunny shower curtain says "It's All About Me."

Who is this Happy Bunny? Is he or she the good kid gone bad? The Playboy bunny gone mad? Middle school boys (who may be preoccupied with farting and butts) are attracted to its rude comments: "You smell like butt" and "Kiss me right on the pooper." Girls who want to defy "cute" like the bunny's saying "Cute but kind of scary."

Happy Bunny and accessories go hand in hand. It's funny how accessories still rule—or maybe *especially* rule—when you've joined the chain-and-zipper set. Hot Topic makes it easy to buy accessories that give a girl a certain punk or gothic look, pricing the body jewelry at $6.99. Morbid Metals puts out piercing jewelry appropriate for the middle schoolers as well, with jewels, flowers, stars, hot pink spike balls, and dragonflies. There are also lots of Playboy bunnies and pink and blue rhinestone-studded skull and crossbones with one-inch nails that evoke the early years of punk and heavy metal. To show how mainstream some of these accessories are today, skull and crossbones earrings were recently suggested as an accessory in *Seventeen* magazine, along with lavender butterfly pins, colorful rings, and pink crystal earrings.

The statement made by girls who choose to look punk or goth is that they want to be different but still belong and still be attractive. The point of goth is to look a little scary and morbid and to project an I-don't-care attitude. Nevertheless, there is even a *Gothic Beauty* magazine, with sections on beauty, fashion, lifestyle, events, and profiles, for those girls who don't see themselves in *Seventeen*.

Punk and goth wear (black and big with zippers, nails, chains, and spikes attached) is influenced by the music that preteens and teens listen to. Sometimes it is also about feeling pain. We've known girls who look "cute and pretty" on the outside but form friendships with punk or goth girls because they think these girls may know the pain, the darkness inside, the confusion and the morbid thoughts they feel but are unable (as yet) to express.

A parent may wonder what makes one girl dress up as morbid or alternative while another who feels the same painful emotions chooses not to. A parent might also wonder what makes a healthy, happy preteen dress as if she's depressed. It has to do with permission—the permission given by parents and schools, or the restrictions either makes—and the permission given tacitly by others who dress like this in their world and their schools. And perhaps more important it has to do with the permission they give themselves in a cruel middle school world to reveal (on some level) their own feelings of being ugly or different or in pain.

For those expressing pain, we should remember that some kids have much to feel morbid about and much to rebel against. For some the spirituality that organized religion offers isn't enough or right for them. For others a parent has been neglectful or absent, and they have missed the mirroring which these loving relationships provide that give a child a feeling of wholeness and peace with the world. Some have been put through a terrible amount of judging and prejudging based on gender identity, race, class, or appearance, by other kids and sometimes their own family members. It is difficult to understand the loss that many kids who seem to have come from "normal American families" have faced in their unlucky lives. Morbidity stems from both the experience of loss and grieving and a sense that one is not quite right, defective, or mutilated.

For others, punk and goth and even "emo" (a style of dress based on bands that express raw emotions) are the only choices they have to express rebellion. For some kids from healthy families, fighting a battle over what to wear and what to listen to is a safe way to express difference from your parents and do a little experimentation. What parents might see as risky dress and listening habits may never lead to risky behavior.

Some parents argue with their daughters about their dress by pointing out that others may judge them on the basis of the black gown or the army fatigues. This isn't the best strategy for a parent. It gives the impression of promoting conforming to others' expectations. After trying to understand the insides of the girls who express morbidity and rebellion on the outside, helping them turn that resistance into power can work wonders for that feeling of being defective, the feeling of being angry or of having no hope. Parents can teach girls how they can feel effective by creating positive outlets for the things they love to do or connecting them to activities or groups that allow them to express who they really are—even when they are down on themselves or others. Too often feelings of effectiveness and power are offered to girls exclusively through being sexy. And Hot Topic doesn't shy away from that identity.

Two salespeople told us that the middle school kids often come in with their mothers during the school year (with friends during the summer) and that it's fun to see what the mothers set limits around. Recently they were shocked when one mother bought her daughter a garter belt and fishnet stockings to wear to her eighth grade graduation. Although Haley, twenty-something and with a cheek piercing that looked like a dimple, was shocked, she told us that she played her part as salesperson, saying to the girl, "You've got a cool mother, to let you wear all that stuff." She was actually thinking, "I would never let a daughter of mine wear that 'skanky' little dress." According to Haley, the mom said if her daughter wants to look like an idiot, it's up to her, as long as her grades are up and her attitude is good.

Younger girls also look at—and sometimes steal, we're told—the itty-bitty underwear thongs with Dr. Seuss's *Cat in the Hat* or Hello Kitty Goth Girl images and tangas. (Tangas are the boys' briefs-style underpants cut low.) The sales clerks tell us middle school girls look for one of two styles, super goth or little slut. The so-called little sluts are into anything with the Playboy bunny insignia on it. Signifying what? That they are sophisticated little players? Or, as one girl told us in our survey, that she is "fine" and "outgoing."

The invasion of sexy girl into the Hot Topic set has its counterpart in the parallel universe of pretty, sexy angels with the introduction of metal. A fashion "story" in a recent *Elle Girl* says, "Take two parts frilly. Add a dash of denim and a pinch of metal. Mix well." And so the fourteen-year-old model wears a satin pink shirt with flower embroidery, extremely short denim shorts studded with metal, barely hiding a white lace garter belt holding up thigh-high white stockings. "Isn't it fun to be a girl?" We've asked at the beginning of the photo layout. The same girl poses next to this question wearing a metal chain necklace and a string of pearls, a white lacy top, the same lacy garter belt holding up transparent thigh-highs with stars on them, finished off with big work boots. We have to add that she is standing pigeon-toed to emphasize that little-girl-gone-sexy/bad look. (This look is all too common, and the model is often posed with a finger in her mouth or twirling her hair.) How long will it be before this look makes its way down to size 4? Wait a minute. It has! In a sexed-up Tinker Bell and that Barbie Fashion spread in *Nickelodeon Magazine*.

Our point is that girls can't win if they try to forge their identity with fashion, and the best way around this issue with daughters who experiment, pretend, try on, and take off is to focus on the outer market. A parent can search out the original meaning of the studs and the nails, when they were truly alternative, and then talk about how this look has been co-opted to make money. When a parent has perspective, she can empathize with her daughter's desire to be noticed as special and unique and the difficulties connected with this in a world that jumps to labels and judgments or prettifying and trivializing things of meaning.

These choices offered up as signs of individuality are culturally mediated, manufactured by marketers hell-bent on channeling girls' desire in their direction. They spend millions capitalizing on middle school girls' anxieties about fitting in, looking good, and being chosen—by the right friends, by the cute boy. Parents won't agree about what's okay and what's too provocative or even about the best way to engage their daughters, but the important thing is that they *do* engage their daughters and that they talk about how the array of choices creates the illusion of identity and security.

T-SHIRTS

A wonderful place to engage your daughter is by reading T-shirts. T-shirts give messages and make statements. First and foremost, they tell other kids where a girl shops. Occasionally Ts and sweatshirts advertise colleges that seem cool, but more frequently they market stores such as AE (for American Eagle) or Gap. If Ts expressed who a girl is, you'd think she'd be wearing the T she got at the summer camp she went to, the music festival she attended, or the Humane Society where she volunteers to walk the dogs. But instead they express "attitude" rather than interests, skills, concerns, and hobbies.

We've tracked the changes in popular Ts from middle to high school. What girls tell us they wear and observe says a lot about the culture they are entering.

Let's start with a stroll into Abercrombie & Fitch, a store that attracts hoards of teens and simply screams "teenager" to any middle school girl who walks by. A&F has a sordid past, selling T-shirts that some have called racist and featuring naked young models with copy explaining various forms of group sex and the "supersafe alternative" of group masturbation in a catalog titled *The Christmas Field Guide*. They know from experience that creating a stir pulls in teens who want to be part of the latest controversy. More recently a group of thirteen- to sixteen-year-old girls successfully "girlcotted" A&F Ts that displayed degrading messages like "Who Needs a Brain When You Have These?" and "Available for Parties." A&F turned this bad press around quickly by asking the girls to help them design more appropriate Ts. It was a good marketing move (as if they didn't know what was appropriate before and needed the girls' assistance!).

A&F continues to sell well. Even the tamer T-shirts for girls express an "attitude" about school that is predominantly negative, confirming that it is not cool to be into school, such as "Not the Teacher's Pet," "Math Never Spells Fun," and "Social Studies Is My Best Subject." This last slogan really doesn't refer to school. Like the others, it refers to the stereotype that girls are social, talkative shoppers who care most about their appearance. Others read "If the Shoe Fits Buy More" and "I'll Talk My Way Out of Anything." Compare these to the Ts found for boys in the same store, like the funny "Class President—Now Do What I Say"; the irreverent "I Blame My Parents"; the smart "Math Rules"; and the playfully arrogant "Natural-Born Competitor."

Why "Math Never Spells Fun" for girls and "Math Rules" for boys? It's hard to believe we're still living in the fabricated world of the first talking Barbie doll who said "I hate math" (at least until parents and educators burst Barbie's bubble and forced Mattel to take her off the market). It's also clear that the designers at A&F think boys are far more into sports than girls. Not one sport-focused T for girls? We also ask why a girl can't wear a T that says "Class President— Now Do What I Say" or "Natural-Born Competitor." In the real world girls are elected class presidents and become valedictorians. They get into Ivy League colleges not only by getting the necessary grades and SAT scores but by playing sports, doing volunteer work, and participating in student government. We know plenty of girls who are proud they are smart, but they have to defy two things to be smart: the feeling (which may be more of a creation of the media than reality) that what they're doing isn't cool to their peers, and society's belief that a boy is the appropriate one to be excelling in these things.

Clothing as well as a host of other indicators portray boys as the natural-born leaders while girls are excelling in record numbers. Our survey and experience with middle school girls is that they're proud of their intelligence. So why all these messages about angels, princesses, shopping, and socializing as natural qualities and activities of young teen girls? Maybe it makes people anxious when girls get smarter; maybe these Ts symbolize the discomfort and represent a sort of collective nervous giggle. Or maybe it is something more serious. More girls are going to college than boys right now, and there is a spate of books asking what we should do about boys falling behind. Thus this more public display of the stereotype—boys' smarts and girls' social interests—could be a kind of backlash. Girls taking up the spaces once reserved for boys may trigger a movement to reinscribe those old familiar stereotypes.

What are the Ts that girls really like? Our middle school survey respondents told us they fall into two categories: the cute ones and the ones with attitude or, for some, too much attitude. Cute ones say things like "Angel," "Sweet," "Best Friends," "American Girl," "Baby Girl," and the ever popular "Princess." The ones with attitude start out by twisting the above slogans into sayings that show they're not all cute and sweet, such as "Angel with Attitude," "Cute but Psycho," and "#1 Brat." The attitude Ts also show how girls can wear a bit of aggression and refuse to be anyone's sexual object; they have slogans like "I think it's cute that you think I'm listening." "Do I look like a f***ing people person?" "Not the brightest crayon in the box, are we?" "RTFM" (Read the Fucking Manual)—for computer geeks. "Keep staring. I might do a trick." Other Ts simply state that the wearer has a problem, implying it is cool to have an attitude problem and to be different: "Laugh at me because you think I'm different; I laugh at you because you're all the same." "Oh, crap, you're trying to cheer me up again, aren't you?" "I love my attitude problem." Girls continue to get pleasure out of expressing their aggressive feelings verbally and often through sarcasm and indirect verbal slams. The good side of this is that it provides a kind of free space to be resistant and multidimensional, even if it's in a predictable way.

The too-much-attitude Ts that middle schoolers tell us they notice basically say, "Fuck you." Are they expressing an authentic anger? Yes and no. As we learned from talking to teens about piercings, tattoos, and goth style, they're often expressing a kind of pain that comes from rotten family lives and horrible school situations. They're also expressing a pain about not fitting into the cute or sweet or hot type that the world seems to want them to be. The choices are really cute, sexy, pretty or *not*. Anger seems an appropriate response.

We noticed that when we asked girls what Ts they liked, only a few out of the more than two hundred middle schoolers surveyed told us they wore Ts that reflected their interest in sports. It may have been because these Ts weren't in the stores. It was also surprising how few of the Ts they liked were about cheerleading given the vast number of Cheer Squad–type T-shirts displayed in the stores. Instead of sports the main activity promoted on Ts for middle school and teen girls was boys and sex: "This would look good on your bedroom floor" and "Why have a boyfriend when you could have two?" and, more blatantly, "Do Me" and "Pimptress."

It is interesting to hear girls say that they draw the line when it comes to wearing Ts that sport the b word and the f word and also those that describe a different kind of sexuality than that of boyfriends and crushes. While stores offer them, girls tell us they won't wear Ts that say such things as "You can look but you can't touch" (across the breasts), "Master Pimp," "FCUK like a bunny," and "I am a naughty bitch." As one eighth grader summarized it, she won't wear Ts that have "things like sexy and hot on them, anything that can be really degrading."

It was interesting that so many of the boyfriend T-shirts mentioned in our survey boasted competitiveness with other girls, while so few said anything about girls' friendships. There were the "girls rule, boys drool" types of Ts and "girl power" Ts that boast individual accomplishments, but the Ts the girls thought were cute, provocative, and interesting had more to do with competition with other girls, from shaking "it" better than Britney to stealing other girls' boyfriends. The T that kept coming up again and again had "Don't hate me because I'm beautiful. Hate me because your boyfriend thinks I am." We think girls wrote so frequently about this particular T because it's cute, confusing, and controversial. It shapes an attitude that is validated over and over in middle school and in the culture at large: to watch out for other girls. They are your competitors, not just your friends.

Attitude does protect girls, and we applaud the girls with attitude who shared it with us. But what good is all that attitude if it is used to defy authority about what to wear or to compete with other girls for boys' attention? Is it really a way of practicing to use that attitude in the future to stick up for yourself and other people in the world? Or is attitude a trendy piece of clothing that a girl wears to look older and more sophisticated than the next girl?

Older and more sophisticated, though, is often simply "sexy." It is amazing how frequently and pervasively teens are sold an image of hot and sexy. The message is that that's what women are prized for in the culture at large. That's what makes women interesting. For middle school girls in particular, being sexy is what will get them noticed and give them power. We can't underestimate the power and not just an image of power that teens girls acquire from looking sexy even when it is a dangerous path to follow. Schools try to take up the issue of dressing sexy, but unfortunately they do it through rules and prohibitions rather than helping students look more deeply and carefully at the wider culture and its impact on all of us.

DRESS CODES

Andrea, who is approaching graduation from eighth grade, has been pushing the dress code at her school. She is more than a dress code outlaw; she is a thirteen-year-old who has thought about suicide and who cuts herself at night when she gets lonely or feels stressed. At school, she says, few people know that she is depressed. They call her Miss Popular in a friendly way, and, as she puts it, she has "tons of friends." She complains, however, that she feels as if she's a fake in school, that there are two of her: the school Andrea and the real Andrea. At school her friends have noticed that she keeps checking the mirror. They think it's out of vanity, but she says it's because the girl she sees in the mirror doesn't feel like the real her, the her in her mind's eye.

The school has called her home to complain about what she wears. A mother of another girl in the school called the principal to report that Andrea wore to a school dance a see-through shirt which showed her nipples. Andrea says this woman is "out of her mind" and says she "wore no such thing." When Andrea came to therapy wearing short pink shorts that were folded down at the hips and a somewhat clinging black T-shirt with pink writing on it, Sharon said her outfit was cute. Andrea beamed but added, "Thanks. I got in trouble today for wearing it. They thought that the shorts were too short." The principal brought her into his office that day to tell her that he has spoken to all her teachers and they're going to be watching her carefully in the future with regard to what she wears to school. He told her that she will have to face the consequences of dressing like that and should consider what others are going to think about her.

Perhaps it is good for a girl who has thought about suicide but who has flown under the radar of school guidance counselors to be watched carefully. It is certainly clear that for a long time now the adults around Andrea should have been watching her more carefully, but, as Andrea might put it, it would be better if they were watching the real her and not the girl in the mirror. Dress is one of the ways girls get attention; no one would deny that, given the emphasis on fashion in the magazines they read and the TV shows they watch. But schools need to look carefully at who the bid for attention is aimed at. School personnel assume that it is distracting to boys, and perhaps this is true for some boys. They also assume that dressing sexy or "hot" is a way for girls to get attention from boys. While this is true for some girls, dressing a certain way could also be an attempt to make an identity statement—a way for a girl to identify with other girls and teenagers they see and admire on TV, in movies, in music, and in their neighborhoods. Parents should not assume they know the message a girl is trying to convey and should not overemphasize how others will interpret what they see.

At a time when we're trying to help girls deemphasize what other people will think, this is often a wrong move. When a mother says, "If you wear that, everyone will think you're a slut," and a daughter answers, "I don't care. I know I'm not a slut" or "The people I care about know I'm not a slut," it's difficult to argue. If a mom says a girl should care what others think about her, then she's reinforcing conformity to a whole host of other activities that parents might not approve of at all. But a mom or dad can say it's important to know or anticipate how other people will "read you" and then think about whether or not it makes a difference to you. This important conversation helps you identify the power others have over your daughter's life (and her power to claim her own identity) as well as examine the fears and prejudices of others. You and she can talk about the ways the grown-ups and the kids in her life support or question the global judging-by-appearance that goes on in middle schools. You can talk about conventions and, yes, you can ask for a certain manner of dress for certain occasions, but we suggest you also be prepared to talk about why this matters to you.

While parents can take a more insightful approach, schools have instituted blunt dress codes for decades. No matter how many journalists tell you that teens are really going overboard now—too sexy too soon—remember that back in the seventies the fashion was halter tops, fishnet stockings, and micro-mini skirts. Much of the current fashion trend is actually retro.

Sometimes dress codes or uniforms are instituted in an effort to achieve parity among disparate socioeconomic backgrounds, although girls can find all kinds of ways to announce their wealth through jewelry and possessions. Dress codes are more typically designed for the kids who want to make extreme and even dangerous statements—claiming their gang or other kinds of exclusive group memberships—as well as the kids who need the most attention, but they also affect those who are being quintessentially adolescent, making a statement about themselves through style and fashion. Too often dress codes stifle that impulse by instituting a narrow, often white and middle class version of appropriate attire for all kinds of kids.

The rules vary widely from school to school. Schools prohibit a range of items: Underwear should not be seen at any time. Hair that has a non-human color is not permitted. Any sleeveless garment must have width on the shoulder area of at least four of the student's fingers, and the arm opening should fit the body closely enough to cover the underarm and the side of the chest areas. A middle school in Virginia has so many restrictions that it divides the rules into categories for bottoms, tops, sweaters, and "other" wear. It is clear that attention to these codes is primarily focused on rules that prevent girls from wearing sexy clothing to school (or as one girl reported, the four b's, three of them aimed at girls: no bras, no boobs, no bellies, and no butts).

The second big category in school dress codes is rules prohibiting clothing that seems to identify the kid as alternative—whether it be goth (spikes), mafia (trench coat), gang member (symbols, lettering, belts worn a certain way), or punk (unusual hair color).

Schools and parents give similar reasons for dress codes. The most convincing state something about how students should dress for the purpose of learning and playing or for health, safety, and comfort. Others talk about "instilling discipline" or "school climate" and "freedom from outside influences." Girls often wear provocative clothing because it's in style. Some girls wear sexually provocative clothing simply because it looks like what Paris Hilton or the Olsen twins wore on *Nickelodeon Kids' Choice Awards* or *MTV Movie Awards*. Their belly button is showing, and they're dying to have a piercing there because it looks "totally cool." Sure, they'll acknowledge that it looks sexy, but for them sexy is cool and feminine. To middle schoolers sexy doesn't mean that they want boys to grab them in the hall or that they want to have sex. In fact, many middle school girls haven't really connected looking sexy with sex but with some vague feeling of being desirable. We asked the girls what message they want to give by the clothes they wear, and they said over and over, "That I'm cute."

It is true that some girls in middle school want to be provocative sexually and what they wear is distracting. There are the extreme pleas for help, such as the girl who wore a see-through shirt to school and the girl who wore only her underwear and a trench coat. Girls often want to be noticed for other reasons; they are confused about sexual feelings and sexual attention, or the sexual attention they have received from adults and peers has been abusive, inappropriate, or overstimulating. They can affect an "I don't care" attitude and feel the danger of being seen as a "slut" or object. These girls might even be seen as creating an alternative identity for themselves as "slutty and I don't care." Some of them really are troubled, and to zero in on the sexual attention they want (a route they choose because in this culture we make so much of sexual objectification or the power of sexuality to make people anxious) rather than their deeper need for just about any kind of attention is superficial and neglectful on the part of schools and parents.

We don't advise dismissing sexy dressing as "just the fashion," either. Sexy clothing is marketed earlier and earlier to girls, and they may find it hard to resist the attention they get when they look sexy. You can talk to them about how difficult it is to have people see the "real you" in this glammed-up, hypersexualized world and that it is unfortunate. If she is dressing sexy for school to provoke, remember that provocation is not always bad, and if we can help girls channel that desire to provoke, to draw attention to themselves, to make an identity statement in areas beyond fashion and sexuality, we will have opened up a myriad of possibilities for girls' development. The way to do this is not to prohibit, lay down the law, or tell them that their budding sexuality is unacceptable or makes them a target for violence. The way to do this is to understand why they are wearing what they're wearing and have meaningful conversations about the various influences that affect these choices, as well as about a culture that sends them a heavy dose of mixed messages about sexuality.

Dress codes can seem biased against girls. In one focus group we led in an eighth grade classroom, the boys claimed they didn't even have a dress code (although this was not true). A savvy middle schooler told us about one school's bias. Tierra's middle school had a dress code, but she noticed that girls who were more physically developed were targeted more for wearing spaghetti straps and crop tops. The less developed girls went unnoticed. Others saw this, too, and Tierra quickly gathered nearly one hundred signatures on a petition to the administration calling for the code to be applied fairly. Rules may miss the point and simply create boundaries that reinforce the angel/slut divisions these girls are already buying into, boundaries that they will challenge themselves and one another to cross.

While kids need to know where you stand on issues, it is more important for you to know where *they* stand, whether it's teetering on high heels or in fifty-pound black boots with a hundred lace holes, and even if it is just for this month. You can defy the media's claim that dressing in a certain way conveys sexiness, violence, or anarchy. You can defy the marketers' hold on your daughter by letting her know that if she is dressing provocatively as a means of self-expression, you want to know the self that is hidden or expressed by the clothes she wears and why.

One more word about schools. What if schools let students monitor themselves regarding dress? What if schools or parents set up broad parameters, within which kids can be creative? What if student committees came up with dress codes that seem appropriate with regard to safety and comfort? We might hear from the students that they are not particularly distracted by the girl who dyed her hair blue; after the first few days they got used to it. We might hear that dyed hair is a qualitatively different identity statement from wearing T-shirts with tobacco company slogans. We might hear that it's not okay to wear sexist or racist slogans on T-shirts but that a majority think it is fine to wear short shorts on hot days or spaghetti straps when the weather is warm. We may have a conversation about how insulting it is to boys to think they can't control themselves around girls who wear short shorts, or we might even get requests from girls for the school to do something about how the boys' reactions prevent the girls from wearing what they want. We would definitely hear that kids "read" the various fashion statements differently from adults.

Important questions could then be addressed about social class and race, about violence and gangs, about tolerance and prejudice, about objectification and gender safety. To what extent are girls making statements, without realizing it, about their wealth, and how does that make a girl feel who doesn't have the money to spend on so many different outfits? Why is brand name so important, and how did these companies get girls to be mini-marketers of their brands by dissing other girls who shop at lower-priced stores? How did stores like Hot Topic become the Gap of the goth set? Are kids really making an antifashion and an anticonformity statement when they shop there? Wouldn't it be interesting to see who owns Hot Topic and whether their investments or subsidiary companies actually reflect that "attitude" the kids are buying?

Hot Teens: The Clash Between Image and Self

Is it too late to talk to your teenage daughter about clothes and image? As we said earlier, she's very capable of reading the culture, uncovering hypocrisy, detecting deception, and uncovering manipulations. Unfortunately, it makes her feel humiliated and angry when she thinks you believe she's the one who has been duped. So tread lightly here when talking about how marketers and the media may be influencing her clothing choices. Girls try to say it all through their clothes. Clothes have such great significance to them that although it may be perfectly obvious to a mom that her daughter is conforming to some image she has seen in magazines or TV, to say so would probably end the conversation.

We asked a number of teens about where they shop, what they wear, and the image they were trying to create. Ali, who goes to an alternative high school, said she was kind of punk/goth. With her red hair tied up, her eyes shining, and her jewelry interesting and pervasive, she related that some days she also dresses like a "sexy earth goddess" and the boys like that. Ali hates to shop, but when she does, she shops online on Web sites that offer the specific items she's looking for.

Mindy, like many girls her age, wants to be a fashion designer; she wants to design the clothes, she says, and not just be a personal shopper. She was dressed in what she called "ska" style, which she explained is the style worn by stars like Gwen Stefani. She defines this as mix-and-match items that in the end look artsy and original. When asked why she wants to be a fashion designer, she said she believes we all have the chance to look pretty no matter what we look like and that fashion can make a huge difference. She spoke as if on a mission to help women and girls not feel bad about themselves any longer for not fitting in with the fashion norm; she wants to help them be original and uniquely pretty. When Leigh joined the conversation, Mindy said, "Now there are three types here." These girls knew they were projecting types and not just themselves. Leigh was blond and a bit wholesome/sexy-looking in tight jeans and layered shirts that could have been from the Gap or Abercrombie & Fitch. She didn't want to call herself "preppy" when the other two girls identified her as such and thought that "trendy" fit best with what she was trying to do with her image.

Ali, Mindy, and Leigh were very interesting people; by talking to them about more than fashion, we learned about things they know and do that were not reflected in the way they dressed. Ali is a field hockey player (and doesn't have a tongue ring because that could really hurt in a game). Mindy is a vegetarian for moral reasons and can tell you about the depletion of the rain forest from cattle grazing. Although they all wanted to look somewhat original, special, or not like everyone else, they also agreed that they were trying to conform to a stereotype about the type of girl they are. Each admitted trying to send a message.

We asked why they invested so much energy in image when there is so much more to them on the inside that doesn't get expressed through this image. We wanted to know why they willingly stereotype themselves in their dress when it is so important to them to be original, to be themselves. Leigh's answer was simple: boys. She presents herself as she does to attract boys. She was the one dressed the sexiest. Mindy said because it was fun, it was artistic and creative to put together an image. Ali, the punk/goth/earth goddess, said it was to kind of say "fuck off" to people, to project a negative stereotype. These were their first responses as conformist nonconformists, illustrating what Alissa Quart calls "self-branding" in her book *Branded*.

As we talked further, the girls came to the conclusion that dressing as they did was also to protect themselves. You protect yourself in high school by belonging somewhere, by fitting into some group. We asked some college students to reflect back on that time. One student, Rachel, told us that she and her friends were totally into fashion in high school. They knew all the latest trends and where clothes were bought even if they didn't have the money to buy designer labels. They all wanted to be fashion designers.

At present, though, Rachel is studying political science in college and says her friends are pursuing other difficult majors: none is studying fashion. When asked the question about image versus self, she told us that she and her friends did not really know who they were. They may have been interesting people inside the fashion they wore, but they didn't really know that about themselves yet or have confidence in those aspects of themselves. She added that she did have confidence in being trendy because ever since she was little she had been taught to value fashion. In college she was free to explore other parts of herself that she hadn't felt quite free enough to explore—at least not publicly—in high school.

Image protects in more ways than one. Image protects high school students by giving them a sense of belonging, but it also gives them a premature identity while they are insecure or struggling to forge something unique and personal. Being an aggressive field hockey player, a lover of literature, a collector of quotes, and a questioner may be a part of who Ali is, but she feels most comfortable, *protected*, shall we say, presenting an image that doesn't really speak to any of that. While this may be okay for some who can move beyond image during or after the teen years, others become trapped and stuck in this superficial world. For those who can preserve a self apart from image, the divisions and unhappiness that come with focusing too much on image in the teen years creates too much stress and too much of a diversion from what they could be doing and creating for themselves.

While your daughter may feel protected with an image, she has to fight hard to preserve something besides that image because the culture around her won't reflect back anything but image. The culture mirrors back the same types in TV shows, movies, music, and magazines; these types are picked up and enacted through relationships with peers and friends. For a culture that values individualism so much, we give message after message to be a type of girl. Even the pop stars and rock singers whom girls worship are reduced to types. It appears to be all that is valued about these girls—not that Hilary Duff is also a gymnast or that Paris Hilton plays ice hockey. Individual interests are invisible.

Adolescent girls may believe that what they are expressing is uniquely them, but it's your job to mirror back to them what is really unique and interesting about them. To you they can never be just a prep, a goth, a nerd, an earth goddess, or an artsy type. To you they must always be who they are, and your conversations about clothes with them should always return to the real girl and not the projection. They may need to limit what they show to the cruel world outside, but your job is to help them make choices to express all of who they are.

SEXY "HOTT" TEENS

There are types, and there are girls who tend toward girly and girls who run in the other direction. Anything that is marketed as "girl" to a teenage girl is marketed as sexy. The only other image that comes close to sexy in terms of the sheer volume of messages is sophisticated shopper. All the angels and princesses and feisty little images that were marketed to your young daughter for years aren't gone; they've become sexy innocent, sexy diva princess, and sexy feisty girl. Everything is sexed up, and the best example of this is at Victoria's Secret where teens shop almost exclusively when they need underwear. Because of this, department stores and stores that were primarily shirts and pants stores now have sections of sexy underwear for teen girls in order to compete. Victoria's Secret has three sections that go from hot (cozy and sexy), to hotter (sexy), to hottest (slutty sexy). Victoria's Secret doesn't label the sections of the store this way, but some salesgirls we met do. The collections and sections of the store are called "angels" or "romantics," while individual items are described as sexy, very sexy, and very very sexy, reminiscent of the porn rating XXX.

Victoria's Secret is connecting innocence and the princess feel with sex, e.g., bedroom slippers that have heels and bits of feather boa, much like Cinderella would wear on her honeymoon. The little jock in your house can now wear little boys' brief-type underpants with a sexy twist. And the feisty little girl grown-up can be bodacious and wear red seethrough lingerie or black lace with studs to indicate that she is not just feisty but outrageous—"very bad," slut and proud of it, as her T-shirt might indicate. Let's not blame only Victoria's Secret for turning every symbol of girlhood into a symbol of sex appeal; all the teen stores are doing it.

Our teens tell us they shop at Urban Outfitters, American Eagle, and Abercrombie & Fitch. UO is a store whose clothing gives a girl a bit of a funky, alternative feel. Ostensibly, AE says "teen" and provides a safe haven—safe because teens know they won't be too noticeable or made fun of for wearing clothes from AE. A&F is admittedly preppie (according to the girls we surveyed).

In each of these stores we see innocence, girliness, boldness, and even darkness sold. The catalog writers use words that suggest the same old alternatives: "ice princess," "heat things up," and "mocs that rock." They're selling the same images again: princess, sexy, and diva. Whatever the "feel," it also has to be sexy. Innocence gone sexy has a slightly different look in AE compared to UO and A&F. In AE it might just be the jeans riding low on the hips and a ruffly T above it. In UO it might be a short plaid pleated skirt. In A&F it might be pink string Ts or a camisole with a bit of lace. Sporty gets the same sexy treatment with cowgirl types in boots and miniskirts. Look at the models in the catalogs with your daughter and count how many seem to be saying "Come hither" instead of "I'm a girl having fun."

But girliness hasn't been forgotten. If it had, what would the marketers do with all those accessories that mean girlhood? At UO, for example, surrounding the cool jeans and moccasins are camisoles with lace, sequins, and ribbons, skirts with satin bows and lace netting, flowers glued on to plain shoes, and sparkly tights. These are the same decorative bits that sell girlness to younger girls. This is what "cradle to grave brand loyalty" looks like.

No wonder that an honest alternative to all that cuteness and sexy hot stuff is pain. If you are not the girl that every guy dreams of, the angel in satin underwear that a sixty-year-old Bob Dylan sings to in Victoria's Secret commercials, then what are you? If you're not the kind of teen girl that boys like or that the world tells you boys like, then you're in no-girl's-land—or so you're told. You're a rejected girl. When your body does you wrong by not conforming to fitting the world's standardized sexy, pretty, happy thing, what can a teen do but punish it?

TATTOOS AND PIERCINGS

Tattoos and piercings are a different kind of accessorizing. What was once a statement about being tough and alternative has been commercialized and is now a fashion trend. In our survey, girls told us over and over how "cool" piercings were and outlined in detail where they liked them, where they wanted them, where it was cool to have them, and where it wasn't cool to have them. It was like reading a *Cosmo* article about ten ways to tie a scarf! The same with tattoos. Although not quite as many teens wanted one (too permanent, some said), this once tough biker emblem has now become a fashion trend with, yes, the same old girl images of butterflies (our girls' first choice), angels, hearts, and cute animals leading their tattoo wish lists. Girls also told us that they thought tattoos were very cool when they meant something special and symbolic about the girl wearing it. In other words, they're identity markers. But in a sense, like the store accessories, the variety of tattoos a girl can like or wish for is so limited that we wonder how they can say much at all about her.

Teenagers say that tattoos "express your inner self" and piercings "explain who you are." What about the girl who is "planning to get a rose on [her] ass" or the teen who wrote she wants a ring of red roses around her belly button or a tiny butterfly on her ankle? Well, they are indicating that they are kind of sweet but also a bit daring. They have bought the belief sold to them in stores that by choosing some personal emblem among the five or ten offered, they are saying something unique about themselves, they are claiming identity. It's not very different from buying that charm for a charm bracelet, but it's much more permanent.

Then there are those who pierce and pierce and pierce. One girl told us that she did it because she wanted to feel the pain and that she liked the healing process; the dull throbbing pain was a constant reminder of the pain she felt on the inside. It said to her that she was alive in a period of her life when she felt numb and dead inside. Another girl told us that the pierced image represented how rejected and awful she felt all the time.

We decided to approach a teenage girl in the mall who had many piercings. On a hunch, Sharon walked over to her and said, "I love that piercing that goes diagonally across your face. It's so cool." This girl, who initially looked rejected and scary, harsh and frightening, unapproachable, looked at the two of us and beamed the most beautiful smile. "Thank you," she said warmly and paused before walking on. In that moment it seemed that she felt not only visible but also kind of loved. Our hunch was right: Underneath the pierced identity was someone who didn't really want to be rejected and feared, but a girl who wanted to be taken seriously and seen, even by middle-aged women like us. So daughters who pierce and tattoo may be following fashion, or they may be expressing some pain inside or even be saying "fuck you" to the world. But we believe they all are looking to express themselves using the means the culture hands them. Read it with them. Read them gently; read them with love.

HALLOWEEN REVISITED

Before concluding this chapter we want to revisit Halloween, still a night of mystery and an opportunity for older girls to express a bit of themselves that they can't quite express during the day. We asked about Halloween in our survey. Mostly, older girls want to be devils. Why? "I was a devil dressed all in red and with devil horns because its sexy and boys love the outfit, gives u loads of attention," wrote Maxine. Jasmine was "an angel because my boyfriend liked it." Quite a few were sluts and hookers or sexy versions of schoolgirls and bunnies. They find costumes online or create their own. Girls who looked like Playboy bunnies and sexy kittens told us, "Halloween is the only day girls get to dress up as sluts and nobody can say anything about it." The night offers a release from all the dress codes and adult surveillance. Even a girl who self-identified as a lesbian joined the slut/hooker party: "I was a pimp. i did it cuz i go to an all girls school, and im a lesbian, and everyone knows, so i figured, what the heck, it'll be funny, and i could get my friends to play as my hos, and i had like 20."

Just as all the innocent angel princess clothing turns sexy for high schoolers, so do the costumes. Sure, some of them were still Miss America, cheerleaders, and rock divas, and one was even "birthday Barbie," but most wanted to be sexy versions of those archetypes. Just as being a devil means dressing in a sexy costume, so does being a vampiress, witch, and other evil temptresses such as Medusa, Catwoman, and Poison Ivy from *Batman*. We can see the Halloween issue of *Cosmo* now: "Evil Just Got Sexier!" Except that your daughter's fantasy life has been invaded and taken over by demons (marketers) who tell her to fantasize showing up in a costume for a bunch of boys. If they have their way, all the creative energy you put into art classes, reading, and bringing her the world when she was younger will be used to make her hot.

But it won't necessarily last. Think of Rachel, Ali, and Leigh, whose parents talked to them about their fashion tastes and, more important, about their talents and their future. You may not lose her to the world of sex kittens and hot angels in underwear. You might if you don't talk about these images with her. Even the most shopping-savvy teen or trendsetter wants to understand marketing and image, and those future fashion designers sure need to know. If you can become that observer of culture *with* her instead of being on or at her, you will be able to set up a wonderful relationship of companionship as she makes her way through the crowd of marketers vying for her attention.

The other key to preserving a relationship with your daughter if she has jumped onto the image train and is riding away from you, is to see her fully when she's at home, reflecting back to her all the things she is and loves. Resist buying into the image even if she buys into it heavily. Mirror back the complexity of her inner self, and she'll carry that with her underneath the costume.

And what to do about sexy? Love the new sexual being you see your daughter developing into and even admit it's fun to be sexy and to sometimes get attention that way. If you do, then you're prepared to talk about being sexual versus looking sexy, about feeling desire versus being a sex object. Being sexual is a developing part of your teen that sometimes is expressed in wearing something sexy or acting sexy, as well as participating in some sexual stuff alone or with a partner. Looking sexy or being someone's sexual object is participating in a dangerous game where she runs the risk of being rejected by other girls or treated poorly by boys or, worse, being seen as "asking for it."

So, faced with an all-consuming culture that is hell-bent on marketing sexy girlhood to your daughter at every age, what is a parent to do? Get in there and mix it up. Talk with your daughter. It's hard and it's bound to be messy, but it's the only way.

CHAPTER 2

See No Evil? What Girls Watch

Don't underestimate the power of the visual on girls. We can talk and talk about our own values, but, remember, girls are seeing values constantly acted out by peers and role models (generally somewhat older girls). We also have to consider what it means to live in a media-saturated culture. Getting rid of the TV, turning off the TV during commercials, being highly selective about the movies they watch, and keeping them away from media after school and in the evening isn't always possible or practical. There will be references to and influences from the world of TV and commercials everywhere anyway. Without the benefit of our views on the messages they are receiving, they are more vulnerable and likely to accept them and reproduce them in their daily behavior, feelings, and thinking. Rather than taking an all-or-nothing approach to TV and the movies, we think it is better to know what is out there, make careful decisions, and watch with our daughters.

In this chapter we explore what your daughter watches. We know that new shows, commercials, and movies are introduced constantly, so we highlight some recurring themes that have been around, are still around, and, unless there is a dramatic shift in perspective at the highest levels, will be around for some time to come. These themes are found in many forms of media; TV, commercials, and movies feed your daughter a steady diet of stereotypes. They continue to output types, because in this day and age with licensing agreements worth billions, the types sold to your daughter in the form of clothing at Kmart and Limited Too get their lifeblood from visual media.

Considering the astonishing technology available these days—three-dimensional images and computer-generated people who look and act real—it's truly amazing what little imagination has gone into developing and expanding gender roles. Some shows such as the Disney Channel's *House of Mouse* add new technology and dress up old cartoon characters in modern clothes but stick to the fifties stereotypes. Professor Von Drake is still a crazy male scientist in a white lab coat. Minnie and Daisy are still

girlfriends in heels and pearls, batting their eyelashes at the boys to manipulate them and get their way. Other shows seem to promise something
better but can't quite deliver with conviction. They constantly betray
their bias: Female animals wear pink frills and aprons to indicate gender;
working moms are few and far between—and crazy if not crazed when
they do exist; conventional romance arrives early to narrow a girl's options and crowd out friendships between boys and girls. It seems the more
things change, the more they stay the same.

The old phrase "garbage in, garbage out" applies, unfortunately,
even to so-called educational shows designed to teach our youngest
daughters to read or to be confident and healthy. Little kids believe what
they see, and a daily dose of stereotypes and narrow sexist portrayals of
girls and women is the kind of garbage that is very difficult to get rid of.
The good news is that girls are more likely than ever to see girls and
women on TV. While the world of prime time is still largely a white
male world—65 percent are male, and 74 percent are white, according
to Children Now, a nonprofit organization that promotes children's
well-being and researches the media's impact on them—viewers are
more likely to see a female alien in prime-time TV than a female Asian
or Latina character. Numbers tell only part of the story. It is important
to note what girl characters are saying and doing, thinking and feeling,
and what effects they might have on your daughter. Because she is likely
to watch about three hours of television a day and catch about forty
thousand commercials a year—at a time in her life when she's trying to
figure out who she is and what she values—these are vitally important
issues to consider.

Fiona in Never-Never Land: The Early Years

The Disney Channel has *Playhouse Disney*; Nickelodeon has *Nick Jr.*; the
Cartoon Network has *Tickle U*; The WB has *Kids' WB!*; and PBS has the
Bookworm Bunch. All these programs are geared to the preschool and
younger viewer. The first thing that struck us after watching hours and
hours of TV shows aimed at younger kids was that they were good in some
ways. In this little corner of TV land you are likely to find kids of different
races and ethnicities, sometimes kids of different social classes, kids with
different abilities, and occasionally kids challenging gender stereotypes
(although your daughter may wonder when she gets to the preteen years

how this open and inclusive world suddenly got so white, middle class, and male). In shows for the younger ages, more men show up as caretakers or adult guides, such as Joe in *Blue's Clues*. And there are also the four silly Australian guys who sing their way through *The Wiggles*. But unlike shows aimed at older kids, parents are often around and available for comfort and advice. Friends take turns and learn how to be better friends; people from all walks of life like to play, laugh, sing, and dance; adults and children alike tell the truth, help out, pick up after themselves, and try new things.

But where are the girls? There are many more male lead characters on little kid TV in shows such as *Stanley, Caillou, the Koala Brothers, Rolie Polie Olie, Arthur, Franklin, Little Bill,* and *George Shrinks*; the list goes on. There are a few shows with strong girl leads, such as the intrepid Dora in *Dora the Explorer* and curious Blue of *Blue's Clues* (although most people seem to think Blue is a boy because of her color), feisty JoJo the clown on Disney's *JoJo's Circus*, and practical Emily Elizabeth of *Clifford* on PBS-Kids. Most often, though, girls are secondary characters (little sisters) or part of a crowd of friends.

While shows for young children are easy to distinguish because of their tone, pace, and explicit educational messages, most young children also watch shows geared more toward later childhood such as *SpongeBob SquarePants* and *Rugrats,* so it's actually difficult to define a show for preschoolers. These more sophisticated cartoons have no parent guides on the show's Web sites and have a lot of sarcasm, tongue-in-cheek jokes, allusions to romantic crushes, and fancy gadgetry that is far over the heads of kids under six or seven. They also have a high cuteness factor that can throw parents off. Commercials add to the confusion because these shows tout products geared to both younger viewers and teens. It is all about selling products, which explains the trend to create shows that also appeal to eleven-year-olds while ignoring the developmental needs of preschoolers.

Even more than the actual TV shows, these commercials educate girls and boys about the gendered route they're expected to travel. The few good messages in the shows about being fully who you are or supporting a sense of adventure in girls are interrupted every fifteen minutes or half hour by commercial images of princesses, baby dolls, and diva fashion accessories, reminding your daughter what girls are really about. Remember, until they are about six, children can't separate the show from the commercial. To them it's all the same and it's all reality.

It's hard not to notice a few troubling patterns when watching TV for younger kids with girls in mind. In award-winning (and Department of Education–funded) shows such as *Between the Lions*, stereotypical imagery is surprisingly frequent. In this show a family of lions—mother, father, older son, and younger daughter—live in a library and spend their time exploring the world of books and using the computer to teach their audience reading skills. Male characters in the serial skits that make up most of the show far outnumber the females. This could be about the gender gap in literacy, but more likely they are simply following a pattern found in most of children's programming. There is the magician wordsmith Arty Smartypants who sounds a lot like Steve Martin's *Saturday Night Live* wild and crazy guy; Cliff Hanger (a muscular guy who hangs from a branch on the side of a cliff; why couldn't this be a girl?); and Tiger Words (based on the famous golfer). There is also *Gawaine's Word*, a combination of the popular TV movie *Wayne's World* and knights of the round table who charge each other with letters to make whole words. Female characters are likely to be diva types, glittery-clothed singers, and bossy queens.

Girls do stereotypically girl things; boys do stereotypically boy things, even when the larger message is a good one. In "Shanna's Show," a short segment on *Playhouse Disney*, for example, an African American girl named Shanna puts on skits and interacts with her young audience. In one skit she is dressed in overalls and a farm hat and she gives out three clues (à la *Blue's Clues*), so the children watching can guess what her job is. She says she plants her seeds in rows, she drives a tractor painted red, and she works with animals small and big. Sounds great. But when your daughter jumps up and guesses Farmer, she sees Shanna's little brother, not Shanna, riding the fun red tractor all around. Lucky brother. We guess Shanna will have to gather eggs or cuddle the bunnies.

What is odd about educational TV is that the shows don't really teach much that is new or real when it comes to gender, or at least they don't teach it with much conviction—kind of like the teacher who makes the rule "No shouting out answers," and then after a few minutes lets it slide for the boys. Most shows simply mirror or exacerbate the most stereotypical patterns: dads fix things and read the newspaper; mothers are kind and make cookies; boys are into sports and the outdoors; girls are into ballet and dressing up. There are a few exceptions: Brenda Blue, the woman mechanic on *Jay Jay the Jet Plane*, and Stephanie, the eight-year-old on the fitness and health-focused show *Lazy Town*. Stephanie is especially interesting. While she seems almost over-the-top stereotypical, with her pink hair, pink clothes, pink room, pink everything, she also plays sports, thinks on her feet, and loves computer games. She makes pink a power color but is the only girl on the show.

One would think educational TV would offer children ways to question and suggestions for moving beyond these limited roles. Instead, girls are often sweet, giggly, bossy, overly emotional, and needy. We particularly dislike this portrayal of girls as overly emotional and needy. These ever-present characters can be grating. For example, the only continuing female character on *The Wiggles* is purple Dorothy Dinosaur who speaks in a high voice and skips around in a floppy white hat and necklace. We also caught an episode that introduced a woman space alien, but she's in a beehive hairdo, a metallic miniskirt, and high-heeled boots. (Even space aliens have to conform.) There is sweet Lucy and her doll in *Little Bear*, the bossy Beaver in *Franklin*, the giggly pink Angelina in *Angelina Ballerina*, and, alas, Elizabeth the Emotional Pig in *Marvin the Tap-Dancing Horse*. Like *Sesame Street*, these shows are much better at representing diversity (even if it's diversity of animals or puppets) than they are in challenging gender stereotypes.

There *is* an exception for girl types, but just one: the feisty/sporty girl. Remember the girl who avoided pink clothes? (This is why Stephanie in *Lazy Town* is unusual.) On TV for the younger set she is usually smart and placed in opposition to the ballerina type. (She is often used to make this more girly type of girl seem shallow, annoying, or selfish.) The feisty girl tends to have a close connection to her father and/or a close male friend, like JoJo and best friend Skeebo. JoJo believes in herself and succeeds in her adventures while her mother watches—in necklace and skirt, alas. Fathers and men are often the ones who make it possible for girls to succeed in cartoons, rarely moms.

In *Arthur*, Francine is the cool girl. She's into sports, close to her dad, working class, practical, and good friends with Arthur. She, too, gets compared to a "bad" type. She is a lot cooler than Muffy, the rich snobby girl who is into fashion and gossip.

Come to think of it, almost all the interesting, feisty girls in TV shows are cool because their primary friendships are with boys and they're not girly girls. In the PBS show *George Shrinks*, Becky is George's best friend and co-inventor; Stanley's friends, twins Mimi and Marci, are pretty nifty. And if your daughter has caught the crossover to preteen shows, there is feisty skater (also spelled sk8ter) girl Reggie who hangs with her younger brother's friends in *Rocketpower*. Lexi Bunny is the only female character in the WB cartoon *Loonatics Unleashed*, and Sponge-Bob's friend Sandy, a smart martial arts whiz of a squirrel from Texas, is a great character (but, unfortunately, not great enough to make it into the SpongeBob SquarePants movie). The only other continuing girl charac-ter on *SpongeBob* is Mr. Crab's daughter, an annoying cheerleading whale named Pearl. And that's the point. These cool girls are tokens, and they are pitted against girly types to accentuate the put-down factor: girly girls, we've been led to believe, are awful.

Girls watching these shows have two types to choose from—girly and tomboy—whereas boys have a range of options available to them. They can be brainy, goofy, sensitive, tough, loyal, funny, mean, depressed, or bizarre. Girls can be either for the boys or with the boys. For example, in PBS's *Seven Little Monsters*, only two of the seven monsters are girls, and they match the same pattern. Six is a tutu-wearing ballerina who thinks she is the most beautiful monster in the world, and One is a baseball player who likes to hang with the guys and take charge. While all seven monsters have different quirks, only the girls dress in a way that clearly announces their girl types. The five boy monsters dress more plainly and differ in shirt color and type. They don't need to announce their particu-lar brand of boyness. Kind of like *Seinfeld* for five-year-olds, there are a bunch of differently funny guys and a token feisty girl. As in *Seven Little Monsters* and *Seinfeld*, girls can be types while boys can be individuals.

Watch out, though. Those girls cast in the girly roles in the younger shows will turn out to be the mean, bossy, popular girls in the shows aimed at slightly older viewers, such as Angelica Pickles in *Rugrats* and *Rugrats: All Grown Up!*; Cindy Vortex and her friend Libby in *Jimmy Neutron*; and those nasty captain cheerleaders in shows such as *Kim Possible* and *Lizzie McGuire*. If you've wondered where to find the roots of girl meanness and the competition between girly and tomboy, look no further than chil-dren's television.

One of the things that shows for younger viewers do best, even within the limits we've pointed out, is provide examples of boys and girls playing together. Disney's *Out of the Box*, PBS's *Arthur*, and, for slightly older chil-dren, PBS's *Cyberchase* and *Zoom*, show boys and girls problem-solving, planning, and playing together in ways that move them beyond stereo-types. But as soon as Nick Jr. turns into Nick, crushes and competition and misunderstandings get in the way of anything resembling true friend-ship between boys and girls. Shows such as *Slime Time Live* pit boys against girls in preparation for all those boy-versus-girl reality shows. Boy-girl friendships happen now and again, but mostly they are part of a story of romance and opposite sides. Too bad. Showing real and lasting friendships between boys and girls would do a lot to break down stereotypes and gender inequalities.

We also wonder what will happen to those feisty girls. The girly girls become popular and get the boys as they get older, but what happens to JoJo and Dora? Where do they fit? We wonder how little girls who lean toward feistiness will know how to stay strong into womanhood with so few role models. If these shows are any indication, they become skater girls and the like, hanging with guys or staying cool by putting down girly girls, continuing to get that all-important father-seal-of-approval.

We would like the TV fathers to stay as strongly connected to their daughters over the next ten years of growing, but you'll see in the next chapter that they don't. They are sorely needed because nearly all the mothers in these shows are presented as *uber*-housewives. Like something out of the fifties, they have coifed hair, wear aprons, dresses, and pearls to clean house, and worry about the messes that husbands and feisty girls and their brothers get into. If the reality for most kids is a working mom, what's the deal? Why offer outmoded stereotypes? There are a few exceptions, of course, but they are considered a bit odd—such as Phil and Lil's feminist mom in *Rugrats*. Instead of being in a strong partnership or on her own, she is portrayed as a kind of man in drag with a weak and ineffective husband—as if being overpowering were the only option for women who are strong.

It's important to talk with your daughter about what she is watching. Four or five isn't too early. Help her see the difference between a stereotype and reality. Encourage her to experience and appreciate the real world and the real people around her and to understand that the people on the shows are acting or telling stories. You might ask, "What other stories could they have told?" and "Let's make up our own with these and some new characters." When she says things like "All girls wear pink" or "All girls dance ballet" or "Only boys play with action figures," point out the wide range of difference in her friends, cousins, and the kids on the playground.

Becoming a critic is only one option. Find alternate ways (other than the media) to develop her imagination, such as putting on plays and puppet shows, creating new games and songs, co-telling stories of adventure or making up worlds and new alien beings to befriend. If she has a lively imagination, the world of TV may get a little boring by comparison, and she may turn off the TV herself.

GIRLS ONLY: COMMERCIALS

There tend to be fewer commercials on the educational shows for the very young set, but fewer doesn't mean they don't exist. Marketers have made the most of the fact that children watching cartoons can't easily distinguish when a show ends and a commercial begins. Because nearly every *Playhouse Disney* commercial invokes Disney products, kids really don't know when they're being taught compassion and when they're being sold Mickey Mouse or McDonald's. One minute there is a segment on *Playhouse Disney* in which Clay—an actual lump of talking clay—teaches something or sings a song, and the next there's Ronald McDonald skipping around and singing about how he "loves to be a part of *Playhouse Disney*." The move from show to product is so quick, smooth, and seductive, *we* could hardly track it. From a kid's point of view, it must seem like the playhouse has its own fast-food restaurant. Although PBS doesn't have as many commercials, they are increasingly present in the form of fast-food sponsors such as Chuck E. Cheese's and McDonald's. You can also find them here and there *in* the shows, such as the trip to the Cape Cod potato chip factory in the "now for us kids" break between Arthur cartoons.

The commercials between shows sell more than products; they sell kids on how to be a cool, hip, and "normal" girl or boy. They make no pretense to educate, so they can utilize stereotypes to the fullest—to poke fun and make kids laugh, to grab attention, to create desire where none exists. Whatever it takes. Younger viewers get ads for tween shows, while preteens are pointed toward Teen Nick and PG-13 movies. While TV for young viewers makes some attempt to represent and mingle male and female characters, commercials are almost completely gender-separate spaces. Except for a few sugary cereal and candy ads, toy manufacturers have all but given up on a world in which boys and girls play together or like the same things.

We watched Nick for many hours. On one of our typical watching days, commercials surrounding popular shows like *Rugrats* suggest that only boys play Legos (Alpha Team), that space is the final frontier only for boys (Lego Star Wars), that only boys play Game Boy Advance and PlayStation, that only boys play with fast cars (Matchbox Hero City) and action figures (Spiderman and Teenage Mutant Ninja Turtles—"You have the power!"), that only boys play at war (G.I. Joe: Valor vs. Venom), and only boys "surrender now and prepare to fight" their Pokémon. The girls we know who love Pokémon and are addicted to their Game Boys will never see themselves on these commercials. The commercials are dark and filled with words and images that reflect power, control, and fearlessness; boys fight sinister things and evil forces, and they win. Girls are intruders in this world or serve as backdrop.

Girls, commercials suggest, are princesses (The Disney Princess Collection), fairies (Fairytopia), exotic fashion divas (Bratz World Tokyo a Go-Go), or surfer babes ("Don't you want to be a Cali girl?"). They want cuddly animals to exercise with (Care Bears work out to songs like "Let's Get Physical"; a four-year-old girl on a commercial tells us, "I'm shakin' it"), to hug (Fur Real Luv Cubs), and to sing with (Serafina, a fluffy white singing kitty). They want little dolls that suggest they someday will have lots of babies (5 ♥sie dolls) and do housework (Dora's talking kitchen). And they're really into clothes and accessories they can wear when they go out dancing (Polly Pocket, Bratz, Barbie). These commercials mix hearts, hugs, and giggling girls with "clubbing," hot-tubbing, wearing makeup, and looking cute in a sexy kind of way.

It is not always easy to see patterns in the images and messages your children are subjected to over the course of a day, week, or year, but they are influencing your child's sense of the world. Parents need to appreciate the issues that intersect with sexism, such as racism and messages about aggression. For instance, when Mary Strom Larson from Northern Illinois University tracked TV commercials on shows rated safe for the youngest viewers (two to seven years old), she found an astonishing 37 percent of commercials contained at least one aggressive act. What's more, she found that commercials featuring "white children only" contained the most physical, verbal, and "fortuitous" aggression—aggression not caused by a character but by something like an explosion. Larson concluded that there are a "wealth of models of aggressive behavior" available to children, and she remains concerned that so much fortuitous aggression cultivates fear of a "scary world" in the youngest viewers.

You may think it's best just to turn off the TV. It won't work—at least not for long. Advertisers are aware of TiVo and the option that DVD movies provide of skipping trailers and ads; it is the reason that immersive advertising and product placement in kids' shows are on the rise. Preventing TV is an ostrich-with–its-head-in-the-sand maneuver. It's not just the world of TV that is bombarding your child with products and gender messages; there are also Web sites, fast-food restaurants, movies, billboards, and toys. The real issue is the big corporations that are out to sell your kids everything. So after you join Campaign for a Commercial-Free Childhood (www.commercialfreechildhood.org), bring the healthy snacks and sit down beside her to teach her how to be a critical consumer. If you watch with your daughter, you will be able to know and question out loud what is really being sold to her. That counts for gender messages, too. Preschoolers are not too young to hear (and imitate) your questions and observations, so when you see a gender message that could be destructive, you can turn it into an opportunity to discuss what girls can be and won-der why the TV doesn't show that.

Let's be realistic. Most parents sometimes use TV as a babysitter. You therefore need to know your babysitter. Check references and see what your daughter is being taught. While you're getting that last bit of work done and your daughter is watching cartoons, ask her to come get you when she sees an example of a cool mom or two girls helping each other and succeeding! She'll keep an eye out for the good stuff as well as what's missing. TV can educate, but only parents can be sure the educational messages she gets are the ones you want her to receive.

DISNEY GIRLS

One place to begin this education is with Disney characters. Disney's mo-nopoly on fantasy is so pervasive, however, that it's hard to know where to begin. In fact, Disney is the first thing we think of when people tell us that parents should simply throw away the TV. Disney's version of girl-hood is everywhere—in department and specialty stores, catalogs, books, magazines, movies, TV, CDs, and, of course, the theme parks. The Disney girl adorns clothing, toys, room decor, sneakers, accessories, makeup kits, and purses. Unless you plan to lock your daughter in a tower, the Disney girl needs to be confronted head-on.

Who is she? Consider the catalog copy announcing a set of Princess Dolls, the most popular of all Disney girls for the three-plus set:

> Belle is ready for an evening with Beast, Cinderella is off to the ball, Tinker Bell is full of mischief, Mulan will bring honor to us all, Esmeralda wishes to help all the outcasts, Aurora dreams of Prince Phillip, Snow White longs for her Prince, Ariel wants to be part of his world, Jasmine's ready for a magic carpet ride, and Pocahontas discovers the colors of the wind.

We can tell a lot from this short description and the dolls that accompany it. Disney girls are typically princesses or repackaged as princesses even if they aren't ones in the stories told about them. They're always ready for, longing for, hoping and dreaming for a man, whether beastly or princely. They "want to be part of his world," not create their own world; ride *his* magic carpet, not hers. They care and nurture, especially animals. They are sweet-faced, big-breasted, small-waisted visual delights. Is that all? Because Disney's animated movies create the stories that drive their merchandise sales, we decided to take a closer look at Disney girls in film. We came up with the following themes:

Disney girls are women with Barbie doll bodies. And, like Barbie, one small size fits all. The form-fitting clothing of these heroines proves it. They have the exotic made-up faces of women and the gowns and midriff-baring (Jasmine in *Aladdin*) bikini tops (Ariel in *The Little Mermaid*) of women. Not real women, of course—they're too perfect— but the male fantasy version. They arch their backs (did they use the same template for the Victoria's Secret bra ad as they did for *The Little Mermaid* and *Pocahontas* bursting out of the water scenes?), toss their hair, smile sweetly, and speak softly. They're pretty when they're angry. Let's face it, changing skin and hair color and adding some exotic clothing does not a woman of color make. The one exception to this is Lilo and her older sister in *Lilo and Stitch*. What a relief to see real girls' bodies, faces, and personalities. No surprise—they don't make the princess doll set.

Disney girls and women are gossips and chatterboxes. "Girls talk too much," Peter Pan complains after Wendy accosts him. Women in *The Little Mermaid* gossip around the washtub. Ursula the Sea Witch warns Ariel, "The men up there don't like a lot of chatter." In *Dumbo*, a mean-spirited female elephant announces to her friends, "Have I got a trunk full of dirt."

Disney girls mother and do the housework. And not only Snow White and Cinderella. Wendy mothers the Lost Boys, while the native woman in *Peter Pan* admonishes her, "No dance! Go gettum firewood" (adding a little racism to the mix). The little girl who catches Mowgli's eye in *The Jungle Book* sings, "I will have a handsome husband, and a daughter of my own. And I'll send her to fetch the water. I'll be cooking in the home." The soldiers in Mulan sing about a girl worth fighting for who cooks and waits at home.

Disney girls have lovely voices. From Snow White to Pocahontas, those girls can really warble. It's part of what makes them beautiful. They sing their desire and woes to animals and other nonhuman creatures because, and this is important:

Disney girls have no support systems. Except for Lilo who has her big sister, Disney girls don't have girlfriends and very little family. If they do, they leave them for princes or beasts or bandits (*Robin Hood*). Even after proving themselves, they find real honor with a husband (*Mulan*). They typically don't have mothers, and their fathers tend to be buffoons (*Beauty and the Beast, Aladdin*) or authoritarian jerks (*The Little Mermaid*).

Disney girls can't resist a mirror. Check out Tinker Bell measuring her hips in a hand mirror. She is clearly shocked at what she sees. Are they that wide? Dated, you say? Elastigirl, the mother in the Disney/Pixar movie *The Incredibles*, checks out her hips in a mirror in the same fashion. It seems that saving her family and the world just has to wait. Disney girls can make mirrors out of anything. Cinderella checks her hair in a wash bubble and later in a pond. Lady of *Lady and the Tramp* catches her image in a water bowl.

Disney girls are incomplete without a man. It is not only romance, it is romance in a reality that affirms male power. Male power is what Disney does best, and not just in the old Disney movies. Every Pixar movie to date is a male journey story. Yes, girls exist as primary characters in *A Bug's Life, The Incredibles, Finding Nemo*, and *Cars*, but the main character is male. Men provide the energy, the rules, and the hope for safety (*Mulan, Pocohontas*), while we're reminded with one-liners that girls are crybabies (*Chicken Little*) or need to be rescued (almost every movie). Disney girls will do anything to meet or be chosen by the man of their dreams. Ariel gives up her voice; Tinker Bell betrays Wendy; Cinderella's stepsisters fight over the prince and betray her. Disney is brilliant at retelling history and creating romance where none existed: between Pocahontas and John Smith or between Mulan and her officer. A girl can't have her own story or live a life of bravery unless, in the end, she assumes her rightful place. She is not a Disney girl unless she marries.

Powerful Disney women are evil and ugly. Except for the grandmother spirit in *Pocahontas*, who shows up again in *Brother Bear*, when adult women exist they are typically vengeful and jealous of the Disney girl. They are also powerful and ugly: wicked stepmothers and queens (*Snow White*, *Cinderella*), ugly monsters and witches (*The Little Mermaid*, *The Sword and the Stone*, *Monsters, Inc.*). They are cruel and vengeful (Cruella DeVille in *101 Dalmatians* and the Queen of Hearts in *Alice in Wonderland*). Female power is itself evil: "It's time Ursula took matters into her own tentacles!" It is pretty clear to any little kid watching that dark skin is associated with evil. Check out Ursula or the evil queen in *Snow White* at their villainous peak. And while women with power will meet their demise in the most horrible ways—a stake through the heart, a car accident—Disney girls who recognize male power are rewarded with a place in his world: "Here she stands, the girl of his dreams" (*Cinderella*).

Disney girls are innocent. Tarty female characters in Disney movies pop up in funny places, usually in groups to underscore the Disney girl's singular innocence or to affirm a character's manliness: the busty barmaids in *Beauty and the Beast*, the sexy harem dancers in *Aladdin*, the vampish muses in *Hercules*. They are the girls that male characters like to flirt with but won't marry.

Let's be fair. We have welcomed the feisty, clever, and brave Disney girl of recent years. Look how Ariel defies her father and follows her heart! Isn't it great that Beauty is also a bit of a nerd and defiantly rejects the big handsome lout who pursues her? Isn't Pocahontas fearless, and isn't her relationship with her grandmother wonderful! Mulan really proves girls can do everything a guy can and, in this case, better than any other guy. Who wouldn't want their daughter to have such presence of mind and such impact on the world around her? The problem is that so much of the courage and feistiness is either in pursuit of romance or later put aside for it. Beauty endures horrific abuse to change her man; Ariel gives up her voice for her man; Pocahontas's goal is saving her man as much as preserving her homeland; Mulan's amazing feats dissolve in the presence of romance. This feels like a bait and switch. Draw a girl in with promises of something different and then bring in the same old thing through the back door.

Mulan, for example, was praised for being the first Disney film to present a tough girl, a girl who can fight, but it is ultimately at the expense of both boys and girls. The song lyrics tell at least part of the tale. "I'll Make a Man Out of You" is sung by Mulan's officer (who will fall in love with her) to his new recruits. The officer insults his soldiers by calling them girly men. One has to wonder how a five-year-old girl, who thinks being a girl is a pretty cool thing, feels when she hears the captain sing about the weakness of girls or when Mulan asks, "How about a girl who's got a brain? Who always speaks her mind?" and the soldiers say, "Nah!" When romance and tradition overtake the story, will she believe Mulan's courage really matters very much?

More recently another theme emerges in Disney movies:

New Disney girls star in straight-to-video sequels. Like a low-budget afterthought, *Peter Pan: The Return to Neverland*, *The Jungle Book 2*, and *The Lion King 2: Simba's Pride* all feature lead girl characters. Regardless of their central role, it is hard to get past the fact that girls weren't important enough to feature in the first blockbuster version. Girls in these movies are brave, but they have a lot to prove. Like other Disney girls, they don't have girlfriends; they seek respect in a male world, and so they have to show they're as brave, as strong, and as smart as boys. This means enduring a running commentary about their icky girlness. Ballou demeans Shanti, Mowgli's friend. When Jane, Wendy's daughter, says to Hook, "Not so fast. You'll have to answer to me," his response is "A little girl!" and derisive laughter. Jane has to deal with another catfighting Tinker Bell and with the Lost Boys' insults: "But she's a girl!"

As we saw in our review of girls' clothing, girls have two pathways out of this dilemma: to be one of the boys or to be for the boys (never one of the girls or for the girls, of course). When Jane punches Peter, he says, "You're sure not Wendy!" Nope, she's a true Lost Boy and proves it by learning to spit in her hand before shaking hands. Kiara, Simba and Nala's daughter in *The Lion King 2*, makes the other choice. She falls in love with and redeems Kovu, the son of evil Zira. In the end we "can feel the love tonight," and we also know there is a new king of the jungle, but it isn't Kiara.

What's a parent to do? Well, there are some wonderful movies out there, so you can avoid most Disney movies, especially the older movies that are recycled every few years, where the stereotypes are worse (although the rest of the products are hard to ignore). More important, ensure that movies with really strong girl characters are in your daughter's collection and life, movies such as *Matilda*, *Kiki's Delivery Service*, *Spirited Away*, and *The Wild Thornberrys Movie*. We recommend not showing most Disney films to really young girls or boys. Violent themes and images in *Beauty and the Beast* and *Pocahontas* really aren't for little kids, and do kids really need all that obsession with romance so long before it means anything to them? It is better to find ways to support egalitarian friendships with boys or bravery and a sense of love, loyalty, and compassion that isn't connected to getting a boyfriend.

If they are watching, watch with them. Tell them about the real story of Pocahontas the twelve-year-old girl, and the tragic true story of the Powhatan nation. Most of us don't know this version, but it is easy enough to find in the library or on the Web. Ask them why characters put down girls or why girls have to prove themselves to boys or fall in love with boys at the end of every movie. Ask them what they see that seems unfair, what they have questions about, what they like and dislike. If Disney stories can be used by parents to teach their daughters to notice and question stereotypes, maybe they are useful after all.

WHERE'S FIONA?

How do girls fare in other animated movies? In the first *Shrek* movie, Princess Fiona discovers that "love's true form" is not quite the Cinderella fantasy she had in mind. It's not a bad message and it's a nice antidote to the Disney films. In *Shrek 2*, Fiona has a chance to break the fairy godmother's spell and change both herself and Shrek, her ogre husband, into beautiful human forms. She chooses to stay real, to stay with "the one I fell in love with," and we all applaud her for that. Both movies were hugely popular, in part because they were brilliantly animated, funny, and irreverent, and also because of the decidedly anti-fairy-tale message that looks don't matter.

Wrong. Looks do matter. A lot—at least post-movie. *Shrek 2* was DreamWorks' biggest merchandising campaign to date, with more than eighty licensing agreements, using Shrek characters to promote the likes of Burger King, Pepsi, General Mills, Dial Corporation, M&M's, Hewlett-Packard, Activision, and even the U.S. Postal Service. So big, claimed Ann Globe, head of marketing and promotions for consumer products at DreamWorks, that, "we could 'Shrek' you out from head to toe."

So where is Fiona the ogre? Like Waldo of *Where's Waldo* books, you know she exists and see her every once in a while if you look hard enough, but she's tough to find. She is not at Burger King. The only Fiona they give away in their kid meals is a whirling human princess Fiona. But let's keep looking. She is not on the ogre-sized M&M candy package or in the Dial "You're not as clean as you think" commercials. She's nowhere near the Michelin radial tires or on the Rite Aid Christmas coupon booklet ("Shrek the Halls"). She has to be somewhere among all those male-bonding Shrek and Donkey scenes. Oh, here we go: You can choose her as a character in the Game Boy cartridge; she is in the background on the cover. But she's missing from the fruit gummy packages and the Go-GURT commercials, and she didn't make the Postal Service's "Greetings from Far, Far Away" postmark stamp.

Fiona, that true-blue, martial-arts-fighting, fun-loving spirited ogre just didn't make the grade. Maybe it wouldn't be good to have her around, reminding everyone that there is actually a girl character of real substance in the movie. Maybe we think girls won't want to play with a girl ogre or that they'd be disappointed to get the ogre and not the princess in their happy meal. More likely it's that pesky message she promotes about inner beauty. Can't have that. What would it sell?

Fiona the princess appears more often, we suspect, because she has a product-selling face and marketers always choose pretty over ugly, ignoring the story line. Changing beloved movie characters slightly in order to sell products happens all the time, in fact. When it comes to commodifying girls, it apparently pays to erase all the edgy interesting aspects of a character and replace them with pretty and pink. Maybe the logic goes that we already have one group of girls, the ones who don't automatically go for pretty—perhaps the hardest group to get—so now let's get all the rest.

Take *Nick Jr.*'s Dora the Explorer, for example. Here's a cool little girl, a bilingual map-reading Latina who makes her way in the world in a safari hat, binoculars, and hiking boots. As a toy she is a wonderful alternative to Barbie and Bratz. She looks like a little girl with spunk, and she *thinks*. But check out the decidedly un-Dora-like merchandise in the girls' section of Kmart: Dora in a bikini and flower bracelet or Dora in a yellow princess gown, fully decked out with a bracelet, ring, necklace, earrings, a yellow cone princess hat; her hair is long and flowing, complete with unicorn and rainbow: "Enchanted Explorers" and "Exploradores Encantados." (By the way, if the marketers had meant "girl explorers," they would have used "ex-plorador*as*," *not es!*) In fact, the inventors of Dora are now "chagrined" at these changes, but, alas, have no influence over licensing and sales.

The pattern repeats again and again: An interesting TV, book, or

movie character gets watered down or changed in stereotypical ways, supposedly to make her more appealing to girls—or maybe just to make her
the kind of girl who is into fashion and shopping. Disney does this with
Mulan, the girl who passed as a male warrior to save her country. Forget
that. How about putting her in the princess set? Mattel, with Disney's co-
operation, puts her in a geisha gown so that in the end Mulan, the determined girl and courageous warrior, is just another pretty face. Extreme
makeover: the early years.

It is really hard to support an "it's what's on the inside that really
counts" message when marketers actively work against it. But a parent can
start early. Let your daughter know you see what she sees, and we guarantee
you that she notices these things. Talk with her about the lack or disappear-
ance of girl characters. Make a game of it: Where's Fiona the ogre? Or simply make an observation: "I notice there is a Princess Fiona and no ogre
Fiona toy in the kids' meal, but there are three different Shrek toys." Ask
questions: "Why do you think they have Mulan in a ball gown? That wasn't
part of the story," or "She wasn't happy in the story when she dressed like
that." Encouraging her to be observant and to question what is given as well
as what is given up will help her trust her senses, develop opinions, and hold
on to the part of herself that prefers the ogre over the princess.

From TVs Meanest Meanies to Princess Movies: The Preteen Years

If you thought there was some kind of logical progression from TV for the
younger years to TV for the tween years, we have news for you. Preteens
who responded to our survey told us they watch pretty much everything,
from cartoons such as *SpongeBob* to extreme makeover reality shows such
as Fox's *The Swan*; from teen family fare such as *7th Heaven* to highly sexualized MTV videos and reruns of *Sex and the City*. Their responses ranged
from gushing endorsements of princess movies to irritated critiques of
music videos. Fifth grader Ginny from Illinois said, "I don't watch them. I
can't stand any video where characters act stupid (especially on purpose)
as well as videos where girls drastically change something about themselves to be accepted." (If only most children became as irritated as
Ginny. Forty-nine percent of kids ages ten to seventeen who responded to
a Children Now poll watch music videos daily. More than one-fourth of
the videos feature female breasts, legs, or torsos, while over two-thirds

feature females as props or in the background. The same goes for movies. Preteens watch family movies, princess movies, boy adventure movies, and the high-profile animated movies, such as *A Shark's Tale* that are designed to appeal to kids of all ages. While we can't prepare parents for every TV show or movie that comes out, we can help identify the problems that some of the best ones present.

One of the first things we noticed after watching cartoons and other TV shows targeted at preteens is that the racial diversity seen in the earlier years has waned. Children of color do appear, and there are some shows such as *Little Romeo*, *That's So Raven*, and *The Proud Family* with nearly all black casts. They are relatively few, however, and there are hardly any Asian or Latino characters in even secondary roles. When kids of color do appear, they're much more likely to be trusty sidekicks, not unlike Tonto and the Lone Ranger. In *Hey Arnold!* Arnold has African American Gerald to give him street credibility, while mean Helga has sweet Asian American Phoebe to give her a softer side. Cindy Neutron has African American diva Libby, and nasty Angelica in *Rugrats: All Grown Up* has African American friend Susie, and so on.

Preteens could use a lot more variety. The girls in our survey tell us they particularly love to watch *That's So Raven* and *The Proud Family*. Raven, like Sabrina, in *Sabrina, the Teenage Witch*, is a high school girl with special powers: Raven is psychic. *The Proud Family* is a cartoon about an African American girl, her girlfriends, and the capers they get into. Okay, she has the stereotypical bumbling father and peacemaking mother, but her feisty grandmother, Suga Mama, is a trip. Variety means more than race in these shows. Raven is a girl with a best friend who is a real best friend, and even though her sidekick male friend gets the bumbling jokester part, as usual, at least the show has her hanging with a female friend. Penny in *The Proud Family* has a gang of girlfriends with a variety of looks and personalities. Raven and Penny are not blond, and they're also not skinny. What's more, their attractiveness isn't played up or even that important to the girls in our survey.

But whether they have white girls or girls of color, nearly all TV shows for preteens focus on narrow teenager themes about boys and dances, popular cheerleaders, and mean girls. "I'm going to hook my man," says one of Penny's girlfriends. When they get a job at a department store, they sell shirts to guys by flirting and telling them how muscular they look. Girls will be a certain type of girl in these shows, or suffer. In *Rugrats: All Grown Up*, Angelica has become a fashion maven—no surprise. But so has Lil, that feisty twin and daughter of a feminist. In an episode called "Tweenage Tycoons," for example, Lil says to Tommy, "When you said, 'Let's get jobs,' Tommy, I was thinking of something a little more glamorous—like perfume sprayer at the mall." They are all raising money to go to a Sulky Boys concert. Although they all like rock and roll, the girls like to watch, and the boys like to play. Throughout the rest of the episode we learn that boys invent things, use the calculator, ride the bike, and handle the money. The giddy preteen girls are shoppers and screaming fans of the Sulky Boys.

Studies tell us that children who watch a great amount of TV per week hold more stereotypical views than those who watch less and that fourth and fifth graders who watch a great amount are more likely to gender-stereotype household chores. This is no surprise because women are much more likely to be used in commercials that sell household products. It's also not surprising that a study of the cartoon action show *Pokémon* found that kids rate characters who play *against* stereotype—an assertive girl or a sensitive guy—the least liked and that both boys and girls rate the male Pokémon trainers the highest because they fit the male stereotype of an action figure. But rather than be concerned that TV is exacerbating gender stereotypes, we think marketers love the simplicity of it all. It provides more support for selling girls on crushes and boys on war.

If you are looking for girls and boys in charge, two clear themes emerge: mean girls and smart boys.

THE MEANEST MEANIES

> It was time to turn our attention to the army of skanks.
>
> CADY *in the movie* Mean Girls

In May 2004, Mean Girls was the number one movie in the country. It followed a spate of popular books that addressed the problem of girls fighting but sometimes seemed to be about how to tame nasty girls. Indeed, given all the recent attention to mean girls and girl-on-girl fighting, parents are as likely these days to wonder why girls are so aggressive as they are to ask why dieting and eating disorders are so rampant. When we think about the compulsion that many girls have to be thin and beautiful, we look to magazines, TV, and movies, and complain about the digitally enhanced models, all the talk of dieting, and the lack of healthy body images. Could what girls watch on TV and movies have a similar impact on girls' meanness? Psychologist Norma Feshbach thinks so. Researching TV shows that are popular with high schoolers, she found that in sitcoms like *Friends* and *Seinfeld*, "indirect aggression" (a phrase that describes much of the mean girl phenomenon—"backbiting, negative rumors, exclusions, and sly rejections") is so prevalent that it "assumes the status of a character trait of females."

What are tweens and younger teens viewing that might encourage them to hurt, betray, and undermine one another?

Girl meanness is far from new territory. Wicked witches populate most fairy tales, and we have plenty of stories with evil women in powerful positions. Some images resurface generation after generation. The evil head of the orphanage in *Little Orphan Annie* is much like the evil head of school in *Matilda*, who is much like the evil headmistress in *Daddy Day Care*. And there has always been a place for mean little girls (though they used to be called bossy), such as Charlie Brown's nemesis, Lucy, and Dennis the Menace's annoying friend, Margaret. But unlike Lucy and Margaret, whose know-it-all manner irritated mostly boys, mean girl characters are now more likely to be fixated on one another. The feminine archetype of jealous, backstabbing women common in soap operas and movies such as *Fatal Attraction* and *Working Girl* is now standard fare in TV shows and movies for tweens and early teens. Like the inevitable collision with a fruit stand in action movies (start looking for it, and you'll see it almost every time), nearly every show or movie with more than one female character has a mean girl subtheme. Occasionally it is just a blip, as in *Shrek* (can you find Snow White and Cinderella in a slap fight?), but it's usually there.

Media mean girls take a lot of different forms. Sometimes they are ugly and rude, sometimes deceptively cute and polite, sometimes popular, sometimes outcast and misunderstood, sometimes powerful, sometimes ineffective. But almost all mean girls share certain characteristics: They are manipulative, deceitful, emotionally impulsive, verbally (and sometimes physically) abusive, and self-absorbed. That is, they're stereotypically feminine. They are usually recognizable by what they look like and what they wear, and the depth of their meanness is typically judged against the height of another girl's niceness. In our search for the meanest meanies, we found three prevalent types: cruel popular girls (often cheerleaders), evil super villains, and bossy sisters, babysitters, and/or friends.

Cruel Popular Girls and Cheerleaders

Popular girls make great meanies. They're cast as beautiful, thin, talented, liked by teachers and parents (because they're great at performing niceness for the right audience, such as unsuspecting adults), and sought after by boys. The power all this affords corrupts them further, renders them superficial, and makes them jealous guardians of their place at the center of social life. Their weapons are creating scapegoats, spreading gossip, and deceit. What's not to hate? We love to see their fall from grace. The eighties movie *Heathers*, a dark comedy in which a girl finds herself involved with an outcast boy in a plot to kill the three most popular girls in her school—all named Heather—set the standard for evil popular girl movies. Since then, lighter movies such as *Romi and Michelle's High School Reunion, Bring It On*, and *Mean Girls* get their energy from the same plot: the downfall of mean popular girls and the rise of someone nicer, more real and deserving. The nice girl seeks what the popular girl has and remakes herself in some way to attract a boy who secures her rise to the top of the social hierarchy. The message? Popularity, the right clothes, and doing "nice" the right way can get you a guy and respect from other girls. Is this the fifties? Not exactly, because today's nice girls are not afraid to show their smarts and a little independence, but it is surprisingly close.

Cheerleaders, in particular, have made for enticing villainous subplots in both TV shows and movies. Disney's superheroine Kim Possible fights all manner of evil, but her main rival is the head cheerleader, Bonnie. The down-to-earth normalcy of Disney's Lizzie McGuire comes from her comparison to her nemesis, the snobby popular cheerleader Kate. The Web site descriptions of Courtney Grupling and her friend Miranda in Nicktoons' *As Told by Ginger*, a show about Ginger's so-called life in the sixth grade, sums up TV popular girls and cheerleaders everywhere: Courtney is "totally self-absorbed and opportunistic" and "takes her position as Most Popular Girl very seriously. She prides herself on the diplomatic control and manipulation of her classmates."

On the surface this nasty rendition of popularity might not seem so bad. Maybe it is even good for girls, especially those girls on the margins, to see that superficiality doesn't win and meanness doesn't pay. They certainly get a steady dose of this story line, from cartoons such as *My Life as a Teenage Robot, Atomic Betty*, and *Rugrats: All Grown Up*. Pretty much any girl main character has the popular mean girls to deal with. But, this message comes at a cost. To buy this story line of good girls or bad (and it is fictional, of course, because all of us are more complicated than that) requires girls to be constantly on guard. If badness is one-dimensional, every time a girl thinks a mean thought or does a bad thing, she risks being labeled pure evil. So the pressure to be one-dimensionally nice is very high. Girls see what is in store for those who sway from the supernice path: bad girl labels, rejection or exile, or a fall from grace in the most publicly embarrassing way. No one talks much about the way this stark choice pits girls against one another and encourages comparisons and jealousy.

Evil Super Villains

If cheerleaders and popular girls are one-dimensionally bad, surely we can look to science fiction to take girl meanies to more creative places. Here we would expect to find female heroines and villains who break the stereotypical mold. Well, yes and no. There are certainly female fantasy characters, good and bad, such as Bulma in *Dragonball Z* or Evil-Lyn in *He-Man and the Masters of the Universe,* although we challenge you to find even one of them in the action figure section of Walmart or Toys "R" Us. But in spite of some variation in superpowers, the Web site descriptions make these fantasy meanies sound a lot like super versions of Courtney and Miranda. For example, Bulma, in spite of her ability "to operate and to fix anything," is described as "emotional, self-centered, impatient, argumentative, and given to fits of hysteria." These meanies are "pure darkness" with "bad reputations." (Can you imagine a male superhero being described as having a bad reputation?) Their power is often derived from stereotypically feminine qualities—the ability to change shape, to conjure strange potions, to create illusions, to fade into the shadows and become undetectable, to generate electricity or to use telekinetic power through their eyes or fingertips. They are, stereotypically, "scratching for a fight."

Like the popular girls, evil superheroines are defined by their looks. They are described as sophisticated beauties, supersexy, femme fatales, models of high tech or high style. Or they are the opposite of all this; they wear outdated jumpsuits and glasses or have gap teeth. Those who aren't fashion-challenged are cold, calculating versions of Lara Croft or Charlie's Angels: big-breasted, skinny-waisted, and long-legged, full of sensuality and anger. They are the antithesis of good girls. They don't fake niceness or smile a lot—kind of like the Terminator with big breasts and fashion sense. But they are made for boys—adventure and porn rolled into one.

Bossy Babysitters, Mean Sisters, and Aggressive Friends

This last category is a bit different, not only because it's a pattern almost exclusively aimed at the younger side of the tween set, but because the meanness is directed at boys, rather than other girls. Sometimes it's girls fighting, as with Misty, the female Pokémon trainer who suffers the valley-girl-like teasing of her three narcissistic and sexy older sisters. But mostly it's a pattern of domineering girls controlling the boys in their lives. The old message that girls have cooties prevails, but with a twist: They now also have power, and this makes the world a lot less predictable. The nasty babysitter, who used to be the overcontrolling grandmother type who made little kids eat spinach and watch soap operas, is now icky Vicky in Nickelodeon's *The Fairly OddParents*. Dubbed "the meanest teen in the toon," Vicky is a dominating, self-involved, boy-crazy teenage girl who thoroughly enjoys inflicting pain on her charge, Timmy.

Power isn't derived only from being older. Same-age girls—potential friends—are scary because they are verbally and sometimes physically aggressive. And then there's the romance. There are the nasty Kanker sisters who want to control and marry Ed, Edd, 'n' Eddy, for example, and bossy Cindy Vortex who relentlessly teases and sort of likes Jimmy Neutron. Boys seem baffled by girls' aggressiveness, and the girls enjoy and take advantage of this. Clearly this pattern of mean girl behavior is age related. Girls and boys are simply in different places, romantically speaking. But what strikes us again is the one-dimensional ways in which girls are cast— as nasty, aggressive, annoying, and secondary. It is as though the male creators of these shows are having flashbacks to their awkward prepubescent days and are unable to appreciate how present-day girls with more voice and more power might make better friends, might deserve real names and not the thinly veiled insults they are given, and might want to be genuine allies with the boys in their lives. The divisions repeated here are not between girls but between boys and girls. This is very unfortunate.

We actually don't have a problem with girls acting mean sometimes. The reality is that all of us are mean at one time or another. All of us say things we regret; all of us do things we aren't proud of. What bothers us is the stereotypical ways that mean, bad, evil girls and women are portrayed: obsessed with physical appearance, jealous, and backstabbing, fighting with fingernails or giving the evil eye; shadowy and deceitful and rife with out-of-control emotionality. The dichotomy is stark. If a girl isn't all nice, she's pure evil. Girls and boys alike are led to believe that girls who want power must also want to control them. It's predictable, and it's harmful to girls.

One mean girl stands out from all the rest: self-possessed Helga in the cartoon *Hey Arnold!* When we first watched Helga, she seemed like all the others. Secretly in love with Arnold (a love she confesses in her secret pink diary, while she openly bullies him), Helga's mission is to take out all female rivals for Arnold's affection and decide the relational fate of the other girls in her clique. On second glance she is more complicated. Her personal hell is not of her own making. We are let into the source of her anger: the intense pressure from her dysfunctional parents to be like her beautiful, smart, supernice older sister, Olga (who is herself depressed). Plain Helga fights back. Not popular, she is a self-made queen of her little out-group and threatens all who cross her with her two fists that she affectionately refers to as the "five avengers" and "old Betsy." Helga's angst, invisible to her friends but not to the viewers, gives us a glimpse of how the demands of perfection and beauty leave girls feeling like zeros if they're not tens. Because Helga embodies both mean and nice, she is more truly every girl. We need more girl characters with such dimension. If we had them, a little meanness wouldn't be all that bad.

BOY GENIUSES: YOU SILLY GIRL! THIS IS SCIENCE, AND SCIENCE IS NOT PRETTY

An instructor asks a group of unsuspecting children to draw a scientist. The image can vary in lots of ways—the scientist might be bald or have wild Einstein-type hair, old or young, mad and wild-eyed or benign, wearing a white lab coat and holding beakers of colorful liquid, creating an explosion or looking through a microscope. But almost always the scientist is white, male, and wearing glasses.

In 1989 the National Science Teachers Association conducted such a draw-a-scientist experiment with over 1,600 children in grades two to twelve. Only 8 percent portrayed female scientists even though 60 percent of the respondents were girls. In 1997 another study found similar results. Of the 117 fifth graders (57 males and 60 females) who completed the activity, 80 percent perceived scientists as male and 90 percent as white.

Surely now, in the new millennium, it must be different. Given efforts by parents and educators to convince girls that science isn't just for boys and men (or ugly women), it is reasonable to expect views about science and scientists to change. Girls are now more likely to take upper-level science courses and to take their skills in the laboratory seriously. We expect that they and their male classmates will have widened their image of scientists to include females as well as males, people of color as well as White people. It surely helps that many of the top-rated chemistry sets show pictures of actively engaged boys and girls, White and of color. You might be surprised to learn that although the gap between boys and girls in standardized science test scores is largely closed and there is no real support for any innate differences in ability to do science, fewer than one-fourth of the scientists in the United States are women. According to a more recent study, science fields such as physics and computer technology are still considered masculine subjects and shunned by most girls and women.

This persistent stereotype of science and scientists certainly has something to do with what girls see in the media. Here the mad scientist or nerdy professor—nearly always male—has deep roots, from Dr. Frankenstein to Jerry Lewis's nutty professor, from *The Fly*'s half-scientist, half-insect to the crazed ambitious creator of Jurassic Park. With all their human flaws, "brilliant" male scientists have a long cultural history.

Today we see them all over kid TV. There is Professor Utonium, the clumsy scientist father of the Powerpuff Girls, the rocket-scientist father of Disney's Kim Possible, and the nerdy father-scientist in *Honey, I Shrunk the Kids*, now a TV series on Disney. Any kid will tell you that the most popular cartoon scientists in 2005 are two superbrain legacies of nerdy, mad scientists everywhere: Nicktoon's *Jimmy Neutron: Boy Genius* and the Cartoon Network's Dexter of *Dexter's Laboratory*. Jimmy Neutron, Nicktoon's Web site tells us, is "just your average, everyday, tweenaged super genius" who creates amazing inventions and has a cool robotic dog and goofy friends. Dexter, too, is your typical boy genius who "applies himself to the greatest challenges of his time: creating a super-powered suit for dodgeball, aging himself to stay up late for movies, and, yes, sometimes even saving the world."

But what about girls? There are no girl scientific geniuses. Not one. We scanned TV shows aimed at kids for scientists of any kind. Girls appear as backdrops or very occasionally as friends, collaborators, or assistants. A few are smart, but never are they scientifically brilliant. In fact, since boy geniuses are stereotypically socially challenged, they seem to need the help of precocious, annoying girls to make them look good. Jimmy Neutron's nemesis is smart-aleck Cindy Vortex who, as her name implies, sucks the life out of anything fun with a steady stream of insults. While Jimmy Neutron invents things such as a girl-eating plant, blond, blue-eyed Cindy, "the second-smartest kid in Retroville" and as tough as nails, alternates between liking and cruelly teasing Jimmy.

Dexter's "brilliance is interrupted only by a bubbly ballerina otherwise known as older sister Dee Dee" who "embraces everything whirly, twirly, and girly in the world. She is a catalyst for chaos, dancing and prancing through the lab on her way to a meeting of the All Girl Ballet and Flowers and Fun Society." Satire? We think not. A full-page ad for the show in the *New York Times Magazine* gives us a sense of Dee Dee's place in the story. Above a large picture of Dexter with his nerdy glasses, white lab coat, and chemistry tubes we see Dee Dee jumping rope, a vacant look in her blue eyes. The caption reads: "He skips grades. She just skips."

A few girls do stand out. The Cartoon Network's Atomic Betty and Disney's Kim Possible are brainy action heroes, but the real geniuses are male: Kim's friend Ron and Betty's nemesis, Maximus I.Q. Other smart girls are secondary characters, such as Penny Sanchez in Nickelodeon's *Chalk Zone*. Rudy Tabootie, the male lead character in *Chalk Zone*, is also billed as "just a regular kid from a town called Plainsville." But Rudy has the amazing ability to create his own world with a piece of magic chalk. Penny is his trusted friend and the only other person he has ever taken with him to Chalk Zone. She is smart and into science. But unlike Dexter and Jimmy, for whom a single-minded pursuit of science is "awesome," "great," and "amazing," Penny is described as totally obsessed with science, and her compulsion with a world of "numbers, formulas, accuracy and precision" is pitted against Rudy the "dreamer" and "artist." Just in case we think Rudy's friendship with Penny is too good to be true, we have to hear his Chalk Zone alter ego, Snap, insult Penny's suggestions with chants of "Not listening." While we're excited to see a girl scientist of any kind, it is unfortunate that she has to be put in her place and noteworthy that her science, while useful, is lacking the passion of true genius.

Not surprisingly, those girls who do have a penchant for science or math, whether evil or good, have conventionally feminine characteristics inserted, as if to be a girl means to be fatally flawed and never quite up to the level of brilliance. *Kim Possible*'s wicked biogeneticist DNAmy is a "really big mini-plush-animal fan" who is obsessed with bioengineering two Cuddle Buddies into one. It's hard to take that too seriously. Of course she is ugly and overweight, and has bad hair, glasses, and gap teeth. Other female TV scientists lack passion. Major Doctor Ghastly on the Cartoon Network's *Evil Con Carne* "isn't really intent on taking over the world. She just likes inventing stuff." Female scientists are described as too emotional and hot-tempered, and there is always some flaw in fashion sense, appearance, or something to trivialize or detract from potential genius.

While female stereotypes detract from a girl's power as a scientist, relegating her to less than genius status, male characteristics fill out the already brilliant aspects of boy scientists. The Cartoon Network's *I Am Weasel* is a case in point. "I. M. Weasel is the opposite of everything you think a weasel should be. He's dignified, generous, patriotic and brilliant, with a deep manly voice to top it all off. I. M. Weasel has just the right combination of rumbling machismo and modest heroism to be a winner, no matter what he does." Being a stereotypical girl provides humor and trivializes a girl's intelligence, but being a stereotypical boy adds dimension. Boys can be whiz kids, and superbrains, they can be the world's greatest engineers or rocket scientists; and we never have to know what they're wearing, or whether or not they cook.

There are some other smart girls, such as Jackie and Inez whose skill and love of math foil evil in PBS's *Cyberchase* and the real-life girls who are shown solving problems on other PBS educational shows such as *Dragonfly* and *Zoom*, but given the rich characters and story lines of Jimmy and Dexter, as well as the product endorsements and mega-merchandise sales that go with them, the not-so-subtle message to girls is the same one they get from a commercial selling Dexter's Laboratory gogurt: "Get out of my laboratory, silly girl. This is science, and science is not pretty."

Tween Movies

In 2004 and 2005 we watched every movie that eight- to ten-year-old girls might watch. We realize that when this book comes out, the movies will have changed, but we are confident that the themes and clichés will pretty much stay the same.

This is not surprising, given the finding of a recent study commissioned by Dads and Daughters and the See Jane Program. In their review of 101 top-grossing G-rated films released between 1990 and 2004, they found that 75 percent of characters in G-rated movies are male, only 28 percent of speaking characters (both real and animated) are female, fewer than 17 percent of the characters in crowd scenes are female, and a whopping 83 percent of the films' narrators are male.

In PG movies we continue to see homophobic name calling. In *Cheaper by the Dozen*, the older sister played by Hilary Duff insults her younger sister by calling her "Butch" and in Disney's *Chicken Little* we are set up to laugh at "sissy" Runt of the Litter, a pig who loves Barbra

Streisand. At a time when concern about bullying and harassment in schools is at an all time high, these movies set kids up to make fun of their peers and use "gay" as an insult when they reach middle school.

We stuck with the G and PG movies, realizing that there are a few PG-13 movies that attempt to draw this age group in and do. In fact, there were always younger girls in the audience at every PG-13 movie we attended. The movies we comment on in this section are the ones that put a girl front and center, as in *Lizzie McGuire: The Movie*, *The Princess Diaries*, *Ella Enchanted*, *Freaky Friday*, *Ice Princess*, and *What a Girl Wants*. They are delightful, light, and almost always romantic. We begin by looking at G and PG movies advertised as for the whole family, such as *Shrek 2* with the lovely Fiona, as well as *Finding Nemo* and *Madagascar*, which was popular at the time of writing and has probably become a part of most children's video collections.

TWEEN MOVIES AS JOURNEYS FOR BOYS

A boy-journey story is an age-old genre in which a boy leaves on a quest for something or someone, alone or accompanied by one or two trustworthy friends. The journey becomes the story, and the boy learns important lessons from people he meets on the way. It's great when a girl gets to go on one of these journeys, and the classic girl journey story is *The Wizard of Oz*. But, girl journey movies are much rarer than those made for boys. Boy-journey stories such as *A Bug's Life*, *Shrek*, *Shrek 2*, *Finding Nemo*, *Robots*, *Madagascar*, and *Ice Age 2* involve girls in important ways, yet even when a girl is involved or gets to go along, the quest is the boy's. In *Shrek 2*, for example, Fiona is central to the story, as Shrek tries to make himself handsome in order to be the prince charming he believes she always wanted. The journey is Shrek's alone in *Shrek 2*, not Fiona's, and the adventure, the laughs, and the pals also belong to Shrek. In *Finding Nemo*, Dori accompanies Nemo on his quest to find his father. In *Madagascar*, feisty Gloria the hippo makes the journey to the wild.

It's not just the journey in *Shrek 2*, from beginning to end, male characters from nursery rhymes and fairy tales abound. But who are the rescuers? The gingerbread man, the three blind mice, the three little pigs, the big bad wolf, and Pinocchio. We can't figure out why Mary Mary Quite Contrary couldn't have come along or Bo Peep or Little Red Riding Hood. Any one of them could have been a part of this SWAT team, too, and probably every bit as effective as a cookie or a blind mouse. But the female parts in this movie, as in so many others, are neatly divided into three: the stereotypical good mother, the bad mother (in the form of the fairy godmother, who is a CEO of sorts, and CEOs are often villains, especially when, they are women and dare to have ambition), and, of course, the passive, nice, and kind princess. The movie does have an important message for girls about not putting so much store in people's looks, but it undoes one stereotype as it reaffirms others. Fiona is nice and pretty (when she wants to be, and bravo to her when she doesn't). But she waits passively in the castle for her prince (Shrek) while he has an adventure. Moms will want to point out to their daughters how unimportant looks are and how it is important to follow your heart and develop relationships with those who are kind and funny and smart, like Shrek. But they may forget to look at the other messages their daughters are getting from the movie: Wait for your man. Don't act. Be nice, not funny.

There are two kinds of funny that a girl is allowed to be: fat funny, like Gloria the hippo in *Madagascar* and Aunt Fanny in *Robots*, or ditzy funny, like Aunt Josephine in *A Series of Unfortunate Events* and Dori in *Finding Nemo*. Ditzy is a different kind of funny from the donkey in *Shrek*, who is annoying and a little needy but a wisecracking sidekick. Dori almost makes it as a wisecracking sidekick, but she fits the stereotype of a ditzy blonde too closely. Her short-term memory makes her more pathetic and vulnerable, which takes away her edge.

These family-fare movies are meant for everyone in the family but clearly place boys front and center. Movies about big, happy, but quirky families also belong in this category because they can work with a number of roles and should show some gender equity. *Cheaper by the Dozen*, for example, had twelve child roles to work with. Thankfully, they created Sarah, a little girl with pizzazz. She was the mastermind of the children's plot to dip the underwear of their older sister's boyfriend in meat so that the dog wouldn't leave him alone She was also the one who set his pants on fire, said her brothers. She also seems to be an athlete as well as a smart girl. Before we give kudos to the screenwriter who developed the character of Sarah, though, let's remember that someone in charge gave her a Limited Too shirt to wear while her brother got to wear a cool T stating "I'm out of bed. I'm dressed. What more?" In addition, Sarah's two younger brothers get a snake and a frog, something any self-respecting tomboy would also enjoy. It is also important to note that they give the tomboy role to a *little* girl because it's fine in Hollywood to be a tomboy before puberty. Big sister Lorraine (played by Hilary Duff) is a totally pink-

and-pretty girl. It's odd that Lorraine isn't more athletic since her father is a football coach; when fathers are athletes, they usually promote sports for their daughters as well as their sons. Instead, Lorraine offers to give cool little Sarah a makeover, but Sarah resists (hooray!). Alas, in *Cheaper by the Dozen 2*, feisty Sarah succumbs to the makeover, but not before she is caught shoplifting some Neutrogena makeup (this movie is filled with product placements). Sarah does stay feisty and sporty, and her mother does remind her that her "crush" likes her the way she is. She gets the makeover anyway.

So, yes, there's Sarah. But then there's Lorraine. Every girl watching sees this character as a model of teenage girlhood and learns what teenage girls do (read fashion magazines and land jobs out of high school working for fashion magazines), how teenage girls dress (pink pajamas and brand-name clothes), what teenage girls look like (skinny, blond, and made up), and what little tomboys turn into. Hollywood knows this and makes the lion's share of G and PG movies that feature girls about this kind of teenager.

But there's another kind of family-fare movie that appeals to the five-to seven-year-old group while at the same time it reaches up through the preteen group to gain a middle school audience. These are the movies that deal with large groups of kids. Often the kids are a bunch of losers who become winners because of a coach who is also a loser but who becomes a winner himself though his involvement with the kids—as in most of the sports team flicks. (Alas, we can't think of a film for this age group in which the coach or teacher is a woman, although *Raising Helen*, about an aunt who inherits her sister's kids, could count and also *Nanny McPhee* who tames seven ill-mannered children of a widower. The theme here is not coaching winners but care-giving lost or wild children.)

Some of these movies are about a bunch of uptight kids who don't know how to be kids. The wonderful thing about them is that because they have so many kid parts to work with, the writers can give the girls more than stereotypical roles. But just as the culture at large believes that boys hang in tribes and girls prefer to have best friends (a belief and not a reality), team films (except for the cheerleading team) seem to be made for boys. The sports teams are composed primarily of boys but may have the occasional tomboy who gets accepted by the boys, as in the remake of *The Bad News Bears*. (Even this winning tough girl pitcher gets a romantic interest and a kiss at the end of the movie.)

The School of Rock is a fabulous film about a loser rock-and-roll guitarist who takes over a preppy fourth grade class at a snooty private school and teaches the kids "to rock." The most prissy, uptight characters are represented by three females: the girlfriend of his weak, passive, and "whipped" best friend who makes him quit the band and get a job; the principal of the school who has the heart of a rocker inside her prissy exterior; and a girl in the class, Summer, who is a "brown nose" and does everything for the grade. Thus, prissy antirock sentiment is contained by the three main female leads to allow the boys to explode and rebel around them. The best thing for girls about this movie is that Summer becomes the manager of the band and does a wonderful job of it; she is brainy and also "rocks" in the end. The worst thing for girls is that they're relegated to unimportant positions in the rock-and-roll project that the class takes on. Who gets to do the computer graphics and light show on the computer? A boy. Who gets to play the drums? A boy. Who is the lead guitarist with some awesome solos and writes the lead song? A boy. A girl who played the cello gets turned into the bass guitarist, but she is a background character and has no solos. Three girls are assigned background singing with some "ooh-la-la-las," and they're great. They take the job seriously musically and don't just glam it up and prance like eye candy. Still, they're the background singers.

If even the best movies pull at us in uncomfortable ways, what about the worst movies? We suspect that children are less careful connoisseurs about movies than their parents, liking almost everything they see and seeing almost everything put out there for them. We have to find ways to enter into that world of moviegoing and enjoy the jokes and the plots, however cliché, with our children while making a space for questioning the roles of girls and women. Princess films are wonderful catalysts for this kind of questioning.

TWEEN PRINCESS MOVIES: JOURNEYS FOR GIRLS

Princess movies are about teenage princesses. While movies such as *Harriet the Spy*, *Kiki's Delivery Service*, and *Madeline* may appeal to eight- to ten-year-olds, this age group is actively being courted and primed for teen worship. They begin this worship through cartoons such as *Kim Possible*, movies such as *The Lizzie McGuire Movie*, and singers such as Ashlee Simpson.

We get princesses-in-training in *The Princess Diaries*, almost princesses in *What a Girl Wants*, peasant girls about to become princesses in *Ella Enchanted* and *A Cinderella Story*, figure skaters called ice princesses, and pop stars who are treated as princesses in *The Lizzie McGuire Movie*.

The story lines follow similar patterns. One pattern is that every girl lead character is super nice and has an embarrassing moment in the first five minutes to make her the kind of girl that girls supposedly want to identify with. The presumption is that girls want to identify with a girl who is self-conscious because she is not too confident (confidence is reserved for the mean popular girl) and is somewhat incapable or clumsy. Like the Traumarama section in *Seventeen* magazine (where girls share their most embarrassing moments) that our survey tells us middle school girls love, these human touches teach embarrassment and self-consciousness to girls just as much as they represent these purportedly "real" qualities. They teach that the sweet, nice girl cares about what others think of her and feels a need to present a poised and perfect exterior.

These sweet girls are stripped of personality and interests, remaining simply sweet and awkward. Personality gets boiled down to clumsiness, and interests are reduced to liking a cute boy (established within the first ten minutes of the film) or relegated to her sidekick who can afford to be a bit more "interesting" without losing some votes. Comparing Ella in the book *Ella Enchanted*, who can imitate people, make up funny tales, and speak several languages like Gnome, to Ella in the movie, who is nice and kind, the difference is clear. In the book, when a girl orders her around, Ella punches the girl and gives her a bloody nose in the first ten pages. A movie princess could never get away with that and retain the nice-and-kind perfection that Hollywood thinks she needs. Instead, Ella in the movie sticks up for a friend of color when another girl is prejudiced and cruel to her. What is important here is that they took away her very human aggression and turned sticking up for herself into sticking up for other people. Self-respect turns into kindness, and all is well. But both are needed in this world.

Ella Enchanted is about a girl who is under a curse to be obedient. In the movie, Ella helplessly flounders under everyone's orders; in the book, Ella is a resister. She finds ways to undermine the cook's wishes. If the cook asks for more almonds, she brings back two almonds and has to be sent back for more. When her mother orders her to do things, she always finds a way to ask "Do I have to?" or "Why?" even as her body forcibly makes her obey. Ella in the movie has lost this cunning way of undermining the curse.

These movies present very sweet and kind princesses by contrasting them with mean girls but rarely mean boys. Mean girls appear in books as well as in movies. It became clear after watching a number of these movies that the actresses who play mean girls disappear into oblivion. It seems that reality and fiction intertwine to help make stars of only the nice girls. This suggests that the actress is not admired for her acting ability but for actually being the type represented in the movie. Think of Kirsten Dunst and of the little ones who have trouble distinguishing fact from fantasy.

In most movies of this genre it takes generally less than five minutes for a mean girl to be introduced to provide contrast to the nice girl. In *Ella Enchanted* there is the prejudiced girl on the playground and then the two stepsisters. In *Freaky Friday* there is Stacey the cheerleader: "She's evil," says Anna (Lindsay Lohan), "an insane psycho freak." In *What a Girl Wants* there is a snotty girl at the beginning of the movie who asks Daphne (Amanda Bynes) where she's going to college, and in England there is the snotty Clarissa who makes fun of the servants and undermines Daphne's every move. Mean girls get their comeuppance in these movies, but not at the hands of the star princesses, for that would make them mean girls, too.

When a nice girl gets a little mean, there is always a boy to bring her back in line, providing the moral lesson that boys like only nice girls. In *Mean Girls* the star gets chastised by the cute boy for becoming too much like the mean girls. In *Freaky Friday* the cute boy rejects Anna after she wrecks a mean girl's exam. In *What a Girl Wants* the cute boy rejects Daphne for acting too much like the self-important Clarissa. Suddenly boys have become the paragons of antibullying morality.

Of course there is the love interest for the teen princess. *Freaky Friday*, that fun story about a girl and a mom exchanging bodies for a couple of days; *What a Girl Wants*, about a girl's search for a father she never knew; and *The Princess Diaries*, *Lizzie McGuire*, and *Ice Princess* all include cute boys and show that they aren't all they're cracked up to be, replacing "cute boys shown to be losers" with humbler cute boys.

The cute boys almost always get to drive cool vehicles. Mia in *The Princess Diaries* has a cool car and Maggie in *Herbie: Fully Loaded* drives a racecar. The rest ride on the back of motorcycles or the passenger seats of ATVs as the cute boys have all the fun.

Eight- to ten-year-old girls aren't really interested in cute boys yet, and most of the reading literature for this age group reflects that. Movies, though, teach them that boys will be important in the years ahead. It is incredibly weird that eight-year-old girls are being taught to look at boys' "cute butts." Comments about them recur in all these movies. Ella claims that Hattie is only interested in how cute the prince's butt is. Transformed Shrek comments on his "taut buttocks," and when the adoring maidens want to give him a massage, one exclaims provocatively as she fights her way in: "What's left for me to rub?" Yes, in movie after movie we were surprised to find such comments along with sexual innuendos and a few scenes of teenage boys taking their shirts off. If the roles were reversed and boys were making comments about girls' butts or watching them disrobe, the movie would be deemed inappropriate for little girls. Why isn't it inappropriate for girls this age to be introduced to scanning a boy's body in terms of its sexiness?

One very sad thing about almost all these movies is how female friendship is not treated as an important part of a girl's life—this at an age when girlfriends can be everything to girls. It takes a backseat to the romantic interest. Best girlfriends are introduced as an accessory to the lead girl, but they are rarely developed as characters and rarely go on adventures. They never rescue friends and very seldom become part of the plotline. (Heaven forbid the princess should run off with the princess.) The exception is Lilly in *The Princess Diaries*. She is a real character with whom the lead has a number of discussions, intimate moments, fights, and resolutions of fights, just as happen in real friendships. She is a confidante but not a rescuer. We also love *Miss Congeniality 2* for this reason. The writers threw out the princess mentality of the first film and gave her a female buddy. How many buddy films can you think of that have two girls? Very few, we're sure. But here, Sam Fuller (Regina King) is the bodyguard for Gracie Hart (Sandra Bullock), and in the end she rescues her from drowning and becomes her best friend.

In all the other princess movies, if a princess needs rescuing or needs someone to accompany her on a journey or to teach her the rules of some new land or role, it is not her best friend and never her mother. Mothers are almost always against the journey, like the feminist mother in *Ice Princess* who would rather her daughter study physics at Harvard than go figure skating in short dresses. Companions on a journey are almost always male figures. Confidants are often grandmothers or male servants (such as the butler or chauffeur).

This is not always true of good literature, which provides more variety, but even literature likes to present children who learn about who they are by separating from their parents. Gaining some separation from parents is a life task that boys and girls need to deal with, and turning to other adults and friends broadens their experiences and leaves them feeling less vulnerable in the world. But why are cute boys, grandmothers, and butlers the continuous source of this wisdom for girls? Hollywood seems to believe that middle-aged women have little to share and that girlfriends are competitors or frivolous, not wise helpers.

That girls are frivolous is reiterated in subtle ways. By emphasizing shopping, fashion, and jewelry many movies stray from the books they are based on. "Jewelry. Now that's a language every girl understands," says Lizzie McGuire in the movie. It must be so because jewelry is featured in almost every princess movie: a special charm bracelet, a special locket, a special bracelet, or an identifying necklace.

A gratuitous shopping or fashion modeling scene, as in *Freaky Friday* and the remake of *Parent Trap*, usually culminates with the appearance of the lead girl or a mother in a white dress. All the lovely interests that girls have in horses, languages, sports, and politics get washed away in a sea of white glittery fashion. At the end of *Ella Enchanted*, even most of the dress gets washed away to reveal a mini white dress and white high-heeled go-go boots.

It's not all bad. Each of these movies has elements that move them beyond Disney's version of *Cinderella*. *The Princess Diaries* created a girl with lots of interests but perhaps gave her these interests because she is painted as a nerd who is transformed into a princess. She is also given a best friend and a Mustang. Shrek's princess, Fiona, chooses character over looks. *Freaky Friday*'s girl has a realistic relationship with her mother, a mother who is not, portrayed as a demon because she works. The daughter also plays lead guitar and is given a mean solo. *Lizzie McGuire* shows that boys and girls can be best friends. *Ella Enchanted* screenplay authors give Ella a sword in the swordfight at the end.

Each one also has elements that undermine a girl's confidence or, worse, teach her that it is somehow better to lack self-confidence than have it. Each creates a vision of girlhood that can be too frivolous, boy-crazy, and disconnected from her friends. In this way PG princess movies set up girls for the full-blown fashion, partying, and sexual activity going on in the PG-13 ones. Do your daughter a favor and instead of *Shrek 2*, check out *Spirited Away*; instead of the Princess movies, try *Fly Away Home* or *Whale Rider*. No princesses in sight, just plain girls in troublesome spots who meet interesting people and solve seemingly impossible problems. If she is bound and determined to watch the blockbuster PG movies, watch them with her and hone her critical skills with some of the following questions:

1. Who does most of the rescuing, and who is rescued?

2. Who is full of personality? Why can't a lead girl be the one with all the personality?

3. Is the best friend of the girl in the movie a real friend, or is she dropped as a character early on?

4. Who gets to drive the cool vehicles? The motorcycles and ATVs?

5. Does there have to be a girl-meets-boy romantic ending? Can you think of another happily-ever-after scenario?

6. What does she wear at the end of the movie? A white gown? Why?

7. Are there girls that reflect your daughter's race, class, or sexual orientation? And why are so many people in this movie white and rich?

8. Are the partyers in the film stereotypically people of color?

9. Is there a gratuitous scene where the girl tries on clothes, goes shopping, or appears on a catwalk?

10. Do the parents have cool jobs (football coach, author, artist, rock-and-roll singer) or real ones?

11. Are feminist moms or businesswomen the enemy rather than a resource?

12. Who holds the powerful jobs? (Children Now reports that 71 percent of lawyers, 80 percent of CEOs, 92 percent of officials, and 80 percent of doctors on TV are men.)

13. What are the lead girl's interests, talents, skills, and hobbies?

14. Why do they make the mean girl so one-dimensionally mean?

15. Why are there so few women producers, writers, and directors?

(When a program has at least one woman writer, a female director, or a female producer, the TV show or movie has 5 to 10 percent more female characters.)

While you're at it, keep an eye out for the following sketchy scenes and sexual innuendos in the movies your little girl watches:

- Mentioning boys or men having "cute butts," boys unbuttoning their shirts to pose as teen idols, girls calling boys "hott" and vice versa

- Parodies of strippers, such as when the cat in *Shrek 2* does a "chair dance," sticks out his chest, and pretends to pull a cord that showers him with water

- Martini glasses at parties, mimicking girl talk scenes of *Sex and the City*

- Suggestions that boys are always out to see girls naked or "get some": "Hey, I can look at myself naked," says Fred in *Scooby-Doo* after he switched bodies with Velma.

- Popular boy bimbos making moves on girls. "Women are just drawn to me" says one in *What a Girl Wants*; or, "the curve," a technique to lure women used by boy bimbo in *Lizzie McGuire: The Movie.*

- Sexy costumes that don't match the movie roles, as in the Giants in *Ella Enchanted* wearing the then popular halter tops and miniskirts with ruffles

- Push-up bras, go-go boots, and lingerie on girls

- Drug jokes meant for older teens, such as the catnip joke in *Shrek 2* and the many drug references in *Scooby-Doo*

Don't forget about previews. We found some very strange previews to PG-rated movies, such as the one for *Shall We Dance*. "You've got to hold her like you're gonna have your way with her," said the dance instructor to the open ears of all the little girls in the audience waiting to see *Ella Enchanted.*

Including these sexual jokes and teasing scenes assures kids that they are part of the life they are told to want and have as teens. It is important for girls to understand sex and sexuality and their beginning feelings, their fears, and their bodies. But these innuendoes are about the "nudge-nudge, wink-wink" sex-is-dirty undercurrent that pervades our country's thinking about sex. While kids may not get all the jokes and innuendos, many have older brothers and sisters who do and can explain them.

Magical Girls and Extreme Makeovers for the New Teen

The middle school girls we surveyed watch just about everything the surveyed teen girls watch. For example, the nighttime shows such as *The OC* and *One Tree Hill*, which are chock-full of teen idols to admire, including Mischa Barton and Chad Michael Murray, and are filled with the teen drama of drugs, sex, boyfriends, crushes, and problem parents, were hits in 2005 with middle schoolers as well as with teenagers. Although teenagers are more likely to be watching shows such as MTV TRL (Total Request Live), the middle schoolers also tune into music video shows such as *106 & Park*, TRL, and Countdown. Given their story lines about sex and drugs as well as the sexual dancing and general coarseness, we were surprised to learn that parents aren't limiting the shows their middle schoolers watch. Instead, parents seem to be focusing on one or two shows they think are problematic. The girls we surveyed told us *South Park* was one " because of the cursing," and *Charmed* or "anything psychic," for "Christian reasons." One parent didn't like *Will & Grace* because she thought watching it would make her daughter gay (according to the daughter). A few parents banned *Real World* on MTV because it's "trashy." It seems that parents aren't really clued into what goes on in the regular fare their kids are watching, but when they see something outrageous (such as something about "butt lubrication" on a *South Park* episode), they draw the logical conclusion and prohibit it. For every child whose parent has set a limit on a TV show or movies, there are two middle schoolers whose parents let them watch whatever they want.

With regard to movies, a few parents prohibit PG-13 movies, but most middle schoolers see them before they're thirteen; moviemakers ensure that audience by placing "must-see" stars in them: like Adam Sandler and Drew Barrymore in *50 First Dates*, Jennifer Garner in *13 Going on 30*, and Drew Barrymore again in *Fever Pitch*. Then there's Daniel Radcliffe and company. Nine- and ten-year-olds flocked to *The Goblet of Fire*, the latest Harry Potter film, rated PG-13 for its dark themes and visuals. But they also saw a buffed-up Harry in a grotto hot tub and the intoxicating Beaubaton Academy girls floating like "stoned butterflies" and then cheerleading at the tournament.

More frequently parents draw the line at R-rated movies, but not the majority of parents, according to their children. Many of them make exceptions and in so doing communicate to their daughters that they think they're mature enough for this or that film. Our survey indicates that these exceptions are horror films, and we believe they make judgments based on how easily frightened their child is and not on whether or not there are sexual scenes in the film.

Showing your daughter she's mature by giving her the gift of a TV show or movie is never a good idea. It defines maturity as the ability to understand things such as sex and drugs and cursing. While some girls say, "My parents know that even if I watch that stuff, I won't do it," at the same time they are betraying a certain pleasure in being grown-up enough to make their own decisions about what these movies are normalizing. We are reminded of the mom who told the salesgirl in Hot Topic that as long as her daughter keeps a good attitude and her grades up, she can wear whatever she likes. But good attitude and good grades don't tell us what is going on with the whole girl psychologically. Being able to watch sexually explicit videos and movies and *not* act out on them is not the goal. We contend that these movies create desires and understandings about what it means to be a girl or woman that invade your daughter's psyche, crowding out other potential ways of being. This is a harder argument to make with your daughter, and turning off one particular show or one particular kind of movie won't make a difference. Talking about the movie will.

In the end it is not about maturity or particularly offensive shows but the overall messages your daughter is getting about girls' lives from these very grown-up images, the limits and stereotypes reinforced even while they seem to be challenged, and the absence of real girls with real interests and problems on these shows and in these movies.

MAGICAL GIRLS WITH SPECIAL POWERS

Remember *Bewitched* and *I Dream of Jeannie*, two seventies shows about women with magical powers? TV is filled with their progeny: girls with special powers. The middle school girls we surveyed like to watch reruns of *Sabrina the Teenage Witch*, *Charmed* (which reruns so frequently you can watch six episodes a week if you have cable), *Joan of Arcadia* (new to TV in 2004 and gone by 2005), *Tru Calling* (also new and gone), and *That's So Raven*. We discussed the latter earlier since it is geared to a slightly younger audience. *Sabrina* and the three sisters in *Charmed* have a myriad of witchy powers. Raven and Tru are psychic. Joan gets special messages from God. Melinda Gordon (Jennifer Love Hewitt) of *The Ghost Whisperer*, talks to dead people, as does Allison DuBois (Patricia Arquette) in *Medium*. They're female versions of superheroes, sort of. They have the power to make things happen, see the future, and kill off bad guys, but they rarely have the superstrength of Superman, which would make them too unfeminine. Combining girls' interest in fantasy and the occult as well as their desire to be special and different from other girls, these shows allow girls to have power in magic.

There are some lovely components to these shows, and we see why girls like them. We enjoyed watching them. Amber Tamblyn (*Joan of Arcadia*), like the interesting Claire Danes of *My So-Called Life* reruns that girls still watch, is intelligent, angst-ridden, and leading a fairly normal teenage life. The writers don't seem to always need a subplot about a love interest, which shows a bit of faith on the part of Barbara Hall who created the show. In fact, it's probably the only show with a teenage girl that didn't make a crush a central part of the weekly plot, at least until Joan hooked up with Adam who cheated on her. Oh, well.

What's cool about *Charmed* for all its sexiness is that it shows the three sisters doing all sorts of martial arts, sword fighting, and acrobatics, putting some oomph to the spells that fight evil, and saying things like "Anyone else want a piece of this?" to demon wrestlers. *Charmed* as well as *Sabrina* show intergenerational relationships with strong women who came before them and are some of the only shows on television that demonstrate strong mother-daughter relationships unmediated by a bumbling father or father figure. (A strong mother scripted against a bumbling father can be seen as early as *The Dick Van Dyke Show* and in the more recent *Everybody Loves Raymond* and even *The Simpsons*.) But the mother's character becomes unimportant in relation to the daughter. She is there to show common sense and maturity in opposition to the bumbling, immature father.

How different are Joan, Sabrina, and Raven from their TV foremothers? Samantha and Jeannie used their powers in stereotypical ways. Samantha twitched her nose to shortcut the cleaning of her house. Jeannie tirelessly served her master until she messed up or wanted too much independence, and he sent her back to her bottle. Today's girls also use their superpowers in somewhat stereotypical ways. If the show is a comedy, the girls will change an outfit with a spell or get some revenge on the snobby girl at school with a curse. If it's a drama, the girls don't stop bank robbers or political graft, nor are they concerned with nuclear proliferation or world hunger; instead, Joan focuses on individual acts of compassion to save troubled peers. In the end, it's not so much God's talking to her that makes her special but that she is really a very nice girl.

Like Jeannie and Samantha, it's who these characters are when they're not special that teaches girls conformity to feminine standards. Samantha tried so hard to be the good suburban housewife, and Jeannie twinkled and teased her way into her master's heart. For today's younger audiences, magical girls like Raven and Sabrina have crushes; for the teen watchers of prime-time shows, angst-ridden magical girls like Joan have boyfriends (which will lead to an episode about whether or not to have sex with them); for the looser girls on WB, HBO, or cable, they're having sex with boyfriends and learning how their careers (substitute magic) can interfere with a love life.

A frequent subplot is that although a girl is made special by her magic, in true *Bewitched* fashion her devotion to the magic or her sister witches or her mission to end evil often gets in the way of her other purpose in life: to be somebody's girlfriend (for Samantha it was keeping husband Darren happy). Sure, it's good to learn early that it's hard for women to do it all and have it all, but the regressive messages that career will always interfere with love serve to remind girls that this is an inevitable drawback to power and accomplishment. Sometimes the lessons are subtle, but more often they're right out there—as in *Charmed* when one sister says to the other, "There's a whole generation of women who . . . followed their careers. . . . You don't want to wake up someday and discover all you have is your career." Well, no, but you also don't want to wake up and discover that you haven't pursued your passion or don't have a way to support yourself, either.

While these shows have great fun creating evil and incredibly sexy villainesses, it is rare that they show adult women in powerful roles. At least *Bewitched* had Endora. Joan's mother is an art teacher, while her father is the local police chief. Raven's mother is dead, as is the mother of the girls in *Charmed* (although she comes back in the afterlife as a guide).

Joan of Arcadia is normal, more obviously so by comparison to her best friend Grace, the boyish daughter of a rabbi, a science geek. Like so many of the other magically powered girls on TV, in the movies, and in the books that middle school girls are reading, Joan is liked but not popular; she's just a little odd and freaky, but not too; she is beautiful in her own way but not snobby. And still, in many ways, she is full of the teenage awkwardness that makes girls want to identify with her. This personality combination would be a death sentence in every other TV show, teen book, and movie, but the magical girl can be typical because she has powers that lift her out of the mundane and make her special, something boy protagonists in shows like *Malcolm in the Middle* don't seem to need. This led us to wonder: Would Joan or any of the others hold the interest of their audiences without their magic? The critically acclaimed *My So-called Life* (about a girl a lot like Joan but without the magic) was canceled after just one year, while its contemporary *The Wonder Years* went on for so long that Fred Savage, who played Kevin, grew into near adulthood. Without their powers, would girl leads be worthy of their prime-time audience's time?

The girls who have staying power without magic have powers of a different kind. Take a look at the girls on the extremely popular series *The OC* or *One Tree Hill* or *Laguna Beach*. In one season of *The OC*, girls who are richer than anyone that most girls will ever meet have had sex, gotten drunk, two-timed their boyfriends, developed a drug habit, exposed a disorder of some kind, and run away. Their power comes from taking familiar types of girls (the good girl victim, the sexual bad girl, the feisty tough girl) to the limit and beyond. This is pure soap drama, and although fun to watch, it glamorizes problem behaviors and neglects to develop the girls as people with interests outside of partying and romance. The personalities most often written into the script are stereotypically "good girl but troubled," "spunky, fun friend," and "snobby, evil girl." Look for them. If you watch old episodes of *Dynasty*, *Beverly Hills, 90210*, or *Dallas*, these types were around back then. When *90210* ended its long run, actress Jennie Garth said it all: "After being the *90210* designated victim for a decade, having been shot and raped and stalked . . . week after week, . . . it was just refreshing to have some fun." Even the show most popular with our middle school girls according to the survey, *7th Heaven*, seemed to be boosting ratings by having the on-screen teens that viewers grew to love go wild.

Can a teen show be more real and have staying power? Take a look at the award-winning *DeGrassi: The Next Generation*, imported from Canada. There are many lead characters, and they are equally girls and boys. There are types like nerds and jocks, and even though there is a fair share of dating and hooking up, the scripts play against type in ways that open up rather than pigeonhole a character or reaffirm old stereotypes. There's Paige, once a cheerleader snobby type, but she can be sweet at times. (She may be the only cheerleader on TV or in the movies who has more than one dimension.) There is also Emma, who likes science and is not hot but simply pleasant-looking. Even though she likes science, she isn't a nerd in a stereotypical way. There simply is more personality to these kids than you see in other shows. They are playing characters, not gendered straitjackets, and they look like real teens. *Veronica Mars* is another TV show for teens that seems to play against type with Veronica, a detective who is rejected in high school, pursuing the killer of her best friend. And her best friend is a girl! There is a missing mother, alas, and a supportive father, but there are also girl computer geeks and a myriad of other interesting characters.

Middle school is also the time when girls begin to understand the satire in shows such as *The Simpsons* and *King of the Hill*. In these cartoons, girls and moms are presented in stereotyped fashion because the writers realize that this is the stereotype. They poke fun at the way Marge will stand by Homer no matter how stupid he acts, and the way Lisa is concerned with grades and the Goody Two-shoes. Lisa is the moral center of *The Simpsons*, the conscience and political voice that is slammed constantly by her family's stupidity and the depravity of the world at large. Poking fun at the perfect girl and the model minority stereotype of Asians, Connie, the Vietnamese American girlfriend of Bobbie Hill in *King of the Hill*, is also one of those too-good-to-be-true children.

Reality shows, on the other hand, take girls in the opposite direction. There is no satire or social commentary here. Just roll the film *24-7*, give it to a group of people hell-bent on ratings to edit it down to forty-five minutes, and let the fun begin.

IS THERE ANYTHING REAL ABOUT REALITY PROGRAMS?

The Miss America pageant is a tradition. Even during the heyday of feminism, when so-called women's libbers picketed outside the auditorium in Atlantic City with signs proclaiming the event a degrading meat market, the show still brought in viewers, plenty of them female. The show taught girls who were beginning their teen years what to aspire to: beauty, poise, talent, and intelligence. But these qualities really boiled down to doll-like beauty, an unceasing smile, an interest in a social issue that reinforced for the audience the girl's femininity, and an ability to answer a couple of questions about world peace.

The Miss America Pageant may be a shadow of its former self, but today's middle school girls watch an endless array of beauty contests in disguise: *America's Next Top Model, The Bachelor, For Love or Money, Who Wants to Marry My Dad?*, *Sports Illustrated Swimsuit Model, Outback Jack*, and *The Swan* are just a few of the shows that line beautiful women up for the choosing and do a version of the swimsuit competition. (There are a few Mr. America pageants, such as *The Bachelorette* and *Average Joe*, but not that many, and none have extreme makeovers or underwear modeling.)

As in the pageants, all the women involved are quite beautiful in stereotypical ways; if they aren't, they soon will be after the plastic surgeons, dentists, and personal trainers are through with them. Almost all have long, flowing hair; almost none are anywhere close to being flat-chested or wide around the hips; and they all smile as if they live in Stepford. In these shows the women join the bachelor or dad in the hot tub as a kind of swimsuit look-see, the camera showing them in all their glory as they step out of the cabana to approach their man in the tub. The producers also include events such as lingerie competitions (*The Swan*) or challenges such as modeling naked with other women (*America's Next Top Model*) for the voyeuristic pleasure of the men in the audience. Then there are the ceremonies that involve dressing up the women in evening gowns à la the evening gown competition of Miss America. They sometimes put them in out-of-context settings—wearing gowns, spiked heels, and all (*Outback Jack*)—to reinforce their girly (read sex kitten) qualities: scared of spiders and snakes, dependence on a strong man. In these ceremonies the women are spangled and bejeweled and in a ruffled sexy femininity that rivals Lingerie Barbie! Women of color fare badly in these shows; the few that appear are made to seem hypersexual or hyperbitchy and controlling.

Although all the women are beautiful in a certain predictable way, the role of the audience is not to enjoy their beauty; instead, we are enticed into dissecting their features and arguing who's the prettiest and who has the problem eyebrows. As the plastic surgeons ooh and ahh over their swan/Frankensteins, girls getting together to watch them on TV say, "I don't like what they did with her mouth" or think to themselves, "She still looks kind of fat to me." The intention is to make us all judges, the way we were in middle school, evaluating and rating friends and foes alike because, so we were taught, that's what women do for each other and to each other. No one on the show asks of the many swans who are mothers, how will their young children react? If a child shrieks when a mother cuts her hair or a dad shaves his beard, how will she feel when Mom gets a new face? What becomes of the newly found self-esteem after all the attention is gone? Will a new body really transform a bad marriage? Who pays for the upkeep of the hair extensions? We are seduced by the moment—the shocking transformations, the cattiness, the competition—not the future.

Miss America wasn't judged on personality; it was assumed that all the women in the competition were poised and sweet. We saw just how little personality counted when, in 1984, the talented and personable Vanessa Williams was forced to renounce her title because nude photos taken years before the pageant were printed in *Penthouse*. In the beauty competitions that continue today, girls who are poised and sweet still win the day in large part because they are contrasted with other girls who are bad in one of the following ways: out for money, not love; slutty; catty; dishonest; or uncouth.

The producers can lie to contestants and the bachelor can fool around with all the women at once, but the woman who does anything of the same variety gets crucified on screen. She is set up by the producers to play the role of the bad girl, and the other women (including those in the viewing audience) are the ones set up to throw the stones.

On *Who Wants to Marry My Dad?* it was revealed that an aunt of the daughters (who are the judges) has been hiding among the gaggle of women auditioning for the part of their new mother. Shock of all shocks, she reveals to the daughters and father that one woman has a potty mouth. The producers replay a scene of the soon-to-be-ousted participant in a limo, laughing with the other "girls" and using the b word in a story she is telling. Cut to father, auntie, and daughters as they react, aghast that she could be so crude. Now remember, in a TV show where daughters are deceptively watching through a hidden camera while their father makes out with multiple women in bikinis in a hot tub, a woman who uses the b word is sent home for ethical reasons.

One by one every option is eliminated as a so-called shocking little secret is revealed about each of the women. For example, Tammy is ousted by the daughters for her slightly feminist inclinations. We find out that Tammy does not plan to change her name even if she gets married. "It's who I am," she states plainly; however, the girls see this as defensive and uncompromising. *Compromise* was an odd word given that there was no

compromise offered; she was asked whether she would yield to their father's wishes to change her name, and she said no.

This is an important lesson for girls beginning romantic journeys in
life, that the girl who wins the guy is the traditional girl, the sweet one (or
the one who does the best job feigning sweetness or even the one who
doesn't get caught in a potty-mouthed moment). Echoing the princess
movies of the preteen years, middle school girls are learning other stories
about romance: that girls will and should give up anything for true love
and that to get true love you have to compete with other girls for sweetest,
most poised, and most beautiful.

The whole idea of sweet and poised is a source of anxiety because so
few girls can be so nonstop. Why else would all those Embarrassing Moments or Humiliating Moments columns be their favorites in teen magazines? While they long for girls on TV to show them awkward moments
that make them real, they also long to know that they can overcome this
awkward feeling of being "too real" to be chosen the princess or America's
next top model or Miss America or the Bachelorette.

Do girls fare better in *Miss Seventeen*, a reality show all their own? In
this show, girls are judged by girls their own age on how sweet, nice, and
honest they are, while the cameramen (yes, men) catch them in embarrassing catfights and betrayals behind the scenes. Girls can log on to *Seventeen*'s Web site to get the inside dirt and talk about the girl eliminated
that week. The only thing more interesting would be watching girls and
their friends, and here it is: MTV's *Laguna Beach* is a docu-soap about the
lives of a group of rich California high schoolers. It has the allure of *Real
World*-meets-*The-OC*. Beautiful teen people with too much time and
money illustrate how to gossip, shop, and make out.

Reality shows are best turned off unless you're prepared to watch
them with your daughter to discuss the content. When a mom or dad
watches such a show with his or her daughter, it's a good time to talk
about how we're induced to pick apart and distrust other women, how
they set the women off against one another, and how it might be a more
interesting show if they showed how the friendships were developing between the women backstage. (We get only a glimpse of that, and rarely if
ever does a magazine follow up to discuss which women have remained
friends after the show is over.) Groaning every time they set up a woman
as a bitch and wondering aloud what interesting things she has said that
they've edited out or added in in order to portray her as the bad girl can
work. Cheer sometimes, too—like when Stefanie and Danni, two very

athletic and powerful players on *Survivor Guatemala*, won competitions, earned each other's respect, and made friends.

Dating shows can introduce talks with your daughter about real interest, which spawns real romance. Rarely do we see the people in these shows engaged in a conversation where the bachelor listens to the woman describe her interest in the small business she's developing or her trip with Habitat for Humanity or even the amateur volleyball team she belongs to. The message to give young girls is that *interests* and activities make you interesting—and that's why these people rarely end up staying together after the camera crew goes home. Even people who look plastic and beautiful and perfect have real lives with interests and talents and jobs that have their ups and downs, and it's how they talk about these, what they share of themselves, that sparks an interest in someone after the initial attraction.

As girls are voted off or sent away from these shows, they are often in tears. Their hopes were high for being chosen. Explain to your daughter that some of that sadness is about not really being known, not being given a chance—and that's the premise of the show. The producers set it up so that none of them is given a chance to be a real person but instead is judged by looks or superficial qualities alone. That's a heartache that every middle school girl understands.

THEY'RE PURE EVIL: HORROR FILMS

The princess movies in the tween years taught a few lessons about love and meanness, but in R-rated movies that middle school girls watch, love gets upped to sex, and meanness gets upped to evil. Evil versus innocence has been a theme from the Bible to fantasy literature, as in the *Lord of the Rings* trilogy. But girls learn important lessons about how to keep their place in this division as they scare themselves silly watching horror films.

Ever since Regan in *The Exorcist* spewed pea soup, twisted her head 180 degrees, and yelled profanity, audiences thrilled to the sight of female innocence gone bad. Little girls in white cotton dresses see things and know things their parents don't believe, as in *The Inhabitants*, and little girls with wide eyes and long black hair do bad things, as in *The Ring*. A male psychiatrist tries to help by saying, "You don't want to do bad things," but the evil girl in *The Ring* says, "Oh, but I do."

It's hard to keep our daughters away from scary movies even though we want to, so it's important to know the varieties that exist. There are the suspense thriller horror movies like *The Ring* and *The Exorcist* and *Poltergeist*.

(Older films are included here because girls do rent them for a scare.) There are also the slasher films that feature Freddie and Jason, the guy with the chain saw, and the *Predator. Jeepers Creepers* features a winged scarecrow evil guy, and *Shredder* has a skiing maniac who doesn't like snowboarders who don't follow the rules.

Some girls like to be scared, and parents make choices about what kinds of horror movies their girls are permitted to watch based on how easily scared they are. They ask their daughters if they will be up all night because of nightmares. Instead they should ask whether they really think teen girls do stripteases for their boyfriends and have hot sex in hot tubs at wild parties. Stripteases? Hot tubs? In horror films? The truth is, it's very difficult for a parent to know what is in a horror film based on the rating. PG-13 movies generally don't have crude language or sex in them, nor will girls actually see heads cut off and blood spurting out. When someone is electrocuted, it generally happens off camera, and while the audience may be surprised and scared by the all-of-a-sudden appearance of a murdered person, rarely do they get to watch a stab-by-stab murder. Severed body parts are the stuff of R-rated horror movies.

Our survey shows us that parents are letting middle school kids see R-rated horror movies—maybe not in movie theaters where they do check IDs, but at home, at sleepovers, on cable, or rented from video stores. Not all R-rated horror flicks are alike. Compare what is done by the girls featured in *Jeepers Creepers* to what is done by those in *Shredder*. In *Jeepers Creepers*, a busload of high school students gets terrorized on a deserted highway. In the latter, college coeds break into a deserted ski lodge. In the former, three cheerleaders accompany the boys' basketball team— one blond, one brunette, and one black. (Why not the girls' basketball team?) In *Shredder*, girl snowboarders (one blond, one brunette, and one tomboy) go off for a wild weekend with college boys. In the former, the R rating is for the violence when Scarecrow Guy swoops down and chops off heads and plunges pointy things deep into chest cavities. In the latter, while heads are chopped and chests are skewered, soft porn relaxes us between the scares. In the former, there seems to be a bit of a moral: The scarecrow sniffs fearful people, and the most fearful of the high school boys are the ones who are prejudiced against gays and blacks. They must die. In the latter, the moral seems to be that snowboarders should be more considerate of skiers.

The major difference, though, has to do with the sexualizing of the girls in the films. Most of these movies feature an assortment of girls. In

Jeepers Creepers they aren't sexualized (e.g., although cheerleaders, they're not in uniforms). In *Shredder,* blond, beautiful Kimberly is featured in the shower soaping her body. The camera follows her hands as she soaps between her legs but stops short of an N-17 rating. The college kids play strip drinking games. Robin, the brunette, seduces a college guy, and we see him suck her breasts and fondle her naked butt. Kimberly gets in the hot tub with a fake Euro-hunk, and the two have wild sex. The remake of *Texas Chainsaw Massacre* lies somewhere in between these two R-rated movies, with the girls wearing sexy little shirts lit by the director in ways that accentuate their breasts. A perverted policeman feels the private parts of a dead girl covered with plastic wrap and says, "She's kind of wet down there. What have you boys been doing to her?"

The sex is kind of shocking to the parent of a middle school girl, but it's the message that is also a problem. Girls in horror films continue to be used to represent the good girl and the bad girl. There is a virgin and a slut, and you can bet the slut is going to die. Even in the PG-13 *The Ring,* a film that middle school girls absolutely love, Becca asks Katie about her trip to the mountain lodge with Josh: "You did it, didn't you?" She did do it, and a few minutes later Katie gets it. Let that be an abstinence lesson! Do it and die.

The good news is that women are playing more and more exciting roles. They're not just being chased by a slasher through the woods (tripping and falling, of course). And they're not always the ones who stupidly say, "Let's go into the basement" or "Let's split up." Some of them *are* the evil ones, as in *Shredder.* When they're not the evil ones, they are given weapons to hold and the opportunity to slash back, punch at evil creatures, shoot guns, and run them over with big vehicles. They're still the only ones in the movies who scream, but at least they get to do something after they scream.

Middle-aged women are represented in this genre only rarely and as mothers, but messages about motherhood abound. These messages are always very conservative. In *Chainsaw* the lead girl, Erin, saves a baby, making her a "good mother." In another film, *The Hand That Rocks the Cradle,* a woman terrorizes a family because of the loss of her baby. In *The Ring,* sixty-six miscarriages drive a woman crazy. Other mothers will do *anything* to protect their child, and more often than not, their child is in danger because the mother works too much.

Don't let middle school girls see the R-rated films unless you've seen them first. But realize that PG-13 horror films are going to be part of your daughters' lives at some point, including at friends' houses and sleepovers. Although they are filled with the same kinds of stereotypes that they'll see in other films, moms and dads have a special opportunity to bring gender questions into their critical conversations. Middle school girls want to be able to take a sarcastic, irreverent, and critical stance on these films, so it's a wonderful opportunity to talk about the problems. Why aren't there any close girl friendships in these films? Do two best girlfriends together ever *ever* kill the monster? Oh, no, are they putting down working women again? Why did they make the girls cheerleaders instead of basketball players, too? Why can't the bad girl live to get married someday?

These gender questions can be intertwined with the fun observations we all make about the horror movie genre! For example, remember to joke with your daughters: "Why don't they ever turn on the lights?" "Oh, look, it was just a cat. We're all supposed to feel relieved now so it will surprise us when the real attack comes shortly after, so get ready!" This will naturally lead to "The girl's running. Is she going to trip?" and "Will they give the pretty girl the gun, or are they going to let the tomboy shoot him?" In this way you let her know what's really scary about these films.

Friends, Sex, and R-rated Movies: Real Teens

Movies, TV, videos, and DVDs—these are an enormous part of the entertainment lives of high schoolers when they are not involved in schoolwork or extracurriculars. More savvy than their middle school counterparts, teens are critical of what they watch even as they continue watching it. They tell us they like shows with "real" teens and "real" friendships. When they see a relationship between two best friends on *The OC*, *Sex and the City*, or *Laguna Beach*, they like to say, "That's just like me and Cathy!" Fiercely independent, or so they believe, they think they're in control of what they take in and are loath to think that the shows might be influencing them. They watch lots of what middle schoolers watch as well as sitcoms and movies that are considered more adult. They believe they are adult, and what better way to prove that to themselves than to be able to enter the world of sex—if only virtually. It seems like everything they watch is either about sex, has a sexual component, or makes sexual jokes.

The girls we surveyed said they watch *Friends*, *Will & Grace*, and *Sex and the City* religiously. These shows teach girls important lessons about what is normal for their age group: friends and boyfriends, although the characters are often older.

Why is that damaging? Aren't relationships great? Aren't girls good at relationships? We should celebrate the ability to connect with others, but let's give girls the freedom to be other than that. Let's let them be action adventure heroes or the more mature senior lawyer, cop, or FBI agent. It is a good thing that the most popular TV show today, the original *CSI*, has women in strong investigative positions doing their jobs, and only occasionally do they show us the private lives of the women or relationship struggles (although we do learn that the senior female CSI is a former showgirl). Still, they are women who are as invested in their jobs as men. The result of this is that young women are now expressing interest in a career in forensics, and it is now one of the most popular majors for girls.

There is another problem about TV shows and their representation of women: If they're not into relationships (as mothers, teen alcoholics, whatever), they're into sex. Sex is everywhere on TV—in the prostitutes on *Law and Order*, the antics of the playboy plastic surgeon on *Nip/Tuck*, the beaches of California's Orange County and Laguna Beach, and the sex toys, weird deaths, and strange S&M practices that are standard *CSI* fare in Las Vegas, Miami, and New York. It's found more innocently in teen dramas such as *Everwood* through heartfelt discussions about whether a couple should "do it." There seems also to be a constant stream of wisecracks about girl-on-girl kisses in sitcoms and in commercials for them. Indeed, sexual scenes on television have nearly doubled since 1998. Among the top twenty most watched shows by teens, including *The OC* and *Desperate Housewives*, 70 percent include kissing, fondling, and talk about sex. If a show is particularly geared to teens, the message they're given is that they should be thinking about this now. If the show is for a general audience, it teaches girls that what makes girls interesting to the culture is their sexuality.

Over the past few years these shows have introduced topics to teens that we would guess 90 percent of sex education classes don't cover: masturbation, vibrators, blow jobs, switch partner parties, faking orgasms, female horniness, hookups, and more—all this in an era where the government supports "abstinence only" education. (By the way, a recent report to Congress showed that these programs have inaccurately taught teens that they can catch AIDS from sweat and tears, and that girls can get pregnant from mutual masturbation.)

With sex ed so brief and so wrong, your teenage daughter is learning about sex from two sources; her friends and the media. This is bad because it is a distorted education, every bit as distorted as the "abstinence only" courses offered in high schools. By watching TV and going to movies, your daughter is more likely to learn that boys love it when they can watch two pretty girls kissing each other (from sitcoms), how to set up a romantic scene in a sunken tub (lots of candles and rose petals à la soap operas), and how to give a blow job (from the movie *Old School*) before she actually knows and understands what's what and what it is called on her own body!

We believe that sex education for children and teens is woefully inadequate in the United States. We know that research shows the more thorough, complete, consistent, and persistent a sex education a girl has, the more likely she is to grow up to find sexual pleasure, to accept herself as a sexual human being, to have protected sex if she chooses to have intercourse, and to avoid early sex and pregnancy. We think that topics such as masturbation and vibrators *do* belong in sex education courses. So what's wrong with these shows for teens?

The purpose of these shows is to entertain, not to educate. And parents have to seriously question who should teach their daughters about sex. A thirty-something group of Hollywood writers, mostly male, looking for ways to make people feel anxious and laugh about it? Writers who are continually looking for new trends in sex and sexuality to make a joke of? Who find ways to create intricate relationship problems because of sex? Who tell your daughters that this is a fast way to feel powerful? Yes, there is power in being sexy, and it's the same power that has been sold to women for ages: the power to get men to pay attention to them.

Knowledge is power. Knowing about sex makes a teen feel sophisticated and older. She yearns to pick up on sexual practices by watching TV at the same time that she's finding new anxieties about sex to worry about. Why? It's simply cool to know. To be older. To be the one in the know. Having this information gives her social cachet. But does she also have to perform? When she does, what she is interested in performing is often a reproduction of the forms and sexual practices that she has seen in the movies or on TV. Where else would she get information about "how to do it"? Watch these embarrassing sex and sex talk scenes with her. Enjoy the girl talk, but remind her occasionally that when Hollywood tries to defy stereotypes of women by creating girls who can talk sex and hook up like guys, they go way over the top and miss something important.

FROM ROMANCE TO PORN

Before looking a bit closer at the kind of sex your daughter is learning about in the movies, let's answer a general question about film. Why are there no R-rated chick flicks? Is it because teenage girls who want to see a "girl" movie will dip down to the PG-13s? Is it because anything that a teen girl might want to see has to be made accessible to teen boys? Yes to both. But a major reason is that teen girls in movies seldom get raunchy or obscene as the boys do in *Road Trip* or *Old School*. As soon as they do get raunchy, it becomes a boy's film, and the raunchy girl is no longer the sweet girl that our daughters can identify with. In fact, she'll be disposed of by the end of whatever buddy saga prevails.

A teen girl may think she has a myriad of choices at the movies when she is out with her friends. She can see a romance that is a step more sophisticated than the princess movies. She can see a romance/comedy that includes a bumbling, rude, but lovable male character (typically played by a comic actor such as Adam Sandler or Will Ferrell) that draws the boys into the movie too, similar to *50 First Dates* and *Fever Pitch*. She can see a horror film that may have a strong woman in it, but if it is rated R, it will make this strong woman porn-star sexy (as she runs in the rain, for example, from her stalker, her blouse will get wet, and her nipples will show through). A teenage girl can see a "boy comedy" where all the girls in the film will serve as types the boys can choose from; there is always a sexy girl and a good girl among them. Or she can go to an action movie where the woman looks like a blow-up sex doll that a boy puppeteer is controlling on the set, keeping her sexy during all her leaps, flips, and laser saber fights. She'll be the kind of woman who appeals to boys—so strong that she's over the top and so busty that she's over the bra. She's a fantasy woman, but she's no girl's fantasy.

The PG-13 romances show the same old girl types, too. *The Boss's Daughter* with Tara Reid, *Wimbledon* with Kirsten Dunst, and *Thirteen Going on Thirty* with Jennifer Garner are all chick flicks of a certain kind. They all have sweet actresses who have edges that make them a teensy bit real. They are a little "feisty" but not too much so as to eradicate the need for a mean girl or a really feisty or awkward sidekick. Sometimes a PG-13 romance will have a fun guy like Adam Sandler in order to attract guys to the movie theater who will love the scenes about farts and vomit and poop. It will be *their* language, not the language of the female characters, that makes the movie PG-13. Their "boy talk" about sex will also change the rating from a PG to a PG-13. From middle school through high school, this is it. There are no R-rated romances aimed at teen girls except when the romance features a lesbian relationship such as *But I'm a Cheerleader* or *The Incredibly True Adventures of Two Girls in Love*.

There are some R-rated teen movies that involve romance, but the story line takes place within a big raunchy journey story about guys being guys by not being girls. Because the real purpose of the movie is to give guys a theatrical joy ride that involves car chases, embarrassing moments, farting, and sex, girls are made into reactors. Are there girls in *Road Trip*, a buddy story? Two guys take the trip to get the videotape of one of the guys hooking up with a girl who is not his girlfriend, but that's it for girls. In *Old School* the women are there for the following reasons: (1) to look sexy and have sex, (2) to get mad at the boys for being immature (as their mothers might), and (3) to be made fun of for being too prudish or un-knowledgeable about all things male, which includes sex. In *Old School* there is a rather famous scene where a gay sex educator is brought into a women's get-together to teach them how to give a proper blow job, telling them that "the secret to a good blow job is focus." The women look stupid as they fondle long vegetables showing they don't know how to do this very important act.

A new kind of black exploitation film is part of this same genre where guys develop and change, and women simply react. *My Baby's Daddy* features some lovable bumbling guys who always want sex. Rather than create female characters whose innocence and longing for romance make the guys look crass, as in *Old School*, the girlfriends in this movie are all sexy and sexual, hot and horny. "You're wearing that top I like," says a boy at a party. "That's because I want you to take it off," she replies, as if they're making a porn movie. In another scene one of the three hot women whom the boys are dating is pictured reading an ad in a magazine for "strip aerobics." As these lovable African American boys warm the hearts of the audience through their awkward, anxiety-ridden, stupid moves in life, they still find time to make sexual wisecracks about women. *My Baby's Daddy* is a title that might appeal to girls, but every girl in it is "made to order" for men, just as they're made and made up in porn. The women all succeed by getting their babies' daddies to marry them, and in the end the stupid, crude, bumbling, funny guys become successful entrepreneurs. Just as the white girl is sold a story of power through withholding and innocence, the black girl is sold a story of power through sexuality—which gets you a baby, which gets you a man to take care of you. Even though romance films are awful in their own way, we have to complain here that girls of color, with the exception of JLo, are simply not permitted romance; they are stereotyped as aggressively sexual, stupid girls looking only for a guy to buy them jewelry and take care of them.

What about lesbians or girls questioning their sexuality? You won't see them very often. The only girl-girl kisses allowed in movies or on TV are those between two beautiful women who are performing a sex act for the guys watching. They do this not to exclude guys but to turn them on. Why is lesbian sex okay in the movies when guys are watching it and making jokes about it and not okay when it's for women? That's a good question to ask your teen daughter.

The better comedies that feature Mike Myers, Will Ferrell, Steve Carell, and Adam Sandler (none of the female stars of SNL) appeal to teens because they focus on a ridiculous lead character like Austin Powers. The women are created for these guys to play off of. Even Beyoncé as a sexy spy played the straight woman to Austin Powers's ridiculous antics. *Anchorman,* which takes place in the seventies, tries to get around the exploitation of women as sexual objects by making the romantic interest of the lead character a smart feminist. Those who make movies like these may think they're undoing stereotypes by making the girls the smart and powerful ones playing against the stupid guys, but who is the movie about and whom do we love? The stupid bumbling guy. And who are we never going to see? A stupid bumbling girl with a guy playing the straight man against her. Picture the scene in *Dodgeball,* a PG-13 movie, in which a dog is licking Ben Stiller's crotch and, half asleep, he's saying, "That feels good," thinking a woman is doing that. It's hilarious, to kids especially. Could a woman make that scene funny? The only kind of woman who could is the kind who wouldn't be given a leading role in a film.

The sex in these comedies is often so funny because the guys are such bumblers; the women, however, are completely satisfied and transported to new dimensions. We worry about idealized bodies on the screen and how they affect girls, but what about idealized sex? Watching sex from the guy's perspective (as in many of these movies), a girl learns to watch herself, to turn herself on, and to feel turned on by looking at her own breasts or at a man admiring her. She learns that this admiration and worship of her body, as shown in scenes of her arching her back while on top of a guy through camera work that shows the outline of her body, is the sexual part of sex. She learns to act as if she is totally absorbed and transported when she is not. She learns that all women must feel satisfied and fulfilled after intercourse. We would argue that just like idealized body images, idealized depictions of sex ultimately make teen girls feel inadequate or think they need to put on an act. Can they focus on their own sexual experience, or must they learn techniques, lap dances, and blow jobs to make them desirable, sexy, and powerful in bed?

FRIENDS AND *SEX*: THE OLD NEUROSIS IN A FRIENDLIER PACKAGE

Friends, Will & Grace, and *Sex and the City* are now in syndication. *Friends* has grabbed the coveted time period of after school but before supper on many stations. It is about white people living middle-class lives with interesting jobs that they care little about. All of these shows feature women who are powerful and creative but spend most of their twenties and thirties looking for Mr. Right. There is nothing new about this format. The twist in *Friends* is that they do it in a friendship group, showing that friendships can sometimes turn into problematic love relationships (perfect for teens). The twist in *Will & Grace* is that the man she loves most is her best friend, the gay man she lives with. The twist in *Sex and the City* is that in their search for Mr. Right they have sex with lots of different guys and talk about whether or not they really should be looking for Mr. Right.

In these shows, teenage girls are given women to identify with, the same as in the princess movies of the early years. These women all bumble a little in their quests, but they are pretty and nice. They have sidekick girlfriends who are the sluts that they aren't. In the end they all want princes.

While these shows have a freer attitude about sex than the parents of most teenage girls, they also preserve ideas of what good girls do. Good girls want to get married. Good girls put relationships before careers even when they think they shouldn't. Good girls want to have babies eventually. They also give lessons about what girls like to do together. Rather than share their interests, girls love to eat together, drink together, club together, and shop together. Careers give girls money to shop for designer shoes and go to clubs. Sex gives girls power—and makes them vulnerable.

All of these shows do discuss the vulnerability of girls who have sex in a world that will call them sluts if they make one wrong move. The powerful women are often depicted as having power by taking on the traditionally male attitude of "wanting it" (sex, the job, everything). Girls who watch these shows tend to think of sex as something that enhances or creates a certain identity of being cool in the same way boys create coolness by cultivating an aura of being a player. The girls we've talked to who buy into this idea of cool, who give blow jobs for fun and like to show other girls it's no big deal to them, let us know that there's power in acting like a boy. In fact, *Sex and the City* plays around with the boundaries of this while in the end reassuring us that all these women are still girls. They want husbands and babies and to be taken care of.

In the end, teen girls don't get a different idea of power, just the idea that for a time girls can grab that power by acting like guys, walking that thin line between sexual and slutty. And the girls who are trying on this power identity, the ones who dress up and surprise their boyfriends in sexy lingerie underneath a trench coat or who talk dirty or who give blow jobs as if they were handshakes, may momentarily feel cool in adopting this power sex persona. But when you speak to them about sex, they are not enjoying it very much; in fact, some don't know how to or feel it is inappropriate to masturbate. Many don't feel much sexual pleasure while they have sex even though they may have fun. So what they're adopting from TV is a carefree persona about sex rather than permission to be a sexual person in their own way.

MTV GIRLS

They jiggle their booties in the background of hip and dangerous-looking male rappers. Or they look mysteriously sexy swirling around male balladeers. They seduce, betray, scheme, and endure. They dance on bars and laps, and they wear feathers and sparkles and see-through clothes and high heels. They suck on lollipops seductively and, in one recent video, even have a pillow fight in their short shorts as the men sing about taffy! These are the girls on MTV, from the music videos to the *Real World*. The power they have on the videos is always a sexual power to overwhelm through being over-the-top stimulating as porn is meant to be. Or they excite by withholding, becoming the woman of mystery that all men want. Sure, you'll find a few female performers who sing it or rap it without jiggling and showing it at the same time, but for every one of them there are a dozen background jigglers.

This is not just a video fantasy; check out MTV reality shows. Sexual power is conveyed by all the shots of girls in bikinis hot tubbing as on *Real World San Diego*. Look, there goes another one fondling her breast implants for the camera in *Real World Philadelphia*. These girls are given the power to scheme and manipulate, to be "typical girls" and "play" people as the game requires. The producers have selected girls who have these qualities and capacities, and they set up situations to evoke them. What gets play time? Sex, deception, seduction, and catfighting. What gets lost on the cutting-room floor? Probably the boring hours in between when people with little interests outside of their bodies and their chance for stardom are sitting around with nothing to say. Maybe it's better than that. Maybe those cardboard cut-out twenty-somethings talk about politics, share stories about their grandparents, read novels, practice their instruments, and study for the GREs—making them much more interesting people than we'll ever be shown. We'd like to hope so.

What to Watch and How to Respond

How do parents respond to the onslaught of images their daughters will be watching? Token girls on male journeys. Mean girls and catfights. Disney princesses and reality makeovers. Girls who get male attention by batting their eyelashes or acting sexy. Girls who feel powerful when they're looking sexy and getting that attention. A mother responds by acknowledging how persuasive these roles sometimes seem, how narrow and simple, not by offering up an alternative that pits good girl against bad. Parents may encourage their daughters to be the nice girl or the princess, the one who appears all in white at the end of those movies, all eyes on her, and they may do that as a way to protect her from the only other way to be—the mean popular girl or sexy dancer on the bar, all eyes upon her. While a parent acknowledges the persuasiveness of each of these ways of being, it's also important to acknowledge how difficult it is to get that much attention for the other things her daughter can be and can do. If a parent chooses to talk about decency versus sluttiness or nice versus mean, she'll be playing into the divisions that society teaches girls and supporting the anxiety that her daughter has already developed about how far a girl can go without being condemned.

It is not a good idea to tell girls to be afraid of being judged; a girl should rarely have to limit herself for that reason. Instead, tell her what you hope for her as a person, not as a stereotype. The more girls and women are simplified and objectified, seen as types and not people, the easier it is to treat them with less respect and compassion. Parents who watch and listen to media with their daughters and openly communicate about what they see can help inoculate them against harmful messages by ensuring they develop a more critical stance toward the narrow types repeated over and over.

She'll need to talk with you about sex *before* middle school; otherwise the media may well become her sex adviser or "sexual super peer." Watch shows with your teens that may have a sexual component but aren't about sex or don't play up the weird sexual practices angle, such as *The Gilmore Girls*, which has a mother-daughter relationship at the center; *Alias*, which has a tough, smart, confident woman who manages to have very good close women friends; and, very popular with teens, *Lost*, which has plenty of female characters that are set up as types but who reveal different histories and more complexity than anyone would expect. Wouldn't you know, the credits reveal women as producers, directors, and writers!

If you can talk about the sex in these shows or other, more problematic ones, tell her clearly and directly that there is a lot about sex that they never show on TV. It is different from the jokes, the dancing, the implants, and the outfits in the bad shows; it is different from the crushes and the "opposites attract" of the better ones. Tell her that she needs to learn about herself as a sexual person from the inside out before she decides to express it in some contrived culturally permissible way. Acknowledge the attention she will get for looking sexy, and always confirm that understanding and wisdom about sex is more important than the way she looks and acts.

The bottom line is this: If you let your daughter watch TV and go to the movies, you're essentially enrolling her in a sex education course written primarily by boys and men, using traditionally sexy women as their teachers. Is this the curriculum you want? Are these the teachers? You need to decide whether you want to emphasize to her that her own pleasure is important or that you believe sex is better in a loving relationship and more ethically placed there. Otherwise, it will be sex toys, swinging singles in animal costumes, bondage and discipline, hot tubbing, pole dancing, and doggy style. Your daughter may learn all about these before she knows the word *clitoris*. Think about that!

MOVIES THAT FEATURE STRONG GIRLS
AND FEWER STEREOTYPES

Because of Winn-Dixie

Bend It Like Beckham

Corinna, Corinna

Fairy Tale: A True Story

Fly Away Home

Girlstown

Harriet the Spy

Herbie: Fully Loaded

Kiki's Delivery Service

A League of Their Own

Lilo and Stitch

A Little Princess

Little Women

Matilda

Me Without You

Miss Congeniality 2

The Monkey Kid

Norma Rae

Prancer

Princess Diaries (if you must
see a princess movie)

Rabbit-Proof Fence

Real Women Have Curves

*Sisterhood of the Traveling
Pants*

Spirited Away

The Story of Ruby Bridges

Ten Things I Hate About You

To Kill a Mockingbird

Whale Rider

The Wild Thornberrys Movie

For older teens:

Bastard out of Carolina

But I'm a Cheerleader

Erin Brockovich

Fried Green Tomatoes

Girl Interrupted

*The Incredibly True Adventures
of Two Girls in Love*

Love and Basketball

Manny and Lo

Princess Mononoke

Stepford Wives (original)

Thelma and Louise

Tumbleweeds

Welcome to the Dollhouse

And see if you can get hold of these documentaries:

5 Girls

*Beyond Killing Us Softly:
The Strength to Resist*

A Girl's Life

Girls Like Us

*Killing Us Softly, Still Killing Us
Softly, Killing Us Softly 3*

Mickey Mouse Monopoly

Playing (Un)fair

Reviving Ophelia

Slim Hopes

Ugly Ducklings

What a Girl Wants

CHAPTER 3

Do You Hear What I Hear?
What Girls Listen To

Little pitchers have big ears" is an odd and old-fashioned saying, but the sentiment is very true. Children listen to the world around them with great interest. They listen to what adults say. They listen to rhymes and chants and songs (some carefully chosen and others picked up on the playground or heard on a borrowed MP3 player). They listen to phone conversations, their parents' complaints about work, kids in school hallways, and radio DJs. When they're young and with us all day, we forget just how many of the words around them they are absorbing. When they're older, off on their own in a trendy visual wonderland of TV, movies, and videos, or in school with friends, or out in the world, they're also vulnerable to the sounds around them, the words that hurt, the stereotypes that are thrown their way, the sex in lyrics, and the girl-typing that insidiously pervades many remarks about girls and women. Perhaps parents are attuned to and concerned about the lyrics that their middle schoolers and teens hear, the antiwomen rap, the rough sex descriptions, and rightly so. But life in school and with peers mimics the sentiments expressed in song, and your daughter is just as likely to get an auditory assault on girls while waiting in the lunch line as she is listening to the radio.

What They Hear from Us: Body Talk and Girl Typing

By age six, children not only show a strong preference for thin figures but rate such figures as better and having more positive characteristics than fat ones. By the time they are ten or eleven, children rank drawings of obese children lower than any other group, including children with severe disabilities. Some studies suggest that as many as 80 percent of early adolescent girls are dieting at any given time. You can see where this is leading. Preventing this pattern means starting young and starting at home.

Anthropologist Mimi Nichter defines the "I'm so fat" language pervasive among girls and women as "fat talk," and she describes the way this language has become an accepted social reality in some female circles. Young girls get ideas about how bodies should look from the fat talk that surrounds them at home. It's in the media, but at six or seven it is more likely to come from mothers and other adult women in their lives.

YOU SAY	SHE HEARS
I can't have that potato. I'm on the South Beach diet.	Got to be on watch about weight gain; got to obey the rules.
These are the huge thighs of the Nelson family.	We bond or belong by putting ourselves down. Your body (whether the thighs are huge or not) will become a great source of disappointment to you.
I'm going to be bad tonight and have that ice cream.	It's bad to enjoy food. Ice cream is a sin, and you must feel appropriately guilty.
She really doesn't have much willpower *or* She's really let herself go.	We sit in judgment of other women and girls, but not boys and men. Weight is a matter of self-control and willpower. If someone puts on weight, it's a real tragedy.

Your daughter hears "fat talk" and learns how to look at and rate her own body. She feels the impact of your anxiety and sees how happiness is affected by food control. She may grow up believing she can be happy only if she is thin, and talking about weight, dieting, and food is a major focus of female bonding as well as female criticism. She learns that not loving her body can be a source of connection with other girls. She learns that loving her body sets her apart from most girls and women. And she learns to pay close attention to what she's eating, how other people see her, and how she talks about her body to other people.

Because it is difficult for most adult women to completely stop discussing weight and food in typically negative terms, a better solution may be to talk honestly with your daughter about when *you* first got these messages about what girls should look like and how hard it is not to take them in and repeat them. She'll learn from your honesty, and you'll both benefit from the conversation. Bond over the struggle to ignore or resist these messages, not over the fight against chocolate!

YOU WANT TO SAY	YOU ACTUALLY SAY
I can't have that potato. I'm on the South Beach diet.	I wonder why there's such a fuss about carbs. I love potatoes. They're delicious and nutritious. Surely, they'll be back in everyone's diets soon.
These are the huge thighs of the Nelson family.	Look at these thighs. They're just like Grandma's. We were born to be strong and solid, like shot-putters or runners.
I'm going to be bad tonight and have that ice cream.	Let's all have ice cream tonight together!
She really doesn't have much willpower *or* She's really let herself go.	You noticed Aunt Mary put on weight? Yeah, me, too. TV teaches us that everyone is supposed to stay the same pencil-thin size all their lives, but people change. People put on weight when they get older.

It is okay to acknowledge that too many carbs and too much ice cream really *isn't* that healthy, and also to let your daughter know that we all look at other people and sometimes judge them: "Sometimes I, too, see a fat woman and think, 'Boy, she's really heavy. I'm glad I'm not like that.' So then I think 'Why am I so concerned with another woman's size? Isn't that silly?'" This honest approach may be the best one because it helps your daughter be a little more reflective about the way the culture shapes our thinking. And you might add, "We don't know anything about her or her life" to help your daughter see there's more to know about a woman beyond her looks.

While you're at it, think about whether you downplay your abilities or women's abilities in front of your daughter. If she starts saying things like "I'm bad at that," most likely she is mimicking things she's heard you or others say. Remember also that if you talk about, put down, or gossip about other women or girls, she learns this behavior as well. Girls pick up not only the content of what you say but how you say it. If you're not direct about your thoughts and feelings with someone who has treated you badly, she won't be. If you shy away from conflict or keep your strong feelings from her, she might do the same. But if you say what you feel and think, have the courage to try something new, and seek out close friends for support, she'll follow your example.

YOUR DESCRIPTIONS OF YOUR DAUGHTER

One of the most important things girls hear is how you describe them to themselves and to other people. Parents label their children in subtle ways. If a girl has a brother, it's very common for parents to make gender comparisons that either fit stereotypes or proclaim how their daughter doesn't fit the stereotype. Either way, they're informing her that there is a "way to be" if she's a girl. Parents may say, "She's a girly girl" or "She's a tomboy."

We've heard many friends stereotype their boys as well. Even feminist moms have told us, "I thought it was all socialization until I had one of each, and lo and behold, my daughter played with dolls and my son played with trucks." Parents are willing to jump to biological explanations when it's their own children and their own child-rearing practices that seem in question. But the world outside the home is reflected and presented in the home in unacknowledged, unnoticed ways. Children of two and three live in the world, too, and girlhood is represented to girls in ways that draw in even the youngest. The late Beverly Fagot examined how gender roles were inculcated in one- to three-year-olds in the day care centers she studied. These toddlers policed each other—rewarding the boys who played with boy toys, the girls who played with girl toys, and excluding the girl who wanted to play with the trucks!

Whether parents label their daughters girly or not, they are still rein-forcing the idea that there are two types. Perhaps the best way to combat all the stereotypical definitions of what it means to be a girl is by never us-ing those terms to define her.

Consider some of the following stereotypical labels and phrases used to describe girls and think about how you can rephrase them.

She's bossy. "She's a natural leader. She just has to learn the gentle art of persuasion."

She's a shopper. "She's in a shopping/fashion phase now. She and her friends love to hang out at the mall, and what else is there to do there but shop? At least she has a wonderful artistic sense about colors. I hope she continues on in art."

She met up with a mean girl in school *or* **Girls can be so mean to each other**. "She and her friends are having some difficulties now. One girl is taking out her own issues on my daughter, and it hasn't been pleasant. I hope we can find a way to reach out to her as well as protect my daughter." (Don't buy into the senseless division of girls into mean and nice.)

She's a girly girl *or* **She's all girl**. "Recently, she loves to wear dresses. I think that comes from when she was little and loved to twirl around in them." *Or:* "She loves pink and purple everything. They have been her favorite colors since she was small."

Girls really are such good little mothers. Be specific about what she takes care of. "She's so great with our dog; she is very attentive to what he needs each day. I hope she will take care of herself with such sen-sitivity when she grows up."

She's acting like such a teenager. It is better not to call surliness a teenage trait. Every little girl has a right to say no and a right to be an-gry, emotional, and upset at the world. In a recent episode of *That's So Raven*, African American Raven proudly exclaimed, "My dad's been teaching me to say no ever since I was little." (Nice for dads! Moms can do this, too.) Instead of calling her a teenager, simply say, "She's been feeling upset and angry lately and has been very private about it. I hope to find out what's been bothering her." In other words, stick with descriptions and resist locking her into simple categories that the culture offers. (Remember, your job is to open up possibilities, and these limiting categories often exist to make it easier to package and sell her something.)

You can turn these stereotypical criticisms around and find a way to describe her strengths. At the same time you can look at behaviors as situational and temporary rather than confirm something permanent or essential about who she is. When other moms and dads describe their daughters in this stereotypical limited way, subtly suggest to them new ways of seeing the behavior and the stereotype. If parents can't refrain from labels, how can we ever expect school kids to stop?

WHAT THEY HEAR FROM TEACHERS

In their book, *Failing at Fairness*, David and Myra Sadker reported their years of work analyzing gender bias in the classroom. With a relatively simple coding scheme, they sat in the back of classrooms and recorded whom the teacher called on and what kinds of comments or instruction she or he tended to offer students. They found three interesting patterns: (1) Boys are called on more often than girls, sometimes two to three times more often; in part this is because teachers spend more of their time disciplining boys, and calling on them helps maintain order in the classroom; (2) Boys are likely to call out answers more often than girls; (3) Boys and girls receive different kinds of teacher feedback when they're called on. Boys are likely to be asked to elaborate on their answers, and they also receive more criticism. Girls are more likely to receive general praise and simple acknowledgment. In fact, the only comments girls receive more often than boys concern their appearance, the neatness of their papers, and their conformity to rules.

Your daughter, unless she has a vigilant and well-informed teacher, is likely to hear boys' voices more often in her classroom. At the same time she is less likely to receive important constructive criticism on her schoolwork. Instead, she may hear nice things about how pretty she looks in a certain color, how nice her hair looks pulled back, or other comments that have little to do with critical thinking or educational excellence. This is something to be aware of and to talk about with your daughter and with her teachers. You might ask her teachers if the school has arranged gender bias training, and, if not, consider recommending books such as

Failing at Fairness and the American Association of University Women's book, *How Schools Still Shortchange Girls*. You can combat this tendency at home as well by praising her for taking risks, being strong, sticking with a hard problem, speaking up when it's not easy—that is, by focusing more attention on what she can do and what she's willing to try rather than on how pretty she looks.

WHAT THEY HEAR FROM PEERS: GIRL STAIN
AND OTHER WORD VOMIT

"Word vomit" is an expression you're more likely to hear from a sassy middle schooler, but it's an apt description of the uncontrollable spew of sexist comments that girls hear about being female. It is sometimes said in the unlikeliest of places and even by people they love and trust. These girl slurs can take the form of insults hurled across the playground—"she throws like a girl" or "girl stain"—or they can be more subtle put-downs heard right in her own home about female bodies or feminine qualities. Those throwaway comments about girls can be heard just about anywhere but also, shockingly, in what your four- to seven-year-old listens to.

Timon and Pumba, in the beginning of *The Lion King II: Simba's Pride*, for example, admire the new baby lion, and Timon indulges in a little nostalgia: "It'll be like old times." "But Timon," Pumba reminds him, "it's a *girl!*" And we know what he means: There will be no reliving the good old days, no group burping, no farting, no eating bugs, and no fun. As often as we hear insults like "girl cooties" or "yuck, that's too girly" on school playgrounds, we're just as likely to be reminded, as Timon and Pumba are, that being a girl just isn't as good, as much fun, or as cool as being a boy.

What is different these days is that you're as likely to hear these comments from girls as you are from boys. Putting down girly stuff is all the rage in the younger set because it's all the rage in the media. The mixed messages are constant. She hears lots of insults about girly girls in G-rated movies and TV shows, and at the same time she gets messages about how she should be into fashion and appearances. You can counter this toxic information by helping her notice it and name it as negative and unfair.

To be fair, in many girl-versus-boy movies or girl-triumphs-over-the-boys TV show episodes, antigirl comments serve to show the chauvinism of boys. They are featured before the girl proves that she is actually better than the boys at some activity nobody expects a girl to be good at. Remember that this is not to show you that girly is fine but that the one girl they thought was a girly girl actually has more *boy* characteristics than they thought and deserves praise because she's more like the boys than not.

It's tricky to handle this kind of talk without devolving into an "all kinds of girls are acceptable" lecture, setting her up for the parade of girl types in *Seventeen* magazine and so on to come, a false tolerance that excludes far too many girls. You don't want her to overvalue pink and pretty and all that frilly stuff. Yet there are things associated with being a girly girl that should be an option to her, too, and not rejected out of hand because boys don't like (or aren't supposed to like) that stuff. That is why we criticize the name caller. Say to her, "That's a put-down!" or "That's a stereotype of girls. Girls don't only do that stuff. There are lots of other things they like." If she likes pink, you can say, "Girls can be into pink and not be boy crazy or think only about their appearance."

The fourth and fifth grade girls told us they call other girls "by their names" or "not bad stuff." But by age twelve, sixth and seventh grade girls in our survey cross that invisible barrier into the land of adult insults, using names like skank, slut, bitch, prostitute, puta, ho, whore, cunt, hooker, tramp, dick licker, and cock sucker. Lisa, age eleven, says, "Some girls call this girl in my school a slut. They really hate her." Maddy says, "They talk about kissing and having sex and grabbing people's butts and how big your butts and boobs are and if you have started your period and puberty and all kinds of stuff like that; that people want to have s** with other people. I think it is gross." In a little more than a year girls have gone from talking about "who peed on the bathroom floor," "getting your period," and "rumors about who likes who" to talking about "nasty things such as thongs, sucking dicks, sex, making out" or "sex, seeing boys' dicks, having sex," and "who they wanna do it with or who they've done it with, and how to do it."

Leora Tanenbaum begins her popular book, *Slut! Growing Up Female with a Bad Reputation*, with a chart. On the top left corner are positive expressions for a sexually active man (there are twelve); on the top right are positive expressions for a sexually active woman (just two). The bottom left lists negative expressions for a sexually active man (only three); the bottom right lists negative expressions for a sexually active woman (a whopping twenty-eight). It's a pretty impressive display of the old double standard. Our surveys of ten- to thirteen-year-olds tell us that girls know this standard all too well; some are uncomfortable with it and some do their part in keeping it in place.

"Bee-Ahtch" is the fun way to call someone a bitch, and it sends seventh graders into giggles if they haven't already developed a mock sophistication about such things. "Slut" seems to be used by girls against girls a bit more regularly than by boys. "Lesbo" can be used by boys or girls as a joke or to make a girl seriously unhappy, bringing her in line. If they're caught saying "ho," girls will protest that it's just a "garden tool." While college students may joke around with words like "man-ho," generally "ho" is something a girl does not want to be.

Girls' intelligence is also routinely commented on, as it was in the focus group we did in an eighth grade class. In response to one of our questions about girls and conformity, one boy yelled out, "Because they're a bunch of airhead snobby idiots." There was no response from the teacher or other students, as if this kind of talk went on all the time, and it was better to ignore it.

While many parents may be tempted to point to this name-calling as an example of why girls should be careful about their image and whom they act sexy around, think this one through. The message is not, "Don't dress sexy because other people will call you a slut"; the message is how unfair it is that girls are so closely watched and so easily put down. It is doubly unfair that just as she's learning about sex, she learns far more about supposed bad girls than about relationships, her body, and understanding desire.

WHAT ELSE THEY HEAR FROM PEERS: GOSSIP

Thanks in part to the tween marketing campaign and its obsession with sexy looks and crushes between eight-year-olds, by the time they're twelve most girls are looking forward to the teen years. They have been exposed to and are actively seeking TV shows, movies, clothes, and magazines that vault them into full teen mode. Even the youngest of the teen magazines have articles about being a good kisser, and the rest have monthly tips about how to keep boys happy and avoid being the school slut. Versions of slut and bitch are all over notebooks, bath products, and cute novelty T-shirts. There are the nighttime soaps such as *The OC*, reruns of *Sex and the City*, *Desperate Housewives*, and reality shows filled with catfights complete with words the girls list on their surveys and a few extra. When a teenage pop star freely talks about her "friends with benefits" (hooking up with friends for sex) relationship, girls are taking notes.

Don't believe everything you read. Not all middle school girls join this trend of early teenagerhood. We know plenty who love their bikes, play games like Magic and hang out with their parents on weekends. Still, there are crowds in the middle school years that take on the job of defining the norm through cliques and gossip. The girls we surveyed told us that the latest gossip is about bodies and appearance, attitude, relationships, and sex. These are the things they have to monitor in themselves carefully if they're going to be "normal" girls and have good reputations. It begins to be a moral failing if a girl does not take care of herself, which means buying and wearing the right things. Friends start dropping old friends who don't fall in the middle ground of cool. If you can "other" a girl, which is a way of saying the kind of girl you're not (that is, the "other" girl is a slut or a bitch), then you're indirectly saying who you *are* (a nice, nonslutty, nonbitchy girl).

For certain groups the boy factor is big in middle school. It is not by chance that girls tell us boys call girls names like sexy, hot, fine, and babe, while girls call girls the harsher slut, ho, and skank. Good girl reputations are constantly at risk when, as one thirteen-year-old said, "everyone talks about perverted things all the time." In this climate, putting down other girls is driven by fear and the desire to maintain one's own reputation.

Some of the girls in our survey struggle with the gossip and rumors spread about them. They've seen where it can lead. One twelve-year-old knows "it's about me and Gordon and Drake. People think that all of them like me, but I try to tell them it's not true. But they never listen." Some are embarrassed or disgusted by all the sex talk, and some choose to "ignore crude rumors going around my school." From some we got the feeling that it matters because they insist so adamantly that it doesn't. One thirteen-year-old said, "It doesn't make me feel anything. I don't listen." Another said, "It is really perverted. It doesn't bother me." Others got irritated and defensive when asked about labeling and name-calling in their schools: "What kind of question is that?" they wanted to know. "Why are you asking this question?" Some readily admitted that the gossip "about sex or sexual things is kind of embarrassing and sometimes degrading" or that such talk is "horrible and makes me feel unsafe" or "makes me feel like punching kids." We know that bullying and name-calling has preceded shootings in schools. We know that girls continue to snipe at each other with humiliating, reputation-damaging words. It is not always the case that boys externalize their rage and girls internalize it, but the higher levels of depression, eating disorders, and self-cutting behaviors that girls display give us a sense of the long-term impact these words have.

The sexual double standard is as old as Jezebel, and parents need to do more than talk with their daughters about name-calling and gossip. All gossip has the power to hurt. Calling someone a slut, ho, or skank is almost always directed at girls. The name caller gets power because these names do a particular kind of damage, not only to the other girl but, in the bigger picture, to all girls who find themselves walking that fine line between hot and slutty.

Sometimes, though, we underestimated the maturity of middle school girls. One thirteen-year-old wrote that sexual rumors are often "about the girls who feel okay in their bodies, so they show a bit of skin. People call them tramps and say, 'Oh, yeah, she had sex with so-and-so and so,' and it makes me mad because it's not true." Good for her, but what can she do about it? Ignore it? Parents can teach girls to speak up. Girls can actively undo rumors. By naming they can fight naming. Teaching daughters to name gossip as gossip and rumors as rumors is a first step. The girls we heard from can do that for us, but there have to be more girls doing it so they can feel safe sticking up for others and themselves with peers. Here's an example:

> LUVRGRL90389: Jody did it with Brandon at the library during the school dance. I swear it.
> MISSYME1090: I don't want to hear that gossip. That's hurtful stuff, and if we spread it, then next time it could be us. BFF ☺.

WHAT THEY HEAR MAY BE DIFFERENT FROM WHAT THEY DO

A special note on middle schoolers: Most people think that Seven Minutes in Heaven, Truth or Dare, and the age-old Spin the Bottle are middle school games played to give kids a structured entry into the world of sex and teen romance. They are practice games, so to speak. We think there is something more to them. Girls love these games because they create stories to tell, information to pass on or to keep secret, knowledge about areas in which they're not supposed to know too much. Like the *Gossip Girls* books they read and the PG-13 movies they watch, party games give them information, and information equals sophistication.

It's interesting that what *doesn't* change for most girls is actual experience. Lyn finds that in her middle school coalition groups—even with those girls that school counselors and kids alike think are sexually experienced—girls ask the most basic questions about sexual behavior. (Is sex just intercourse? Can you get pregnant the first time? Does it hurt for boys?). They are also confused about definitions of the simplest terms such as blow job, clitoris, and orgasm. It turns out that a combination of things can get a girl labeled a slut, the least of which is her sexual history. Believe it or not, early breast development is enough to get a girl labeled fast. If two boys like her at the same time and another girl likes one of the boys, forget it! If she has a tough exterior, a big attitude, a difficult home life, past sexual abuse, or lives in poverty, she is vulnerable to being seen by other girls as a slut. In reality there's not much she can do about most of these things, so it's not so much what a girl has done but how she comes across to others that gets her labeled.

Girls are curious about other girls' lives, but it's knowing more than other girls that gives girls a particular sense of superiority. When a girl knows what oral sex is or what "C" "U" "N"ext "T"uesday really means and shares that information with a friend or a group of girls at a slumber party, she's no longer a child but a sophisticated *Sex and the City* girl. It's knowledge about what's going on in their middle school—Who slipped someone the tongue? Who appeared to have an erection at the school dance? Who went off with whom at a party? And who has tried this or that with a boy? There is power in being the one who has the information.

Why does sexual sophistication (being knowledgeable about sex rather than doing it) give a girl such power? While getting too much experience can render her "slutty" in the eyes of peers, knowing about it is a way of being grown up. It's fantasy play of a kind. In play, children test ideas without consequences. In talk, girls test opinions, acts, and reactions with no consequences to themselves. The harm is done only to the girl whose secret is revealed.

While you can talk to your daughter about what gossip is and does, one of the best ways to counteract this problem is to give them real information in as unstimulating a way as possible. Demystify, detoxify, despectacularize sex for them, and they will gain a different kind of sophistication. "I know all that already. My mother told me."

Music to their Ears

> I like good songs—not the ones that tell you to make bad choices.
>
> —SANDRA, *fifth grader*

"I Must Not Kiss the Boys"
—*song by teen group* PLAY

Preteen girls are just beginning to get into popular music, and the culture is introducing musical taste into their lives at a rapid pace. But what about the four- to seven-year-old group? They're in it, too, up to their ears, so to speak. Just as your daughter hears about how to be a girl from family, friends, and teachers starting at a very young age, she also hears these messages in music. Nursery school rhymes, jump-roping songs, Kidz Bop, and Disney spell out the romantic fantasies that future songs will repeat ad nauseum throughout their growing-up years. Music today is so much more than just a voice and a guitar; it's a full-course feast of visual and auditory delights. Marketers know this. Kids hear pop music in the G and PG movies they love, the Web sites they visit, and the TV stations they tune into (on the shows and in between them). Channels such as Nick and Disney play videos and film personal spots with their star actors turned artists, including Hilary Duff and Raven, to capture the attention and loyalty of tween girls and even their younger sisters. Magazines such as *Girl's Life* and fan sites on the Web keep girls updated on their favorite artist's every move. Their favorite movies showcase their favorite artists, who make videos with clips from their favorite movies. Girls as young as six or seven buy their first CD and stash it in those fur-lined CD cases that Toys "R" Us markets to them, blurring the line between stuffed animal and teen toy. Most are listening to their older siblings' music.

While eight-year-olds are likely to have different tastes in music and more parental monitoring in this arena than middle school girls, you'd be surprised at how similar some of the themes are: romance, relationship problems, efforts to be one's own person, and sex. The marketing to girls stays the same but intensifies, and what they hear is as much or more about all the other stuff that goes with the music as about the music itself. For the younger kids there are the dolls, karaoke machines, and as they get older, the clothing, posters, and books.

Involved parents have a lot to absorb and talk about with their kids. And it can feel overwhelming. We suspect there's not a parent out there who hasn't "discovered" the shocking lyrics that go with a catchy tune their child has been humming and has wondered whether to allow or ban the song. Sharon's student who interviewed seven- to thirteen-year-olds about the lyrics to Britney Spears's "Hit Me Baby One More Time," a song they were all singing in their housing project, found that the seven-year-olds thought it meant something else, "not real hitting," but couldn't say exactly what it probably meant. The thirteen-year-olds thought it meant something about sex or drugs.

Take a look at these lyrics:

> Imma bring da cool whip/Then I want you to strip
> *from "Slow Jam" by* KANYE WEST

> Don't wanna squeeze triggers, just wanna squeeze tits
> *from "Hey Mama" by the* BLACK EYED PEAS

> Shut up, just shut up shut up/
> Stop the talking baby or I start walkin baby
> *from "Shut Up" by the* BLACK EYED PEAS

> She start feelin on my Johnson right out of the blue,
> Girl you super thick so I'm thinkin that's koo
> *from "Tipsy" by* J-KWON

> Girlz call me Jolly Rancher cuz i stay so hard
> You can suck me for a long time
> *from "Laffy Taffy" by* D4L

These are some of the lyrics girls told us they listen to and sing to themselves. Can you imagine? A 12-year-old girl listening to beloved Jack Black, from *School of Rock*, one of the coolest PG-13 movies kids own, singing "Fuck her gently" as his alter ego, Tenacious D? Or Ludacris singing about "rough sex" and "make it hurt"—"In the garden or in the dirt."

You may be thinking, as we did at first, that the lyrics and artists who are most popular today are different from the ones your daughter is listening to, and that to speak to your daughter, you have to know the artists she's listening to right now. Not true. In music, the more things change, the more they stay the same. You've probably already begun to worry about some of the lyrics she's hearing. Typically, parents respond in the following ways: Some don't let teens listen to certain artists or buy CDs with parental guidance ratings on them. Some give up, thinking they'll hear this music at friends' houses or on the radio, so they tell their kids, "That's disgusting" whenever they hear it. Some ignore the lyrics and have fun with the music. There's a different approach that combines all these responses.

First you should know this: we love music. Beyoncé and Usher have marvelous voices. It's fun to dance to Black Eyed Peas and sing along with Gwen Stefani. Good Charlotte did some interesting musical distortions at the end of "Bloody Valentine" to show that the narrator of the song who killed his ex's new boyfriend is a twisted kind of a guy. Musically, these artists are creative and talented.

Because of this, you can't just dismiss an individual performer or group out of hand. The same group that sings "Don't wanna squeeze triggers, just wanna squeeze tits" and the song "Let's Get Retarded" (after all those years we've tried to stop kids from using that word!), is the same group that asks "Where is the love?" in a beautiful antiwar, antiracism rap: "If you don't have love for your own race, then you only have room to hate." Dismissing a group or an artist because of one song is only going to make you seem reactionary and out of touch.

Let's not forget that in the sixties the Beatles were considered junk by many parents, mindless noise that was corrupting the ears of youth. Today we think of their music as almost classical and savor the love songs as well as the ironic and experimental tunes of their later years. Tastes change, but music still says something about the listener as well as the artist.

Take into consideration what music can mean. Music is unlike so much of what we have been talking about in girls' worlds. It's not something to watch, although it can be; and it's not something to do, although it can be. Music and lyrics together form an emotional combination that changes the experience of a moment. Whether background or foreground, it has the capacity to reach kids at some level that words alone or pictures cannot. The capacity of music to create a variety of emotional experiences and thus possibilities for a young girl far exceeds what TV, movies, or video games can do alone. Why else do movie directors add soundtracks with music that urges you to release a few tears at the climactic moments in their dramas? Think of the "Allelujia" song at the end of *Shrek* and the way it deepened the feeling and message of this funny movie. The music added a poignancy that dignified the frivolity of the cartoon and emphasized the message about how good love is in any form. Why else do girls, preteens and teens, turn on music to soothe or enhance emotions when they retreat to their rooms? Parents worry about angry music and lyrics because they sense their power and take it seriously.

In particular, lyrics speak to teens personally and help them express themselves. The girls who answered our survey told us about lyrics that have taken hold of them and what they find themselves singing aloud or in their head throughout the day. Here are three examples, mistakes and all:

> so now i come to you with open arms nothing to hide,
> since your here by my side
>
> from "Open Arms" by JOURNEY

> Cant this family have one day to get away from all the pain?
>
> from "The Other Side" by SMILE EMPTY SOUL

> We're growing up, its unstoppable! Wen uve seen, seen,
> too much, too young, young, souless is everywhere!
>
> from "New Born" by MUSE

When they sing along, they express emotions they already have and try on new ones, evoking similar feelings in themselves. A girl who has never had a boyfriend can experience the vulnerability of approaching someone, arms open wide, as well as the pain of being dumped. She can practice it in her head and heart. When an artist sings a song relating to their lives, even if it's "Can't this family have one day to get away from all the pain?" they feel understood and comforted. Of all the categories we've studied, including clothing, TV, and books, music offers your daughter the greatest variety of experience.

So what's the problem? The problem is that in the music girls listen to the lyrics all too often confirm the stereotypes and misinformation we've seen in magazines, TV, and movies. The messages about girls in relation to making music and loving it are also terribly insulting at times. Here are a few:

- Boy bands are cool; girl bands are wannabes; groupies are the bottom feeders.—"These chicks don't even know the name of my band," sings D12. (Yes we know Eminem is making fun of the boy band, too.)

- A girl's place is looking sexy in front of a band of guys.

- If a girl isn't singing about teen angst, she'd better be super naughty, dirty, and hot.

- Some girls don't even have to sing well to get in front of a band. Being a celebrity gets you everything, including a band, a recording studio, a few songs, producers, and more.

- Guys like you if they can depend on you, but they don't want to depend on you so there must be something very special about you to get a guy to trust you. And you'd better be careful with his heart because if you're not, you'll turn him into a hard guy. Guys also like you if you're a rebel or if you're hot and dirty. Guys want to "fuck you hard." (Sorry to be so blunt, but this book is, after all, for parents, not children, and this image of the "rough fuck" is prevalent throughout much of today's popular music.)

We don't underestimate the beauty of music, so never underestimate the power of words to hurt and damage, especially when put to music. Yes, acknowledge that the music feels good, but listen closer to what they're singing—not only when they are teens but when they are smaller, too, even while jumping rope. Our section on music lyrics begins there.

JUMP-ROPE RHYMES

Mastering the skill of jumping rope is almost a rite of passage for children. For most five- and six-year-olds the ability to coordinate the arms and the swing of the rope is a thrilling accomplishment. It is great exercise, and girls especially spend hours practicing, advancing from a simple skip to some really complicated double-Dutch maneuvers. Similarly, lots of girls about this age learn to play clapping games that go fast enough to make your head spin. Jump rope and clapping moves are accompanied by songs, rhymes, and chants, some passed down from generation to generation. However, most of the rhymes and songs girls in our survey told us they remembered singing to each other in the course of playing jump rope or clapping games have to do with the same stereotypical themes we've been questioning in this book: romance, nurturing, and narrow gender roles, with a sprinkling of unintentional racism.

Still, aren't jump-rope rhymes pretty innocent in the grand scheme of things? We don't think so. A well-known Russian developmental psychologist, Lev Vygotsky, wrote extensively about how our inner lives are first experienced through our social interactions, through the words and concepts we take in as children: the songs our parents sing to us at night, the rhymes we memorize in school, and the chants our friends teach us. They help build our views and assumptions. This is why as thoughtful parents we choose our words carefully when kids are around, why we do what we can to ensure our children are around people who model respect and speak kindly to others, and why we provide our children with a range of venues and opportunities and expose them to a diversity of people and experiences. It's good for them. This variety widens their social worlds and as a result enriches their inner lives. The fact that rhymes, songs and stories are repeated over and over in the safety of home and the pleasurable context of play gives them all the more power.

Singing chants and songs that repeat gender, racial, and other stereotypes are not doing irreparable damage, but added to other experiences that are equally narrow and stereotypical, they aren't doing much good, either. "Cinderella, dressed in yella, went downtown to meet her fella. On the way her girdle busted. How many people were disgusted?" Girls still chant this one.

Like the other songs that follow, the chant is sort of about romance, but it's really about the anxiety of humiliating feminine moments, anticipating the ubiquitous "Traumarama" and "Most Embarrassing Moments" columns in teen magazines. Why has the Cinderella rhyme lasted more than forty years? (Today's six-year-old would have to ask, "Mom, what's a girdle?") It looks ahead to the anxieties to come, just as the kissing songs do. Kissing songs are both thrilling and incredibly funny to little girls. Take this different version of Cinderella: "Cinderella, dressed in yella, went downtown to kiss a fella, made a mistake, and kissed a snake. How many doctors will it take? Ten, twenty, thirty, forty, fifty . . ."

And then there's:

Down by the meadow where the green grass grows, there sat Georgia as sweet as a rose. Along came David and kissed her on the lips. How many kisses did she get? Strawberry, blueberry, blackberry pie, who's gonna be your lucky guy?

Mailman, mailman, do your duty. Here comes [name], Miss American Beauty.

She can do the pom-poms. She can do the twist.
But most of all she can kiss, kiss, kiss, k-i-s-s.

Under the bramble bushes, down by the sea, boom, boom, boom.
True love for you, my dear, and true love for me.
And we're gonna get married in California.
How many children will we have?
1 2 3 4 5 6 7 8 9
turn around, touch the ground, do
the splits, wiggle your hips, ten!

The kissing songs are about girls waiting for true love and catching fellas, a theme they'll revisit in pop music just a few years down the road. It is not a terrible theme, but it's the *only* theme, and it starts her down a very narrow path.

Mom's havin' a baby, a sweet and chocolate baby,
while Dad's goin' crazy.
If it's a boy, give it a toy.
If it's a girl, give it a curl.
If it's a twig, wrap it in a newspaper,
throw it in the elevator.
First floor stop, second floor stop, third floor stop,
and don't stop till your hands get hot.

When there's a baby, boys will get toys and girls will get curls. To her this all seems very fun, normal, or expected. This is what girls are learning—expectations. But why do we give them so few?

Sometimes girls come home with cute songs that are problematic for other reasons, such as this one:

I went to a Chinese restaurant to buy a loaf of bread, bread, bread.
She put it in a five-pound bag, and this is what she said, said, said.
My name is Ky-yii-yippee-yii-yippee-yii-ky-yii-humblelyberry-ky-yii-
   yippsee-chow!

A few of the rhymes that girls told us confirmed what we knew already: that girls learn very early how to diss other girls, making them feel ugly and unwanted. These are for people you don't like.

Extra, extra, read all about it.
Girls are tough, so we're gonna shout it.
Ugly. You ain't got no alibi, you ugly.

Two, four, six, eight, who's the person we love to hate? Big loser, loser.

One has to wonder about the sheer repetition if there's no signifi-cance to these rhymes. When stereotypes and chants of romance appear in the innocent songs of little girls, we are inclined to think that some-thing genetic put them there, just as psychologists once thought that playing with a doll signified some internal girliness being expressed. But remember, at five a girl has lived in this world for five years. That they like romance and embarrassing quasisexual themes in their chants is an ex-pression of the world they're striving to understand. They are beginning to practice the customs of that world. They may not understand the con-notations, but they practice these themes over and over.

We suggest that parents simply call attention to the overabundance of romance themes or inappropriate assumptions about race and make suggestions for creating new songs. When Lyn's daughter, age six, came home with the Chinese restaurant clapping chant she heard at school, Lyn suggested changing the song to be about hobbits, which delighted her daughter. Small changes can make a big difference. Their song began like this: "I went to a Hobbit restaurant to buy a loaf of bread, bread, bread."

Creative parents can make up their own jump-rope songs about the kinds of interests their daughter has. They can switch genders for some of them. They can play around with gender, too: "If it's a boy, he doesn't get a toy. His daddy takes a whirl and gives his hair a curl." The idea is not to take the fun out of play with lectures but to expand the play into territo-ries that reflect the larger world you want your daughter to be in.

MUSIC FOR FOUR- TO SEVEN-YEAR-OLDS
THAT HIJACK CHILDHOOD

We remember the songs and singing games our children loved to play. Many of them were passed down from one generation to the next, such as "I'm a Little Teapot," "London Bridge," and "Itsy-bitsy Spider." As they got a little older, the songs became longer, faster, and sillier, inviting new stanzas and goofy antics, such as those in "Down by the Bay" ("Did you ever see a moose kissing a goose down by the bay?") and "I Went to the Animal Fair," and the "Boom, boom, ain't it great to be crazy" song.

Parents sing these songs, and some buy CDs and tapes by child-friendly singers such as Raffi. Although most of the animals mentioned are identified as "he," moms do figure in the songs, both girls and boys get their names twisted, and both girls and boys are invited to picture themselves in the ridiculous settings these songs provide.

Unfortunately, kids are more likely these days to *see* the songs they sing rather than just hear them, thanks to videos and DVDs. No one markets songs with more visual zeal than Disney. On the Disney Channel there is always lots of music, some of it good, some of it bad. For example, a few years ago Disney's parody of Ricky Martin's "Living La Vida Loca" played repeatedly on *Playhouse Disney*: "She's got Mickey on the brain/Outside inside out/She's living la vida Mickey./That's what she's about,/Living la vida Mickey." A child may watch Mickey's attempts to escape Minnie's sloppy kisses, coy behavior, and shopping sprees, but it's the catchy tune that stays with her. The theme is Disney-consistent: Girls live in a boy's world.

Now, thanks to a steady stream of Disney's "Sing Along Songs" videos, kids can hear and see this theme over and over again. These videos are compilations of songs from Disney movies grouped under a general theme. They're introduced by an owl teacher who's male and professorial (why are all the "wise" owls male professors?) in a classroom of little birds, who tells his little charges they'll learn that "music's fun for everyone!" He then explains that the words of the song will appear on the screen so they can sing along. Of course the songs are fast-paced, and the words and concepts are way over the heads of younger kids, so kids don't really sing along. This setup gives the video a pseudoeducational feel.

We went to our local video store and chose what appeared to be a strong-girl collection, Mulan's *Honor to Us All*. We were attracted by the picture on the cover: Mulan the warrior with her sword. Moms who choose this collection might think they're getting songs about honor if not about brave girls, but they would be wrong. Even though songs like "Honor to Us All" are meant ironically (older women tell Mulan to primp and be obedient as a "recipe for instant bride"), a four-year-old, doesn't understand irony. The tape also features the song "Zero to Hero" from *Hercules*, where baby muses with tiny waists and big breasts sing, "When he smiled, the girls went wild." This will certainly give girls an idea about who to playact in their dress-ups. It won't be superstrong Hercules, or any strong woman for that matter. The songs "A Dream Is a Wish Your Heart Makes" from *Cinderella* and "A Little Thought" from *Beauty and the Beast* make perfectly clear that girls ought to wish and dream for a man rather than find adventure in the world. Goofy and his son in the song "On the Open Road" are permitted adventure. While they drive to a camping trip, a trio of Dolly Parton–busty cowgirls and other stereotyped figures show up in the other cars on the road. Another song shows Aladdin and his father doing father-son things around the palace while the genie, dressed as a busty blonde, acts as a guide. The messages are clear: Fathers and sons do goofy, fun things together, and busty women are accessories to this fun. Mothers are absent, and romance is the only adventure a girl will have.

The video ends with the song, "I'll Make a Man Out of You," where Mulan and her fellow soldiers are called "daughters" by the officer to shame them. Mulan starts out weak and then becomes "a man" because being a girl is too insulting! This isn't a video sing-along about honor after all, unless it's honorable to be the kind of girl who gets a guy or, in one case, the kind of girl who is a guy. Do you really want your daughter singing these lyrics and learning these lessons of romance? Give up what you love, know your place, clean and make a nice home, wait for your prince . . . and if all else fails, be a better guy than he is? Whichever path she takes, the guy takes center stage. Compare these lyrics to the fun and goofy "Down by the Bay" that Raffi sings, and you can see why we think Disney has all but hijacked childhood. Romantic themes, sexist and racist stereotypes of girls and women, and jokes at girls' expense threaten to take away the sense of genuine fun, power, and possibility that we want girls to feel when they're five and six. There is more possibility than being a boy's girlfriend or a busty backup singer, and other ways to get power than dressing up as a man.

KIDZ BOP

Disney is not the only one in the hijacking business. Take the popular Kidz Bop music. Kidz Bop is a series of CDs, advertised incessantly on Saturday mornings, in which preteens sing "Kid-Friendly Versions of Today's Hits." The logic goes something like this: Today's music is inappropriate for younger kids, so let's remix and clean up the lyrics of the most popular songs, give them to cute preteen kids to sing, and we have pop music that kids love and that parents will support. Preteens who look a lot like the neatly dressed girls and boys on preschool shows such as *Barney* and *Out of the Box* belt out the likes of Maroon 5's "This Love" and Avril Lavigne's "Sk8ter Boi." The placement of the ads and the ages of the Kidz suggest these CDs are marketed to the four-to-seven set and, really, aren't many preteens already into the real Avril?

The way it is pitched on TV with those cute ten-year-olds riding bikes and singing (this is the age that five- and six-year-olds look up to), it seems innocent enough. But don't get taken. Changing words—and most of the words actually change very little; "sexy" might become "cutie," for example—does not a kid song make. These songs are written for teens. As one critic said in an online review of "Hey Ya!" a bouncy song by Outkast about dumping a girl because he was in the relationship only for the sex, "Getting rid of the word 'come' does not give the track merit as kids' music." We agree. The message is in the way ideas are conveyed and the way the lyrics hold together to paint a picture of, say, loving your baby, hot bodies, and addictive love. This refers to Britney Spears's "Toxic," a "Kidz" remake, which is still about sex and is filled with drug references: "I can't wait" (she needs a "hit"), "baby give me it." She sings that he's dangerous but also says, "I'm lovin it." She reveals that she's "addicted" to him even though he's "toxic."

Wal-Mart tells us on their Web site that " 'Toxic' gets reworked in the hands of the Kidz Bop Kids, and while it musically sounds very much like the original, the lyrics about addictive love sound entirely different when presented by the pre-pubescent set." Really? To us it sounds even *more* scary because kids aren't fully aware of what such a sick relationship might hold. Girls come across in lots of teen songs as the ones addicted to love, used by boys, and jealous of other girls. This is hardly the message we want to send to seven-year-olds. Maybe the Kidz Bop Kids aren't swearing up a storm, but their version of *The Rocky Horror Picture Show*'s "The Time Warp" is just plain creepy. We don't believe the "kidz" have a clue about what they're singing and why. It comes down to money: By opening up pop music to a new and younger market, many more CDs are sold of these and the older versions of the songs.

While her ears are young, play your daughter tunes by Dan Zanes and Laurie Berkner, or the group Hot Peas and Butter. Corny songs, Americana, and simple lovely folk tunes provide a musical foundation in childhood that can stand her in good stead when she is inundated with the prepackaged tunes of early adolescence.

WITH A SONG IN THEIR HEART OR STARS (POP STARS) IN THEIR EYES?

As we roamed malls, hung out at school functions, and talked to music teachers, we discovered that tween and middle school girls listen to a variety of music that is not popular. Their parents are still very influential at this point in their lives, choosing what radio station to listen to in the car and putting their own music on at home. Because of this, some girls this age love musicals like *Grease, The Wiz, Wicked,* and *Guys and Dolls.* One girl told us she mostly listens to classical music. Some mentioned the Beatles and Aerosmith, and with MP3 players, kids who can afford them have a lot more choice about what they can listen to and where. If girls choose a pop star to listen to, they may choose someone they've seen on the Disney Channel or Nickelodeon or in a movie. Sound tracks from movies, especially the "princess" movies, contain songs by a variety of artists and a few solos featuring the girl they've come to love as a character in the movie.

What do nine-, ten-, and eleven-year-old girls listen to? The young critics on the Web call it "bubble gum"; the PR people call it uplifting, positive, and fun. The girls who like this music and answered our survey think the tunes are catchy and fun to dance to. Take, for example, the kinds of tunes that are a mainstay for Hilary Duff and Jesse Mc-Cartney, two tween-type stars that our survey says girls this age liked to listen to in 2005. Musically, what they are hearing are the same four or five rock-and-roll chord progressions when the song is a rock-and-roll song, and a repeating bass line when the song is a rap song. When the song is a sad "break-up" song, the same five chords wrap around a minor sonority.

The music that Disney and Nickelodeon introduce is highly manufactured, catchy, and fun, and it is primarily about creating a pop star, not about the music itself. For example, loving rock-and-roll used to be about a bunch of teens or older kids getting together in rec rooms or garages and imitating their favorite groups until they started pounding out an original sound. This way of creating sound is a form of sharing or even committee work in which the sum is greater than the parts. Today, most of the music your daughter hears is dominated by electronic backup, and while the pop star singing the tune is live and in full living color, the rest of the music seems to be composed and played by nameless, bodiless phantoms moving from computer to instrument and back to computer. You can wonder aloud with your daughter about who is playing in the background and why they don't seem to count. Help her to hear the parts behind the girl singer up front, the bass lines, the drums, the occasional trombone, even when this manufactured music can have an originality that might spark her interest.

Then focus on why a girl is up front singing. Is this girl power? Hilary Duff is a musical pop star not because she created a sound or wrote an original song but because she was a blond and pretty TV star who had a pleasant singing voice and young girls wanted to see more of her. When she is not singing, she's selling Barbie fashions. And is Jessica Simpson a pop star for her original sound or her TV show produced by her father about her marriage, *Newlyweds: Nick and Jessica?* Lindsay Lohan, well established in PG movies, used her fan base to launch her singing career. In the summer of 2004, a twelve-year-old named Stevie Brock was promoted because he was "young and hot" (according to one Web site). One kid who listened to Stevie's first CD said, "If you are ten and like bubblegum pop such as Aaron Carter and Britney Spears, you might actually love this album." Another little girl wrote, "I think this is the man for me." Man? Still another wrote that she bought the CD because she thought he was "the cutest boy ever." In the following summer, Jesse McCartney was the "cutest boy ever." So it goes.

Potential idols are supremely aware that who they are and how they look are just as important as how well they sing. The judges of *American Idol* remind them by commenting on weight, clothing, style, and attitude. Even the sassiest contestants become nice and humble by the last few shows to conform to the kind of pop star their audience wants to admire. The *American Idol* show of 2004 saw an absolutely wonderful vocalist, La-Toya London, get booted before the mediocre Jasmine Trias, to the judges' disbelief, simply because LaToya seemed aloof and confident while Jasmine seemed vulnerable, humble, and nice. In the next *American Idol*, in the spring of 2005, it seemed possible that Vonzelle remembered LaToya's defeat, for she mugged cuteness for the camera throughout the season even though she had a mature voice ready to belt it out. In spring 2006, girls are informed to look hot but also sing songs appropriate to their age group. For this age group, sweetness and humility, nice and cute go a long way toward making a pop star. Sweet and cute is about all a girl can be on *Idol.* Watch them all get voted off until the sweetest is left.

Avril Lavigne may not fit into this sweet and cute image, but she appealed to younger girls because of her interesting first hit, "Complicated," which was about what fifth graders call "posers"—kids who try to be who they're not, something they can all relate to. Avril stands apart from other female vocalists that girls this age like because she writes her own songs. She is also not conventionally pretty like blonds Britney, Hilary, and Jessica, all Barbies of sorts who market themselves as everyday girls. Brunette Avril was a skater girl who gave young girls an alternative that is not too far from bubble gum as sort of an introduction to the more rebellious girl singers and punk bands that they'll start to enjoy in a few years. However, once again, magazine covers have recently turned Avril into yet another blonde with a pretty face.

The "like me" factor is big for this age group, meaning that girls worship the stars who they want to be like or who they perceive are like them in some ways. In fact, marketers of pop stars first create a likable personality on TV or in the movies, as they did in 2004 with Raven, Hilary Duff, and Lindsay Lohan. Their packaged personalities are similar to the characters they played: vulnerable, self-conscious, and awkward like tween girls. To transform her into a pop star, they give her a song (one that is uplifting or about a breakup she'll survive), and an accompanying video. It is played either between shows on TV or inside the tween movie. They set this song up on Web sites such as RadioDisney and Nick Jukebox so that tweens can hear parts of it. The music video mimics older music videos by dressing the pop star in cool outfits that are mildly sexy (see Raven's push-up bra effect on "Supernatural"), but unlike the MTV videos, they focus on the girl's sweet and innocent face rather than her body. Once a fan base is created, the promotion continues, and fans argue over whether the person is talented or not and whether some other girl pop star is trying to steal her thunder. Why can't more than one girl be at the top? Why do they assume if Lindsay Lohan is getting attention for a new movie, that Hilary Duff is suffering and in competition?

Many girls who study music and sing in school choruses have good ears. They know who among the *American Idol* contestants can really sing and who are simply attractive to them because of who they are. Constantine Maroulis, heartthrob of the pre-teen *Idol* set of 2005, blew it and was voted off after a "pitchy" rendition of a song they knew well. His fans had to admit that although he was cute, he couldn't sing in tune. When it comes to girls, though, it seems as if they forgive them their lack of talent and care more about the girl herself and the guys she dates. They don't realize that the girl they see is an extremely packaged personality. One fan of Hilary Duff wrote that she may not be a great singer, but her songs are great and she's wonderful. They really know nothing about the personality of the actress and don't seem to realize that her style is identical to that of ten other superstars. And because sweet and nice can't last forever, when she gets repackaged into an adult form of girly, almost always soft porn, marketers are hoping your daughter won't bat an eyelid.

Along with supergirl pop stars, girl groups are marketed to tween and teen girls as a bunch of girls getting together to have fun. The Cheetah Girls, one of the few young, racially diverse groups, appears frequently on Disney. The group stars Raven Simone of *Cosby* fame, has made a movie, and has a book series. Musically, groups like The Cheetah Girls are more interesting than girl pop stars who don't play instruments and just stand there and sing. These girls do harmonies similar to the girls' a cappella groups that have spread throughout college campuses and became more prominent than the barbershop quartets from which they originated. The group No Secrets, composed of four fourteen- to sixteen-year-olds from Los Angeles, was marketed by Disney in a way that accentuated their personalities as well as girl friendships. They are a "dazzling blend of hot music, cool fashion sense and intense quest for fun." In the minds of marketers, all girl groups must be into fashion and fun as well as music, making the listening of music evoke the experience of shopping with your girlfriends. One of their songs was in the movie *Jimmy Neutron*, which shows how young an age group their publicity people are aiming for. Movie placement, like product placement, is essential to the success of a group. The Swedish group Play, which consists of teen schoolgirls, gained some popularity by appearing on Aaron Carter's video *Oh Aaron*. This was a wise choice, given that they are marketed as dreamy romantics: "If you've ever fallen in love, looked for love or lost a love, you've got something in common with the young ladies of the Swedish pop quartet Play," says RadioDisney to its eight-year-old listeners.

The lyrics of the songs that these tween stars sing are unobjectionable. In fact, The Cheetah Girls and many of the others have discovered that "girl power" is big money and produce songs that decry "I've got the power to make it all happen" and "As long as I do my best, it don't matter what no one says." On The Cheetah Girls' "Cinderella," they say they'd rather rescue themselves than be rescued by a prince. How can *Ella Enchanted* (the movie) and the song "Cinderella" be at the top of lists for eight- to ten-year-olds simultaneously when one is about being rescued by a prince and the other proclaims that a princess would rather rescue herself? Clearly, the girl power in "Cinderella" is not taken as seriously as we'd like. Parents can and should use girl power songs to make connections to other things in girls' lives, but they need to also point out the contradictions in this world that take advantage of girl power slogans without backing them up.

What happens to all this girl power when girls switch over from following the very few girl bands or groups and start identifying with girl fans of boy groups? In a culture that centers on male artists, girls move from center to margin. As preteens they have their Jessicas, Avrils, and Lindsays and see the world through their eyes, feeling the power. They may later listen to JLo, Mariah Carey, or Madonna, but soon they identify with these women not as musicians but as sexy objects and girlfriends. The girls they listened to when they were eleven move on: Jessica becomes Nick's squeeze, wife, and ex-wife; Britney becomes a wife and mother. The male musicians they listened to grow up to give concert tours, and the female stars grow up to become sexual objects or wives and mothers. This is where parents need to help their daughters question what is going on. Why do we need to follow their trek into marriage and motherhood? This should come right after the question: "Why do they all turn blond?"

You can sing along with your daughter if she buys these CDs and let her know you love music, too, but there are many conversations to be had about the pop stars: about the realness of their sweet, vulnerable, awkward personalities; about whether they are up there on stage singing because they're blond and pretty or because they are talented; about why they have tutors, BMWs, and mansions before they're eighteen but haven't taken the time to learn an instrument; about why your daughter likes one girl more than another and what differences she sees between them; and about what these girls could be singing about in their lives other than "crushing on a boy." When a pop star tells your daughter she "has the power," agree with that and take it from there. Wonder aloud how the girls getting all the attention on the stage are using their "power" to change the world.

INTIMACY, CONFESSION, AND INSPIRATION

From middle school on, girls listen to confessional music. We call these songs "intimate" rather than "angst-ridden," because "angst-ridden" sounds as if we're mimicking the intensity of emotion that middle school girls feel and want to feel. The sings are about painful feelings and are sung in a confessional format. Take, for example, the lyrics from "Tiny Vessels," a song by Death Cab for Cutie: "And we'll pretend that it meant something so much more . . . And you are beautiful but you don't mean a thing to me." This kind of song cuts across genres. Boy bands sing intimate, soul-searching songs as do hip young girls. Bubblegum pop song can be intimate, too. There is also "emo," the genre of music defined by its angst and confession. "Intimate" can be found in rap. And it is especially a part of rhythm and blues. In fact, the blues *created* intimate, painful confessions in American song: "My man done left me."

Girls feel the emotion in these songs. Sometimes the songs express feelings they can't put into words. "Wake me up inside. . . . Save me from the nothing I've become," sings Amy Lee of Evanescence in the song "Wake Me Up Inside," which speaks to girls about emptiness and phoniness. Sometimes lyrics teach girls about pain to come. Most girls haven't had a real boyfriend yet but look forward to it and even to the pain of betrayal: "Have you ever been loved? Have you ever had a friend that let you down?" sings Kelly Clarkson, the first American Idol, in the song "Low."

Most of the intimate songs that the girls we surveyed wrote about concern boyfriend/girlfriend heartache—all heterosexual as far as we could tell. It seems as if teachers, friends, and parents rarely give kids enough heartache to sing about, although we know that's not true. "Perfect," by the group Simple Plan, was the only song about family relationships that girls listened to. It seemed to be about parents putting too much pressure on their kids to be perfect: "I'm never going to be good enough for you," and "I just want to make you proud." It turns out that it's really a boy's song to his father. Fine, but too bad for girls. In spite of the fact that mother-daughter relationships can be deeply moving and conflicted, mothers don't feature in the songs that girls listen to (except for "hot mamas").

One group of intimacy songs is simply about feeling bad, which can mean bad as in depressed but also empty, lonely, or frozen inside. Amy Lee of Evanescence, in pure pain, asks God to be her "tourniquet" and stop the metaphorical bleeding. These songs about pain seem existential, but many focus on the pain of breaking up.

Both female and male vocalists sing about the pain of breaking up, but when male vocalists sing, there seems to be a plea in the song to girls to comfort them. Instead of calling on God to help him, the Blink 182 vocalist calls out to "stop this pain tonight," saying he "needs someone tonight." The male singer in Twelve Stones who hates the way he feels inside also "needs you in [his] life." Usher tells us that one side of him is telling him to move on, and the other side wants to break down and cry. In "Confessions, Part 2," Usher needs his girlfriend's forgiveness and comfort because he's so confused. While we want our girls to be sympathetic, we want them to put their own welfare first and not be taken in by guys who two-time them and then need comfort.

On the other side of the pain of heartache is friendship and how friends give you inspiration to go on. There are songs teens like that reach out to them and tell them things are going to get better. Good Charlotte in "Hold On" tells someone whose mother has gone and whose father hits her that "we all feel the same way as you do, and we all have the same things to go through." The song encourages her to hold on and says that it gets better. It's a friend telling your daughter she's not alone. What else could a parent want? Like Carole King in the seventies singing "You've Got a Friend," the Beau Sisters offer the all-encompassing promise of friendship to an uplifting tune. And it is the only such girl-to-girl promise in any of the songs that girls told us they listened to.

Think of these songs as diary entries your daughter could have written. "My songs are a direct route into my brain," said Vanessa Carlton, the New York singer-songwriter-pianist whose interesting voice and lyrics make her more of an alternative singer than a pop star. Her album *Be Not Nobody* goes directly to the heart of middle school girls who are searching to be special and feel that if they're not special, they're no one.

Listening to those songs can reinforce feelings of emptiness and teach lessons about the need to be special. You don't want your daughter feeling special only because she feels so deeply or cares so deeply about boys in pain. Girls are frequently complimented for how sensitive and caring they are, leading them into primary caretaking positions in life and in work that put them at risk for caring too much for others and not enough about themselves. You can remind your daughter that some of the things that make these singers special are their talents. Vanessa Carlton worked hard at piano lessons, wrote songs constantly, studied ballet for many years, and did so well in school that she got into Columbia University. Michelle Branch is an awesome guitar player. Fiona Apple is a great singer-songwriter. These people don't just feel the pain, they work on healthy ways to channel and deal with it. (And you might tell your daughter about a coping skill she can use when feeling pain: Put it in words.)

As you hear these songs with your daughter and express sympathy for the pain they feel, you can remind her that you'd like her to come to you if she ever feels bad. You can also ask her if she has friends she can turn to or talk with when she feels lonely. Tell her that in your experience these songs leave out moms as helpers and tell girls to first turn to friends while they also teach her that she can't trust other girls. You can help her know whom to turn to, whom to trust.

THE SONGS OF DRRRTY GIRLS, TOUGH CHIX, AND YOUNG INNOCENTS

Amy Lee of Evanescence began writing her songs of pain, intimacy, and inspiration in the following way: "My little sister was really getting into these, I don't want to offend anyone, but like really fake, cheesy, slutty, cracker-box idols, and it really pissed me off. . . . She started dressing like them, and she was like 18 years old. So I gave her the talk and I wrote a song." We love this story. The new "talk" is not the one about the birds and the bees but about the media, the marketing, and the image!

From middle school on, girls listen to songs about pain, but they're also attracted to songs about power. How exactly does a girl become powerful (in song)? Well, there are two alternatives: She can be a "naughty girl," or she can be some mutant form of a "riot girl." As a naughty girl she can act sexy, do sexual things, and offer her virginity up to the right guy. As a riot girl (which no longer refers to girls loving girls and playing punk music together) she can do mischief as boys do. As long as she is competitive with other girls and true to her boyfriend, she can be bad. There is also the "rich girl." We think she's just a variation of the other two—rich enough to be naughty without being slutty, and riotous without repercussions, à la Paris Hilton and Nicole Richie.

There is also innocence. Innocence alone has no power; to be innocent and still marketable to the preteen crowd, a girl has to be innocent in sexy ways. Just listen to the songs of Kelly Clarkson, an American Idol who appealed to middle school fans. After winning, she needed to be sold to a broader, older audience. Her lyrics are innocent. Her look is sexy. It's the same with Mandy Moore and Hilary Duff. Both starred in preteen movies that middle school girls have watched, so their promoters know they have to keep them sweet. Their look, though? Budding dirty girls.

In Britney Spears's first video, *Hit Me Baby One More Time*, she was blond and Mousketeerish in her school uniform, sexed up a little to show her midriff. Sexy young innocents walk the line between clean and dirty for a few years before they become, well, "toxic." Your daughter bought an innocent Hilary; she is now used to her, loves her, will grow up with her, and will eventually get down and dirty with her. Growing up equals getting sexy, and that's the whole story for the pop music scene.

Britney went from sexy young innocent to a full-fledged dirty girl. The bigger she got in name, the more she had to be for everyone. That requires a lot from just one girl, but she did it. Watch her in *Toxic*, the video in which she goes from blond to brunette to redhead, and dressed in sparkly white to dressed in sleazy black, in less than three minutes. Then check out Gwen Stefani in *Hollaback Girl*. In just three minutes she goes from funky to drum majorette in mini-miniskirt to cheerleader in sexy red. It's no longer about being sexy but about being sexy in all ways for all people. She is a product that has to appeal to all. (It is interesting that her new line of clothing was announced just around the same time as this video filled with sexy costume changes. Even more interesting is her Teen Choice Award in 2005 as a "visionary." (She won the award for being an "endlessly stylish icon to teenage girls.")

The pop star manages this transition from sweet to sexy without being seen as skanky and slutty. Her appearance as a real person outside the video and the song seems to be important. For example, Britney's early pronouncements about her virginity kept her just this side of slut. When she does get sexy, it has to look uncalculated, as if she can't help herself. These stars must give an image that sexy is what *all* innocent girls become and that the transition happens as they are swept up by some guy. "Swept away," as Carol Cassell wrote over a decade ago, is the excuse good girls give for being bad. As this notion continues to pervade music and books your daughters read, it becomes obvious how it supports the continued lack of real sex education they need as well as the lack of contraceptive use. They have to be swept away; they can't actually *plan* to be dirty girls. But they *can* be tempted.

Britney's former Mousketeer friend, Christina Aguilera, in true sexy/innocent fashion, tells us that her body says let go when her heart says no. With the metaphor "genie in a bottle," Aguilera brags she can make a guy's wish come true if he makes a big impression on her. But it has to be the right guy, she warns girls. In "Drrty Girl" there is no waiting; she is out of control: "I want some action"; "Gonna get dirty"; "No questions."

Li'l Kim? She never went through an innocence stage but hopped onto the scene as a totally sexy, dirty girl. There's a long history of racism that simply doesn't allow "sweet and innocent" as a category for African American girls over the age of seven or so. Presumed sexual and raw, Black preteens are bounced into the world of jiggling butts and cleavages of dirty girls immediately with their idols. Destiny's Child seemed to offer something different at first, but these great singers got gobbled up and spit out as just a few more sexy bombshells. What about Beyoncé herself? What a beautiful voice and what a great dancing song "Naughty Girl" is. But it's all about "feeling sexy" for some guy's pleasure.

Is your daughter just dancing and forgetting about the lyrics? Probably not. She is probably imagining being that naughty girl for some special guy.

We're not sex negative when it comes to girls. We know that middle school girls feel sexy, and that's fine. But these songs are telling them how to experience these feelings and what to do about them. In short, the message is this: wait for the right guy, but it's hard to wait because when you feel sexy, you just want to forget about waiting and be naughty. Perhaps things have changed; the girls who withheld used to have the power. Now the sexy, the bold, and the addicted have a power all their own. The power comes from being looked at, from being acknowledged as out of control, a dirty girl, free, better than other girls: "Don't cha wish your girlfriend was hot like me? Don't cha wish your girlfriend was a freak like me?" sings the vocalist in The Pussycat Dolls. A girl can be bold, have power, and be hot—hot, not slutty. We're not sure of the difference. But people say that some girls can be hot without being slutty, can be dirty and stay powerful. We suspect it's short-lived.

Tough girls don't like sweet and sexy ones. Rather than rebelling against controlling boyfriends, they save their anger for other girls. If a girl isn't tough, if she has a pretty face and likes ballet, for example, as in the song "Sk8ter Boi," she has to be weak and superficial. A tough chick like Avril is gonna end up with that cool sk8ter boi (because underneath that tough exterior she really has more heart than the sweet girl). And she's going to rub it in her face. Gwen Stefani is going to fight all those girls who gossip about her until there is no one left standing in "Hollaback Girl." In the end what does a tough girl get credit for? Being good to her boyfriend, caring (for the right people), and dissing other girls.

The message in these songs is that being sweet and innocent, being a dirty girl, and even being a tough chick is all meant for the boys. Promoters of tough girls say she is an expression of girl power, but she is constantly dissing other girls left and right and loving boys right and left. Where's the girl power in that?

Sweet, dirty, and tough. We think the saddest thing about these three types is that they all transform into sexy girl at some point if they want to stay alive in the business. Or they become "alternative" and develop small followings of loyal teenage fans. That's not the best way to fame, glamour, money, and this specialized form of girl power.

SEX IN SONG

Sex has been a topic of song for centuries. We hear it in the double enten-dre songs of the twenties, thirties, and forties, for example in Andy Razaf's 1928 song about a handyman who helps out a lady, she sings, when he "shakes my ashes, greases my middle, churns my butter, and . . . strokes my fiddle," or in Cole Porter's lyrics to "Let's Fall in Love"—"Birds do it. Bees do it. Even educated fleas do it." Later there were those indecipherable lyrics of "Louie, Louie," and Roger Daltry's unforgettable song about a "Squeeze Box" that keeps Daddy up all night. Songs can and do create scandals. Still, parents need to separate the deliciously scandalous songs of sex and seduction from the crass, repetitive, degrading songs. If your ado-lescent daughter thinks you think she's too young to hear about sex, to lis-ten to songs with sexual messages, and to understand the double meanings, she will tune you out and work her hardest to obtain the sophistication to laugh and act shocked with the rest of her peers. But if she thinks you're talking to her about being discerning, about what you want for her as a sex-ual person, you give her the sophistication she longs for on your terms.

Sometimes it is tricky to tell the difference between seduction and degradation; sometimes it's quite obvious. For every look of disgust a par-ent gives in response to a lyric, it may be a good idea to offer a word of respect for these artists when possible. Take, for example, Kelis's "Milk-shake." Kelis is the sex symbol who once studied violin and who states she admires her jazz musician father. A parent can really trip up discussing her little rap, "My milkshake brings all the boys to the yard." Your first reac-tion may be: She's teaching my girls to shake it for the boys. The song continues, "Damn right, It's better than yours, I could teach you, but I'd have to charge." Is she advocating being paid for shaking it, for stripping, or for sex?

There's something a little clever and a little subtle about the word *milk-shake*. Is she shaking her breasts? You can see why this would be amusing to a teen. It's also a very danceable song. The narrator who likes her milkshak-ing is teaching girls a lesson that's sad but true—"You must maintain your halo, Just get the perfect blend, Plus what you have within." You can ask your daughter, "Do you think, honey, she might be talking about how you have to act sexy to get boys' attention but that you can't act too slutty? It's so hard for girls. There are so many restrictions." You can tell her: "Even in a song like this that seems to be about feeling sexy, powerful, and attractive, there's a thin line you have to walk." Object to the expectation, not the song. In the end, your conversation will be about subtleties in the song that relate to her life and girls' lives, and not about how the rap or the rapper is bad or dirty.

Another conversation to have about songs is the one about how hateful some of the lyrics sound about girls and women. If she says she doesn't listen to the lyrics, teach her a little bit about subliminal messages. Kids love to hear the story about when subliminal messaging was first discovered: Movie theater owners flashed signs every five seconds at the subliminal level of one three-thousandths of a second during a film, telling customers to "drink Coca-Cola" and buy popcorn. They can even look up on the Web the experiments on this practice that took place in the fifties and the FCC laws about subliminal messaging!

Some messages are more obvious. Eminem writes some really hateful lyrics about girls and women, specifically his female fans, making fun of how much they like him in his song "My Band": "Becky oh my fuckin god it's Eminem . . . Please Marshall please let me suck your cock." You may not want to discuss these lyrics with your daughter, but it's important to do so. You don't have to go on about the use of the f word. That's really insignificant compared to the message, which is that Eminem sees the girls who look up to him or to boy band members as a bunch of stupid sex slaves. Your daughter might want to distinguish herself from other girls by saying, "But, Mom, there *are* these groupies that just do anything for rock stars." The point isn't that you're worried about her doing what's portrayed in the song. The point is that you want your daughter not to join him in dissing girls who are excited to see him and love his music. Isn't it hypocritical that in one song these guys are all over a girl for sex and then in the next disrespecting her for doing it?

Quite a few of these guys are writing hateful lyrics. J-Kwon describes a girl as having an "expression on her face like she ain't got a clue." Or Right Thurrs's "fatty girl"? It's disrespectful, and a parent can call it that.

It's harder to talk to girls about the explicit sex in the songs. Dirty sex, hard sex, rough sex—we call it "porn sex." Abstinence education has risen in the schools thanks to conservative agendas, and teachers are not permitted to teach anything about real sexual relationships. Parents are struggling to find the right way to have these conversations. Kids are learning everything about sex through porn and watered-down porn in the movies and media. What we mean by "watered-down porn" is talk or visuals about sex that don't actually show body parts but imply sex in other ways: stripping, moaning, pole dancing, and jiggling. We hate that girls learn about sex through porn, because that is not what sex is all about. Porn does not depict real sex; it is fantasy sex that makes girls into sex toys. When a guy seems to be admiring a girl in a song, he's really admiring her performance as a sex show for him.

The sheer volume of degrading messages in song should shock and awe parents. For example, she's "the type of girl that'll get ya up and go make ya grind. I'm thinking bout snatching her up dirty, making her mine." Does he really admire this girl? Later in the song he offers to give her $300 to strip and asks if he can taste her cat. J-Kwon admires one girl's "baby ass jiggle like she want more" and even if this sounds admiring (and God help us if girls hear it that way) help your daughter to notice that in the next verse he says he's got to move on to the next "whore." Ludacris demands "gimme the lap dance." Usher sings "We want a lady in the street but a freak in the bed." Even when it seems about pleasing the woman, what woman is going to leave a guy because he doesn't "keep her coming every night" except in some porn narrative that Maroon 5 made up for "This Love"?

Girls told us in our survey that they listen to these songs. What do you think they picture as they hear lyrics about guys longing to do it "hard" and "dirty" and "rough"? How confusing and maybe even frightening it must be to imagine, even before you've had your first boyfriend, that that's what grown-up sex is like. The message is not that sex is about love or communicating or even pleasure; it's about domination, having her, doing her, getting her, nailing her. And she's supposed to moan in ecstasy when "nailed."

The answer is sex education. And educators who don't include lyrics, movies, and TV as jumping-off points for sex ed are missing the best opportunity to address what kids are learning from people more powerful than their health teachers. With middle school girls and even teenagers, you still have the power. Listen to the lyrics, and don't be afraid to use them.

MUSICAL PACKAGING AND PROHIBITIONS

In our perusal of the top fifty *Billboard* list going into the year 2005, we noticed that all the women artists are "produced" by males. They're young, they're beautiful, they're sexy, and they're either self-denigrating ("Take a chance you stupid ho," Gwen Stefani tells herself on "What You Waiting For?") or hot-to-trot party girls ("the sex was crazy then and crazy still" sings Ciara in "1, 2, Step," and "Boy you got me doing things that I would never do," says Ashanti in "Only You"). It doesn't work to prohibit your daughter from listening to an artist even if you could. Instead it helps to show her the packaging and the person who is doing the packing. This information is easy enough to find. Check out a bio on the MTV Web site, www.mtv.com/music. It will tell you who discovered the artist, who gave her her first chance, who produced her first CD, who she sang backup for first, and who she danced behind on that sexy MTV video. A guy, a guy, a guy, and another guy.

Like their daughters, parents react to these pop stars as if they are artists in their own right and not produced, packaged, and put on display in particularly narrow ways by exclusively male producers. They need to take a broader view and wonder what kind of music she would truly like to make in a world where all kinds of great music was funded and all kinds of people get to sing on a stage because of their talent.

We asked girls what their parents prohibit them from listening to and found that although parents don't prohibit much, they prohibit what they do because they think the artists are bad influences. Listen to the teenage girls, though, and you'll hear what it is they admire in these prohibited artists and their music. Maritza, seventeen, from South Carolina, told us her parents prohibited "Christina Aguilera because they reckon she shows too much of her body and that she can't sing. I think that she can sing, and showing her body off sometimes shows confidence." Becca's parents prohibit Nirvana. "I like Kurt Cobain. My father doesn't agree with his music, though, especially the song 'Rape Me.' That's pretty self-explanatory. My argument is that Kurt Cobain was a brilliant man. Despite what he thinks, I can listen to whoever I want to. It's not like I'm suicidal." Chanel's parents prohibit 50 Cent "because he is a bad person, a thug who degrades women and has no respect for others. Some of 50's songs are catchy, and even though i don't have a real good argument, I listen to his music! . . . I like some, not most, of his lyrics." A few parents prohibit Eminem particularly. Kara's parents say, "He gets in trouble with the law. His language is horrible. I think he's a genius and says all the s*** everyone else is afraid to say." Christine's parents also hate Eminem. "They don't like rapping in the first place, but they think he uses language or talks about in his music things that would influence kids to do things that their parents would disapprove of. I think that no matter what kids listen to, they're going to do what they want to no matter what songs say."

If we listen to what these teens are really saying, they're liking what they interpret as the boldness of the artists, whether it's in dress or lyrics, not just the catchiness of the rap or the melody. They hear artists saying "what everyone else is afraid to say." They also laugh at any idea that they are so simpleminded they will go out and imitate what a singer says he does in a song, or behave and dress like a pop star simply because they like her music, even when we know that they do imitate them. Why else would these same stars have clothing lines and signature fragrances? Still, if you listen to this voice of resistance, they will come to value that part of themselves. Prohibiting music because you fear the influence demeans your teen. Believing that your teen can take a critical stance and offering her the language and tools to do so supports that critical stance.

We advise you to encourage all kinds of music. Knowing that your teen likes boldness, point her to the boldness of more political songs or female singers who honestly say what it means to be a girl, a woman in today's society. For example, there are protest songs. There are groups and artists from the sixties who sang about peace and love as a form of protest and whose music survives today. Ani DiFranco, Dar Williams, India.Arie, and female artists like them, who have been singing songs of female protest for over a decade on subjects such as girl-to-girl competition, guys rubbing up against a girl in a crowded subway, buying things and then wondering about turning a profit for some "big man's business," and AIDS. Social critic Ani DiFranco, who has a production company, can help your daughter turn her angst into anger with regard to the cultural messages she's receiving about her looks and her behavior.

Point out the maleness of the world of pop music. For the most part, men own the companies and produce the artists and the CDs, control what gets airtime, and film the MTV videos. They're also overwhelmingly the ones in bands (U2, Green Day, Simple Plan, Yellowcard, Death Cab for Cutie, Maroon 5, Korn, and so on). Men are also overwhelmingly the rappers. What does it take for a girl to make it into a band, a rap studio, or the business? Not just talent but beauty, dancing ability, a sexy body, and what Maritza mistakenly sees as the "confidence" to show off your body. When you point these things out, your daughter will probably bring up Missy Elliot, the once overweight female rap artist who has made it. Agree with her and then ask why there aren't more like her. Why did she suddenly lose so much weight? Why do these men think boys and men won't buy music from a plain-looking girl if her guitar playing rocks and her lyrics are right on?

If you can, take her to the places where there are talented women rockers, punks, "emo" girls, goths, acoustic artists, and real riot girls—not the one Good Charlotte sings about. They may be in independent rock bands and playing for local dancing crowds, in coffee shops, or in bookstores on a Sunday. Their messages are usually not the mainstream messages your daughter hears in radio music. Encourage her to listen, to play, and to open her heart to a variety of sound.

Even in packaged CDs there is a lot of interesting music for teens that is not exactly pop or rap or mainstream or listed in *Billboard*. We encourage you to help your daughter find these CDs so she can hear some real creativity and get to know female artists who haven't been packaged by men for men. She will be tempted to want to show her identity through the music she likes, narrowing herself down to the kind of girl who likes hippie/folk music or boy bands or hip hop or country. If so, enter that narrow view by listening and learning, and then sharing and expanding. Parents who think they have no influence over this area of their daughters' lives may be surprised.

CHAPTER 4

Reading Between the Lines: What Girls Read

As a group, girls learn how to read earlier and read for pleasure more often than boys. Parents and teachers love this about them and are inclined to think they don't have to worry about girls in this area. It is common knowledge among publishers, teachers, and librarians that most boys won't read books with girl protagonists. Because boys lag behind girls in reading, the common solution has been to give them reading material they like, and this means books and magazines about boy-led adventures and sports. Girls *will* read about boys, so publishers should just publish stories with male protagonists. Right? Wrong!

It's surprising that more people don't question this faulty logic. It's unfair, and both girls and boys learn the deeper lesson of who is more important and more naturally the center of things. The more equitable and simpler solution is to begin with nonstereotypical reading choices earlier for boys and girls. Younger boys will read about girls as well as boys if the story is exciting or funny and the pictures are bold—and if parents and teachers offer them with enthusiasm. The stories told to children have a profound impact on their worldview, so in the long run it is well worth it to offer those in which boys and girls share a range of experiences and emotions, where they work and play and go on adventures both separately and together.

Books aren't the only thing children read, of course. They read the backs of cereal boxes and sexy plotlines on the cover of magazines at the check-out line. After a time, notes from friends and bathroom graffiti are likely to make more of an impression on your daughter than anything her teacher assigns. Web sites, magazines, and popular series books about gossip and boys offer junky brain food.

While we realize that girls read so much more that is full of stereotypes, from the cereal boxes dominated by male characters to the birthday cards that tell them how pretty and "special" they are, but feature boys having wild, rollicking birthday fun, we've limited our discussion to the core reading material marketed to girls: books and magazines.

Books for Little Girls

GENDER STEREOTYPING: WHICH BOOK IS THE FAIREST OF FALL?

One of the first things to be aware of when you read books to your little ones are the ways illustrators and authors stereotypically assign tasks to one gender or the other based on the most old-fashioned of stereotypes. This happens especially in books that celebrate special events and holidays. It may be because such times evoke nostalgia, comfort, and familiarity, however, these books often show a world that is truly foreign from the real, however, these world.

In a 2004 display at Barnes & Noble of books for younger children about fall activities such as apple picking and pumpkin carving, we noted over twenty books on tables and display racks that featured tractors on farms and lots of apple pies. In book after book, not one woman drove a tractor, and not one man baked or served an apple pie, although men were often shown enjoying the pie that a daughter, wife, or grandmother baked. Stereotypes, plain and simple. Looking closer, we noted that not one picture showed a mom wielding a knife to carve a pumpkin. In our experience, moms do every bit as much carving of pumpkins as dads. And who owns the apple orchard or farm? It's a proprietor, so it must be a man.

Now let's look at who gets to enjoy the fall season. Pooh and Scooby Doo and Clifford and Biscuit the dog are all familiar characters to young children, and they are all male. In one princess book, *Who's the Fairest of Fall?*, Disney manages to cram two stereotypes into one title: a princess and girl-against-girl competition. There is Arnold in *The Seasons of Arnold's Apple Tree* and several books where two or more children go trick-or-treating or apple picking. As usual, when there are two, one is a boy and one is a girl, and she's in pink or bows. When there are three kids, two are boys and one is a girl. As we paged through these books, we noticed boys in puddles but girls keeping neat by holding the umbrella, boys playing baseball and girls looking on, boys lifting a big pumpkin and girls asking for help lifting that pumpkin. In *The Pumpkin Book* the boys get to decorate the pumpkins and the girls admire it.

This is so consistent that when you open a picture book, the first thing you could and should ask is what the girls are pictured doing. Are they helping, admiring, gazing, baking, or nurturing? If you look at these books, be sure to say to your daughter, "Where are the girls?" or "I wonder what face those girls would carve on a pumpkin" or "Can you imagine driving a tractor in the orchard? Let's go!"

WHERE THE BOYS ARE: CALDECOTT WINNERS

A safe bet might be Caldecott Award winners, wonderful books aimed at younger children and prized for their beautiful art. Looking at the covers you see wolves, rabbits, mice, pigs, ducks, a dog, a dragon, some frogs, an owl, and a cat. You notice that the only females are a cat and one of the four pigs.

These books contain stories about presidents (all male, as we know); about a Frenchman in *The Man Who Walked Between the Towers*; about *Snowflake Bentley*, the Vermont man who experimented with snowflake photography; about the boy in bed waiting for *The Polar Express*. Rapunzel, waiting for her savior wearing traditional princess garb, is easy to find but you almost miss the little girl in *Owl Moon* because the author and artist have made her so gender neutral that you can only tell by reading the copy on the inside flap of the book cover that the child is a girl. On another there is a boy saving a cat. And there are *Golem*; *Song and Dance Man*; *Joseph Had a Little Overcoat*; *Hey, Al* (and his dog Eddie); *Saint George and the Dragon*; *Officer Buckle and Gloria* (at least Gloria the dog is female); and *Grandfather's Journey*. The list goes on and on. By the time you get to *Mirette on the High Wire*, the only book in the past twenty years that features a girl in an adventure, you know this isn't coincidence.

The stories and the art are indeed beautiful, but girls are often left out of the adventure, the thrill, the plot, the *picture*. Who goes on the *Polar Express* and who watches her brother open a present when he returns from his adventure? Who gets in trouble? Who's the inventor? Who takes a child owling? Who explores America? Males—boys and men. Who is rescued by a handsome prince? Rapunzel. She participates through good grooming habits, but she needs a prince to figure it all out. There are other women in these stories, but they play traditional roles for girls and women. Grandmother from *Grandfather's Journey* is along for the ride, looking pretty with her parasol. Sisters watch brothers grab at Christmas presents. Women are wives of presidents and influential schoolteachers.

Snowflake Bentley's mom supports him, and little girls watch his slide show of snowflakes (though, when it's time to build a snow fort, we see four boys and only one girl).

Caldecott Award winners represent twenty years of beautiful art for your daughter to linger over, but your sharp daughter may notice the minor roles for girls; she may begin to think that adult women can only be witches, wives, or mothers.

"THINKING FUZZY THINGS": THE SHAPE OF GIRLS IN DR. SEUSS

If it's Dr. Seuss, you know the tale will be magical, wise, and wonderful. Generations of children have been introduced to reading through *Hop on Pop*, *One Fish Two Fish Red Fish Blue Fish*, and *Green Eggs and Ham*. Once little tots have mastered these primers, they graduate to a collection of whimsical rhythmic stories, filled with odd, funny creatures, many of whom are engaged in morality tales that cause young and old to give pause. When Horton the elephant insists he hears "a world all full of persons" on a speck of dust and risks his life to save the Whos, we're humbled. When Horton solemnly vows to hatch Lazy Mayzie's egg, hunters or no hunters ("an elephant is faithful 100 percent"), we're rooting for him and everyone else who keeps a promise. When little Yertle defies the tyrannical turtle king whose pleasure depends on others' pain, we'd like to think we'd be as brave. And when the Grinch's heart grows three sizes one day, our hearts grow a little, too. Dr. Seuss's penchant for hard truths even caused *The Lorax*, a cautionary tale of environmental exploitation, to be banned from some libraries.

Surprisingly, there are no girls leading the way. In the forty-two books for children Dr. Seuss published in his lifetime, not one features a female lead character in its central story. To be fair, some females are quite important, but they are cast in secondary roles, often looking and doing quite stereotypical things, as in Whoville, where they push strollers or lead Who children by the hand, carry groceries, sweep floors, or work as Who receptionists in the town hall.

Sisters are the most common girl characters in Dr. Seuss books, and as in *The Cat in the Hat*, they tend to be less active, allowing their brothers, typically the narrators, to take action. Sally's brother does things like capture Thing One and Thing Two, while she reminds him of their mother's rules. Sisters also come in animal form, as in *The Glunk That Got Thunk*, a story about a young cat narrated by her older brother. When the young cat dares to imagine more than "friendly little things/With smiles and fuzzy fur," the large, frightening "Glunk" she conjures quickly becomes more than she can handle. In comes brother to the rescue. After helping, he gives his sister "Quite a talking to/About her Thinker-Upper" and she goes back to smiles and fuzzy fur. Unlike the boys who imagine a multitude of fantastic creatures in *If I Ran the Circus* and *If I Ran the Zoo*, with no ill effects, girls are cautioned to think a little smaller, a little cuter.

In *One Fish Two Fish*, the sister rides a one-hump Wump with her brother, but he holds the reins. She rides the three-person bike with him, but he sits in front and steers. Opening cans with the horns of their pet Zans, she holds the cans while he pries them open. He milks the cow while she watches. He tosses the ring on the Gack while she waits her turn.

In other stories, girls and women can be lazy, like Mayzie who hands her egg off to Horton so she can take a vacation. Or they are mean and calculating, like the mama kangaroo who rallies the Wickersham family of monkeys to take Horton's "dust-speck" from him. Most often they are fancy, vain, and jealous, like Gertrude McFuzz, "a girl bird" disappointed by her "one droopy-droop" tail feather in comparison to the magnificent feathers of Miss Lolla-Lee-Lou. *On Beyond Zebra!* has Miss Fuddle-dee-Duddle, one of few females in a book of male creatures noted for their abilities and odd habits, whose "tail is the longest that's ever been heard of!/So long and so fancy, she'd be in a fix/If she didn't have helpers. It takes about six." We wonder if this is the first diva that little girls encounter! Female characters in Dr. Seuss books don't heroically stand up to big business, bravely shout down tyranny, risk their lives protecting the weak, or stand up for what's right.

As we would expect from Dr. Seuss, there are some surprising subtle twists in his books that children are unlikely to miss. Lyn's student, Emily Brostek, who helped us with our research, found something wonderfully inventive in the illustrations. Unlike Disney and other cartoon characters on which eyelashes—usually batted coyly—always identify a character as female (think Minnie Mouse and Daisy Duck), Dr. Seuss used eyelashes on males and females alike to express emotions such as surprise and sensitivity. The mama kangaroo has no eyelashes until she finally hears the cries of the Whos and vows to help Horton protect their tiny world from further peril. The eyelashes soften her face. The Grinch is shown with lusher eyelashes after his heart grows three sizes. Horton has eyelashes that suggest his loyalty to and love for the little egg he is determined to hatch.

Even if you don't find the girls you're looking for, you'll still want to read these wonderful books. Enter your daughter's world and have a little creative fun. Change *he* to *she*. Let eyelashes stand for what they will. Do whatever it takes to make your child feel as if she could be brave Horton or bold Yertle or any one of the clever brothers *while still being a girl*. Girls understand that times change, so you can point out to her that the books were written at a time when grown-ups didn't know that girls also wanted to run the circus and hold the reins of a one-hump Wump. They used to think girls only wanted to "brush, brush, comb, comb" their pet's blue hair. You can show her how other books in her collection have girls climbing, saving, and inventing. And don't forget to ask her what kind of animals she would include if *she* ran the circus. Tell her you're not afraid if she thinks up a Glunk either—she can handle it!

GIRL TYPING IN BOOKS FOR GIRLS

If you are still searching for girl protagonists, the good news is that there are lots of them these days. They may not be winning the awards, but they're out there. Children's literature is the best place to see the early introduction of female "typing" that will follow your daughter through high school. She can be the "girly girl" in pink and bows; she can be the "power girl," the one who wants to have it all: good grades, high heels, painted nails, and basketballs; and she can be the resister—a clown sometimes or an aggressive girl—who basically says, "To hell with it. I'll find my own way alone or as one of the boys."

Angelina Ballerina (written by Katharine Holabird and illustrated by Helen Craig) represents the girly girl. Not actually a girl but a cute little mouse. (In other words, a small, meek animal.) Angelina loves ballet. In the introduction to this series we see that she wears ruffly dresses adorned with multiple bows, and a present of a pink tutu is a life-changing experience. As in much of children's literature, older women are presented in this work as opposers of little girls' dreams. In the story we meet her mother, who is pictured cooking and sewing and who doesn't want her to be ambitious. Above all, she wants Angelina to keep her room tidy. A neighborhood lady is angry because Angelina dances in her flowers. After her *father* gets her a tutu and ballet lessons, she is good. How does the book present "good" for us? She keeps her room tidy, gets to school on time, helps her mother *bake*, and sometimes lets boys catch her on the playground. The first three are the typical ways girls are supposed to be good, but why in the world would she let boys catch her on the playground? She does not want to oppose the boys' wishes? She does not want to make them feel bad for being slower than her? Help your daughter to open the back door and let this mouse escape!

Olivia is a pig in the book with that title by Ian Falconer. That's something. At least we know she can be dirty and squeal. We're told that she's good at many things. That's a big hint we're dealing with the "power girl." The embodiment of girl power for advertisers is a girl who can "have it all." She doesn't have to give up makeup, boys, or fashion. She can do all that just as she does sports, leadership, and drama. Olivia puts on lipstick and high heels, loves the Degas painting of ballet dancers, and has to try on everything—so we are reassured that she is not too unlike other girls. She also builds the Empire State Building as a sand castle and does a Jackson Pollack–like picture on the wall. But while Olivia has a few good qualities, we're too often reminded she's a typical (read stereotypical) girl.

In *Olivia Saves the Circus* she is told she can "always accessorize" when she doesn't like her costume; she adds a purse and a bow. In *Olivia and the Missing Toy* she demands that her mother sew her a new soccer shirt so that she'll look different from the other girls, introducing competition among girls as a power girl theme and fashion as a weapon to make herself superior to other girls. Olivia rides a camel and plays soccer—that's the power part—but it comes at a cost. As in *Angelina Ballerina*, Dad saves the day; he promises to buy her "the best new toy ever." Saved by shopping!

There are a few books out there of resister girls, but none for the youngest ones that have so captured the interest of parents as *Olivia*. There are some good old standbys, though. Motherless Madeline, in the book with that name by Ludwig Bemelmans, has the courage to stand up to a neighbor boy's cruelty to animals, to take in a lost soul in winter, to save a drowning dog, and to proudly show her appendix scar. She stands apart from the eleven other little girls in her midst because she's tinier, braver, and tougher. Of course that means for true friendship she's drawn to Pepito, the neighbor boy and reformed bully. Why couldn't there be a bad girl turned good to befriend?

Kay Thompson's series has six-year-old Eloise, who lives on the top floor of New York's Plaza Hotel, "darling," and "skibbles" and makes "a really loud and terrible racket" in the halls doing what she pleases. "I am a nuisance in the lobby," she tells her young fans. The effect that Eloise has on a girl who listens to her brazen antics or looks at the picture of her sprawled across her bed is infectious. She seriously takes her own pulse, her hair is messy, she has a picture of a boxer behind her bed. She also has a monthly chart with ★'s (for NEAT) and O's (for UNTIDY), and it is filled in with O's. Eloise gets away with it all because she's pampered and rich. But what girl doesn't love to imagine herself riding an elevator on her own, wearing Kleenex boxes on her head, and using a screwdriver to adjust the thermostats when she needs to? Alas, she has an absent mother and no girlfriends.

Junie B. Jones, in titles such as *Junie B. Jones Is Captain Field Day* and *Junie B. Jones and the Stupid Smelly Bus*, is a more contemporary and typical six-year-old created by Barbara Park, but she is no less funny and bothersome—an opinionated, bigger-than-life-character. Junie mispronounces words with all certainty, talks too loud, demands too much, and exasperates adults and other girls. She has a mother, but once again adult women (her mother and her teacher) stand for all that is proper and polite. She has female friends, but she is often jealous and competitive with them. Whole books have her pitted against her "girly girl" friends, the fashion mavens of the first grade, now known as "mean girls." Just like those feisty girls on TV for the youngest set, the one really loyal, kind friend to Junie is a little boy named Herb. We like this girl-boy friendship—there aren't enough of them—but we wish it didn't come at the expense of girlfriends.

Frog and Toad, a series by Arnold Lobel. Toot and Puddle, a series by Holly Hobbie. You name 'em. There are plenty of boy-boy, guy-guy adventure series for young ones. But none, zero, zip, nada girl-girl partners who storm the halls of early children's literature. If occasionally a story is written about two girls who are best friends, the story pits a girly girl against a feisty girl who learn from each other. Rarely can they be full characters together, on adventures, off on their own, creating, investigating, and demanding attention!

Books with girl lead characters teach lessons critically important for all children, and given the pressures on girls to be cute little fashion mavens, they seem especially important for girls. Jamie Lee Curtis's *I'm Gonna Like Me: Letting Off a Little Self-esteem*, for example, features both a girl and boy, but clearly the self-esteem issue is a big one for girls. Mia Hamm's *Winners Never Quit!* offers an important lesson about how to lose gracefully and stay with whatever you love to do, even or especially when it gets hard. This message is great for all kids to know, but the fact that it's Mia and not Mike loving to play soccer has real significance for girls (although we do wish another sport or two would surface as often as soccer). Janell Cannon's wonderful *Stellaluna*, about a bat raised by birds who comes to embrace difference, and the more recent *Penduli*, about a hyena teased for her big ears, her stripes, and her prickly fur, offer life lessons that all children need. The fact that these characters are so brave and clever guides girls toward behavior and feelings the social world doesn't always associate with being female. If a book is about bravery and action, you can count on its being a useful book for girls who have been given a big helping of Angelina-type wishing and hoping and dreaming.

SOME ARE BRAVE

Look long and hard, and you will discover there are authors who can be counted on to create brave, interesting female characters. Jan Brett's Treva in *Trouble with Trolls* is the ultimate quick-thinking girl, and Kevin Henkes's little mice, such as Sheila Rae, the Brave, are anything but meek. New ones pop up all the time. *A Bad Case of Stripes* by David Shannon is about Camilla, a lima bean–loving girl who doesn't say what she loves for fear of not being liked. As a result, Camilla gets a case of vivid colored stripes that take the shape of others' desires. Only when an "environmental therapist" tells her to "breathe deeply and become one with your room" and Camilla melts into the wallpaper do we see what is really at stake. The remedy arrives at the door in the form of an old woman who gives her . . . lima beans! "The truth is," Camilla finally admits, "I love lima beans." The old lady remarks, "I knew the real you was in there somewhere." It's great, even essential, for girls to know that giving up who you really are to please others starts with giving up the little quirky things you love. It is powerful when a woman—and it would be great if it were a mother now and again— recognizes what is real in a girl and brings it forth.

Some of the best girl-centered books take on stereotypes directly, and this can provide relief and comfort to a girl who is told by adults that people are all the same inside and she can do or be anything, but who experiences a world in which her appearance really does make a difference in the way she's treated. *Amazing Grace* by Mary Hoffman tells the story of a girl who acts out adventures she reads about in books as well as ones her nana tells from her home country, Trinidad. When her class does the play *Peter Pan*, Grace wants to try out for the part of Peter. One friend tells her she can't be Peter because she's a girl; another tells her she can't because she's black. After her concerned nana takes her to see a beautiful Trinidadian ballerina playing Juliet on Broadway, a newly inspired Grace practices and wins the part. Best of all, she has both a mother and a nana who support her.

In *The Paper Bag Princess* by Robert N. Munsch, a brave princess uses her smarts to outwit a haughty dragon and save her prince. Instead of thanking her, the prince insults her for showing up in the brown paper bag she hurriedly put on when the fire-breathing dragon burned off her clothes. In the end, the princess decides this isn't the prince for her and skips down the road on her own.

Such books show the importance of self-respect, and they show that bravery doesn't require brawn or machismo. It is often about a girl's presence of mind when the unexpected occurs, as when Angela pushes the wrong buttons on an airplane and finds herself flying and successfully landing the plane (*Angela's Airplane* by Robert N. Munsch), or when Astrid Lindgren's creation, Pippi Longstocking, thwarts the burglars. Thankfully, these books about bravery often undo stereotypes that women only cook, sew, and think fuzzy things. They have wonderful women teachers such as Ms. Frizzle, the quirky science teacher in *The Magic School Bus* series by Joanna Cole, or wise older relatives such as Barbara Cooney's *Miss Rumphius*, who advises her grandniece to "do something to make the world more beautiful." They encourage girls to think big, explore the world, get messy, and be brave.

The really good books breathe life into characters with the whole range of emotion, including anger and frustration, and because of this they can be funny. The girls in them are outlandish and silly, observant and smart; they are not frivolous but sincere, more concerned about being right than being liked. They take themselves seriously, which gets them in trouble but also takes them places most girls don't often get to go. This makes them the perfect lead into other books with feisty girl characters such as *Ramona the Brave* by Beverly Cleary, *Harriet the Spy* by Louise Fitzhugh, *Matilda* by Roald Dahl, and *A Series of Unfortunate Events*, by Lemony Snicket, which they can read on their own in third or fourth grade.

These are books that focus on the many ways girls can announce their presence in the world and live rich, meaningful, and fun lives. They are your best alternative to Bratz and Barbie, TV divas, and mean girls. A heavy dose of these characters can provide not only a corrective to the bad press that girls get for being only into their looks, boys, or shopping, but they can actually inoculate girls against that anemic version of girlhood. You can check out *Great Books for Girls*, by librarian and former Caldecott Award committee member Kathleen Odean. If you're ever contemplated writing a children's book, give us a Thelma and Louise of the younger set, but please don't have them drive over a cliff in the end. We need that great girl buddy book series to appear and succeed. They don't have to be brave alone.

Books for Preteens: American Girls, Newbery Girls, and Real Girls

It's not unusual for a preteen girl to have two or three different books going at once or to read the same book two or three times. Through reading, preteen girls find fantasy figures to identify with, go on harrowing journeys and adventures, and confront real-life problems. They explore social and moral issues, consider new options, and imagine the possible. But reading can also channel their desires and invite them into the world of gender stereotypes—shopping, gossip, romantic love, and the world of flawless beauty and emaciated bodies. The sheer numbers of book series targeting eight- to ten-year-old girls in the past few years tell us just how lucrative some publishers believe this invitation can be.

Serial books for preteen girls aren't new. *Nancy Drew, Sweet Valley High*, and *The Babysitter's Club* have made millions. Why? Because they're a bit like fast food: You can get through one quickly. They're not very demanding emotionally or intellectually. You get to know some likable characters who, like cartoon characters, have quirks a kid can identify with and are reassuringly the same book after book. You know what to expect.

There are plenty of series in which girls take care of animals. Horse stories predominate: there is the Black Stallion series, Phantom Stallion, Pony Pals, Thoroughbred, and, finally, Heartland: Healing Horses, Healing Hearts. There is also the Animal Ark series that varies the animal in each episode. All except the Black Stallion books feature girls as main characters, and *The Black Stallion* features a boy most likely because that was the original character in the novel from long ago. The message is clear: Girls love animals, especially horses. While horseback riding is a wonderful sport for girls, asking them to take control, to take risks, to jump, and to increase their speed from a canter to a gallop, horse books seem to focus on girls' preparation for nurturing roles in life, beginning with a special animal all her own.

There are also plenty girl books that educate girls about girls in history. In the Dear America series, we read the diaries of immigrant girls. Girls of Many Lands explores the lives of girls around the globe. In this regard, the American Girl series deserves special mention.

A SERIES TO BUY FOR

The original five dolls of the American Girl collection from the Pleasant Company, created by Pleasant Rowland with the goal of creating an alternative to Barbie, were Molly, Kit, Samantha, Felicity, and Kirsten. They are all white and represent places and periods in history such as the Colonial era (Felicity), the Great Depression (Kit), the Victorian era (Samantha), the mid-nineteenth-century Minnesota prairie (Kirsten), and World War II (Molly). The company later added girls of color: Addy, an African American who escapes her slave master through the freedom trail; Kaya, a Nez Percé Indian growing up in 1764 ("the *first* American Girl"); Josefina, who lives in 1824 on a New Mexican rancho; most recently, Jess, whose parents, Japanese American and Irish American, are archaeologists; and Latina Marisol Luna, whose move out of the "dangerous" neighborhood of Pilsen in Chicago caused Pilsen residents to call for a boycott of the doll in defense of their neighborhood. The dolls are designed to teach girls about their place in American history and about the value of family, courage, and independence. Each doll is described in the catalog and in the book she comes with that introduces her story.

These girls, with non-Barbie regular girl bodies, are adventurous, spunky, hopeful, strong, courageous, resourceful, imaginative, and, of course, kind. They are also expensive (about $80). You can also buy additional books about the girls' adventures. These books have a cata-novel (catalog and novel combined) feel. Each subsequent book introduces a new outfit and/or accessories. For example, the outfit associated with the book *Changes for Kirsten*, the "pioneer girl of strength and spirit growing up in Minnesota in 1854," costs $60. To buy the whole collection of outfits, accessories, and furniture for Addy, an ex-slave living in Philadelphia, you would have to spend $1,098, and $50 more if your daughter wants to wear a matching nightgown. Clearly these dolls are marketed to middle-class girls who are likely to subscribe to *American Girl* magazine, peruse the AG Web pages, watch AG movies, and receive the company's many catalog sale emails.

Perhaps it's unfair to complain about the endless accessorizing and outfits for each doll. Pleasant Company is, after all, a *company*. Their purpose is to make money. But there's something that feels just a little wrong about this celebration of American girlhood when you read a book and pick up on the "product placement" within—and this began long before Mattel bought the company. Do marketing executives make suggestions to the books' authors about including a darling little change purse in the story, for example? Or perhaps the authors unconsciously write into the plot a brightly colored necklace, imagining it pictured in the catalog?

Consumerism has long been associated with femininity, and women are the biggest catalog shoppers in families. We in the United States decry "Coke days" at elementary schools and find it distasteful that commercials are shown along with educational videos in some classrooms today. But how is the intertwining of shopping and reading in the American Girl books any different?

American Girl dolls and books evoke mixed feelings in us. It is rare that girls are the brave heroes of their own stories. Each book ends with "A Peek into the Past" that provides girls with photographs and information about being a girl in a given era that they would rarely get from their U.S. history book, but there's something about the medium that undercuts the message. These girls save people, horses, parents, and the environment. They ride horses, start newspapers, defy cruelty, endure hardship, and make a difference, but they do all this staying pretty and accessorized.

As a result, the books provide lots more than history lessons to girls. The books are infused with the words *pretty* and *pink*. By page 12 in *Meet Felicity,* the word *pretty* has been mentioned four times—"a pretty maid," "so tall and pretty," "pretty one," and a "very pretty" nose. Kaya's horse is "the prettiest," and her big sister is "the prettiest girl in the whole village." Molly daydreams about a pink dress; Kirsten wishes she could wear "pretty dresses."

By contrast, in *Meet Addy* (about the African American slave girl) no one is called pretty or beautiful. Instead, the dresses she desires are called "fancy"; the cowrie necklace is described as having great personal meaning rather than "pretty." The cruelty and torture on the plantation, the loss of her father and brother, and the escape north are told in such vivid detail that "pretty" doesn't seem to fit. At the end of the book, Addy gets her fancy dress. It is pink and "prettier than any she had imagined." It's rather depressing that the symbol of freedom at the end of the book is that dress, as if to say that at last Addy can be a real girl, pink and pretty!

Boys don't fare better. As troublesome, mischievous pests, they are set up in opposition to showcase the niceness of girls. The trouble with making boys an opposing team to girls is that it gives the boys all the qualities that would make the female characters fuller and more real. We know that girls can also be mischievous, nasty, bothersome, and even "frog-faced," especially to their siblings, but they never are in the American Girl books. When boys are mean, girls must be nice, and the dichotomies box us all in. Also, it gives the message that boys can't be deep and loyal friends to girls.

Another troubling theme in these stories is the portrayal of mothers; they are not the role models they could be. Instead, they're often portrayed as the one who upholds a former and earlier version of femininity that the girl is rebelling against. This leaves teenagers and grandmothers to provide the wisdom. This war against mothers reflects society's devaluation of mothers as resources and confidantes of their daughters. Molly's and Josefina's mothers are dead. Kirsten's mother is sick and almost dies. Addy's mother is brave but almost dies because she doesn't know how to swim and Addy has to save her. Kaya's grandmother is the wise woman while her mother mends. It's Kaya's father who teaches her how to ride and gives approval to her racing in the end. Molly's mother simply isn't very present until the end of the book when she gets the kids to stop warring. Kit's mother wants her to be a girl who likes pink and frilly rooms, although in the end she gives up her tea party ways.

Teenagers or young women, not mothers, serve as figures of idealization for the girls in these books. Yet they are rarely idealized for their accomplishments. Kaya watches her pretty older sister in a courtship ritual. Cornelia, the girlfriend of Samantha's uncle, is idealized for being pretty and modern, not old-fashioned like her repressive grandmother.

What mothers in these books teach their daughters is restraint. In fact, the moral messages in many of the Meet series have something to do with the lead girl learning restraint. Addy, the courageous girl who flees the plantation master, is made to eat worms and saves her mother from drowning. She doesn't learn at the end that she has amazing abilities and resources, although that's implied. Instead, her mother compliments her on learning when *not* to express her emotions—how to keep her feelings inside. Molly learns *not* to be aggressive and seek revenge. Felicity learns *not* to be so impatient. Kaya learns *not* to brag. Josefina does learn how to stick up for herself (with a goat, however).

Let the buyer beware. As a product line there is much to celebrate about American Girl dolls and books: real-looking bodies, choices of skin and hair color, and varied stories that pull girls to the center rather than push them to the margins of history. But teach your daughters to be critical. When you scratch the surface, it's hard to avoid upper-middle-class notions of prettiness and perfection, and it's hard to miss the way the catalogs promote self-indulgence and consumerism over social justice and the realities of the world. Look a little deeper and it's hard not to see the same old stories of disappearing mothers and boys against girls. Go ahead and buy the books and the dolls if you can afford them, but don't mistake them for truth—either historical or contemporary.

NEWBERY ABSOLUTE WINNERS

Librarians are a wonderful resource and often point us to books with complex characters and interesting story lines. They know literature and also know what kids like, but they also feel responsible for helping children find the right book for the right age. They often turn to the Newbery lists. The Newbery is the top award given to the author of the most distinguished writing in a children's book. As with Caldecott winners, when a book wins the Newbery medal, it is imprinted on the front of the book. The book is often kept in a separate section in bookstores, bought by all school libraries, and suggested to schoolchildren by librarians everywhere.

While more female authors have been awarded the Newbery than male authors over the last twenty years or so, male leading characters still outnumber the female leading characters. The book jackets seem to follow stereotypes, more frequently picturing close-ups of sad girl faces. But, more important, let's look at what the girls are doing, their issues, the obstacles they need to overcome. The loss of a parent is a prominent theme in many of these books, and this is equally true for boys and girls. As in fairy tales of old, losing a parent or becoming an orphan makes a child vulnerable and sets the scene for bravery. But there are some subtle plot differences.

Here are some examples of plots involving boys. One boy whose mother has died is accused of a crime he didn't commit and must flee. In his travels he is befriended by a juggler mentor. Another orphaned boy becomes an apprentice to a potter, is mentored by a crippled wise man, and goes on a dangerous journey. A third motherless boy searches for his father and is befriended/mentored by men in a jazz band. A fourth boy, the only lead male character with two parents, is wrongly accused of a crime, gets sent away, and escapes a camp for bad boys with his friend. Another boy, given the most precious job of his community after long training with a mentor/older man, escapes. Another homeless orphan has adventures, runs away from his aunt and uncle's home, confronts prejudice, and is able to run faster than everyone else. A boy with an absent father befriends an author. And, in a different vein, a boy finds an abused dog and tries to protect it from its angry owner. These boys escape and travel. They get accused of crimes they didn't commit. They fight injustice. They search for fathers, and while they search, they learn that there are substitutes in strong male mentors. They do some nurturing too, thankfully: one boy nurtures a dog; another takes a younger boy with him when he escapes; and a third escapes with a baby about to be killed.

Here are some examples of plots involving girls. A girl cares for a mentally ill mother before taking siblings on the road to find their grandmother. Because her father lost his job, another girl must live at her grandmother's house and cope with the change of schools. A girl whose mother died from despair when she bore a daughter instead of a son goes on an adventure to overcome evil powers. A girl goes on a dangerous mission to save her best friend. After her foster mother's death, a girl and her foster father go on a car trip to deal with their grief. A girl walks to be united with her missing mother and hears stories of other motherless girls. A girl whose mother dies because of an accident stays during the dust storm and copes with a physical injury that prevents her from playing piano again as well as the guilt from having killed her mother. A girl, abandoned by her mother, is apprenticed to a midwife and discovers she's not ugly, stupid, or alone.

Girls may not escape from bad circumstances as much as boys, but they do go on missions. While boys generally look for fathers, girls undertake missions to help or save other people and may be more likely to take care of or protect others through their adventures. Girls also may be more likely to be asked to cope with a difficult situation rather than escape from it.

These are wonderful stories and far different from the faux literature girls are reading at this age about boyfriends, shopping, and gossip. These books bring girls into the world of girls at other times who deal with strong emotions and powerful events in their lives. Unlike the series books about girls in other historical periods or countries, the girls described in these books are often very complex and capable creatures, with individuality and real quirkiness.

As you read the good literature with your daughter, don't be afraid to ask questions. Is this book about rebellion? If it's a book about a boy, ask whether a girl can rebel. If the book is about staying at home and coping, ask why the author didn't have the girl run away. Is the book about adventure? Can a girl go on an adventure to find herself, or does it have to be to save others? In horrible circumstances, must a girl stay put and cope, or can she escape? Is the girl given the traditional role of caretaking? Are there male caretakers in the book? Does a girl have to find romance at the end of the book? Is it realistic for that age if she does? Are her looks described? Is a girl described without reference to whether she is attractive or not?

Remember, these books reflect a culture that gives girls and boys permission to do different things. If some of the best literature limits our daughters in subtle ways, think of how oppressive the junk literature can be.

HERMIONE GRANGER AND OTHER REAL GIRLS

If you want to raise a girl who loves adventure, doesn't measure herself and others by looks, and feels free to pursue a myriad of interests and hobbies, you should probably point them to fantasy and science fiction. Too often contemporary or "reality" preteen books give them more of the same—suggesting that they become a nurturer, be proud of being a pretty girl (whatever that means in whatever time or culture), and get ready for crushing and divadom. What is missing? Athletes (all sorts), girls skilled in the wilderness, girls on adventures who don't have to take care of their siblings, brilliant mathematicians, clever, science-oriented girls, dashing computer whizzes. But if you look to fantasy, you will find girls who invent things and save the world. Best of all, these books can transition into wonderful teen literature, the kind where girls don't stop to comb their hair and check out boys before saving the world.

One of the best series of fantasy books for preteens is Lemony Snicket's *A Series of Unfortunate Events*, about three children who are quirky and interesting. The oldest is Violet, an inventor, a role rarely given to girls and women. When we first meet her, we learn that she is good at skipping rocks and that she has a "knack for inventing and building strange devices." (Alas, watch out for the movie, where Klaus, her younger brother, gets credit for some of her inventions and saves her, while in the book she saves herself.) She wears a ribbon in her hair, but only because she wants never "to be distracted by something as trivial as her hair." Of the three children, only one is a boy; usually the girl provides the variation to the male norm. The evil villain is Count Olaf, but there are loads of both female and male villains throughout the books. There are also plenty of women in prominent places, as officers and justices and on the "council of elders." This is a series that earns its acclaim as three orphans try to make it through the world depending on their wits. Girls and boys both love these oddly irreverent books, and although they can become tedious, as all serials can, they gain our respect for giving us two interesting girls who defy stereotypes. They don't nurture or cook or take care of animals, or if they do, they don't do so any more than their brother, Klaus.

Although the Harry Potter series has a lot more male characters than female, Hermione Granger is evolving into someone a smart, brave, and feisty girl can really look up to. Hermione thinks on her feet and is wonderfully creative, solving the most pressing, dangerous, and complicated puzzles and problems. Her quick mind saves the day over and over again. She is a better magician and in some ways more strong-willed, in control, and focused than either Harry or their other best friend, Ron. Her parents are "muggles" ("non-magic folk"), and she faces head-on and with dignity the nasty taunts of "mud-blood," which make her the object of the worst—and potentially deadly—prejudice in the wizarding world.

We weren't so sure after the first few books in which Hermione stood waist-deep in a cauldron of mixed messages. The very qualities that define her bold character marked her as stereotypically difficult, both to the woman author who created her and the girl who plays her in the movie adaptations of the books. In early interviews, author J. K. Rowling repeatedly described Hermione as "annoying," a view clearly shared by the character's Hogwarts classmates. Even Emma Watson, the actress who plays Hermione, couldn't distance herself fast enough from her character: "We're completely opposite," she said in an interview after the first movie. "[Hermione's] bossy. She's horrible. I hate her!" Imagine the disappointment felt by little girls everywhere when they heard that!

In the first books Hermione carried the heavy baggage of any smart girl who speaks her mind and is unconcerned about her appearance (she has big teeth in the early books, and it doesn't bother her). She is described as a bossy know-it-all, hissing at the boys "like an angry goose."

And we're repeatedly reminded of her (weak) femininity when she runs to the bathroom in tears or is found cowering in corners or "sunk to the floor in fright." Words such as whimpering, shrill, and panicky follow her through the stories like a house elf. The boys accept Hermione as she becomes nicer and more relaxed about breaking the rules, and also because she so surprisingly proves her loyalty and cunning.

Because the boys have accepted her as one of their own, we unfortunately have to be constantly reminded that Hermione is a girl. In book four there is a predictable *Cinderella* scene where Hermione arrives at the ball transformed, her too-large front teeth reduced, "her hair no longer bushy but sleek and shiny," and wearing "robes made of a floaty, periwinkle-blue material." The boys are mesmerized; the jealous girls gape in "unflattering disbelief."

Still, Hermione becomes more and more her smart, outspoken, aggressive self. Romance and shiny hair take a back seat. She grows into a determined political activist, creating S.P.E.W. (Society for the Promotion of Elfish Welfare). And in book five we finally see a budding female friendship for Hermione, as Ginny also grows into a witty, irreverent, athletic character worthy of respect. For the first time ever there is a kind of gender parity in the battle with evil.

We wish there were more girls in the series. Male characters are so plentiful that they comprise all variation of moods and qualities. They represent the height of pure goodness, the depth of pure evil, and everything in between. Other than Hermione, the female characters emerge as secondary or backdrops. And the one powerful female character who emerges in book five, Professor Umbridge, "Hogwarts' High Inquisitor," turns out to be more misguided disciplinarian than evil monster. Her worst offenses are her toadish appearance, syrupy sweetness, dangerously false smile, and girlish voice. Listen up, girls! Hermione, nevertheless, is a lesson to us all—that girls who are laughed at, called crazy, teased because they challenge expectations, or are different from the norm can stay strong and true to themselves.

Like Hermione, there are certain girls in books who seem to exist to show the world what good literature can do to present characters that are rich and interesting and fully developed. Tamora Pierce deserves special attention in the world of teen fantasy books for introducing a girl who by proving her skill and loyalty receives a special royal decree to train for knighthood. While Alana begins her journey passing as a boy, she eventually proves herself as a strong young woman. Pierce's books are full of daring adventure and feminist activism.

But we think Lyra Silvertongue in Philip Pullman's series The Dark Trilogy has to be the best of the bunch. In the first book, *The Golden Compass*, we meet her when she is about eleven years old. She is hiding in a wardrobe with her daemon (an animal-form soul mate that humans travel with at all times), trying to discover political intrigue at the college where she lives. Daring and curious, it is her daemon, Pantalaimon, who plays the role traditionally given to goody-goody girls in literature, telling her to watch out or she'll get in trouble—the Jiminy Cricket to her Pinocchio. We learn in the beginning: "In many ways Lyra was a barbarian. What she liked best was clambering over the College roofs with Roger, the kitchen boy who was her particular friend, to spit plum-stones at the heads of passing scholars." We also learn: "She was a coarse and greedy little savage." In fact, when she and her friend Roger found a bird, Lyra says, "It had a hurt foot. I was going to kill it and roast it, but Roger said we should help it get better." What? A girl who'd rather kill a bird than nurse it back to health? We don't find that too often in literature unless the girl is a problem child who will learn kindness by the end of the book. Not so for Lyra. She remains complicatedly rough and loving, depending on beast, person, and situation. Lyra is also chastised for not being clean enough or polite enough. In this way we know at once that the author has made her tough enough for adventure. She searches for an expedition lost in the Arctic; she befriends an armored bear; she learns how to work a complicated scientific instrument; she scrambles away from danger; and she bites, punches, and spits at grown men who hold children captive.

These books also present female characters galore. They represent powerful evil, and there are also good witches, soldiers, tough mother figures, and a scientist who has made the most important scientific discovery of her time. Gendered qualities are divided among characters so that no one girl or boy represents girlish this or boyish that. Women are given roles that are good and evil, powerful and weak, nurturing and treacherous, and often their personalities are a mixture of all of these. Love is represented in so full a way that the romantic crushes of teen literature seem silly in comparison. Girls who read these books are given a story that tells them that they, too, can think about big issues such as politics and religion, that they can have adventures, that they can aspire to being the scientist who can figure it all out, and that they can have love without having to give up expeditions, friendships, and their selves. While these books may be hard to read for some middle schoolers, we urge parents to read them aloud or check out the audiobooks in the library.

Serial Books—from Preteen to Teen

They may be selling expensive dolls, but American Girl books can lead the way to more complex historical classics such as *Anne of Green Gables*, The Little House on the Prairie series, *Little Women*, and on to Willa Cather novels. There is something to be said for tried and true, since once girls become preteens, reading becomes a more independent (and less easily monitored) activity. Girls talk about books, recommend them to friends, borrow them, and buy them with their savings. Girls who read well will look for books beyond their grade level because books are not visible to parents in the ways TV shows, clothing, and activities are. Parents may know little more about a book their daughter loves than what she or the book jacket tells them.

As a result, there's an increase in series books that blur the preteen-teen boundary. When Nancy Drew moved from intrepid detective to hot-teen-in-trouble books some years ago, with covers that resembled *Baywatch* ads, we knew a desire for sales would win out over content. The newest trend is the graphic novel version of Nancy Drew. With that Japanese comic "manga look"—all wide-eyed and a body like Lara Croft—and a pumped-up OC-like George at her side, a new hybrid car, cell phone, and lots of Internet talk, Nancy is a fully wired teen. *The Demon of River Heights* is a first in a new graphic series that, as Meghan O'Rourke of *The New Yorker* says, brings us "a contemporary Nancy . . . more attuned to emotional issues than the old Nancy, as one can only expect in our therapeutic age." There is little description and lots of word balloon explosions and screams, which accompany shadowy angles that emphasize Nancy's big breasts.

Serial books can range from educational to trash. For preteen girls and up who are looking forward to teen culture, there is a range of serial books purporting to teach them what is ahead, from the cata-novels produced by the Limited Too stores to the Gossip Girl books meant for teens but read by middle school girls. Some series books try to take being a girl seriously; they look quite good compared to the above two series that are rather extreme. Even within the good books, the characters teach girls the importance of shopping, boyfriends, being understood, and hating math.

TOONE IT OUT

Limited Too has a book series called Tuned In, and it is by far the most disgusting example of selling out preteen girls. Written by a purported young and hip Julia DeVillers, who PR people reassure us knows what girls are about, these books are a new genre of literature, cata-novels. Similar to the American Girl books, but ten times worse, they are catalogs for Limited Too products and events disguised as novels. According to a sales-clerk and based on the level of the writing and size of the print, they are sold to girls younger than middle school age although the girls in the stories seem to be in junior high. To any mom who has loved the literature their girls bring home, selected lovingly by their school librarians or teachers, these books are absolutely horrifying.

The store's name is mentioned in every other chapter, and most important, the action of the novels takes place in the store or at a Limited Too event. The lead girl and her friends become consultants to Limited Too, and by so doing we get a behind-the-scenes look at how interested the company is in girls and how much it cares. The girls never question why the marketers "care" so much about them.

The stories revolve around a girl named Maddie who has self-esteem problems because she's klutzy. In book one she is "bumming" because she didn't make the cheerleading team and all her friends did. In book four she is trying to get up enough confidence to try out for cheerleading a second time. Her self-esteem issues are never resolved but are treated as a personality trait that makes young readers easily identify with her. Like so many novels for this age group, so-called mean girls are introduced in the story early, stereotyped, and used to show the niceness of the unidimensional lead characters. Nice girls are *not* self-confident; mean girls are overly confident. That is a self-esteem dilemma for any eight- to ten-year-old and the beginning of an important lesson: Low self-esteem or pretending to hate yourself may win you friends; confidence will certainly make you lose them.

Limited Too products appear on page after page of these books; pillows, frames, hats, sunglasses, charm bracelets—any kind of merchandise gets worked into the story and never rejected. When Maddie almost rejects a "Property of Cheer Squad" T-shirt, her friend, sounding like a salesgirl, says, "You don't have to be a cheerleader to wear it. It's just fun."

Girls are identified primarily by their hairstyles and how pretty they are. For example, Maddie's three new friends are described stereotypically: One is "the cutest girl," another "should be on a runway somewhere," and as for the third: "If the other two girls are way pretty, she is even prettier than that." They are all given "hobbies" written in a slambook at the beginning of book one, presumably to show their uniqueness. Their interests are easily dismissed, however, when we learn that their primary interests are fashion, modeling, crushes, and stars.

These books are marketing the L2 girl, the kind of girl who gets rescued by the "mall guys," who makes best friends by bonding over looks and hair, who deals with sad feelings by buying lip gloss, who needs tutoring in math, and who delights in being a runner for stars at a Toopalooza concert, an actual concert that L2 has produced with pop stars and from which they make CDs to sell in their stores. By doing so they've managed to introduce concert-going and star worship to the pre-middle-school group. If they get them younger, they'll have a customer for longer. Let the makeovers begin! In one novel the L2 concert actually has an "interactive tent" in which eight- to ten-year-old girls can get makeovers. In the Friendship area they can contribute to the largest bracelet in the world. How's that for girl power? There are dance contests and Twister contests. Finally, in the fashion area, we see some real action. What's more interactive than being able to walk down a model's runway, "learn what it's like to be a model and get some tips." We can't understand why the Girl Scouts would deliver an audience to the L2 concert billed as a special concert for them when it seems obvious to us that L2 was trying to "brand" these girls early.

The saddest thing about all this is the disrespect for girls' friendships. Not to idealize these friendships, but they generally are about more than mutual admiration of one another's hairstyles. Perhaps the saddest thing about these books is that they are billed as "empowering" girls. Power to little shoppers everywhere!

Next to cata-novels, the worst of the series books are those that shamelessly promote television shows such as *The Cheetah Girls* and *Lizzie McGuire*, and, of course, the ever popular Olsen twins. Drama and divadom are all that's available for girl protagonists, while boys get series like *Captain Underpants*, in which two "behaviorally challenged" and "disruptive" boys rule their school. Along the way these disruptive boys meet up with Melvin, the "school brainiac" (yet another boy genius). One of the few women in the Underpants series is a mom, and she's pictured reading a book, *How to Lose 20 Pounds in 3 Days*. Do we need this? Why can't a girl be "trouble"—like Meg in Madeleine L'Engle's *A Wrinkle in Time*? Why can't a girl have over-the-top, almost offensive prankster fun in books? They're too busy crushing or nurturing or healing their horses, we presume.

FULL-FRONTAL SNOGGING AND GOSSIP GIRLS

It's very easy to see where preteen serial books are heading. Teen series books, even when written by award-winning authors such as Phyllis Reynolds Naylor, tend to contain a lot of stereotyping because they're written very quickly and depend heavily on clichés. One author we interviewed who worked for a company that published books for girls told us that as editors and writers sat around a table brainstorming an idea, the editors made sure that writers would make their girl characters more likable by putting some spinach in her front teeth and the like. Having the girl do something embarrassing or humiliating in the first ten pages is a cliché of these books. If your daughter continues to be surprised by this, you might help her read more critically by asking, "Does every girl in a book have to embarrass herself in front of a boy?"

When these series become very successful, they frequently are no longer written by the author whose name is on the front cover. Instead, as in the Sweet Valley High series (one of the first successful series books for girls), the author plots out the next book, and the publisher finds a starving graduate student to write the whole book in six weeks.

The topics for these books are generally boyfriends, magic, shopping, girl talk, and dreams—the usual. Since the hyped-up mean girl pheonomenon, a new spate of books about girl-against-girl competition has arisen, as in several series: The Clique; The It Girl; and The A-List. Take a look at the two series recommended to girls in *Teen* magazine in July 2004. The first was a new series by Todd Strasser called Impact Zone, which was about a boy: "cutie Kai as he breaks hearts and rides the best waves to a surfing championship." The other is a series by Catherine Hapka called Star Power, about a rising pop star named Star who searches for her missing family. His books are titled *Close Out* and *Take Off*; her books are titled *Supernova* and *Always Dreamin'*. It is clear that "action" for girls is becoming a star, as supported by similar fare like *Confessions of a Backup Dancer, Backstage Pass*, and *Pop Princess*.

One cliché of these books is that the lead girl is dissatisfied with herself and her body. The message we think they're sending is that to be a girl you have to be somewhat down on yourself and awkward. We challenge the notion that every girl has these worries. Sure, early adolescence is an awkward time of life, but there are other things girls are concerned with and this awkwardness comes and goes.

Using this idea of awkwardness, the series books that feature "magical" girls, such as *Daughters of the Moon* and *Fearless* (about a girl who was born without the "fear gene"), describe teenage girls who find their special powers useful but freakish. (Editors probably presume it wouldn't work to have them completely embrace and enjoy their powers. Girls are taught to be humble about their talents, not conceited or proud.) In like fashion, the British quick-witted Georgia Nicholson series (*Angus, Thongs and Full Frontal Snogging*) by Louise Rennison and the Mates and Dates series by Cathy Hopkins feature girls who are very uncomfortable with the size of their nunga-nungas (breasts) or their beauty in comparison to other girls. Books in the Girls series (*Girls Under Pressure, Girls in Love*, etc.) as well as the Alice series feature everyday girls encountering cliché problems because of their low self-esteem (too much dieting, jealousy over another girl's attention to one's boyfriend).

These books have all jumped on the *Reviving Ophelia* bandwagon, but rarely do they have an author like therapist Dr. Mary Pipher, and rarely do the lead characters really have reason to doubt themselves. The authors always let their girl readers know that the lead character is actually quite good-looking: "Half the boys at school have crushes on you," Vanessa of *Daughters of the Moon* is told by her friend. Gaia Moore is "blatantly beautiful" in spite of her ninth grade attempt to dye her hair orange. This is a problem for girl readers because in real life the answer to their problems is not always going to be "realize you're too hard on yourself." Would a series book about an overweight nerd with a great sense of humor work? We think so. (Think of *Napoleon Dynamite*, the popular movie about the loser boy.) But publishers seem too unwilling to try it out.

As in children's literature, myths, and fairy tales, these books also tend to show parents are useless or dead. Perhaps this is a common concept because mothers are so important to children; however, it also means that we rarely see good mothers represented. In the Alice series, Alice's mother died when she was five. Ellie's mother is dead (in the Girls series).

In the Fearless series, Gaia's mother is dead and her father is gone. In the funny books, like the linguistically entertaining British books, authors keep the parents alive to make fun of them. The mothers are absolutely useless with their old-fashioned ideas and are totally clueless about their daughters' lives. Only in *Daughters of the Moon* does the lead girl, Vanessa Cleveland, have a mother who is approachable and reasonable (although this mother is not her biological mother but the woman who found her at the side of a road when she was six). This killing off of parents, particularly mothers, serves to create an isolated girl world that the book centers on.

Sooner or later some kind of competition is set up between the lead character and the more beautiful girl. There's always a girl who is prettier than the lead character and is a source of jealousy. Quite often the author makes her snobby or unlikable, undoubtedly because the way to save girls' self-esteem is to teach her to say, "At least I'm nicer! At least I'm not her!" These girls are called things such as complete airhead (Mates, Dates series) or, more flatteringly, gorgeous and confident (Fearless).

It's clear that not a single editor thinks a girl wants to read a book about a girl who isn't interested in boys. There is always a boy to have a crush on, and this could be the conflict. Gaia (Fearless) who can "kick just about anybody's ass" has three wishes. The first two are quite noble and poignant, and the third is to be kissed by a boy. Georgia Nicholson (*Full Frontal*) goes on about her pent-up snogging (making out) deprivation. Vanessa Cleveland (*Daughters of the Moon*) thinks of that boy she likes: "He made her feel all fire and ache down to her bones." All she has ever wanted is to be able to do normal things like "kiss gorgeous Michael Saratoga without disappearing right in front of him." Sometimes there is a "dishy teacher" (Girls series) to fawn over. And yet we know so many girls who seem to go through entire years of middle school or high school without a boy to crush on.

In issue books there's always a girl who is far worse off than the lead character. For example, if a girl is dieting too much, she gets to know a girl who ends up in the hospital because of her dieting. If a girl is fooling around with boys, there's always another girl who is the slut. This device keeps our girl "good." It also divides girls into good and bad, sick and healthy.

There is often shopping. Even for Gaia; her memory of her dead mother is of going out to the Gap. Shopping, like boyfriends, can be a plot device used to stir up excitement in the reader. The same goes for dressing up. In most of these books the outfits are described with fashion magazine detail: Serena wore a "yellow tulle skirt" over a "sheer clingy red" dress. Over and over again best friends are featured bonding over clothes and makeup in stores and malls rather than on the soccer field or tennis court or in the park or science class. In the funny British books, the school scenarios are merely backdrops for more discussion about boys and "snogging"; in our own country's girl books, other interests besides the girl's self-doubts and crushes are barely mentioned.

There is one activity, however, that is mentioned in every book. Authors seem to feel compelled to tell readers that their lead characters hate math. Like stumbling in front of a cute boy, hating math most likely makes a female character likable. Alice struggles with her algebra. Gaia hates math and pretends to be bad at it to get a different teacher. TJ of the Mates, Dates series is "first at everything. Except math." The message is clear—math and girls don't mix. But how sad given the number of careers that math leads to. Indeed, even though TJ's whole family has gone to medical school, she is planning to opt for writing or psychology so she can skip math and "help people." (Little does she know but statistics is a part of every psychology major.) Why can't just one of these girls actually like math? We've met girls who tell us they like math or that they're good at math. We therefore suppose that in the minds of these authors if a girl likes math, she would have to be a nerdy sidekick rather than the kind of girl "real" girls would identify with. Still, we wonder who the "real" girls are that they're thinking about. The funny thing is, girls in middle school are presently doing just as well at math as boys. Researchers don't know why they've been found to drop out of the higher level math electives in high school. Maybe these books are part of the reason, or maybe after adding fluff high school courses like fashion design, there wasn't room in their schedules.

The book series that moms and dads should read with their daughters is the Gossip Girl series. One of our surveyed girls says, "They make girls imagine a life that is there but we just don't have!" For example, "Here's my recipe for senior stress management. Mix one gorgeous boy, a nice new pair of leather boots, a new cashmere sweater, a long night out, and several drinks." This was said by GG (short for Gossip Girl).

These books are no-holds-barred trashy novels about very rich girls gone wild. Written by Cecily von Ziegesar, these books show a set of friends who live in penthouses, go to elite schools, and have lots of money. The reader is meant to distance herself from these spoiled leading characters and hope for their downfall, taking the attitude of GG, who is the reader's friend, supposedly, and emails the reader all the gossip. But while the reader loves to hate Blair, the bulimic senior, and her friend, boarding school dropout and jet-setter Serena, she is also supposed to be enchanted with their lifestyle. These girls go for "Brazilian waxes" and receive presents of Manolo Blahnik shoes. They shop at places like Barney's and wear cashmere constantly. The absent parent cliché is taken to the next level; the parents are totally and ridiculously unavailable and variously neglectful, gay (stereotypically cast as a sign of narcissism, we presume), troubled, or gone.

These books celebrate the pleasure of gossip and the belief that there is a set group of *other* girls, girls who think too much of themselves and who have far too much, who deserve to be humiliated. Maybe there are such girls. Why aren't girl readers invited to have such pleasure at the expense of entitled boys in the series? There's Nate, who thinks about his girlfriends in a degrading way: "She wasn't the best dressed or the skinniest or the tallest girl in the room, but she seemed to sparkle a bit more brightly" or, comparing his new girlfriend to his old one, "incredible breasts" versus "nice but nothing spectacular." It is interesting that we're not really meant to hate this character or bond over his humiliation as much as we're meant to hate and bond over Serena and Blair. On their college admissions trips the girls are made to look like fools when neither can think of a book she has read, while Nate, who also doesn't read, is rescued as he impresses the counselor with his passion for sailing. The moral center of the book lies with the poorer New Yorkers: a rather sweet boy named Dan who spouts Goethe and Shakespeare at his college interview; his pure sister, who is described as cute and orders seltzer instead of alcohol; and the girl of his dreams, the punk Vanessa with a shaved head, black dress, and Doc Martens (showing us that even poorer goths need name brands). Girls are divided evenly into good and bad, but the boys are more mixed. Why? Because it's not as pleasurable to make fun of them. Even gossiping girls like to give boys a break no matter how awful they've been.

There are implicit messages in these books and in similar series, Cliques, It Girl, and The A-List. Many are about where to shop and what brand of mascara is the most sophisticated. There are also explicit messages, particularly about sex and drugs: "No one really wants to go to college a virgin." "There's nothing worse than frozen weed." "The candlelight was making her horny." Vanessa shops at Victoria's Secret for her date and appears before Dan in lacy see-through briefs. The author writes elsewhere, "Was Blair about to 'give it up'?"

What can a parent say about these books without seeming to dismiss them out of hand or criticize the rich girls, thereby supporting the good girl/bad girl stereotype? Some suggestions: "I know it's fun to imagine girls as superficial as that, but I think they exist more in our fantasies than in real life, to make the rest of us feel deep." Or "Boy, that author is so hard on those girls. I bet she thinks girls like you love to hate rich and pretty girls, and never give them a chance." Or a more snide "Yeah, it's fun to gossip—until it's you they're gossiping about."

ISSUE BOOKS: THE GLAMOUR OF PAIN

It is not always easy to distinguish between preteen and teen when it comes to cata-novels and romance series, and the better preteen readers might cross over to teen books before going to middle school. But one genre seems firmly situated in teen territory: girl-issue books. Girls want to be special without being considered odd or weird. While authors of book series respond to that desire by creating strong female characters with magical powers, girl-issue books mark girls as special in a different way. They present girls who are anorexic, who cut themselves, who develop a drug problem, who have been raped, and who go too far, all of whom eventually find themselves and their voices and get better. While great literature often poses a problem for a lead character to overcome or learn from (loss of a parent, a developmentally disabled sibling, a horrible accident), these books portray girls developing and dealing with age-related psychological disorders and symptoms. We contend that these books are also about being special, and because the characters are presented as being special, they unwittingly invite girls to try these self-destructive, angst-ridden acts as ways of self-expression.

Parents who want a reality check on how disorders, specifically eating disorders, are glamorized can check out the online girl-created eating disorder Web sites, where girls gush about their friend ana (short for anorexia), teach each other how to throw up and starve themselves, and cheer each other on with pictures of their favorite anorexic movie stars: You, too, can be special like Mary-Kate Olsen, look like her, have her willpower. Is this kind of "special" a female version of what we used to call adolescent grandiosity or invulnerability? There is something very adolescent about pushing boundaries, and we've constantly told girls that their power lies in their bodies. So, while boys are testing their physical invulnerability by driving cars real fast, girls are going deep—trying to feel something that no one else has felt—and pushing their psychological limits. They sometimes do this by controlling their weight. It is not surprising that for girls who have heard beautiful princess stories their whole lives, the focus of their tests of invulnerability would be on their bodies. It is not just *their* focus on their bodies but others' focus on their bodies. When the princess appears at the top of the ballroom stairs (always the climax of any Cinderella story), all eyes are on her, and she feels the rush of power.

Having read about girls' lowered self-esteem for the past two decades, parents may think this search to be special, visible, and understood springs from mistreatment and sex bias in schools. Sometimes it does, and sometimes the source is darker: abuse or trauma. A far more pervasive influence is the media indoctrination of girls which tells them that to be anyone they must be beautiful, popular, and/or special. Earlier in childhood, fairies, angels, and princesses were special, and identifying with them made a girl feel lovely and unique. (After all, there is just one princess up in the tower, just one person that the shoe fits.) In the middle school years it would seem that being "popular" is the pathway to being special. Even if you hate the popular girl, you can't take your eyes off her. This sets up a competition because often it's only one girl or one group that gets labeled "popular." We see the destructiveness of this kind of thinking in middle school girl relationships. If only a few can be popular and the opposite of special is invisibility, then girls will look for other means of being different.

Haley, the salesgirl at Hot Topic who guided us through "what they wear," reminded us that many middle school girls are choosing a goth look because it expresses something internal, something deep that they feel is different from other girls. Along those lines, a destructive and glamorous way of being special is to take on a disorder. Take cutting, for example. Almost every middle school girl has heard about a girl who cuts. She has seen a TV After School Special on the subject, paged through the teen magazine human-interest story, or read a book that describes the feelings of not being real or alive that precede cutting. By high school many girls have given it a try. Adults are freaked out by it, and understandably so. But researchers tell us that cutting is not as severe a symptom as it may seem. It serves two purposes: It brings stress relief when a child feels overwhelmed, and it helps her feel real in a world that doesn't know her, doesn't see her.

The publicity around this social issue is constant and serves several purposes, some intentional and some not. It helps girls who suffer from this symptom feel not so alone. It educates girls and parents about the causes of the symptom. It shows ways to get help. On the other hand, these symptoms can be glamorized, and we think they are intentionally glamorized in teen magazines as well as on book covers.

We're not advocating that these kinds of symptoms be ignored or trivialized, but we believe that parents should look at them in the context of the massive amount of pressure telling girls that to be someone, to be visible, they need to be special, not ordinary. One of the most successful treatments for anorexia and bulimia, psychodynamic in nature, rarely mentions the disorder and instead, over time, works on building a sense of self in a girl that is based on something other than her looks or her thinness. One builds a sense of self through interests, meaningful work, hobbies, skills, engagement with the larger world, and engagement with other people's lives.

These issue books describe problems like anorexia in full-blown detail, showing what it is like to have the disorder and how friends and family are clueless. They speak to all preteens and teens in the way they present the loneliness, anxieties, and fears of this age group. But they also often focus on the symptoms of the illness, showing that the author has done her homework. They are read by girls for information but also for the drama that these illnesses provide. Many of the authors use the metaphor of voice and silence that has come to be a bit of a cliché in girl literature—the silence about the illness or trauma, the voice that shows she has found herself. The best of these look at a unique girl who has gone through some traumatic experience or is in the process of developing a syndrome. The worst of these look at the illness and forget the girl.

We looked at three books about issues that are popular with the middle school set: *Speak* by Laurie Halse Anderson, *Fat Chance* by Leslea Newman, and *Cut* by Patricia McCormick. All these books have been "front tabled" (set out in a display for young readers) at our local bookstores. It is important to note that these are books middle school girls recommended to us. They are books about rape, bulimia, and self-injury.

Speak is one of those rare books that is about a girl and not the issue. *Speak* draws young readers in to a familiar world of adolescent angst and desire. Girls identify with the narrator's interior struggle: her desire to be real in a world full of hypocrisy and fraudulence. Something happened at a high school party that led Melinda to call 911, and thereafter her best friend and the other kids in school won't talk to her. Three-quarters of the way through the book we discover she was raped at that party, and then three important moments follow. Her former best friend begins to date Melinda's rapist, leading Melinda to finally "speak" through a note she passes to her friend telling her she was raped by the guy. Reading the bathroom stalls, she finds that she has company; other girls have written (spoken) about their experiences with this boy. And finally, when her rapist—upset that she has warned her best friend off him—confronts her and threatens to rape her again, she yells "no" and repeats herself: "I said no."

We think that most authors could learn from this kind of writing. First, Anderson creates a person, a real character, who is a critic and ob-server. Witty, Melinda says the school changed the sign outside from "Home of the Trojans" because it "didn't send a strong abstinence mes-sage." She's an "outcast." We see her go through many classes in school showing an interest in art, playing tennis, and writing a paper on suffra-gettes who fought for the right to have a voice. Aside from creating a real girl as a character, the author never has her demonstrate a list of post-rape symptoms. Melinda simply exists as a character who has been raped. Her salvation isn't only in self-expression through art but also through the feeling of solidarity with other girls when she finds the writing on the bathroom stalls. Because of this the book is not an issue book at all but lit-erature that has deservedly won a slew of awards.

Books such as *Cut* and *Fat Chance* describe the development of self-injury and bulimia in accurate ways (according to psychiatry), but they're different from *Speak* in that they rely on the drama of the illness to sell the book, leaving out character development or interesting plotlines. *Cut* has a characterless character whose cutting represents her self-punishment for her belief that she caused her brother harm. (Many of these authors have a cinema-like idea that every disorder can be traced to one wrong belief or traumatic moment that if addressed or remembered or relived would cure a person. While it is dramatic, it's not psychologically true.) *Fat Chance* is the diary of Judi Liebowitz, whose character is limited to her feelings of low self-esteem, admiration for the thin girl at school, and recitation of how much she eats on a binge.

From a clinical perspective, many of the pieces of a disorder are accu-rately portrayed in these stories—the dissociation in the bulimia, the relief in the cutting. The message to the girls who read them is mixed. While these problems are presented as warnings to girls (this could happen to you), the suffering is glamorized. These books are invitations into a way of being different that is dramatic and into a way of making typical adolescent pain that finds no safe expression into an exciting illness. They are manuals of a sort.

Readers who write reviews online seem to be mostly interested in the accuracy in an author's portrayal of the illness. Of *Fat Chance* one girl wrote, "I'm in seventh grade and I thought this book was very unrealistic." And for a book on anorexia, *The Best Little Girl in the World:* "Still caught in the hell that is this disorder, I found this book insulting and quite revolting."

More interesting, though, are the warnings to other cutters and "eds" (eating disordered people) out there about "triggers." One girl wrote that a book about anorexia "gave her tips on how to hide [her] problem more." Another who read self-injury books wrote, "Don't read this book if you are easily triggered." One girl was "a bit inwardly glad that the book did not suggest any way to 'cut' other than with a pair of scissors." A girl who identified herself as a "cutter" who loved *Cut* said, "It describes the feeling. The relief of a cut. The joy in the feeling it allows you for [a] split second. The addiction to it, and the withdrawal of it." She added, "I don't suggest this book if you still cut or think of it. I had a relapse in reading it myself."

Considering how popular issue books are with girls, it strikes us that these books imply that the only interior life girls can have or that we take seriously is the result of pain or loss. In most of these books the implication is that the other girls, healthy girls or popular girls (and they can actually be the same girls), have no interior lives, that they are fraudulent, superficial. There is something deeply problematic about this. We've noted how it divides girls, but it also connects pathology to girls' "true" nature, leading them into a billion-dollar self-help industry. Girls who are complex, real, and have deep feelings are those who are deeply *troubled*. Is this an invitation to a girl? We think so.

Don't fool yourself into believing that reading a novel on the subject is a good substitute for talking about these issues with your daughter. Parents need to deglamorize these problems by having real conversations about the feelings that underlie them and not the symptoms themselves. Because these books present destructive ways of self-expression and coping with pain, parents need to counter them with detailed and realistic alternatives. Pointing out all the ways that the culture, her peers, and her school conspire to make girls feel so unspecial unless they are Ophelias is a good start. We also think parents can point out to their daughters that the command to stand out sets her in competition with other girls who are also trying to be different and stand out. Joining with other girls could be her also salvation. Girls can express real feelings and passion in healthy, constructive ways by reaching out and doing good, and these are not only as deep but ultimately more powerful.

The moral of all these books is that when we teach girls to express the range of feelings, including their anger, when we teach them that the striving for perfection is fruitless and that growing up involves building a strong sense of self through investment in activities, they are less likely to cut, throw up, or starve themselves. This message has to start young, but it is not too late to welcome that critical, complex voice in an active and proactive girl in middle school.

Magazine Reading

To some parents any reading is good, but we disagree. A constant diet of books that reinforce girl stereotypes or that have succumbed to product placement, magazines that sell image, and spin-offs from TV shows tell us that some reading can be actually harmful. The research on girls reading magazines supports this. Psychologists have shown that even with elementary school girls the more they realize that thin and sexy is the ideal, the more they want to attain it, and the less happy they are about themselves.

THE NATURE OF GIRLS: MAGAZINES FOR THE YOUNGER SET

With great names like *Spider*, *Cricket*, *Your Big Backyard*, and *Zoobooks*, the magazines younger girls are likely to read are gloriously gender neutral. It is not until she's a few years older, when she's introduced to "girls' magazines" that point her in the direction of *Cosmo*, will your daughter receive the explicit message that boys and girls are almost nothing alike, that they inhabit not only different worlds but different planets, and that "planet girl" revolves around crushes, embarrassing moments, and the latest fashion. For the time being, though, she's on terra firma and the whole world is her canvas—or is it?

We checked out some of the more popular kids' magazines to see if the impression of gender neutrality is a reality. For the most part these are generically kid-friendly and advertisement-free, or at least reduced, zones. But parents do need to be on their toes because gendered messages are subtly and not so subtly present.

For example, while nature stories such as "Going Head-to-Head with Warthogs" in *Zoobooks* have no real connection to gender, we noted that the illustrations show more male animal handlers and scientists. Women are shown admiring a spider's web or engaging in traditional activities such as weaving. If both men and women are present, the man might hold a sea turtle while the woman measures its shell. A man looks through the microscope, and a woman holds up the beaker. It's interesting how nature can be framed in gendered ways. An issue of *Ranger Rick* has a feature called Living Lace: "Nothing says summer like a field of white lacy flowers. But there's more to these beauties than just looks. Read on." We then see pictures of camouflaged insects and animals seeking food, accompanied by a pretty blond-haired girl crouched in a field of Queen Anne's lace and looking at the camera. (Why isn't she at least discovering one of those camouflaged insects in the flower petals?) Alongside her photo are sidebars with directions about how to press flowers and color the lace by placing bouquets in dyed water. In the same issue a fictional account of discovering real dinosaur eggs in a natural history museum features an intrepid boy and his paleontologist father. The next story is about dinosaur bones and shows a boy goofing off, pretending his arm is caught in the jaws of a large skeleton, while a girl tries to pull him away. The message? Girls are pretty and cautious; boys are fearless and fun.

Girls and women are more likely to be featured in these magazines when the topic turns to food preparation, crafts, or child care. In *Ranger Rick* we see a photo of girls sitting in a doggy diner; the story includes a recipe for homemade dog bones. In *Highlights* (ages two to twelve) an explanation of how a camel keeps the dust out of its eyes is illustrated with a cartoon of a girl riding a camel and holding a young child in front of her. In the same issue a Bahamian tale about Sister Felice, "a woman of magic" and "the best cook on all of Andros Island," tells a story of how mischievous elfin creatures called chickcharnies are tricked into eating guava duff and turn into chick hens. Readers are directed to the *Highlights* Web site for guava duff recipe.

More than any of the other magazines we reviewed, *Highlights* has very clear gendered messages. We would say it hasn't adjusted to the times, but the newer magazines don't fare much better. Sports stories nearly always feature stereotypical boys, and the illustrations, especially those geared to younger kids, tend to be more stereotypically coded: boys playing Ping-Pong, making maps, getting lost in caves; a matching game with one girl pig dressed in a pink dress holding flowers and four boy pigs—a baker, a baseball player, a carpenter with his tool belt, and a pig in shorts with a book. (This last pig could be male or female, but given the really pink pig, it seems more like the other boys.) A feature about two boys, Goofus and Gallant, teaches good manners (as though girls don't need these lessons), The Bear Family's grandma is in a pink dress and pearls. Another feature, For Wee Folks, connects play and work with stereotyped pictures of girls having tea parties and mainly boys playing with trucks.

Many of these magazines have fictional short stories, which are generally fun and interesting. Still, messages about the "true nature" of girls and boys come through more often than we'd like. In one issue of *Spider*, a story, "The Pickle Queens," begins with brother Marcus and his dad heading out for soccer practice. This leaves the house to mom and the girls who are pickling tomatoes for their elderly neighbor, Mrs. Banks. Mrs. Banks has "the cheeriest smile and the cheeriest ankles in town" because, as she told the girls, even if you needed two canes to walk, as she did, if you dressed up your feet in bright pink ankle socks, "you fooled your feet into thinking they could still dance." The girls decide to pickle "something pretty" for their cheery neighbor, so they fill a jar with pink socks and label it Pickled Pink. Mrs. Banks sounds a lot like *Highlights'* Miss Dinsmore in "As Cheerful as Cheerful Can Be," who lives all alone and can't decide what color to paint her drab house. When she ends up with a houseful of neighbors, she realizes what real cheeriness is.

Cheerful, pretty, and cute are exclusively reserved for girls. The cover of an issue of *Click* (for ages three to seven), has a little boy looking at a turtle, and inside we read about Amy and Martin and Grandpa fishing for rainbow trout. Amy says things like "Ooh! I bet they're really pretty!" and (about some ducks) "Oh! They're so cute!" Although both kids wade into the water, Martin does the frog catching. In the same magazine is "A Pond for Maddie" in which Maddie and her family find an old artificial pond behind their new house and decide to clean it up. "Even with big, thick gardening gloves, [Maddie] didn't want to touch anything." When they buy plants for the pond, Maddie asks, "What about water lilies? . . . They're the prettiest!" In a *Highlights* regular cartoon feature, The Timbertoes, the kids are brainstorming what to do for Father's Day. The girls want to make breakfast; the boy wants to sweep the shop. When the girl picks flowers, the boy thinks, "Silly idea." Pa likes them, of course, but in the few minutes it takes your daughter to read this simple cartoon, she is treated to a series of stereotypes about cooking, pretty flowers, and the differences between boys and girls.

There are a few stories and features that went against type, especially in the nature-focused magazines but also in some of the others. In *Ladybug* (for ages two to six) we read about "Max and Kate." Kate finds her grandpa's old fishing things, and Max gets a little scared. He says, "These are nice to look at, but I don't want to catch any fish." But Kate's not afraid: "Look, I've caught two big fish already" (two stuffed animals in a net). Such stories tell girls that they can take initiative and be bold; they tell little boys that it's okay to be afraid every once in a while.

There are lots of wonderful stories and activities in these magazines, and maybe because there is some awareness that advertising is not good for little kids or that nature and reading are for everyone, they are an oasis amid the ever-increasing competition for product loyalty. (Although you might want to nix *National Geographic Kids*. It is loaded with advertising for junk food, cartoons, movies, and computer games. There are other ad-free magazines that do nature better.) Because children can't really distinguish between fantasy and reality, it is especially important to question gender stereotyping when you see it. For example, kids this age are too young to understand the generic use of the pronoun *he*. When you don't vary pronouns or when boys and girls are repeatedly associated with certain things—girls with pretty, boys with sports—children think this is really how the world is. We suggest that while reading with your daughter, you ask questions, pose alternatives, and change pronouns. And then discover with your daughter what it's like to go head-to-head with a warthog.

SEVEN GOING ON FOURTEEN: MAGAZINES FOR TWEENS

Once girls have left *Highlights* and *Zoobooks*, they're introduced to magazines designed specifically for girls. With a few exceptions this means girls move away from being educated about the world of nature, entertained by goofy jokes and riddles, and challenged with puzzles and mazes, to being educated about a world of fashion, beauty, and boys.

The average reader of teen magazines is twelve, which means many ten-year-olds are reading them. There's a difference in tone and content between magazines designed for nine- to ten-year-olds and those designed for twelve-year-olds and older. In some cases it's a difference of degree. For preteens, boyfriends are called "crushes," beauty has to do with hairstyles and products, and fashion focuses on the brightly colored accessories from Claire's, "Smackers" lip gloss, and cute tops from Limited Too. Leaving the teen magazines such as *CosmoGIRL!* and *Seventeen* for the time being, we'll focus on those aimed at the younger set: *American Girl Magazine*, *Discovery Girl*, *Girls' Life*, and *New Moon*.

We were struck by the trend to define a teen girl as younger and younger. Still, these preteen magazines are better than the teen magazines marketed to middle school girls. Yes, there are regular features, captions, and stories that make us cringe: false girl power promises like "the fun and freedom to accessorize" and "the great debate: looks or talent" (surely there are greater debates), and lots and lots of stories about crushes on and rejections by boys. But there are also stories by girls themselves about getting messy, staying close to Dad, daring to be different, and surviving tragedy, and also about girls from around the world.

The most popular preteen magazines are *Discovery Girls* (for girls seven to fourteen), *American Girl* (seven to twelve), and *New Moon*, the "Magazine for Girls and Their Dreams" (eight to fourteen). We also include *Girls' Life*, or *GL* (for girls ten to fifteen), because it includes preteens in its targeted age range.

Seven to fourteen is a ridiculously wide age range. This means the magazines most often shoot to the middle or high end of the age range, figuring younger girls want to feel or appear older and can be easily brought along. None of these magazines are appropriate for seven-year-olds.

Because these magazines sell a version of girlhood, girls reading them try to figure out what a normal girl should feel, think, and act like and what she should wear or buy to create the image of normal. Each one of these magazines has a decidedly different view of American girlhood.

American Girl is the youngest of the preteen magazines, although the letters from girls suggest that readers are as likely to be twelve and thirteen as they are eight or nine. Content and photos suggest American girls are squeaky clean and like pets, cooking, giggling with friends, foolish fun, and crafts. They shine, have heart-to-hearts, volunteer in their communities, and lend a helping hand. They also play sports, explore the natural world, and do brave things. They say "I'm sorry" a lot, make pretty cards, and have bedtime blues. They are encouraged to be nice, be cheerful, and change the subject when something irritates them. For this reason, *American Girl* magazine has a finishing-school feel to it. The few ads are either for expensive AG products and such things as boarding schools. ("Every day I practice English riding at the stable. . . . This year I brought my own horse, Audacity, to boarding school.") American Girls are supernice, but they don't seem particularly real or very deep or complex. We know lots of eight- and nine-year-olds who are living with family stresses and personal struggles. Advising them to smile through it, drink herbal tea, or just keep trying doesn't quite do justice to their lives. AG's "normalcy" is once again that perfect girl image that is too hard for real girls to live up to.

Unlike AG, which seems mostly age appropriate even if its view of girlhood is limited, it is hard to understand why *Discovery Girl* is marketed to seven- to fourteen-year-olds. According to their publisher, "*Discovery Girl* provides a forum for girls to speak out about the challenges they face each day . . . helps your daughter connect with girls across the country" so she can "become the self-confident, creative, and healthy young woman you want her to be." There are lots of stories written by girls; in addition, girls of different sizes, races, and styles grace the pages rather than digitally enhanced supermodels. We especially like their Behind the Scenes and Over There sections that showcase real girls around the United States and in other countries. Discovery Girls discover more than their own voices. Along with the purple and pink pages enhanced with cartoon girls and lined with stars, flowers, and hearts, they discover a world of consumerism through boys, fashion, and beauty. There is a blatant teen edge to the magazine that is absent in *American Girl*. Gotta-have-it fashion spreads, shopping tips, CD and DVD reviews, and hair advice with lots of product placement prepare girls to "dare to be different"—by buying the same things. The DG girl has more problems than the AG girl, but they are all personal and relational: Her body is changing; she fears rejection; she's into guys, shopping, and popular culture. This is hardly the stuff of most seven- and eight-year-old girls' lives, but it's excellent preparation for teen magazines such as *Girls' Life*.

GL is a teen magazine shamelessly masquerading as being for a preteen audience. GL is fun, no doubt about it. It is filled with quizzes, advice, and celebrity interviews, as well as a few good regular features such as One Girl/One Solution. The primary problem with GL is the series of contradictions that are too mature for ten-year-olds to grapple with: "free to be me" ads for products girls must have to be cool; advice about being your own person with suggestions about how to attract, kiss, and keep boyfriends; information about healthy body images interspersed with ul-trathin girl models. There is very little diversity. Not surprisingly, this magazine marks the beginning of "mean girl" talk, boyfriend jealousy, makeup, popular culture, and consumerism. Filled with thin blond mod-els, ads for "boy crazy" trading cards ("So many boys, so little time"), and makeup, GL is a not-so-subtle education about the material world of prepackaged girl culture and promises a straight-line prequel to more highly sexualized teen magazines like CosmoGIRL!.

New Moon makes a different promise. It is the only magazine for girls without any advertisements. It is also the only magazine with an editorial board made up of girls. New Moon sees itself as "an international magazine for every girl who wants her voice heard and her dreams taken seriously." While "dreams" buys into the stereotype that girls dream and boys like ac-tion, NM is more blunt about its purpose—"to build healthy resistance to gender inequities"—and they have zero space for fashion and beauty prod-ucts. To that end, their departments have names like Women's Work, Girl Talk, Girls on the Go, Herstory, and Girls Act Out. Their girl-written features—"Visit the Birthplace of Mother Teresa," "Hot on the Trail of a Disease Detective," and "Look at What's Hiding Behind Harry Potter"—give a sense of action, independence, and media savvy. Our favorite is their annual twenty-five-most-beautiful-girls issue, an in-your-face re-sponse to People magazine's fifty most beautiful people issue. While People goes for outer beauty, New Moon redefines beauty as "good hearts, great works, and activism" and showcases a diversity of brave, unique, creative girls. The normal New Moon girl would rather do than be done to, see rather than be seen, and create culture rather than consume it. Like the other magazines, though, New Moon seems geared more to ten and up than eight and nine. But more than any of the other magazines it provides a view of girls as people of substance.

Magazines like GL and the rest of consumer culture see the spark of young girls and want to direct it toward buying and posing and becoming interested in pop stars. (Why read about real girls when an Olsen twin may have an eating disorder? When Paris Hilton's life has gotten even more glamorous?) A magazine like New Moon may be too real and no longer work when girls get to be thirteen or fourteen. They have devel-oped anxieties that teen magazines promise answers to and may no longer believe in the values that a magazine like New Moon espouses.

We want to teach moms how to help their daughters stay invested in the real and the reality of their lives in the fullest sense, beyond looks, crushes, and decorating. When they read magazines about their interests—for example, *Track and Field*, *Figure Skating*, and *Mac Addict*—and not magazines about their gender, that will be a start.

ARE YOU A HILARY OR AN AVRIL? COSMO GIRLS CATEGORIZED

> I read [magazines] from beginning to end. I like reading
> about fashion and makeup and hair tips.
>
> —RACHEL, *age twelve*

Teen magazines are everywhere a high schooler or middle schooler goes. She sees the covers of these magazines on a weekly basis, and these covers tell her what she should be interested in and what she should be anxious about. Magazines such as *Twist*, *J-14*, *YM*, and *Teen* are more for the middle school set. The letters written in and the humiliating experiences of real girls presented show the age range as eleven to fifteen. Magazines like *Seventeen*, *Elle Girl*, *CosmoGIRL!*, *Teen People*, *Teen Vogue*, and *Glamour Girl* are purportedly for an older teen crowd (their similar letters and experiences of real girls show the age range of fourteen to nineteen). Unfortunately, in spite of these age ranges, our survey tells us that both middle school girls and high school girls are reading them all—cover to cover.

Rather than expose the repetitiveness of stereotypes about bodies, consumerism, and romance in these magazines, we thought we'd look at a few problems that are less blatant. It's obvious to even the youngest girl in these groups that all the models are thin and pretty, but maybe not as obvious to most white girls that there is very little racial diversity. If a girl is African American or Asian, she will have to look hard to find a girl like her in these magazines. The July 2004 issue of *Seventeen*, showed eighty-one white girls, five African American girls, one Latina, and one Asian girl.

These magazines try to sell girls a sorry substitute for diversity. After all, today's generation was raised in schools that gave clear-cut messages about diversity and tolerance, and advertisers have known since the old Benneton advertisements that diversity is hip. The type of diversity these magazines pretend to offer are diverse categories of girls. Fashion shoots, faux stories, question-and-answer columns, and special inserts all provide girls with a variety of categories with which they can label themselves. The magazine's message about girls being individuals is really telling them they need to fit into a set number of boxes. Those ever-present questionnaires will tell girls after they count up their scores whether they are a chilled-out chick, fair weather fan, or sunshine sistah. Fashion features will have them label themselves as either a busty babe, hippie gal, curvy chick, or skinny sistah, or just label their body shape as star, pear, apple, or tube. These articles answer that all-important teen question "Who am I?" over and over via predictions and advice. They take advantage of your daughter's genuine self-analysis at this age and make a mockery of the heartfelt questions she has.

Surveys in teen magazines seem harmless enough, and of course the girls who take these quizzes don't take them totally seriously. The incessant categorization, however, gives a stronger message: You will be categorized, so get a jump on it and do it yourself. Moreover, the most important categories are about style. You will be read by your style, they proclaim, so you need to know everything you can about it.

These questionnaires not only categorize girls but also the crushes and pop stars the girls love, asking them to use the same makeup as their "role models" but never explaining why a pop star deserves to be a role model. How they sell products is sometimes very subtle. For example, *J-14* has virtually no traditional advertisements; however, in a feat of immersive advertising, every feature story about a star sells something. For example, the writer may guess at the makeup a star uses, never actually saying "Mary-Kate Olsen uses it" but instead "Shimmer like Mary-Kate." The feature then has several photos of Mary-Kate and several products beside her with brand name and price for a girl to choose if she wants to shimmer like Mary-Kate. We're sure Mary-Kate's publicist doesn't mind because while the article sells the makeup, it is also selling the star, her future movies, her CDs, and her upcoming line of clothing.

Below we've listed the kinds of stereotypes about girls that are presented over and over in these magazines with examples of headlines and text from the articles. If you want, you can play one of those teen magazine matching games—a game you'll never see in one of these magazines. Match the stereotype with the article title below:

Stereotypes

Girls love to shop

A makeover fixes anything

Girls are catty and can't get along

If two girls are popular, there has to be a rivalry between them

The most important thing in the world is getting a boyfriend

To get a boyfriend you need to look sexy

Articles

"Look Sexy in Those New Jeans" or "Score Sexy Summer Lips"

"Finding Your Inner Super-Model"

"Who's the Queen of the Divas?"

"Who's your Primetime Boyfriend?" or "Discover Summer Lovin—
Is He More Than a Friend?" or "Who's Your Hip Hop Honey?" or
"What's Your Favorite Dating Style?"

"How Does Hilary Handle the Haters?"

"I Want Her Hair"

"Dreamy Sleepover" (Featuring outfits for sleepovers)

If you matched each and every one of these to "Girls love to shop," you
are right on target! (Of course other stereotypes abound, too!)

There are quite a few articles titled in a way that ask girls a question
or invite them to respond, feigning interest in the real girl: "Tell us about
your best kiss." Sometimes there are contests pretending that they want to
know how girls really think: "Express yourself!" These questions draw girls
into the magazines, teaching them that self-analysis at this very superficial level is an activity of girlhood. Boys' magazines (what few there are)
don't ask boys to rate themselves, categorize themselves, or analyze their
style. It seems tragic that girls buy into this superficial interest in them
when the intent is to shape their interests toward buying more.

One of the most infuriating aspects of these magazines is the way they
sculpt girls' actions and activities by showing what's typical and what's acceptable for them to do. An interview with Paris Hilton was particularly
revealing. Most articles about her go on and on about her embarrassing
porn video, her TV series *The Simple Life*, her fight with Nicole, her little
dog, her exotic pets, her sense of fashion, and the parties and boyfriends.
When asked what would be the most surprising thing about her that her
fans don't know, she answered that she was an ice hockey player in high

school and one of the best on the team. That fact says volumes about the girl. Do you know what it takes to be a good ice hockey player when you're a girl in high school? We now have a totally different picture of Paris—as a disciplined, incredibly strong girl who woke up every morning at six o'clock for practice, who pushed her physical limits, and who probably got quite aggressive on the ice in order to be one of the best players. Rather than pursuing this interesting side of her in the article, it is mentioned and thrown away, like the wrong answer. In the summer of 2004 there were many articles about Paris Hilton, and only one mentioned this major aspect of who she was and, we bet, still is. Ice hockey is not the kind of activity these magazines want to encourage because it doesn't lead you into beauty and fashion and promoting movies and CDs.

Sports aren't cool, at least not for girls. Publishers and editors pretend to be interested in girls and sports but often use a sport to categorize a girl or sell fashion. *Teen* had a two-page feature called "Sporty Girls" (remembering once again to categorize girls who play sports as different from other girls) that told of four summer camps or competitions featuring tennis, surfing, skateboarding, and . . . cheerleading. Sports are mentioned a second time in the same magazine in an article entitled "Where the Boys Are." If a girl wants to meet boys, she should hang out at the tennis courts or the arcade "and look pretty." Remember not to "challenge him and beat him at his game!"

A "summer fragrances" ad said it all. Featured were a girl and a boy and a surfboard on the beach, and written across the two kids were the words "For all the ways you play." Clearly *his* form of play is surfing, given he is the one holding the surfboard. Her form of play is teasing him. In a bikini bottom but no top and a six-button shirt that has only one button buttoned, she is certainly playing something. What fun!

In an effort to promote girl power, though, these magazines teach girls to get angry at any boy who says that girls aren't strong and can't play sports, reinforcing the stereotype that girls need to fight with their words and not with their bodies. In a feature about what boys say and what they mean, they have a boy saying "Girls don't surf" and claim that what he means is "Stay away from me—I'm a sexist pig." Yet in an entire summer issue the magazine does not show one single girl surfing. They are virtually saying, "Girls don't surf," but never "Stay away from us."

What activities are acceptable for girls besides the fashion, makeup, and boy-chasing activities that pervade? Because we were looking at summer issues, we found a few articles on summer jobs and how to spend time during those free summer days. Remembering that girls can't have real jobs until they're sixteen, here is what's recommended. In "Cash In on Fabulous Jobs" the authors recommend walking dogs, explaining the Internet to senior citizens (which is rather patronizing to seniors but at least suggests some technical skill on the girls' part), baking and selling cookies, organizing someone's basement, becoming someone's "supersecretary," designing a Web site for someone else, going grocery shopping and running errands for someone else, babysitting, house sitting, holding a car wash, setting up a mini carnival for children, making crafts and selling them, taking care of others' plants or gardens, tutoring, and holding a garage sale. With very few exceptions this sounds to us as though they want these girls to practice being a traditional *uber*mom. Baking, organizing, crafting, gardening, taking care of kids and old people! What's absent? Did you guess mowing? Mowing people's lawns is probably the best way to make some cash before you're old enough for a real job, that and babysitting. But mowing was outside the box for these *Teen* authors. And instead of baking cookies and selling crafts, why not collect old CDs and rock-and-roll albums and sell these? How about just returning people's empties? How "fabulous" are these jobs? Well, not too. But as moms we can also vouch for the fact that taking care of our gardens, organizing the basement, tutoring kids on their schoolwork, and holding a garage sale aren't too fabulous, either.

What *should* daughters be doing with all that free summer time? According to these magazines they should be watching TV, going to movies, and reading trashy novels. According to *Teen*, here are some "ridiculously cool things" they might also try: write down the lyrics of their favorite songs, lie on their backs and say what shapes they see in the clouds (how original is that?), and learn how to read palms. (Mildly interesting, but "ridiculously cool"? We think not.) *J-14* thinks they can check out soaps, practice their karaoke (an okay plan if they want to be a diva), give their rooms a mini-makeover, make their own lemonade (again in the kitchen?), show off their "fave swimsuit" at the pool, send someone an e-card, or have a summer fling (just what we want our daughters to do when they're bored—have meaningless sex with someone).

We can think of other choices, such as volunteering to work on a political campaign, illustrating a book they like, writing a short story, helping out at summer camps, learning how to play guitar, practicing their basketball skills, or holding a mini soccer camp rather than a carnival, offering to assist at their church or synagogue, learning how to surf, sorting food at the local food pantry, or walking dogs at the Humane Society shelter. Instead of being a mommy's helper, why not be a professional woman's helper for a day and learn what her day is like?

These aren't the kinds of things magazines suggest to girls who they believe hope to be divas and have hot boyfriends by the end of the summer. Pretending to be a girl's best friend, they tell her secret after secret, whisper tips as if standing right behind her at the mirror, and dish gossip galore. These magazines are fickle friends. Look how they treat the stars! On one page they will make a reader feel like Lindsay Lohan's BFF (best friend forever) when reading about her intimate woes; on the next page the reader learns about her catfight with another star. By showing no loyalty to any star and their willingness to betray any confidence or share any tidbit of gossip, magazines re-create the middle school scenario of cliques and status problems.

EMBARRASSING MOMENTS

The middle school girls who answered our survey told us they love the embarrassing moments sections of teen magazines the best. Every magazine for this age group has stories from real teens about humiliations, accidents, and embarrassing situations. Although the magazines set up the "perfect girl" image over and over again as something girls can and should work to attain, they also say that perfect girls are snobby, mean, full of themselves, and untrustworthy. So the embarrassing moments offer signs that girls who buy these magazines have an imperfect side. Just because they're flawless on the outside doesn't mean they are not vulnerable on the inside. While no one can be exactly like the perfect models in the magazine, they can share imperfections with them and still feel included. Embarrassing moments is a great hook; it is a way for girls to insert some of their own reality into the fantastic unreality of the pages before them.

These embarrassing moments feature lots of surprise happenings: skin revealings (bathing suit tops fall off), bodily sounds at the wrong time, accidents that reveal bodily functions (spilling a backpack and having supersize tampons roll out), eating too much, misunderstandings with boys. Anything that breaks the false image of put-together perfection will do. One girl wrote the following embarrassing moment about eating birthday cake in the now defunct YM (our commentary has been added):

After blowing out the candles and giving everyone a slice [*of course she's polite*], I dug right in [*but she's real, with hunger*]. It was so delicious that I wolfed it down [*and a bit bad*]. A little too fast, though, because I started choking and ended up coughing out a spray of crumbs all over the place. I was beyond mortified. [*That will teach her to enjoy eating!*]

This normalizes things. The normal girl is the one who carries tampons in discrete places, suppresses farts, doesn't reveal too much skin, and is mortified when she shows her messy humanity in public.

In the girls' groups that Lyn runs, the girls love to hear about the embarrassing things that happen to others. The less popular girls especially love to hear these stories because they feel they are being let in on something that makes them more like the popular ones. A bonding takes place that has to do with fitting in and status; social heirarchies momentarily disappear when we realize that everyone farts.

We agree these embarrassing moments stories have a wonderful quality about them. However, they don't suggest to girls that we are all complicated, that all of us present various selves to the world and struggle to integrate these selves into a whole person. Instead, they merely remind girls that it's better and even normal to present a false front most of the time and then reveal the cracks in that front so that other girls will like them—but not too many cracks or guys will not want them. What a thin line to walk.

GOOD GIRL AVRIL, BAD GIRL BRITNEY?

Most of the magazines that girls are reading feature their idols, and although idols change, you can be sure they will be contrasted as mean versus nice, good versus bad, hot versus innocent, alternative versus girly, and so on. We look at Avril Lavigne and Britney Spears as types that shift with each issue.

Avril Lavigne began her career as the skater high school girl who hung out with boys and didn't take her clothes off to get attention. She was the alternative to Britney. She actually played guitar when she sang and jumped up and down with punk excitement rather than thrusting her boobs and hips at us in MTV dance form. She was a girl rocker, and she was so popular that they just couldn't let her be. To get a larger fan base, to reach more kids, they had to mainstream her. The marketing ploy was to clean her up, feminize her, keep her unique but not too unique, and make her a little more sexy once she reached eighteen. Voilá, the new Avril.

This repackaging takes away what was really unique about her (and possibly still is in reality) in exchange for broader appeal. Someone out there thinks that she's more appealing when she's presented more like a stereotyped "everygirl." That couldn't be right. You might ask your twelve-year-old daughter, "Why do you think you have to be liked by everybody?" But if you ask marketers and packagers why a cool and decent kid like Avril has to be liked by more and more preteens, and stay popular with those preteens when they become teens, the answer would probably have something to do with branding and selling and, in the end, making more money.

Listen to the way *CosmoGIRL!* writes about her:

- Avril, a self-described tomboy, says she's become "more girlie as she's gotten older."

- Avril says, "I love clothes and going to the spa to get facials and massages."

- Avril thinks Jessica Simpson is "sweet and pretty. . . . If I wanted to look like anyone else it would be her."

- "But for all the bad girl behavior and punk rock bravado, Avril is still just another girl who gets crushes on cute movie stars and musicians."

The same month, the same year, and, not coincidentally, the month her new album was being released, *J-14* was writing that Avril is "misunderstood."

- She's not a loudmouth.

- She's not a total tomboy. "I am actually really girlie. I love shopping. I'm really into face products, hair products, sleepovers, facials, and stuff."

- She's not just a guy's girl. She "has female BFFs [best friends forever] as well."

- She's not closed off to love. "Just like many girls, Avril daydreams about boys and being in love." And to top it off this tomboy, skater girl, pop punk rocker says, "I'm looking forward to getting married and having a family."

Her new album, supposedly full of songs from her diary, is advertised as a "girl power" album, but we mainly hear typical songs of teenage romance, defining girl power as the power to wait for the right time to have sex (as in "Don't Tell Me"). She uses the powerful metaphor of voice and choice (à la reproductive politics) to teach girls that they have choices about who they can go out with: "He wouldn't even open up the door/he never made me feel like I was special/he wasn't what I'm looking for. . . . We've all got choices, we've all got voices." Girl power—the power to pick the right guy. And the right guy is someone who makes you feel *special!*

Magazines will play up the sweet Britney and now the Mommy Britney angle. But what will girls think when they see her packaged elsewhere? Check out the photo of Britney that promoters sent to such tween girl Web sites as RadioDisney. It is one from 1999 where she looks like a tween—cute, vulnerable, and awkward. Talk about bait and switch! Her pop bubblegum music appealed to younger girls from day one; her blond Barbie looks won admirers in even the three- to five-year-old set. Her first video, set in a school and with her dressed in a school uniform, created an image of a rebel schoolgirl that would appeal to fifth graders, tenth graders, and, unfortunately, grown men. In fact, two years after the success of that video, she hired Gregory Dark, porn director, to direct "From the Bottom of My Broken Heart."

Fast forward a few years to the video *Toxic* and we see Britney as a sexy flight attendant (male fantasy), who transforms into an evil villainess type, curls around on the floor in a glittery white leotard looking like a sexy kitten, and does some dance moves reminiscent of a lap dancer/pole dancer/stripper in their evocation of oral sex. Where can a girl go from here? In her video *Everytime*, she playacts a suicide. Naked in a bubble bath she is saved just in time by her hunky shirtless boyfriend who jumps into the tub and gives her mouth-to-mouth. So many of us make fun of girls for being drama queens, but at the same time we give them horrible ideas of how to create drama when they're feeling alone and depressed.

But how do you talk to a little girl about pornography when, hopefully, she hasn't seen any or has seen only intimations of it in cartoons, TV shows, and movies? One suggestion is to say, "I wonder why Britney keeps trying all these different ways of being sexy and not different ways of being her?"

BAIT AND SWITCH: THE LURE OF GIRL POWER ON WEB SITES

We'd be remiss if we didn't mention the plethora of girl power Web sites in cyberspace. Web magazines are another source of garbage for girls, so don't be fooled by the bright pink flashing *Girl Power* titles all over the Internet. Almost as soon as the phrase was coined, girl power was snapped up by the media and just about everyone else trying to sell your daughter something. What it sells is an *image* of being empowered. Once girls buy into that desire and go after that image, they're told that the way to get that power is through makeup, clothes, and boyfriends.

A case in point is the Web site gURL.com, which is a creation of the writers of the book *Deal with It*. The book has a shocking pink cover with an equally shocking cartoon girl in a yellow raincoat. Her back is to us, but clearly she is opening that raincoat to flash an unseen audience. What is cool about it is that the girl is not ashamed of her body. Inside the book there is a ton of information about girls and their bodies and sex and sexuality. There is also info about pimples and mood swings. It would seem that the point of the book is to give girls information to empower them.

Cut to the Web site. When the book came out, we joined the Web site in order to get monthly emails from gURL.com. Month after month we've been receiving tips on how to do our hair, what to wear to proms and winter balls, quizzes about our "aura," and information about how to please our boyfriends. We can make our own "cyber-sweetie" or create an on-screen "boy band." Why a "boy band"? Probably so that girls can stand in front of it, sing, dance, and look pretty, or just be a groupie. But why not a band she can play the drums in? We guess she's too busy with makeup, hair, auras, and boyfriends. The authors of the Web site lured the girls in with a promise of information and power, and then continued to turn them into *Cosmo*-tweens.

Over and over again girls are sold a promise that their voice counts, that they have potential to do great things, that they are part of a larger world where what they do matters, and even that they are unique. Then the promise boils down to makeup, hair, clothes, and boys.

How can you make your daughter more savvy about this bait-and-switch tactic? Help her decode words such as funky, hip, cool, and awesome when it comes to style. All those words really stand for an attitude that defies convention. Funky = original = neat = weird in a good way. Talk about how companies are trying to sell *funky* to her, to mainstream it, to make her feel original and unique while telling her that everything that truly makes her original and unique also makes her vulnerable to being laughed at and left outside. You and your daughter together can make up words that capture this hypocrisy in action, such as faux funky or false funk or fake funk.

Steer her to some of the online resources we list at the end of the book. Looking at sites ending with .org is a good place to start, although not always reliable. These nonprofit agencies are usually very girl friendly and are short on ads. Take a good look at MySpace and ask your daughter if you can see the photos of her "friends." Don't be surprised if she has around two hundred of these friends. While the media (always interested in teen sex scandals) might scare you into believing that MySpace has tons of teen porn on it, more than 60 million teens are now using it to show who they are to the world. Some of them buy into a sexed-up image of themselves. Many of them show their faces, their pets, their interests, their musical loves, and more. Real kids, no matter how they represent themselves, are so much more interesting to talk about than lingerie models or other media stars.

Most important of all, decode the promise of "girl power" for her! Point out the problems of "Girls Rule" slogans when they're attached to shopping and sex. Admit that looking good and looking hip does make a girl feel more powerful, but then suggest that it is a problem when it's the only way girl power is described. She can be special and wonderful and do great things, but the world has taught her to *feel* powerful and special and wonderful only on good-hair days.

"BECAUSE YOU'RE MORE THAN JUST A PRETTY FACE"

This is the tagline for the magazine *Teen Voices*. You have only to look at a cover to know you're seeing something unusual. The three or four or five girls smiling back at you are all different. They have different body sizes and different styles of clothing; they look comfortable in their differently colored skins. Their sweaters, T-shirts, bandannas, braids, jeans, and braces make them "every girl," not the airbrushed, media-constructed, Hilary Duff kind of every girl but every "real" girl, the kind you'll see in your high school hallway. The girls have supremely confident smiles, arms around each other, and are leaning forward, posing in a way that suggests being a cover girl isn't their primary goal in life. Around them are the magazine's promises of more reality inside:

"Different Races, Different Proms: A Teen Takes on Racism"

"Latinas in Hollywood: Fed Up & Taking Charge"

"Cutting Classism: Are You Defined by Your Status?"

"Teen Novelist Brings Sheroes to the Shelves"

"Coming Out? Read 'Dear D' First"

"Going to the Gyno: Your Questions Answered"

"Taking Over the Turntables: Women DJs Chat Coast to Coast"

Here's a teen magazine "written by, for, and about girls" that takes girl power seriously. No girl-hating "you're failing to be beautifully perfect, so buy this product" messages. "*Teen Voices* only accepts advertisements from companies which do not exploit their audience or employees." Rather than makeup and hair products, they advertise colleges and girl-positive Web sites, books, magazines, and music. Now there's an original idea!

The real power of *Teen Voices* is that it takes seriously the notion of gender diversity—that there are many ways to be girls of substance. You won't see the old familiar types here—girly girls and tomboys; mean girls and nice girls—or the typical features touting makeovers and where to find the coolest accessories or prom dresses. Their interviews are with such people as outspoken Carol Moseley-Braun, edgy comedian and political commentator Janeane Garofalo, and such girl-inspiring music artists as Fefe Dobson. Under The Contents of Our Minds they list regular features such as "We Are Family," "Health," "Arts and Culture," and "Cultural Harmony." Their departments—"SHOUT! Notes," "Girl Talk," and "Top 10"—give girls the opportunity to speak out, ask hard questions, and create their own worlds.

Teen Voices is for girls who take genuine pleasure in the things real girls do, who feel and think and know they are on this planet for reasons other than shopping. The media would classify girls like these as nerds or activists, making them feel like outliers—different. The truth is that there are thousands of them. This teen magazine reflects and supports real girls, reminding them that romance, makeup, and fashion are just *part* of their lives, not their whole being.

BOOKS AND SERIES THAT HAVE STRONG GIRLS AND FEW STEREOTYPES

Our Recommendations in This Chapter

Speak by Laurie Halse Anderson

Pinduli by Janell Cannon

Stellaluna by Janell Cannon

Ramona the Brave (and other Ramona books) by Beverly Cleary

Magic Schoolbus series by Joanna Cole

Miss Rumphius by Barbara Cooney

Walk Two Moons by Sharon Creech

I'm Gonna Like Me by Jamie Lee Curtis

Matilda by Roald Dahl

Sheila Rae the Brave by Kevin Henkes

Amazing Grace by Mary Hoffman

Ella Enchanted by Gail Carson Levine

Pippi Longstocking series by Astrid Lindgren

Angela's Airplane by Robert N. Munsch

The Paper Bag Princess by Robert N. Munsch

Junie B. Jones series by Barbara Park

Protector of the Small series by Tamara Pierce

His Dark Materials (Golden Compass, Subtle Knife, The Amber Spyglass) by Philip Pullman

A Bad Case of Stripes by David Shannon

Eloise by Kay Thompson

Recommended by Trusted Librarians, Authors, and Parents

The Sisters Grimm by Michael Buckley

Landry News by Andrew Clements

The Report Card by Andrew Clements

The School Story by Andrew Clements

Bloomability by Sharon Creech

The Wanderer by Sharon Creech

Because of Winn-Dixie by Kate Di Camillo

The Birchbark House by Louise Erdrich

Coraline by Neil Gaiman

Julie of the Wolves by Jean Craighead George

Hannah, Divided by Adelle Griffin

Chester's Way by Kevin Henkes

Letters from Rifka by Karen Hesse

Out of the Dust by Karen Hesse

Witness by Karen Hesse

Born Confused by Tanuja Desai Hidier

Casa Azul by Laban Carrick Hill

The Canning Season by Polly Horvath

Everything on a Waffle by Polly Horvath

My Great-Aunt Arizona by Gloria Houston

Journey to the River Sea by Eva Ibbotsen

Devil in Vienna by Doris Orgel

The Great Gilly Hopkins by Katherine Paterson

All Alone in the Universe by Lynne Rae Perkins

Jojo's Flying Side Kick by Brian Pinkney

Sorceress by Celia Rees

Witch Child by Celia Rees

How I Live Now by Meg Rosoff

The Serpent Slayer and Other Stories of Strong Women by Katrin Tchana

A Complicated Kindness by Miriam Toews

Each Little Bird Sings by Deborah Wiles

Love, Ruby Lavender by Deborah Wiles

CHAPTER 5

Wanna Play? What Girls Do

In the world of play—from dolls to sports to musical instruments to slumber parties to cheerleading to instant messaging to kissing and more—there is a common belief that when the child herself chooses a game, activity, club, instrument, or toy, she is expressing her individual personality and cannot be coerced by old-fashioned rules of gender. This belief couldn't be more wrong. Choice is coerced every day, and not only by marketers but by other people who pick up on societal ideas of what is normal and important for girls compared to boys. When a girl chooses a doll instead of a truck, decides to sit and watch rather than join in, selects the flute instead of the trombone, or picks a Barbie Fashion Design computer game instead of a racing game, we are inclined to think her choices express something unique to her. Examined in light of the pattern of most girls' choices over childhood, however, these aren't freely made choices. They are choices made within a very narrow definition of girlhood, a definition that is getting narrower all the time.

As developmental psychologists we admit that this chapter about what girls do makes us the saddest (and maybe the maddest) because play is everything to a child, and girls should have the opportunity to experiment, practice, invent, and imagine anything in play. Instead, as in the magazines they read, the TV shows they watch, the clothes they buy and the lyrics of the songs they listen to, they are being sold a version of girlhood that will feel satisfying to them when they conform to it but will also limit their possibilities in the future.

A parent may disagree and think that girls these days have it better than they did because there are less obvious restrictions on girls. Psychologists are saying that girls' social worlds are now less scripted and controlled than boys'. It is true that girls can freely embrace what used to be "boy territory" in ways boys could never venture into what is still "girl territory." Playing sports is fully acceptable for girls; playing dolls is still out of bounds for boys. Girls can move between dresses and jeans with nary a thought. Not so for boys; just the idea causes panic. Girls can get wild at slumber parties and roam the streets. In high school they can have sex and brag about it, even put notches on their belt. But it's not all that simple. Bragging could get her labeled a slut, not a player. And, sure, girls can wear jeans, but they are "pretty," and soft, and stylish, calling attention to her body. Boys can wear rough and tough clothes that can withstand an unself-conscious freedom of movement, clothes that stand up to whatever and whoever they tackle.

This pattern holds for nearly everything girls do—whether it's an activity they share with boys such as bicycle riding or computer games or whether it's considered by most to be "girls only," such as dolls and slumber parties. It may look like a prism of possibilities, but the assumption that a girl has full and unfettered access to male territory is an illusion. Whatever she chooses to do, she is told in a number of subtle ways that she needs to do it like a girl. This means doing it with attention to style, doing it with grace, doing it nicely or with a sexy, flirty air, and doing it knowing that others will see and comment on her doing it. This promotes a self-conscious concern with appearance and an assumption that girls are primarily responsible for relationships, nurturing, fashion, and decorating, all of which will have very real implications when she reaches adolescence and adulthood.

This script is easily seen in the dolls versus trucks activities of the younger children, but at ages eight, nine, and ten, kids take on a new level of extracurriculars: music lessons, sports, horseback riding, dance lessons, tae kwon do, and more. Parents want their children to have these extracurriculars; the more they do, the more chance they have to be good at something, to develop adult-child relationships that are supportive, and to become resilient when adolescence descends on them. It's not just how much but what they do that will shape their middle school and teen years.

Girls don't throw themselves over wholesale into the world of boys, glamour, and gossip. Yet from middle school onward they live in two worlds: the world of what they actually do (school, homework, sports, reading, music, babysitting, learning languages, drawing, playing computer games, getting tutored in some subject, training to be a lifeguard, taking care of a neighbor's dog) and the world of being a teenager (parties, IMing, clothes, boys, and shopping). Many kids do fine balancing these two worlds. They do all the everyday things while keeping a finger in the teenage pot, attempting to build a sense of self that is both authentically theirs, grounded in family, while still staying connected to peer culture. There is a lot at stake and lots of anxiety because life is in flux. Bodies are changing, romance enters the scene big time, and music, TV, and magazines catapult girls into new places and new choices.

Parents worry that their curious and lively girls will drop all the interesting things they have been pursuing—the activities that lead to careers and hobbies—and take on media-induced activities that channel them into being a teenager in a certain way. We worry, too, because there are few examples in the media of the glamour of training to be a lifeguard but plenty showing teenage girls looking pretty in a bikini while lounging poolside with a cool drink at her side. Will she make it into high school pursuing a developmental path that plays out her interests and talents, or will she direct her energy into a cardboard cutout teenage persona that is mostly style and little substance?

The girls in our survey told us that by high school they still engage in a lot of those great activities but are also very interested in a world of hyper-heterosexual romance, girlfriends and gossip, drugs and adventure—things they have learned are part of being a teen.

The Games She Plays and the Toys She Loves

> It's Great to be a Girl!
> Little girls love to play with dollhouses. . . . It's their way of learning about who they are and who they might be someday!
> Your little girl can . . . collect a dollhouse family just like her own. . . .
> Making decisions about what kind of furniture she likes and where it should go puts your little girl in control. . . .
> The road to imaginative fun and adventure is just ahead . . . recreating the familiar—like running errands around town. . . .
> Make her house a home with lots of Loving Family accessories.
> —FISHER-PRICE *flyer, 2002*

TOYS "R" US AS ALIEN CULTURE

A saunter through Toys "R" Us or Wal-Mart will teach you most of what you need to know about kids' toys. Three things will be apparent: (1) boys' toys and girls' toys are in separate aisles; (2) boys' toys are action toys, and girls' are homemaking, nurturing, or fashion toys; (3) boys' toys are red, blue, black, and green, and girls' are pink and purple.

Most parents have made these observations on their own. The way toys are advertised and sold, you'd think boys and girls came from different planets. The truth of the matter is that if men are from Mars and women are from Venus, it's because they've been educated in the language, customs, and behaviors of these stereotyped pseudo-planets from birth—and a lot of this education has been through toys. Even people who accept a strictly biological version of gender acknowledge that brain chemistry is affected by socialization. Repeating social responses to infants, for example, can affect the way the brain grows and functions. Giving girls crafts to make, houses to decorate, and dolls to nurture will predispose them to accessorizing, decorating houses, and caring for babies. Caring for babies is, of course, essential learning, but it ought to be essential for everyone.

In fact, boys and girls aren't all that different, especially at four, five, and six. If you ask kids this age about what it means to be a boy or girl, they'll say such things as boys are wild and rough, and girls are calm and gentle; girls wear bows in their hair, and boys wear bows on their necks; girls play with Barbies and stuffed animals, and boys play with action figures and trucks; boys play sports, and girls play dress-up. They know what you're looking for. Psychologists call this a "cognitive schema." But ask the kids what they *really* like to play, you'll get a more complicated response. We call this the real world. Lots of girls will say they like sports and fast cars, and many boys—at least those not teased about it—will say they like to dress up and play with stuffed animals and even Barbie. Girls can sometimes be quite wild and boys can be quite gentle. How can kids compete with the likes of major corporations that are relentlessly pushing a strictly gender-coded version of beauty and toughness? Maybe they can't, but you can offer even young children words and questions that open up possibilities and help them hold on to all the things they love.

This will be hard to do. Sharon's student went to Toys "R" Us to buy a present for an eight-year-old niece. The salesclerk asked. "What does she like to do?" He replied. "She likes to swim." The clerk took him straight to the Barbie aisle and pointed out the pool set.

Since we're talking about planets, let's imagine we're aliens sent to Earth to gather information about human beings. We land in the girls' toys section of Toys "R" Us, Wal-Mart, or Target, thinking that what we see represents the people of this planet. Here is what we learn about these supposedly imaginative, industrious, and somewhat volatile earthlings:

Humans are obsessed with pink. Pink is such an important color that they dress all their babies in it. They decorate their make-believe houses and furniture; their bicycles; their dress-up clothes; their beauty sets, dishes, tea sets, blow-up chairs, doll strollers, karaoke sets, sleeping bags, cars, castles, jewelry, diaries, games, and building sets almost exclusively in pink. Other colors show up from time to time, but humans avoid them as much as possible unless they are being trendy or fashionable.

Humans nurture everything but especially babies, and they practice with baby dolls. Their dolls have names like Little Mommy: Nurture, Love, Grow, and they want unending attention from their owners. They have doll carriages, high chairs, cribs, changing tables, and armoires. Dolls coo and cry and demand food. Earthlings live to nurture even if they do not have families; for example, Happy Family Baby Doctor Barbie nurtures other human families. Humans also nurture stuffed animals, mostly cats and ponies. Humans who aren't baby doctors are veterinarians.

Humans must look pretty and fashionable. They must also make everyone else look pretty and fashionable. Trendy is another word for fashionable and means wearing tight, form-fitting clothing such as low-rise miniskirts, skintight pants, and crop tops. These can be found in bright colors, often with pink and black somewhere. Humans practice from age two at looking trendy with such things as Little Tykes Fashion Time Talking Vanities, which tell them to "play at the lighted mirror and choose an accessory," while a "magical" voice prompts: "Your hair is beautiful," "That's a pretty color nail polish," or "Don't forget to put the dryer away." (Humans are very neat, too.) By ages four and five they practice wearing fashionable makeup and hairstyles that are glam. (Note: *Glam* is another word for fashionable and trendy. Having so many words for the same thing is a clue that this thing is very important to their survival.) They wear trendy purses in order to carry what they need to stay glam, and they create fashionable accessories to enhance their trendy look. They buy small plastic dolls called Polly Pockets with hundreds of pieces of fashionable clothing to try on and they buy these dolls fashionable cars to take them to fashionable "clubs" where they meet other fashionable dolls, sit in hot tubs, and pretend to drink fashionable drinks.

Humans love jewelry and accessories, either to wear or to decorate with. They love them so much that they spend a lot of their time sitting still indoors making them. They are told on the packaging of these products that "the right accessory can make the outfit," and they take this seriously. They make rings, bracelets, earrings, necklaces, barrettes, porcelain lamps, trinket boxes, picture frames, window decorations, pot holders, and dolls. Even toys that seem as if they could be used for building buildings, bridges, and vehicles are used to make decorative crafts, such as Lego's Clikits' Cool Room Frames, the Ultimate Jewelry Click-N-Store Jewelry Set, Pillow Décor-N-More, and Ultimate Design Studio. Clikits' motto is "Change your mind? Change your design!" so maybe humans are known to be indecisive.

Humans love to decorate houses. They have toy houses where they practice decorating with fancy furniture, rugs, and accessories. More importance is placed on having a nicely decorated house than on the people in the house or what goes on in the house. We know that the humans in the house are a happy family or a loving family, and almost all the families available are white, two-parent, two-child, and middle class. These houses come in different sizes, but they all suggest that all humans live in large, gorgeous, comfortable homes containing a happy, loving family.

Humans clean, cook, and entertain. They have many ways to practice these activities, including ironing boards, mops, brooms, plastic fruit and vegetables, toy pots and pans, sinks, stoves, and microwaves. They have a mini baking oven that cooks food with a lightbulb. They especially like parties where they sit their dolls and stuffed animals around a table for what appears to be high tea.

Wearing the right accessories is critically important. A human cannot be seen in public without properly accessorizing.

Humans shop. They love to buy new things. There are rows and rows of things to buy, and the things they buy tell them to buy more things. Buying stuff is the most important activity they can do, and there is no downside to buying everything they want. For example, they have more clothes than they can use. Barbie Fashion Vinyl Clings, tiny two-dimensional dolls that stick to vinyl backdrops, offer more than 135 different outfits for Barbie and her friend Kayla. Dressing Barbie means associating her clothes with the activity of shopping and then coming home to a fancy house to get ready for a night of clubbing.

All humans are queens, brides, princesses, fairies, ballerinas, and mermaids, or they are sexy shopping divas, pop stars, and cheerleaders. Princesses and divas alike wear tight, form-fitting clothes; they have big breasts, flat tummies, and long, skinny legs. Divas wear clothes that show more of their bodies and have lots of accessories such as cell phones, makeup compacts, purses, and hair clips. Most of the sexy divas have dark skin while most of the princesses and fairies have light skin. Sometimes there are creatures called "boys," and they have cars, skateboards, and surfboards. Otherwise, these humans exercise by dancing at clubs or at the beach, shopping, and dressing up.

Humans are really happy about all this. They want more and more of it. They smile all the time and shop a lot, and encourage this behavior in others.

Aliens would probably conclude that this is a lovely, if not strange, culture, full of warmth, lightness, and interesting things. Their commanding officer might, after looking over those notes, decide that humans from this planet would be excellent domestic helpers and swoop them up to serve their alien masters who have more active, empowering, or intellectually challenging things to do.

Like those aliens, at some time or other we all have looked at this world of pink bows and teacups and thought, "How delightful." But what's missing? The rest of the colors of the rainbow, to start. And, there are no really challenging activities. No building sets for actual building. No rockets or science kits (unless mixing lip balm flavors or makeup colors constitutes science). No balls or bats, motorized toys, or action figures. In other words, nothing that encourages adventure or exploration outside the home or the local dance club. Nothing that requires activity or testing physical limits except those cute accessorized bikes. This version of girlhood does not prepare girls for a life of real possibility.

NO ONE WINS IN THE DIVA DOLL WARS

Let's meet the (relatively) new dolls in the hood. Barbie had barely turned fifty when Cloe, Dana, Jade, Sasha, Yasmin, Fianna, Nevra, and Meygan moved in on her territory. In a brazen act of disrespect to the icon of the doll world, the Bratz (with a little halo over the *a*) girls brought their "stylin'," "funky," "kickin'" selves to Toys "R" Us, KB Toys, Wal-Mart, Target, and other popular toy retailers throughout the country. Fashion mavens such as Groovy Girls and Polly Pockets have done pretty well, too, but Bratz have cleaned up.

The queen of pink, however, didn't go down without a fight. Marketing Executive Barbie must have been paying attention because she quickly diversified into the multicultural My Scene Barbie and the urban street-smart Flava dolls, complete with a graffiti-covered cardboard "street stand" so she has "a spot to hang out." Flavas flopped. (Were we to believe this represents all urban girls?) Barbie also lightened up considerably by breaking up with boring steady, Ken, and finding a new Aussie beach boy. Still, if our local Wal-Marts are any indication, the war is all but won. A walk through the diva doll aisles found four separate sections of Bratz and Lil' Bratz dolls and their Boyz ("W'sup! My name is Eitan."). In addition, there was a full section of scenes such as the Lounge Loft and Sun-kissed Summer Pool Set, and cool rides on an F.M. cruiser and "rev your engines for a blazin'" motorcycle (for the Boyz, natch). Compare that to two small sections of My Scene Barbie, and an even smaller section of Cali Barbies (the California beach scene dolls with the Aussi hunk). The layout in Kmart was similar.

There is no doubt that the spunky, sassy, girl-of-the-millennium attitude of the Bratz dolls has given Barbie a run for her money. If sales are an indication, girls and parents alike see something cooler and more fun in these multicultural dolls. Bratz dolls don't share Barbie's "body issues," at least not the ones parents have complained about for years. They can stand on flat feet, for one thing, and they don't wear a double-D-cup bra. But like Barbie there is just one body type—thin—and their big heads and feet make their skinny bodies seem even more emaciated. A kickin' attitude clearly doesn't translate into criticizing the fashion industry for promoting a body type that most girls and women can't attain.

Barbie has long been called a bad role model for young girls partly because of her obsession with an all-things-pink fashion. It didn't help that in a country with a rapidly changing demographic and an emerging girl power message, Barbie was so predictable, so suburban, and so white. (Even young girls could see that the Barbies of color were just white Barbies with dark skin.) MGA Entertainment Inc. saw an opportunity. In the face of this unrealistic icon of womanhood, Bratz dolls could be credited simply for being *not Barbie*.

But are Bratz dolls all that different? Don't let their sassy, funky, girls-gone-wild descriptions fool you. In actuality these dolls are stereotypically feminine. Unlike Barbie, who sort of recovered from the bad press of saying "Math is hard" some years ago by morphing into everything from Dr. Barbie to President Barbie, the Bratz dolls are unapologetically focused on—no, obsessed with—fashion and boys. There *is* no other career unless maybe it's modeling the animal skin miniskirts and bikinis they come with. These are "the girls with a passion for fashion"—period. But in case they should come off as too hard-core for moms of younger girls, the funky edginess of their clothes are softened with cute names and descriptions. Blond, blue-eyed, sexy Cloe, who is pictured resting her right palm reservedly against her cheek, says, "My friends call me 'Angel' because that's what I am!" (It is no surprise that Cloe is Barbie's real rival; she's the doll most coveted by preteens.) Dana's nickname is Sugar Shoes because "when I step out, I do it sweet!" Nevra is sweet "like honey," which is why she is called Queen B. Yasmin's nickname is Pretty Princess.

One thing that distinguishes Bratz from Barbie is the Bratz Boyz. They're not Ken-like steadies for these girls on the town, but more like friends with benefits. But their nicknames are as stereotypical as the girls': Viper, Fox, Dragon, Blaze, and Panther. A few of the Bratz girls have animal nicknames, too, but they are of small and cute animals. Kool Kat and Bunny Boo.

Like Barbie, the Bratz dolls come with different accessories. In fact, they make Barbie look as though she's saving for college. There's no mere pink convertible for them. The funky world of Bratz includes all kinds of rides and loads of "kickin' accessoreez," such as movin', groovin', coollectible cards, a fashion organizer ("input names and birthdays to see if you make good fashion sense"), dazzlin' door beads, and an electric funk matchmaker journal. ("Is your love life superstylin'?" "Keep your love life organized." "Rate your love match.") Is this really what eight-year-olds are into? Bratz sassiness may have the feel of independence, but it's the same tired message in new kickin' garb: Get a boyfriend and shop.

Still, what makes Bratz work for preteen girls *is* the pretense of choosing a lavish lifestyle. Barbie invented this, but Bratz takes it to another level. It's not only the frenzy of consumerism but also the lifestyle itself. Barbie had a dream house to come home to, but her nightlife was ours to create. Bratz gives the dolls a variety of scenes to choose from and tells us how the girls experience them. The Funk 'N' Glow collection has the Bratz dolls "hitting the town and dancing the night away" in soft, feathery boas, midriffs exposed, covered in fairy-like glitter (hence Funk 'N' Glow). These are the girls who "know how important it is to be seen!" Let's practice being sex objects.

The Bratz dolls also exist to highlight gender differences. The Sun-Kissed Summer Pool Set prepares the girls for a "super stylin' day at the beach," whereas the Bratz boys' complementary Sun-Kissed Summer collection describes them as getting ready for a "super sizzlin' day at the beach." The girls are there to look hot; the boys are there for fun. (The Toys "R" Us ad for this scene shows the girls in bikinis sitting in a hot tub, mixing drinks [!] while the boys play guitar and stand with their surfboards.) The Slumber Party is girls only, as is the Super Stylin' Runway Disco, the Stylin' Salon 'N' Spa, and the Stylin' Hair Studio.

Can My Scene Barbie and friends compete? Mattel has given it a whirl, with collections such as: School, Surf Rider, and In the Tub. They have sold out girls to keep up. School is now about being popular: Madison tells us, "I'm a shoe in for Best Dressed at school this year. But that's the thing about style, you always have to outdo yourself. So I think I'm gonna have to take an extra class. It's called shopping." And don't miss the Aldo shoes product placement in My Scene.

Here's where My Scene Barbie makes a fatal mistake. The "cute boy" refrain, the obsession with being popular, and the explicit love of all things "girly" give My Scene Barbie an air of desperation. The Bratz girls are big because they present a front; they disguise these same obsessions with a sassy know-what-they-want attitude. Really popular girls don't talk it, they walk it. With Bratz's videos, their own Twentieth Century Fox movie, the Girl's Toy of the Year Award (please!), and Property of the Year Award by the Toy Industry Association for 2004 under their belt, we have to wonder if this is really the kind of girl the public wants to endorse.

In all fairness, Barbie still has her devotees. Search out reviews of Bratz or My Scene Barbie on the Web, and you'll find a diva debate that you'd never imagine—loyal Barbie enthusiasts attacking Bratz for being too sexy; Bratz lovers accusing My Scene Barbie of being a wannabe Bratz. Barbie as Beta Girl. Who would have predicted it?

No matter. We suspect both MGA and Mattel enjoy this online scrap. Like boys watching girls fight over them, the companies know they're off the hook, and they expect to have a sizzlin' good time with the money they rake in.

EDUCATIONAL TOYS

Toys "R" Us isn't for everyone. Although it is a multinational, multiconglomerate corporation with about sixteen hundred stores in twenty-eight countries, there are alternatives. But before you decide to avoid Wal-Mart, Target, and the like, remember that choosing "educational" doesn't always mean choosing gender equity. Our kids love the Discovery Store and other stores like it. It has all sorts of cool science stuff about space, the earth, biology, and technology. But check out the catalog. Below is a list by gender of what kids featured in the catalog are doing. Guess which is the boys' list and which is the girls' list.

LIST A

Helping mother cut flowers with "home florist system"

Eating a snack

Playing indoor golf

Playing with an interactive educational globe

Hanging with Mom

Flying a kite

Watching someone launch a rocket

Getting money from a play ATM machine

Making a pot on a pottery wheel

Watching a kid use a radio-controlled hovercraft

LIST B

Looking through a telescope with Dad

Chasing a radio-controlled jet

Holding the controls of a radio-controlled jet

Playing a foosball game

Playing basketball

Flying a kite

Launching a rocket

Launching a UFO

Launching an air-powered glider

Using a spy tool off a spy utility belt

Using a metal detector

Wearing a Night Vision Communicator

Using a voice converter system

Playing with a chemistry set or forensic lab

Looking through a telescope alone

Performing a magic trick

Working a radio-controlled hovercraft

Flying a radio-controlled helicopter

Particularly offensive is the thought that girls' play will involve shopping and could make use of a toy ATM machine. Where's the science and discovery in that? Also offensive is that she is used as a prop to observe and admire the boy working the controls for the radio-controlled hovercraft and launching a rocket. The only gender-neutral toy that the Discovery catalog features is the kite. Don't we want girls to discover the world, too?

BOARD GAMES: FIBBING, FAIRY PRINCESSES, AND FASHION

Next comes the wonderful world of board games, something most children are introduced to through the classic Candy Land. Surely this is a genderless category. You may be surprised. We looked at 101 board games for children. We noticed first that a near equal number of photos of boys and girls was depicted on the box covers (43 girls and 41 boys). But in counting cartoon kids there were almost twice as many boys (91 boys and 51 girls).

The idea that male is generic tends to hold true for central characters in the games. Mr. Boddy in Clue is male, as well as the cartoon body in the game Operation. The head popping open with all sorts of trivia for Trivial Pursuit is a male head. When a child gets four labels for naming the four hippos in Hungry Hippos, three names are male and the fourth is Happy. The frog in Mr. Mouth is male: "Watch *his* eyes jiggle." Then there's the old Monopoly guy, Mr. Moneybags, and Mr. Potato Head.

Okay, some of these are older games and are bound to be more sexist. Mrs. Potato Head came later. But take a look at the newer game, Guess Who, which tries to be diverse with African American– and Latino-looking faces to choose from. But there are only five females to eighteen males.

Next, let's consider who's in control. Figures of authority are twice as likely to be male than female. The male authority figures on game boxes were as follows: builder, bus driver, fireman, cowboy, farmer (twice), political supporter, guitarist, he-man, painter, tech support worker, scuba diver, wheeler-dealer, world leader, doctor, millionaire, and astronaut. The game of Life was different, and our survey told us that girls love this one. Still, while a woman ran for office with a male political supporter behind her, the nurse and the shopper are—who else?—moms. Let's not forget the pink figures for females and blue figures for males.

Who's out of control? Any driver of a car is Dad, not Mom. And it's always a guy who is "out of control" in a game, and gets to have wild, kooky fun: a male screwdriver, a boy golfing, a man driving a backhoe. The only "out of control" fun a girl can have is shopping!

Who wins and who loses on these board game box covers? We counted how many girls and boys were shown acting in some way (for example, placing a chip on the board or throwing a bean bag) as opposed to watching, waiting, reacting, catching, or poised to act. Twice as many boys were shown in action (twenty-six to thirteen) and only boys and male characters were ever shown winning the game. This is astonishing when you think about it. Not only do boys win the game, but they are allowed to express exuberance when they play and when they win. Boys are depicted raising a fist with the "yes" sign after making a good move or winning the game; another boy raises both hands over his head (no girl does this on a box), and a cartoon guy jumps up and clicks his heels.

Of the 101 board games we examined, only six seemed to be marketed to girls alone. Hasbro's update of the old Milton Bradley game Mall

Madness is an electronic shopping spree, where girls scramble for sales and trendy looks. Out of cash? Be sure to hit the ATM because the first one to buy six things and make it to the right destination wins!

In Pretty Pretty Princess, girls compete with one another to collect the most jewelry. Fashion was the focus of two other games. In Disney's Princess Enchanted Dream Ball Game, girls become their favorite princess and proceed to gather items they need for the ball: a crown, shoes, flowers, and jewelry. You'd think a cool ride might help? What one wears and looks like is key to getting ready for the "fairest ball of all." After gathering items, the girl meets her prince, and in the end, the first to get Tinker Bell's wand wins. The third fashion game was based on the Bratz dolls. There's a "fashion emergency," it says on the box, and "you've gotta look good." How about that "totally hot halter" the box cover asks girls who are seven years old and up.

More surprising are the games that highlight girls' purported deceitfulness. Truth or Dare has long been a slumber party favorite, and Slam books with their potential to hurt or reveal secrets are thought of as almost always as in the purview of girls. Game makers obviously saw a market niche. Girls eight years old and up are initiated into the world of betrayal by girls through games that make light of this difficult aspect of girls' friendships. Are you "4" real, asks one board game. Are you the "truest of them all" or a "first class fibber" asks another. In Are You 4 Real? the object of the game is to fool your friends by making up a story that they'll believe. Three girls on a rug are surrounded by pillows, popcorn, and drinks, chatting away in supposed friendship. But the object of the game is to be the best liar. In the second game, Fib Finder, the object is to be the "truest of them all." There is a packet of questions to ask each other, teaching girls what should be secrets in their world. There are questions on boys and boyfriends and crushes—secret territory. There are also questions about "bad" behavior such as "Did you ever put a piece of gum under a chair or table?"—as if this is something that a girl would want to lie about to protect her image as the "good girl." Can you imagine a bunch of boys asking each other that? The answer would probably be "Sure. What's the big deal?" Most disturbing, though, was the question "Have you ever eaten a whole pint of ice cream in one sitting?" Why should this be something that a girl should keep secret or be ashamed of? Why should she want to lie about this? Girls eight years old and up are being taught that girls shouldn't pig out now and again because it's shameful to do so. Again, imagine the boys: "Yeah, what's the big deal" or "Yeah, and my mom was so mad because that was for the whole family." The shame or shock is that it is taboo for a girl, something she shouldn't do. A game doesn't give a girl an eating disorder, but the message here and in many advertisements is about secret eating. A girl's pleasure in eating has to be secret because it's wrong, it's harmful.

One could argue that if girls are on the covers of games, at least they're halfway there. Probably there were even fewer girls on game boxes twenty years ago. Yes, but is halfway enough for half the population? Girls want to play. Girls like to win. They want permission to pump their fists in the air and say "Yes!" They play these games, place pieces, move cards, and shake dice, so why not depict them doing so on a box cover? Why not give them games about more than fashion, shopping, and secrets? There is no conspiracy here—just stupid, unconscious sexism that associates winning, action, and skill with maleness.

Physical Play: Bikes, Sports, and . . . Cheerleading?

With all sorts of government calls to action about the nation's obesity epidemic, you'd think that getting girls active and participating in sports would be a priority in most homes. Exercise isn't only for weight loss or team competition; it's key to health and well-being. It's about equal participation in a major form of entertainment and leisure activity. Why does girls' participation in sports diminish from junior high to high school? Why is it difficult to keep girls active? Because the world around them has "prettified" it so much that the quintessential physical activity for teenage girls now is either cheerleading or dance, and if a sport, it's soccer. Cheerleading and dance are fun activities, but why not all the other options? Why not football or baseball for girls? It seems as though we can't see boys and girls doing the same kinds of things.

BICYCLES: RIDE, BABY, RIDE

There are rules for bike riding: Wear a helmet. Signal when you turn. Don't ride on sidewalks when there's a lot of pedestrian traffic. If you're on the street, stay to the side of the road.

There are also rules that show kids how to be certain kinds of bike riders. They're less explicit than the rules of the road; in fact, some are painted right on the bikes. Girl bikes are called Bliss, Sweetie, Teen Talk, Princess Dreamer, and Glitter Express, to name a few. Boy bikes are called

Hulk, Dinosaur, Overdrive, Arrow, and Firepower. Those are just for very small two-wheelers. Go up a few inches and you get Girl Stuff, My Special Things, Star Bright, and Petal Patch, as opposed to Qualifier, Spitfire, Thrust, and "Barebones" (presumably because accessorizing is a girl thing). Even in the older kids' mountain bikes we have Destiny for girls and Challenger for boys. There are no twenty-inch dirt bikes for girls unless they want to ride something called Basher, Prowler, or Big Daddy. No Big Mamas to be seen!

These names are guides for children about how to ride their bikes and how to be a kid riding a bike. They spell out feelings that you can have while riding and people you can pretend to be while playing.

It's not only the labels. Visually the bikes are quite different and give additional lessons about how girls and boys should be bike riders. Almost all the girls' bikes are pink or purple. The boys' bikes are yellow, green, blue, red, maroon, silver, black, or combinations of these colors. Unlike the boys' bikes, most girls' bikes are accessorized with streamers from the handlebars, little backpacks or purse attachments, horns, spoke beads, and the occasional water bottle. These accessories provide more opportunity to decorate the bike with flowers, hearts, or glitter.

All this tells girls that how she looks is as or more important than what she does. It tells them the kinds of movements that are acceptable, who can be out of control, who can be aggressive, who can compete, and basically who can be active. When they ride, they are invited to feel as soft as an "Island Breeze," not ride as wild as a hurricane or go as fast as a Fun Fair's Whirlarama. Boys can "Thrust," "Bash," put it in "Overdrive" or give it some "Firepower." Yes, the movements and icons suggested by the boys' bikes have a violent tinge, but aggression and aggressive movements are part of children's fantasy worlds. The solution is not to take away aggressive images but to allow them in both boys' and girls' fantasy worlds so that they can play with these feelings in fantasy.

Is permission to be out of control a good thing? In some ways. To push one's limits, to really let go is part of being fully embodied. Besides, we're talking about bike riding and children's fantasies, not the real world. Bikes such as Haywire and Chaos give boys that permission. Girls will stay under control with Pretty, Dreamer, and Charmer.

Boys can compete. They can be a Qualifier or a Racer; they can dare others to race them on their Challenger or throw down the Gauntlet. Girls are taught at an early age that they shouldn't or maybe can't compete. Some parents may think this is a good thing and that men and boys get into difficulty for being too competitive. Well, this is certainly true, but just because boys and men sometimes take competition too far doesn't mean girls shouldn't think about competing, qualifying, and winning. Why deprive them of the joy of these activities?

The most striking difference, however, between girls' bikes and boys' bikes is the suggestion of who they can be. Potential jobs and fantasy roles are suggested to boys through such bike names as Judge, DJ, Big Daddy, Road Tech, Dirt Racer, Hulk, Kobra, and Jackal. Girls are given adjectives to describe themselves, such as Pretty and Groovy. They can't be real people with real roles to play—not judges or drivers or technicians. Their job is to look good or aspire to be a Teen, Star, or Princess who always looks good.

Is it different for toddlers who long for a Big Wheel just about as soon as they can walk? On the box for the Cozy Coupe II two boys are driving while a girl stands by and reaches for the teddy bear in the back compartment. Boys drive; girls watch.

But some girls are driving. Look at the box covers of the Pretty in Pink trike, the Princess Rider, the Glitter Girl Trike, and the Little Ms. Rider. The boys drive vehicles like the Rock, Roll 'n' Ride Trike, the Excavator, the Police Car, the Tonka Rider, the Lil Lightning Scooter, the Streethawk, and the Nitro X-treme. Little Ms. Rider is pink; Rescue Rider is red. She's a "Little Ms.," but he's a hero.

None of this is any surprise to a parent who has walked through a toy store. Some smart parents bemoan the fact that their little girls go straight to the pink glitter bikes and say, "Isn't it pretty?" They've been told in a million ways that "pretty" is valuable and they're valuable when pretty. What if there were a big poster of a girl on a hot red and black bike, with an expression on her face of unparalleled joy from speed, racing her older brother and winning while both parents look on smiling. Or, better yet, instead of winning at the expense of a boy, why not have her doing a wheelie on her bike while a group of boys and girls look on admiringly. The bike could be called Wild One or You Go, Girl or Athlete or even Crusher. She'd be actively taking a risk and being admired for her skill, not her looks. Do you remember the joy and freedom of bike riding? There are little girls who would rather ride than walk, who take risks, build their skills, and love to compete. Why can't they be represented in the culture? Can't we make bikes for them, too?

SHE TAKES THE FIELD! GIRLS PLAYING SOCCER

What is lovelier than a fall day in Vermont? A fall day when girls with red dye in their hair get dirty, bounce balls off their heads, and run down a soccer field. Every October in Sharon's hometown, during breathtaking peak foliage, the town's recreation department holds the Newbery Cup competition. Similar events take place across the country. From 8:30 in the morning until 3:30 in the afternoon the town soccer teams compete in short twenty-minute games for a grand prize that marks the conclusion of soccer season. Anyone who wants to challenge Title IX, the 1972 law that gave girls equal access to sports, should come here first and see the fruits of that amendment.

We think it is just as important to celebrate the things that are going right for girls as it is to condemn the things that bring them down. Soccer seems to be going right—at least in Shelburne, Vermont, on these coed soccer teams whose participants are in first to eighth grades. One-third to one-half of every team is girls, reflecting a national average of about 40 percent. In the United States, soccer is a mostly white, middle-class sport, and it's even more so in Vermont where there is so little diversity. But that's a different issue, and city coaches know that funds are needed to bring grassy and water sports to city girls. For now, looking at these players we can say, "Wow, these girls are good!"

The gender equality on the field is impressive. First of all, the girls and boys seem about equal in height and strength, although it's hard to tell from the sidelines. Girls seem just as likely to get into the mix to try to get the ball as boys are and are just as likely to move the ball down the field in one big kick. Both play goalie and seem equally likely to yell "What?" to the ref after a bad call and to block a player or a ball with their full body, sometimes resulting in injury and tears.

There were some differences. Observing two different first and second grade teams and four different third and fourth grade teams, it was clear that the boys tried to kick the ball into the net and go for a goal while racing down the field a little more frequently than the girls. They seemed much more willing or able to take the ball halfway down the field through footwork and good zigzagging. Maybe on these particular teams the boys were in positions that required them to do more of this kind of playing, and maybe this reflected the choice of the coach about where to place the girls, blocking and defending rather than pushing forward. But it was different at a later age. The girls on the seventh and eighth grade team went for the goals just as often as the boys did, which shows, as research suggests, that practice is what gives any kid an edge. Still, like the younger girls, these older girls didn't seem to "take the field"— possess the ball, keep it away from others, and run with it down the whole field—as often as did boys.

Why don't the girls control the ball all the way? Are they passing more? (Girls are supposedly better "team" players.) Is it because they don't run as fast? (It certainly didn't seem so on these teams.) Maybe boys are more likely to block them or challenge their possession of the ball when they run. (Not observed, but a possibility.) Or maybe it reflects a lack of entitlement. Whose field is it? Who *owns* that field? Who feels most comfortable *taking* the field?

In philosopher Iris Marion Young's essay "Throwing Like a Girl," she contends that girls from very early on are taught to use less space and to protect their bodies and their selves. They learn "inhibited intentionality," or, to use a sports term, lack of "follow-through." Is their passing a show of "nice" teamwork on the field or a learned behavior of letting someone else follow through. Girls who stick with soccer throughout their childhood may have to *un*learn inhibiting their approach, their running, and their movements through practice, season after season.

Why wouldn't girls feel entitled to the field? Most of the major sports on TV show men doing it. Most of the coaches are dads. Most of the sports talk is done at school by boys and at home by men. Even the two pickup games observed that day were initiated by high school boys and dads. Did they ask permission to use the empty fields, or did they see a space and claim it? After years of soccer mom participation, why don't we ever see a pickup game with moms and daughters?

We asked who is cheering the girls? "Go, Amanda! Go! Go! Go!" "Take a shot, Olivia." The deep voices of the dads and the coaches, difficult to tell apart, reign at the sidelines. Moms are there, too, in even greater numbers, but they are often quieter. All the coaches observed on the day we watched were men and dads. Even though Title IX existed when they went to school, only a few of the moms were athletes themselves while many of the dads were much more involved.

The two mothers who stood out as real yellers were the moms of girls who were considered stars on their separate teams. Were these girls stars because their moms pushed them out there? Or did their moms feel more pleasure and excitement because their daughters were so good?

Colette Dowling, author of *The Frailty Myth*, suggests there is something called "the dad factor." When dads delight in encouraging their daughters in sports, when they give them tough coaching, girls excel. These girls grow up to say, "I owe it all to Dad." Their pride is not just in their own ability but in their crossing over and being successful at something traditionally male. Is there any way to get around this problem of girls still seeing sports as male territory? What can moms do?

Young girls are twice as likely to be sedentary as young boys. Dowling suggests that it's not good to let girls play all day in the doll corner, under the belief that fantasy and role-playing are good for them. Maybe moms can get their girls outside and start some mother-daughter pickup games. Maybe dad can make dinner while mom tosses a ball around. Moms can make a commitment to develop their own sports skills, coach, and learn the rules even if they haven't had the background that Title IX gave younger moms and their daughters. Both parents can encourage their daughter to try out for teams. They can try to get their town, school, or Boys & Girls Club to take girls' sports as seriously as boys' sports or they can take their daughter to see women's games. If they don't do team sports, they can take their daughter swimming, hiking, skiing, or mountain climbing. And, we all need to stop comparing girls to boys when it comes to athletic ability. Sports is one area where it is okay to learn the rules and pass them on. Then, when you do, scream at the sidelines, "Go, Laura, go, go, go!"

BRING IT ON: CHEERLEADING

One activity in which girls are invited to rave, yell, be athletic, jump, run, and bring it on is cheerleading. But what exactly are they being asked to bring on? We don't think it's the gymnastics' devotion to bodily control and competition. Images of cheerleading are everywhere in your daughter's world, creating impressions about what it means to be a cheerleader that it might not live up to and impressions that cheerleading coaches hate. The girls who quit cheerleading after one season say such things as "It's hard work!" and "The coach was mean." Initially, many thought cheerleading involved having fun, looking pretty, and being popular. The depiction of cheerleading, even when the hard work involved is shown, emphasizes the pretty and popular quotient. Even when journalists such as Cathy Booth Thomas write in *Time* about the high level of athleticism of cheerleaders, they are certain to add comments about jealousy, popularity contests, the expectation to be a fashion plate, and meddling moms.

First, let's look at the impression that kids get about cheerleading from movies. Moviemakers and screenwriters try to have it both ways. In movies such as *Bring It On* and *Bring It On 2* they try to do justice to the new version of cheerleaders as competitive gymnast-dancers, every bit as athletic as boys and girls who do other sports; however, they also perpetuate the old version of cheerleader as the popular blond sex goddess that men long for. If you don't think that second version of cheerleader is still around, just do a Web search and try to make your way through all the cheerleader porn to find a little corner for girls to chat in. It ain't easy. "Bring it on" works as an aggressive, competitive athlete's cry at the same time that it works as the come-hither call of the sex kitten cheer girl.

Girls love the movie *Bring It On*. Here is a sampling of some of the cheer lines featured in the movie: "I'm wanted. I'm hot! I'm everything you're not!" "Who am I? Just guess! Guys wanna touch my chest!" "I'm danger. I roar! I swear I'm not a whore!" Others cheer about being "on speed" and end with the line from the shampoo commercial, "Hate us 'cause we're beautiful" and add "Well, we don't like you, either!"

These tongue-in-cheek cheers come at the beginning of *Bring It On* when Torrence, played by pretty, blond Kirsten Dunst, has a dream about cheerleading that ends with her naked and embarrassed as jocks in the stands laugh at her and cry out, "Nice rack." It's an interesting way to start a movie that purportedly is about "real" cheerleading. Soon after this scene we see "real" cheerleaders in bras and panties in the locker room. Two of the nastier cheerleaders (being snobby is also a cheerleading stereotype) make fun of one girl's "big butt." (It's a tiny butt, of course; no one in PG-13 movies is allowed a real big butt.) We are made to feel that this is the sordid inside story of girls getting together, and when Torrence is elected captain of the cheerleading team, another girl supports the subplot of girl cattiness by calling her a slut and calling the "real" gymnast who joins the team (emphasizing to the audience that cheering can't be "real" gymnastics), an *uber*dyke and a big dykey loser.

To its credit the movie shows that cheerleading is hard work and takes a combination of musical, dancing, and gymnastic talent. The movie also presents a team of African American cheerleaders doing their thing and doing it better than the white team who stole their routines. When the cheerleaders raise money via girls in bikinis giving car washes, we know that even the movie's director doesn't buy the line that cheerleaders give him—that it's really about gymnastics, dance, and competition, not about bodies and looking good. While the credits run at the end of the movie, just to make sure that any good wishes toward a new kind of cheerleading get undermined, the director features the cheer teams doing some dirty dancing and cheering, "C'mon. Give it to me any way you can."

Cheerleaders are a happy bunch in the movies as well as on the professional football field. It's part of the job description. In one *American Cheerleader* article defending cheerleading, the author wrote that cheerleading is every bit a sport because it requires speed, strength, agility, gymnastic ability, hand-eye coordination, rhythm, and dance ability. Moreover, unlike most sports, "it also has to be performed with flair and a smile." Why? Because the central purpose, no matter how difficult the routine or preparation for it, is to look good and help a crowd cheer on other people (usually guys) who are working their hardest to compete.

Cheer defenders will point out that you have to be strong and solid rather than tiny and thin to do the stunts. The girls we know who are on the bottom of the pyramid love it there. They feel strong and powerful; perhaps they are not quite as visible as the perky little girls on the top of the pyramid, but they love the feeling of strength it gives them.

A quick look through *American Cheerleader* magazine gives some indication of what is important in real as well as movie cheerleading. Alas, the articles on hair, beauty, grades, decorating, and careers give the magazine a *Seventeen* feel. The ads are mostly about various competitions, clothes, and fund-raising relating to cheerleading. But in the beauty department, interestingly enough, hair removers are advertised more than makeup, deodorants, or acne creams. One can imagine the importance of hairlessness when you picture the outfits and think about the splits, the tosses, and the short skirts.

Take a look at the featured cheerleaders in *American Cheerleader* who are described as role models for younger cheerleaders. All white, each of them has a quality that shows her to be kind and helpful, a "good" girl. Missy won Miss Congeniality at the Snow Queen Pageant; Lauren coaches a special needs squad; Kristen volunteers as a mentor at her local grade school; Amy volunteers at the hospital; Gina raises money for animal shelters; and Kacie has a near perfect GPA. It's a veritable Miss America pageant of do-gooders. Of the Honorable Mentions, one enjoys scrapbooking, another loves to dance, and a third likes to shop.

Imagine a different set of cheerleaders: Jamie plays the drums and started her own funk/groove band; Taisha shadowed her senator for a day in Congress; Kelsey won a snowmobiling race in Anchorage; Devorah began an ALLY group for friends of gay and lesbian students at her high school; Mara wrote and performed in her own one-woman play at her community theater. Why don't these sound like cheerleaders? Because they don't fit the mold of pretty, kind, nice, helpful, or, as in the movie *Bring It On*, sexy *uber*girl.

Ivy League schools have cheer teams with smart women, so one article implied. It featured eight squads in which there was more diversity in weight, color, and race than in the whole magazine. This seems to suggest that among smart women the idea is being supported that cheerleading is open to anyone who will work at it rather than to certain types of girls and women. This is good.

Does this mean girls can enter this *uber*girl activity and undermine it—make it a sport, transform it so that it's not about popularity, wholesomeness, smiling, showing off your body, and being pretty? Can they steal it away from the porn industry that beckons "Cheerleader sex pics—see them having sex in their cheerleader uniforms after the big game."

Girls aren't going to be able to redefine cheerleading as a sport on their own. Even as they defend their sport on the Internet, arguing in chat rooms that they *are* athletes, they still buy into the image. Look at their chat room names: cheer chick, cheer angel, cheer diva, cheer princess, cheer shopper, hotcheer, blondecheer, sweetasapumpkin, cheerglitter, and preciousgirl. These same girls are trying to convince us that they're athletes. They're the same girls who call other chat room girls bitches and sluts, and who put down other girls for composing negative cheers such as "I dunno what I've been told; Colebrooks' colors look like mold" (which is about as clever as the chants get).

Girls who want to be cheerleaders like to dance and have people look at them. That's not all bad. Dancing is wonderful and a great way to express creativity, talent, and, yes, sexuality. Girls who want to be cheerleaders like to work together to put on routines and stunts. There's nothing wrong with that. It does sound like lots of fun. Just because boys don't have these interests doesn't make them "girl interests" per se. What makes us critical is not the dancing, the routines, or the stunts but the stuff that surrounds it all. Girls are enlisted in this activity not because society gives them greater permission to dance and move their body (which is true) but because they're in the traditional role of cheering on other people. It is connected to social approval and popularity; they are the supportive cast to the athletes. Most girls enlist in this do-gooder army because they want those extra perks for being looked at, sought after, pretty, and nice. If a girl does all the work it takes to be a better basketball player, does being pretty and smiling help? No way. So if your daughter has strength, dancing ability, gymnastic ability, speed, agility, and a clever way with lyrics, but she is moving away from sports, as middle school girls tend to do in hoards, why point her toward cheerleading? Why not dance? Why not competitive gymnastics? Why not rap? Why not track? People will look at her, people will applaud, people will cheer her on—and she won't have to smile unless she wants to.

"Skills": Gotta Have 'Em

Middle-class parents are putting on lots of mileage driving their kids to extracurricular activities. Gone are the days when kids simply come home after school and play. They're preparing for the future in music and swimming lessons, in ballet class, on the field, and even at the computer. After-school programs for lower income kids follow suit when they can, bringing the extracurriculars to Boys and Girls Clubs across America.

All of these things that children do build their skills in some way. The doll playing we discussed earlier builds social and nurturing skills. Soccer builds skill in competition and self-discipline as well as body control. Cheerleading builds athletic skills, too, but the skills are as likely to be social as athletic.

EXTRACURRICULARS

While writing this book we were continuously confounded by the difference between real girls and the media and marketers' views of girls. The representation of girls in sports on TV and in the movies is pathetic. Even in 2004, the year of the summer Olympics, the most commonly represented female sport was beach volleyball. We suspect it was because of the bikinis. The lesson is clear: Girls who play sports get attention when they look hot. After all, the U.S. Olympic swim team posed provocatively for *Maxim* after the competition. No wonder so many girls aspire to being a cheerleader. They get to "do everything an athlete does" and still look hot while doing it.

Even though girls drop out of athletics when they're in middle school, the truth is that quite a few continue to play and play hard, according to our survey. They said they liked to participate in basketball, track, and gymnastics. They also play tennis, badminton, ice hockey, field hockey, baseball, volleyball, softball, football, and golf. They ski, Rollerblade, and rock climb, and they do some trampolining. One wrote that she was about to take surfing lessons. More often than not they wrote that they participate in sports, whether as a school activity or not, because it's fun. One eloquent basketball player wrote, "I love the thrill of running down the court, sweat pouring off your face, and knowing you just made a shot." One soccer player wrote (tongue in cheek perhaps), "I like to kick people."

But twelve-year-old Tamara wrote, "I'm too fat to play sports." Most likely this was her perception rather than reality. She may have gotten the idea via a program at school that emphasized competition over personal achievement and fun, or she may have gotten it from the media, which show so few women playing sports in ads, TV shows, and movies. In these forms of media the bodies you see are not the bodies of athletes—except perhaps for Mia Hamm, one of the highest-scoring players in the history of women's international soccer. Most likely she gets all those endorsements and TV spots not because she is the best player but because she's so pretty. For some sports women can and do look quite solid, strong, and muscular, but magazines want sexy or feminine. So it's not the Olympic softball team that makes the cover but skaters, gymnasts, and select beauties like Anna Kournikova or sensational images such as Brandy Chastain in a sports bra or seductively posing for *Sports Illustrated* with nothing but two soccer balls covering her breasts.

Another reason Tamara might think she's too fat to play is that she's afraid of being teased. This didn't seem to be a problem for several overweight little boys who played in the 2004 Little League championship games in August 2004.

It's too bad that Tamara won't be playing sports because research has shown that girls benefit from participation. Girls who participate are less likely to grow obese or to deal with weight issues via anorexia, fasting, vomiting, or smoking. They are also less likely to use drugs in high school or to get pregnant. They are more likely to delay first intercourse, have better body images, and be more resistant to the media's focus on sexuality and body size. They are also more likely to do well in science and graduate high school. (See the Web site www.gogirlgo.com for a listing of these research studies.)

Between middle school and high school, girls experience a 23 percent decline in participation, and this decline is greater for black girls than white girls. One study of girls ages ten through nineteen showed that by sixteen, 56 percent of black girls and 31 percent of white girls showed no habitual leisure time activity.

What is happening that changes girls' feelings about sports from middle school to high school? Team sports in high school are more competitive (a girl has to try out for a team whereas in middle school almost all are encouraged to participate). It may be that a girl does not want to try out and face the disappointment or the pressure of competition. Another reason may be that other extracurricular work competes with sports—the work of becoming a sexy teenage girl, which requires shopping and boyfriends, and conversations about shopping and boyfriends. As she matures physically, others come to see her differently. When girls are looked at and objectified, when they are seen as more sexual, they become more interested in boyfriends than sports and may not want to be seen aggressive and sweaty. Research suggests that girls' attrition in sports in the high school years may be related to their perception of participation as antithetical to ideals of femininity and popularity. Sports don't give girls the same kind of social capital that they give boys; boys stay in for the girlfriends, but girls drop out for the boyfriends.

Do girls actually feel weaker or perceive themselves as weaker? Boys develop more muscle mass per unit volume of body mass after puberty than do girls. If a boy and girl are of equal weight and height, he will have more fat-free body mass. But there is much more within-gender variation than cross-gender variation, and there are ample opportunities for girls to compete with female athletes of similar strength and ability. (It is too bad the stronger and more competent girls frequently aren't permitted to compete with boys when they want to. The constant separation of girls' and boys' teams serves to support the idea that overall girls can't compete with boys, and that's simply untrue.)

The world around girls changes in middle school. While younger girls have been allowed to compete with boys, challenge them, and test their own mettle, middle school girls have been introduced to a debilitating image of the female sportswoman personified in the few faces we see of serious female athletes and, of course, in the cheerleader. The message to young girls as they reach puberty is that to be anyone they need to be beautiful and thin, and that while it's okay to be smart in school, image is everything and it's better to be a talented actress, singer, pop star, or diva look-alike.

We examined the extracurriculars that middle school girls in our survey participated in to find out what is drawing them away from sports.

Drama, singing, and art were tops in the lists. These are wonderful activities that add depth and beauty to your life and provide a means for self-expression and transcendence. Unfortunately for boys, they've become almost exclusively girl activities starting in middle school because of the self-expressive element that is quintessentially girlish to a twelve-year-old boy. While boys are persuaded to veer off into garage bands, girls do dance steps and choral harmonies in their family rooms. While boys may fantasize about rocking the world with their bands, girls too often fantasize about standing in front of these boys, looking pretty, dancing sexy, and singing their hearts out.

There is another reason that after puberty girls change over from sports to drama, dance, art, and singing. They have been taught to be deeper, more emotionally rich and complicated people, and that drama, self-involvement, and angst-ridden self-reflection are the essence of teenage girlhood. Art, singing, and drama are all positive ways to enact this introspective self.

But when girls give up sports for these more emotionally charged and dramatic hobbies, they miss the rewards of a deeper connection to their bodies. One could argue that dancers have that bodily connection, but the high incidence of anorexia and bulimia among dancers goes against that argument. To summarize the research, girls who play sports simply have a better connection to their bodies than girls who don't, and that has a myriad of positive consequences.

We don't want to set up a dichotomy between the arts and sports as so many schools do, pouring money into athletics while the music department holds a charity auction to raise money for a trip. The arts are just as important as sports, and they aren't only about self-expression, though those who see them as a girl activity (and sports a boy activity) emphasize this aspect. Girls who engage in art, drama, and music (and boys, too, for that matter) learn a lot more than how to express themselves and decorate their science projects. These activities are closely linked to intellectual development. Theater helps kids delve into literature in a deeper way; the visual arts help them develop outside-the-box thinking; and music has an obvious link to critical math development.

The truth is girls can't do everything, and parents can exhaust their children by overscheduling their after-school time. But let's think more broadly and address what schools and after-school clubs can offer all girls that can help intellectual development, encourage self-expression, *and* be physical. In reading the list of all the sports that girls are involved in, it's hard to believe that a girl could find none of interest. We shouldn't accept the notion that a girl is either an athlete or an artsy type. There is some physical activity that every girl can find pleasurable and fun. Resources need to be made available to all girls, including those in poorer neighborhoods, that would allow them an opportunity to see if sailing or golf or horseback riding is something they might enjoy. We need to think beyond the YMCA pools and team sports to find ways to bring diverse physical activities to urban centers and rural outposts.

If a girl is interested in drama and singing, all is well as long as the interest does not become narrowly focused on image. If your daughter loves drama, for example, encourage her to play the evil roles as well as the pretty debutantes, to think of acting as a process of self-discovery and not just creating an image. Encourage script writing and reading of the literature that the play is based on. When girls sing and love to sing, they need to be given an instrument on which to accompany themselves. With an instrument and the skills to read music, they will most certainly go beyond becoming "eye candy" stars like Britney Spears and Jessica Simpson. Teach them to improvise, an intellectually creative skill. When they do art, don't just compliment them or ask them to make things look pretty; ask them to solve problems through visual media and to make interesting statements. When described in these ways, the arts no longer seem gender specific, and girls and boys can share in all these activities.

Finally, the more activities available for kids to choose from, the better. In our survey girls told us about yearbook committees, science clubs, building clubs, language clubs, computer graphics classes, and more. Languages help girls imagine the world beyond their own; math and science help them test the world and open up opportunities they've been prevented from knowing; arts encourage the use of vision, critical thinking, and introspection; physical activity helps them feel strong, competent, and alert. All of these tell a girl that she has so much more potential than has been reflected back to her on her TV set.

MAKING A BIG NOISE

Don't girls and boys participate equally in band? At age nine or ten a child will often be asked to select a band instrument in school. Some kids have already started piano or violin at an earlier age because these instruments are manageable for small fingers; also, teaching techniques such as the Suzuki Method have been developed to start children early on these instruments.

Believe it or not, researchers who have looked at what influences children's choice of instruments have determined that children as well as adults categorize particular instruments as either masculine or feminine. In one study, 96 percent of eight- and nine-year-olds said that boys would prefer to play the drum, and 96 percent said girls would prefer to play the flute. In another study of kindergarteners to fifth graders who were asked what instrument they would like to play, boys selected "masculine" instruments such as drum, trombone, trumpet, and saxophone; girls preferred the flute, violin, clarinet, and cello. In still another, 77 percent of eight- and nine-year-old girls preferred "feminine" instruments, and 73 percent of boys preferred "masculine" ones. Even when girls choose a "masculine" instrument, they still categorize it as a "boy instrument." These preferences stabilize around fourth grade, just when they are asked to make their choice.

It's no wonder. The music world around them supports this difference. Orchestras rarely show female trombonists, and flutists seem to be overrepresented by women. Looking at the rosters for the Philadelphia Orchestra, the Cleveland Symphony, and symphonies in Atlanta, Dallas, and Baltimore, it's clear that men are overrepresented in every category except flute. There is one female trumpeter and one female trombonist in the 2004 rosters, and although many women have large lung capacities and great breath control, few play the tuba. In one study where girls and boys heard an orchestra and were allowed to approach a musician to look at his or her instrument, when a man was playing the trombone, only 2 percent of the girls went up to look at it, but when a woman was playing the trombone, 24 percent approached her.

Why is this a problem? Well, when you play the saxophone, trumpet, or trombone, or when you play the drums or guitar, you are much more likely to be in a jazz band. All those flutists are left out of a wonderful heritage of music and a fabulous middle school and high school performing experience. Also, jazz teaches improvisation, not by-the-book music learning. At the Berklee College of Music High School Jazz Festival you'll see a few girls in each of the jazz bands, but the soloists who win the competitions are most often boys.

Another problem is that when you play the brass instruments, you get to make a big sound. Perhaps girls don't want to make a big sound, but we have to ask why. Are girls supposed to be light, fragile, and delicate like the airy sounds of a flute? Are they afraid to build up their lungs and feel the power of a brass instrument because they will look and feel less feminine? We think so. We also think that their friends, schoolteachers, and parents don't encourage them to make big noises.

One ten-year-old girl told us that she was considering playing the trumpet but thought it might be too heavy. She was the star player on her soccer team and as big, if not bigger, than half the boys in her class. She said everyone had been telling her to play the flute. We gave her a trumpet in its case to lift, and she exclaimed, "Oh, that's not heavy at all."

What we want and what all parents should want for girls is the opportunity to express themselves musically in ways that can deepen their understanding of themselves and their love of music, rather than confirm how society already sees them: little, light, sweet, and fairylike. Music can express all sorts of feelings that words cannot. We want girls to have access to as many of these forms of expression as they need to express themselves.

GAME BOY GIRLS AND GIRL GAMERS

Another set of skills has to do with technology. The general consensus seems to be that there is a world of difference between boys and girls. Girls IM, write fan fiction, keep online diaries (blogs), visit MySpace, shop, and chat. Boys IM, visit MySpace, and play video games. Girls are not as often "gamers."

When we asked girls to name the video games they own and play and to tell us about some of their favorites, the universal response began to sound like a mantra. "None," "I don't play video games," "I don't like video games," or they simply didn't answer that question. One has to wonder about an industry so gendered that the most popular gaming platform is called Game *Boy* and where sports, sexy women, and violence rule the day. Still, we were surprised at this survey response because the girls answered an online survey, which suggests they're pretty well connected to a cyber world. Moreover, research shows that girls do play some games, but they go online to play their games rather than turn on an Xbox or PlayStation.

There is a public outcry today about boys' gaming and the effect it has had on their reading habits. How can we get boys to read more, parents ask. Why aren't we asking how we can get girls to game more? Steven

Johnson explains in his provocative book *Everything Bad Is Good for You* that gaming teaches kids to model complex situations. The games themselves increase in complexity and cognitive demands once a kid gets hooked; newer platforms and changing technology require kids to take in more, think faster, and plan ahead as they play. It could be that when we don't encourage girls to play these games and when manufacturers don't market these games to girls, girls may be losing out on something that is important to intellectual development in the twenty-first century.

If a preteen girl were to browse the stores, wondering if gaming was for her, she would have little encouragement. We checked out the covers on E-rated (for Everybody) games for Game Boy, PlayStation 2, Xbox, and Nintendo Game Cube at our local stores in search of what might loosely be termed girl-friendly games. It's slim pickins. We found only two games with girls prominently featured on the cover: Allegra, a girl extreme snowboarder, and Kim Possible, the high school cheerleading crime fighter.

There were very few other girls on covers (again, on E-rated; there were many busty women on Teen- and Mature-rated covers). There were some games featuring girls, but most are unapologetically sex-role stereotyped, encouraging such things as fashion, shopping, and dance parties, and featuring lots of pink. We found some E games targeting younger girls, such as Disney's Princess game: "Play as Snow White, Cinderella, Ariel, Sleeping Beauty, Belle, and Jasmine" and "search for the magical Tiara of Friendship to make sure that everyone lives happily ever after." There are lots of Barbie games, such as Pet Rescue, where girls can nurture rescued animals back to health; Barbie Horse Adventures, where girls can choose outfits for Barbie and horses; and Barbie's Groovy Games, a collection of simple mini games with a lot of pink in them.

These pink games aren't that different from those targeting to preteen girls, such as the Bratz Dance game that has the Bratz girls getting dressed up to go dancing in a contest, and Mary-Kate and Ashley's Sweet 16, where girls can "collect party points to upgrade your car, clothes, and tunes." Lizzie McGuire On the Go offers girls a chance to play an arcade-type game called When Cheerleaders Attack and keep track of friends' contact information, important dates, horoscopes, and biorhythms.

The girls in our survey who are into gaming don't mention any of these games. One ten-year-old said her favorites included Secret Agent Barbie, but not because of any Barbie fashion statement. She said it was "because I like trying to get to the other countries without being caught."

(And we ask, where in the world did Barbie hide Carmen San Diego, a character who was cool and smart and didn't wear pink.) She also liked Rocket Power Team Rocket Rescue "because I like learning how to do new tricks." If our survey is any indication, the folks designing games for girls are missing the boat. The girls who choose this medium like a challenge, and they're unlikely to get it with dance contests and arcade games.

One ten-year-old's list contained all extreme sports games with girl characters, which may be why she likes them. Of course lots of those characters look like sexy supermodels with breast enhancements, such as the snowboarders of SSX like busty Elise who "has successfully built her snowboarding success with savvy business and modeling careers." And there was "sacrilicious" Marisol, that "sacrilegious/delicious mix of innocence and raw sexuality" who "loves to dance, to surf and to flirt." But there were also characters like down-to-earth, fully-dressed Kaori to choose from, and all the girls' descriptions are more about their skill, confidence, and original boarding styles than their appearance. If it weren't for games like Mia Hamm's Soccer and Soccer Shootout, there would be almost nothing for girls who are into competitive sports.

We'd like to see something other than a violent alternative to fashion or nurturing games. According to a UCLA study, when children designed their own video games, girls preferred nonviolent games with positive feedback for players, and they didn't program "evil" characters or conquer an "evil enemy." In response, Patti Miller, director of Children Now's Children and the Media program, said, "Video game producers need to stop thinking pink. . . . Girls want games that engage and challenge, as well as entertain them, not 'girlie versions' of games originally designed for boys."

There aren't many of those kinds of games out there yet. Maybe this explains why nowhere other than the action figure aisles at Toys "R" Us is there a physical space more explicitly owned by boys. When we were at Best Buy checking out the games, we watched a nine-year-old girl playing one of the sample Game Boys. Behind her a boy about her age waited for her to finish. He stood close and acted impatient with *her* but not with the other boys playing the machines nearby. There was a feeling that she was an interloper, not serious, and ought to finish up quickly and leave. Thankfully, she was too into the game to notice. Wouldn't it be great if there were as many girls playing or impatient and anxious to try the latest game? Maybe soon.

HACKING AND GAMING FOR OLDER GIRLS

Girls are definitely online. A Pew Survey shows that only 44 percent of sixth grade boys go online, while 66 percent of sixth grade girls do. The survey calls older girls, ages fifteen to seventeen, "power communicators" and "information seekers." These girls show much more activity and facility in online activities, looking at educational, game, and shopping sites, than boys their own age and younger. But even while girls are doing all sorts of things online, they represent themselves in our survey and to the public as less technologically savvy than they are. This has less to do with their skills and more to do with their social identity. Roberta Furger, author of *Does Jane Compute?*, found in her research on girls and computing that some girls had all the skills of a hacker but refused to identify themselves as such because of lack of self-confidence and qualms about taking on an identity that might indicate to others ugly-smelly-nerdy more than brainy-hip-alternative.

In spite of girls' facility with the computer, there aren't very many good games for girls. If an older girl plays a "boy's game," like Warcraft or Diablo or Halo or even Tony Hawk Proskater, she is gender-crossing. It's not that hacking and slashing aren't interesting to girls, but when girls do enjoy such games, they are so male-identified that they think of themselves as doing a boy thing. Roberta Furger talked to the executives at Her Interactive, Inc., who had done some research. They asked over two thousand girls what they wanted in a computer game. According to Her Interactive the girls requested "cute guys, dating, shopping, telephone conversations, a prom, and music." The greedy execs gave the girls what they asked for and probably called it giving them a "voice." The outcome was a game called McKenzie and Co. that a girl could play about one day before she exhausted all the dating options available. It didn't fly. Perhaps girls aren't the best ones to speak for themselves here. After all, they have been told from the time they were yea high that they should be interested in boys, makeup, and fashion. Why didn't the girls ask for more action? Perhaps they repeated what they think they should be interested in, what they've been taught girls want. Perhaps they hadn't asked for alternatives because they haven't experienced them. If so few professionals have yet to envision a girl's game that isn't about fashion, how can we expect girls to?

Girls like The Sims, which comes closest to a gender-neutral game that everyone of all ages can like. The Sims puts characters in their own reality show that the child controls. But just as *Survivor*, one of the first reality shows, spawned many romance reality shows, so did The Sims. The expansion packs of Makin' Magic, Hot Date, and Super Star look like they were designed to hook preteen girls. What makes the games interesting is that things can always go wrong. Houses catch on fire, dates fall asleep on you—so it is not your usual dream-girl existence. In fact, a girl is enticed to spice up the game by making someone accidentally pee or die.

Stephanie is a girl gamer who got passionate about gaming in middle school when she watched her mother and aunt play computer games. Furger notes that when mothers compute, so do daughters. Stephanie played only occasionally before then, but after became an avid player of Final Fantasy, a role-playing game with a story line like a book that players navigate through. Stephanie found that the girls featured in the games were often more complex and stronger than those on TV: "They were ordinary people who overcame extraordinary circumstances."

Games like Final Fantasy have male and female characters, and many of the versions have strong female leads that girls think about (and write about on Web sites). This makes them like book characters. We asked Stephanie about girl-stereotypes—such as love triangles and catfights between girls. She said that these stereotypes seem to be developed in the fans talking online and not in the games themselves. Fans talking online, for example, created a fierce rivalry between two girls who love the same character, Cloud.

The makers of Final Fantasy have changed the game to provide a more teenagey, sexy Yuna and friends. In Final Fantasy X, Yuna is fully clothed and looks like a strong peasant-type teenage girl of action. In Final Fantasy X-2, Yuna now has something like thirty-two outfits, and changing her clothes changes her magical powers and abilities. The problem is that she basically looks like a sexy MTV video star no matter what you put on her. It's a lesson to girls, that being brave, strong, and ready to fight can only last so long—the next adventure is fashion, boyfriends, and sex. It's a lesson they're getting everywhere at the age of twelve and after, not just in gaming.

In 1994, the *Wall Street Journal* published an article entitled "Gender Divide: A Tool for Women, a Toy for Men" about computers. But why must this be true for girls? Through the early introduction to girls of a teen life of sex, partying, boys, and fashion, we take girls away from the world of play. Role-playing games full of fantasy, love, story lines, and strong women seem to be what middle school girls would love if they became involved. The grown-up girls who started young and then went on to better games are not nerdy addicts but interesting people who read books almost as often as they play games.

Girls get involved in these games that are more interactive than TV shows and seem to offer girls a facility and interest in technology that they can take with them into adulthood. Remember that once a girl gets into a game, she then searches the Web for cheats, enters chat rooms to analyze and discuss plotlines, and may even take computer animation courses to try her own hand at it. Why don't any of the girl magazines have a technology column? Why don't they sell these games and products alongside the makeup and fashion items? Perhaps we should try to get magazines such as *Teen, Elle, Glamour, Vogue,* and *Seventeen* to broaden their focus and provide alternatives. Parents can accompany their daughters into game stores, talk to the salespeople, and try to find out which games are complex and satisfying, rather than let their daughters look at the cover of a game and choose the Mary-Kate and Ashley stuff.

Schools can join in by creating after-school clubs for gaming. Girls can learn some of the most complex and interesting role-playing games together rather than waiting for an older brother to teach them. After girls start together at a game, they can move on to solitary play or Internet playing where they can exchange weapons and conquer kingdoms with virtual friends all over the world.

We urge moms and dads to figure out some of these games with their daughters. Parents feel more of an obligation to play with their children when they're younger, but middle school girls still want to play. Sports, though fun, doesn't speak to the imagination, but these games with their fantasy story lines do. They give middle school girls an alternative to playing at being a teen.

SHOPPING: IT'S A GIRL THANG

> If you're bored with your life and want to be more like me, Eloise, then buy this book, for Lord's sake, and charge it, please!"
> —*Book jacket copy from* Eloise's Guide to Life, or How to Eat, Dress, Travel, Behave, and Stay Six Forever!

When we look at the images in books, television, and movies, we see that even the youngest girls are barraged with messages of the near-orgasmic pleasure of shopping. Left to their own devices, three- to seven-year-olds would rather hang on the monkey bars than hang out in the mall. But shopping and an endless desire to consume are shamelessly marketed through toys, TV shows, movies, magazines, and Web sites so that girls are brainwashed into believing that shopping is for real girls. For the 2003 holiday season alone, Susan Linn reported in *Consuming Kids*, "Mattel produced at least seven Barbie play sets with a shopping theme." Of course, this was just the tip of the iceberg. Girls and shopping is a persistent theme for marketers, and for obvious reasons. Hook girls early on the pleasures of shopping, and the rest is a marketer's dream.

Fostering the connection between mothers and daughters through shopping is the obvious emotional link for moms. Share an afternoon together, shop, go to a spa, have lunch, and talk girl talk. This seems like more of a preteen or teen hook. How do they reel in the younger girls? Here are just a few examples of products and messages that teach your little girl (they're all marketed to girls ages three and up) that the key to excitement and happiness is shopping:

- Imaginarium, a line of role-playing/dress-up costumes, markets a Purse Play Set with pretend brush, lipstick, keys, cell phone, wallet, credit card, perfume, and makeup compact. It's dress-up, consumer style.

- Barbie's Shop with Me Cash Register is more than a place to put your play money. The Amazon.com Web site says, "Barbie's shopping sprees are legendary." Why not give your daughter all she needs to charge herself into major debt. "Re-create a Barbie shopping spree without leaving the house. . . . Input item numbers from 'Barbie's Shop with Me Catalog,' scan bar codes on price tags, scroll through items in the Barbie cash register, input your own prices—this Barbie cash register adds them up for you. Use Barbie's savings card for discounts and swipe her credit card to purchase."

- Kim Possible's Shopping Avenger online game and plush doll (which is how they get the younger girls who are not yet using computers) shows you what the heroine's real concerns are: "Drakken and Shego are plotting a villainous scheme and Kim Possible must save the world . . . again! But what is she going to wear? Take Kim on a Club Banana shopping spree to get her outfitted for her mission: who says you can't save the world and make a fashion statement at the same time!" (This is on the MSNKidz Web site.)

- American Girl, that provider of girl-centered semihistorical fiction, has loads of ways to encourage your daughter to practice
  spending money. If you've ever been to the store, you know what
  it's like to see hundreds of little girls looking very grown up; loaded
  down with their bright red-and-white shopping bags or taking a
  shopping lunch break with their dolls at the American Girl
  Dreamers Cafe. From purses with "go anywhere accessories" such
  as a compact, hair bands, and a library card to spa kits for the doll
  and her "frisky Westie pup," she's an American girl who plans to
  look right and have money to burn.

- Fisher-Price markets Loving Family dollhouses and dolls along
  with Sweet Streets villages so girls can have a separate community
  of dollhouses that allow them to go on "imaginative adventures" to
  the toy shop and restaurants.

- The Bratz *Starrin' and Stylin'* summer 2004 movie, full of fashion,
  angst, and gossip, included a collectible Bratz purse.

Always in competition with the Bratz divas, My Scene Barbie goes for
"the ultimate shopping spree." Advertised between shows your daughter
loves, such as *Rug Rats*, we're told that "The My Scene girls love to shop
'til they drop, and they always know where to go for the best deals on the
hottest new clothes and accessories!" In the online My Scene Shopping
Spree, each doll shops for something trendy or hot in clothes, makeup, or
bling-bling in a favorite real-life store (so, of course, the ad includes clever
product placement). When your three-year-old says, "Mommy, can we
shop for Mudd jeans?" you know she learned both the importance of the
activity and the brand name from Mattel.

Then there is the ultimate marketing wonder—Neopets! Neopets are
cyber beings that live in an evolving mythical land called Neopia. Kids
from around the world are invited into the free site to create and then
care for their virtual pets, while a team of webmasters update the goings-
on daily. Hugely popular, it has been the number one site for preteens; 39
percent of their visitors are twelve and younger, and nearly 60 percent are
female—a very high percentage for a computer game. In talk with parents
and girls about Neopets, we heard that it's innocent fun in the too-often-
racy world of gaming. Parents like that girls are choosing something interactive and creative rather than IMing their friends.

Don't be fooled. There is nothing innocent here. Neopets is actually a sophisticated marketing scheme disguised as virtual pet care. The object of the game is to gain Neopoints by playing product-placement games or by watching commercials and movie trailers and visiting the Web sites of their sponsors. You can buy food for your pet (such as McDonald's fries; no wonder McDonald's Happy Meals toys in the summer of 2004 were Neopets) and then keep its teeth from falling out with a Crest spinbrush. The company is unabashedly gleeful about using "immersive advertising," which is "an evolutionary step forward in the traditional marketing practice of product placement." Immersive advertising, according to the company's site, "incorporates the advertiser's brand, service and/or message directly into entertaining site content, thereby creating brand affinity with site members."

Immersive advertising is extremely powerful because kids connect emotionally with their Neopets. The game echoes those real and virtual nurturer games aimed at girls in early childhood; they bond with pets by playing, feeding, and grooming them, as well as entering them in beauty and other contests, all the while using well-placed products to ensure the pet's health and well-being. Mattel ran a campaign promoting its Diva Starz dolls in which users could buy a doll for their pet. Products alleviate pets' discomfort, and this affects kids' feelings about the product. Marketers use their entire bag of tricks within this virtual world: They place products strategically, and they make needed products scarce. Pet owners then want them more, and barter and trade for them, building a desire that overflows the game and translates into the real world of "pester power"—using kids to influence what their parents buy. They introduce and teach kids how to connect to real-life products, how to gain Neopoints by referring friends to the site, signing up with real world sponsors, or completing marketing surveys that provide companies with detailed reports about girls' and boys' buying preferences. "We live and breathe market research," says Neopets' executive vice president. Where does that place your living, breathing daughter in the grand scheme of things?

Neopets takes what seems like a natural caring nature in your daughter and finds a way to profit from it. It's legal, but it doesn't seem ethical. What they're doing with little girls has long been done with mothers, playing on their desire to love and care for their children by creating anxieties that can only be met with products. Are you a good mother if your child doesn't have the best car seat on the market? How do you call yourself nurturing if you haven't bought your child's favorite cereal? "Choosy mothers choose Jiff," not the less expensive store brand.

What makes this so egregious is that girls log on for the chance to create and play with a cool, adorable pet. We and our children consider such play a time-out from the real world. We want fantasy to flourish, unfettered by adult tricks, pressures, and con jobs. We want them to invent wild things and make up stories that take them to faraway places. We distinguish fantasy play from the reality of, say, shopping.

Not Neopets. It's all one and the same, and this benefits them and the companies who market through them. Neopets has translated the site into ten languages, and their bottom line is "international development and expansion into offline revenue streams." You may want your daughter to engage in creative play, but Neopets sees your child as a "target audience." They want "repeat exposure" for products that "create a positive and long-lasting impression with site members." It may not be great for her, but it is wonderful for products that come from companies such as Mattel, whose director of their Girl Online Division says: "It becomes addictive. It has tremendous stickiness, and that helps us gain the exposure we need." We think the stickiness comes from the slime of these marketers!

If we want girls to learn how to live right and if in the real world there is concern about environmental depletion, poverty, and overconsumption, why don't we see more toys that teach creative versions of reduce, reuse, and recycle or that play against the girls-as-superficial-shopper stereotype?

ROOM MAKEOVERS: THE NEW HOME EC

Here's a skill you might not realize is being taught to your little girls from day one: decorating. Many young mothers today don't have the horrid memories of home ec class that we older mothers have. Home ick! While the boys were playing with tools, making birdhouses and bookcases, the girls were making dresses for a fashion show or learning how to bake a coffee cake (before many even were drinking coffee). Home ec began in middle school and became optional in high school. Today, girls don't need to learn sewing and cooking any more than boys. With very few exceptions, we buy our clothes and throw out socks with holes in them. We throw things in the microwave or follow the directions on the back of a Betty Crocker box. That's why the new home ec is decorating.

It begins with those little girl bedrooms. Consider the spring 2004 Sears Room for Kids catalog: "The best place to shop for all things kids!"

A place "where imaginations bloom!" On the cover there is a picture of a young girl sitting on a coverlet of purple and pink flowers; she is dressed in periwinkle, has a fancy bow decorating her long curly hair, and is looking lovingly at a white stuffed horse cradled in her arms. The curtains in her room are purple, the rug is a matching purple flower pattern, and surrounding her are a yellow stuffed bear, pink-and-purple-striped boxes, and a pink-and-white lamp. Inside the catalog are pages of girls lovingly gazing, surrounded by "dreamy" fabric, "gorgeous" furniture, and "dazzling" accessories. Just in case she ever left her room "for a day of shopping or simply out to stroll," there's "a must-have" or "sophisticated" purse that fits the theme.

So it goes, page after page. If not princesses and fairies, hearts and flowers, pink and purple, it's the world of pop stardom, with maybe "a fabulous contradiction" of pink, blue, green, and yellow, floral, paisley, and stripes. Add a radio that "changes color with her mood" or a dollhouse for her "fashion dolls and furniture," and you have a complete set of stereotypes! They're marketing to parents, but before buying most parents will show their daughters the pages. And girls will read in magazines that Hilary Duff and the Olsen twins now have their own signature brand of bedroom furniture.

Everything in these girls' rooms is fabulous, dreamy, the cutest, the softest, beautiful, flittery fluttery, pretty, or lovely. It is hard not to compare these with the boys' rooms on alternate pages that have themes like Fly Me to the Moon (Explore the Solar System), Wall to Wall Nature (dolphins and sharks for "little nature lovers"), Bon Voyage (sail on, little dreamers), and Champs (all-American sports). They are patterned in bold colors—lots of red and blue, dark green and bright yellow. In these rooms there are signs of action everywhere—bedding that glows in the dark, space-shuttle lamps, and laundry nets they can "shoot" their dirty clothes into. The boys in the catalogs reach for things, hold soccer balls and walkie-talkies, and make funny faces behind bean bag chairs. Everything for boys is whimsical, vibrant, fascinating, and durable, durable, durable. We apparently know the beds will be jumped on, not just stretched across in dreamy repose. What is the message? Girls' rooms *are* their worlds, while boys' rooms reflect the wide-open expanse they expect to see and discover. Where "imaginations bloom"? More like "where stereotypes flourish."

Girls are told in many other ways that their job is to decorate their worlds in tastefully lavish style. We've seen how toys, crafts, computer games, and TV tell them decorating is fun, it's what girls do. American Girl sells a line of small furniture and accessories just so girls can create and decorate miniature rooms. "Create teeny tiny rooms with your own style and flair." Little girls can learn the important skill of decorating from unlikely places, such as Madeline's Rainy Day Activities computer game. On what planet would brave Madeline give a hoot about the color of the living room wallpaper? And then there are the design kits where you can make your own lamp, picture frames, and other room accessories.

Nearly every catalog and every store that specializes in teen clothing also sells room-decorating items. It might start with Limited Too and a piece here or there to show a "crush" on Johnny or a girl's love of dragonflies. By the time she is a teenager, all that pink and pretty has been replaced by another narrow image: sexy. If rooms are an extension of a girl's identity, and identity is being constructed through *The OC* and Victoria's Secret, why not decorate in the style of a "den of iniquity," otherwise known as the "harem"? This theme has lots of beads and drapes and mood lighting, cotton velvet pillows, brocade bedrolls, and furry chairs for lounging about. All that's missing is the hookah.

Teen girls are schooled in decorating their faces and bodies by magazines, TV, and their friends, but this has now been extended to their rooms, their lockers, and, for the luckiest girls, their cars. What may look to parents like an investment in identity is also an investment in homemaking. Many teens will tell you that they want a career as a fashion designer or interior decorator. But the reality is this: They are practicing skills that will make their bodies and their homes pretty and desirable rather than skills that will get them into a good design school. If your daughter likes decorating, encourage her to decorate her Web page!

Social Life

In the gap between playdates and real dates, children simply play. Developmental psychologists tell us that as early as age five, when the social world supposedly starts to turn boys and girls into species from different planets, girls stop playing with boys. This is called "the birthday party effect." At least until some time in middle school when being with boys takes on a whole new meaning, girls will spend most of their playtime with other little girls.

PARTY GIRLS

Walk through any party store, and you'll get the message: From birthday to slumber to school dances to proms, parties are the center of girls' social lives. Birthday party paraphernalia that is promoted in Wal-Mart, in specialty party stores, and in catalogs serve to make the birthday girl, from an early age, feel special on her day. Later on, the packaging of specialness grows stronger, inviting girls to be divas and boy band groupies—to be "special" for boys while still pursuing their dreams of being a princess. As a result, most girls at one time or another want a princess or diva party where the plates, cups, streamers, and cake shout "You're special."

Feeling special is wonderful for all children, but parties for girls take the idea to new heights. A hot pink feather boa and a princess tiara for the birthday girl mark her queen bee status and introduce her to the all-girl social hierarchy long before it occurs to her to include and exclude. There is no push to celebrate who she is and who she wants to be. The pressure is on to reduce all those unique qualities into something like a generic princess or diva. Not all girls go this route, of course. These days swimming, bowling, and climbing wall birthday parties are as likely to be for girls as boys. But you can bet that parents won't be taking the girls paint-ball shooting or to an arcade or to play laser tag; instead, moms take girls to the mall for a party and give each a little money to spend!

As she gets older, slumber parties become more common. Slumber parties tend to mean fewer girls than for the prototypical birthday parties, so there are decisions to be made about who is in and who is out. Being in doesn't always mean home free. The intimacy of the evening alone can trigger a series of unfortunate events for the invited or for the excluded. When slumber parties turn mean—and one might think that always happens given how they are represented on girls' favorite TV shows and movies—a parent might ask, "Where do they get this stuff?" Watch a little "educational" Teen Nick, and you'll understand how that special princess can turn into an evil queen if given the right encouragement and social setting.

TV and movie slumber parties highlight the gossip, the fighting, and the burgeoning sexuality of preteen girls. Pictured in baby doll pajamas for the boys and men in the movie audience, there is often a girls-gone-wild theme, one that is sexualized. Take the pillow fight, for example. If you've ever seen a real pillow fight, the girls are flushed and athletic and fierce-looking in action. In the movies, in their shorty pj's and baby negligees, they're dainty and controlled, as if putting on a show for boys. If you don't think so, check out a recent MTV video for the song "Laffy Taffy," where grown women are featured in sexy outfits having a pillow fight for the male rappers.

More often real slumber parties are fun and intimate and times when girls can get wild in their own way: running out in the middle of the street at night in their pajamas, making up a persona and pretending to be that person online in a chat room, asking Ouija board questions that scare and delight. Unlike the school dances that begin around this time, girls find that all-girl spaces allow them the freedom to be wild, adventurous, and outrageous without being boys.

A disconnect surfaces around middle school, between who girls say they are and who they feel they need to become around boys. Peek in at seventh graders getting ready for a school dance. They make plans with their friends to go to each other's house after school, pick out clothes to wear, do their hair, and simply anticipate the evening jointly. In many schools girls take over the function of planning the dance, working with teachers to choose the theme, staying after school to decorate, deciding on the refreshments, and helping to make it special compared to other dances.

A school dance can be one of the most disappointing experiences in a middle schooler's life, and the media depiction of the event as a princess ball is a preamble for disappointment. There is too much emphasis on how it all looks rather than on what a kid is going to do there to have fun.

These dances are setups for dating when they don't have to be. Many times the girls and the boys are friends in school. They talk about their homework together, laugh at the substitute teachers, and hang out on the playground swing set chatting. The reality is that there are many girl-boy friendships being forged during this period. And yet the world around them is telling them it must be "romance," it must be "boyfriend-girlfriend," and they ought to feel something that perhaps they don't yet feel.

Parents can help middle schoolers anticipate the social fun rather than view the event as a contest to look special or an exercise in decoration. Consider these dances an opportunity to dance; when treated in this fashion, it doesn't matter who you dance with. The fun is in the dancing. It doesn't need to be a preparation for prom.

The prom occasion can be set up as a highly stylized "date" or as a fun night out. If girls follow the media presentation of them in movies, TV shows, and magazines, proms are always represented as opportunities to be a princess for a night (in practice for princess weddings). Here, playing dress-up takes on new dimensions with flowers, tiaras, gowns, coaches (limos), and fancy meals. Ready for the prom, girls walk down the stairs in Cinderella fashion to the oohs of parents and their date, or they stand posed in their gowns with their awkward dates by their side, parents snapping an albumful of pictures. Girls who invest in this princess moment are apt to be disappointed, however, because there is a whole night to fill.

There are alternative prom options that girls and boys have thought up themselves, such as group dates where everyone dresses up, gets involved in the planning, pitches in to buy the tickets, and so forth. We know of at least one alternative school that has a "no date" policy for the prom. Everyone is invited and comes alone to socialize with all. This school's policy is for the prom to be a secret from the seniors; the juniors prepare it to give the seniors the evening of their life. In this way it is classmates entertaining other classmates rather than a dance oriented around the pressure of a date. What is also nice about this kind of arrangement is that lesbian and bisexual teenage girls feel included in what can seem like an otherwise *uber*heterosexual event.

There is enormous pressure on girls to have a boyfriend in high school, which suggests to others that she is wanted and acceptable. It's the rare high school where lesbian or questioning girls feel safe to experiment in the public way that heterosexual girls can. When the world puts this much pressure on girls, it's the school's responsibility to relieve some of it by making such events inclusive and discussing this with the prom committee.

IM SO INTO MYSPACE

Another form of social engagement occurs online. With teens and now middle school girls getting their own cell phones, there is a lot of talking and listening to real voices. But, we've noticed that even when high school girls have cell phones they enjoy the computer style of text messaging more than talking.

In middle school girls seriously begin to talk to each other on computer email systems such as Instant Messenger (IM). Independent of the rise in the amount of homework, girls are multitasking by messaging their friends while doing other things. They can keep the AOL lines open on their computer while running to the kitchen to have dinner, doing their homework, watching TV, playing a computer game, or checking out strangers' MySpace pages.

While IMing is a surefire way to spread gossip quickly and exchange other information, it is also a way for girls to try out that new middle school sarcastic wit, create a linguistic style, and stay connected to friends. Forty percent of households with children own a computer. When they don't, boys generally find ways to get access by hanging out at an after-school program with computers or at the library. Girls seem to make do with other means of communication.

The problem with IMing and other forms of cyber communication is that they are unsupervised areas that can introduce preteens and middle schoolers to a virtual teen life, a life that makes them *girls* using the Internet, not just kids, and often flirty, sexy girls. While many parents are worried that their child might meet a sex offender online (very rare), more ought to be worried about the stereotypes that lurk around every corner in cyberspace.

The girls who answered our survey told us that of the screen names their friends used, the majority insinuated their gender. While some names identified them as girls with particular interests, such as Cheerchick or Sk8terGiRl, most identified them as being a girl *and* having a girly feature, as in Baby, Luv, Cute, Angelic, or shopper. These names seem clever at first, but when you read them en masse, they tell a different story: Funkygirl, Luv2dream, Luvrgrl, Babygirl, QT, Sassygirl, PurtyFlirt, Justluvly, Rowdychic, Chicky13, MrsSexy, HuneyBunz, LilMzTude14, Imaqtchic, HrtBroken, Dizzyblond, GlitterGal, QT4U, LilAngel, ShoppinLuvr, Fashinadict, Chinadoll, Sexy4U, Hulagirl, Ditzyblonde, FameMiss.

IM names express something fanciful about the person, but in the online social climate of cyberspace, fanciful takes a narrow turn. Often the name is spontaneously chosen when the girl signs up for a messenger system. What comes to mind is telling—that the girl wants to be identified in one of the following ways: cute, hot, ditzy, glamorous, famous, or with attitude. And we can't forget sexy.

Journalist and dean of the Ithaca College School of Communications Dianne Lynch interviewed UWannaLoveMe7 for her research on preteens and the Internet. UWannaLoveMe7 was almost thirteen and says she and her friends message each other "because we're bored a lot." They also sit in chat rooms and look at what other people are saying. When asked how she could make sure the "hott" guy she was talking to was really hot, she told Dean Lynch, "I don't really believe what they say anyway. I just go with the flow. It's not like real life, so I don't really care."

It's frustrating to parents to see their kids typing away only to see the screen going black when they reach the six-foot perimeter. In the old days, many a parent unethically listened in on their kids' telephone conversations with friends out of nosiness, but instant messaging seems so much more private. While a parent may not be able to enter the virtual friendship world of instant messaging, she or he can enter the conversation about selves and identity. We're told by eighth graders that having a cool MySpace page is a way that even so-called unpopular kids can rise in social status. MySpace may be the place where you can pull up a chair and ask to look around your daughter's cyberworld.

What you'll see is a lot of kids, aged eleven and on into their twenties, representing themselves—and in rather artistic, intriguing ways. Some are interested in music. Some do their own art beautifully. Some do the sexpot thing. Some ask readers to take a quiz about what kind of self-mutilation they prefer (photos included)! Rather than present a critique of the names, photos, or other representations, smart parents will realize that their daughters can have multiple names and many ways of representing herself over the next few years. Compliment interesting pages and tell your daughter who among the strangers on MySpace seem like interesting people and who seem troubled. The idea is to open up possibilities regarding how she represents herself. Offer to take cool photos of her doing the activities she loves to place on her MySpace. Suggest looking up MySpaces in zip codes in faraway places. For IM, suggest a few names she can use: Smart1, 1whomustBobeyed, Dragonslayer, Wonderchild, Soccerbud, Hoopster, 82much, Quizzical, WhoIam, AntiFake, thecritic. Instead of Paleogirl788, a dad can suggest Paleopower788; that way her love of dinosaurs defines her, not her gender.

And are the dangers media-hyped? While you can't be over her shoulder reading every word, it's important that you understand the medium, appreciate the cleverness, and also talk about the dangers that do exist. How can you supervise when so much is intended to keep parents in the dark? We recommend you go straight to http://www.sharpened.net/glossary/acronyms.php for a quick lesson if you know less than ten of the following Internet acronyms: 2L8, 4RL, ASL, BFD, BF, BFN, CUL, CWOT, EAK,

EG, EOR, GBH, KIR, LMBO, NMJC, NW, POS, and SLY. Twenty-something Vini Nair, co-creator of Platform Shoes, a nonprofit agency that provides interactive online educational programs for girls such as Zoey's Room, advises parents to become computer literate so they can talk with their teen daughters about the realities of their world. She tells us that parents aren't that far off the technology grid; in fact, they may be ahead in some ways. But Internet lingo can be daunting as teens find new and ever more cryptic ways to create adult-free zones.

Getting to know how IM works and what kids are sending or receiving from peers is important. So the next time you see POS (Parents Over Shoulder), you'll know enough to hang around. When you do, you can say, "Let's look at some MySpace pages. Show me your friends."

DRUGS AND DAUGHTERS

Teens know that the public image of teens is that they are involved with sex and drugs. They also know that getting involved with either has more serious consequences for girls than for boys. Movies and TV show girls that boys are the drug experts and it's a part of teen boy fun. Boys are the providers of a "good time." It's another place where boys can be the authorities.

Drugs are presented as a form of fun for teens, and it's important for parents to acknowledge and question this as a popular image. Acknowledge that, like drinking, it could be fun, but somehow those beer commercials never show a gal hunched over the toilet vomiting. Denying that it might be fun doesn't work. Kids see it everywhere that teen life is presented to them, from TV shows about teens (That '70s Show) to buddy movies about boys bonding over drug experimentation. The culture has always given boys more time and space to experiment with adolescence, and as long as a boy doesn't go over the edge in his drug interest to become a druggie or slacker, he may be considered by school and parents to be within the norm.

A girl who is into drugs raises antennae. After all, the quintessential teen drug addiction book is Go Ask Alice and not Go Ask Al. Check out any show like The OC or the older show, Beverly Hills, 90210; the beautiful teen girl will try drugs or alcohol and become addicted, which will start her inevitable slide to rock bottom.

Plenty of teen girls try drugs and drinking but don't let it rule their social lives. Plenty don't try it at all. The important thing to think about, apart from the obvious health and safety issues, is what public images they may be responding to when they try or invest in drug use and underage drinking. One of those is the idea of risk-taking. Drugs allow teenagers shared experiences of daring and stupidity. To the extent a girl buys into the image of doing drugs as a form of daring, she seems to gain temporary entry into a boy's world of adventure with the potential of raising her esteem among her male peers. "Eve was so wasted" can be heard as a criticism but more likely a sign of her bravado if Eve is the kind of girl who'd rather be "one of the boys" instead of "for the boys." Her actions become high school history: "Do you remember the night Alicia . . ." How else might a girl who wants to be daring get the attention of peers?

There are dangers in such daring for girls. One thing TV and movies show quite frequently is that girls who do drugs or get drunk are at risk for date rape and regrettable sex. This is true, of course, but why aren't there also stories of boys who have regrettable sex or who push a girl too far or who gave in to an aggressive girl's demands because *they* got drunk? We think it's because the media is always showing the difference and not the similarity between girls and boys. When girls get daring through drugs or alcohol use, they risk becoming pathetic and despised by other girls. When boys are depicted throwing up or running down a street drunk and naked, it's an incredibly funny joke. A girl throwing up or taking off her clothes is more likely to be depicted as pathetic or slutty, and the other girls will either feel sorry for her or despise her. A girl walks a thin line between party girl and pathetic loser. As in most of psychology, where women go mad and men go bad, boys who do drugs are treated as badly behaved kids, while girls who develop drug problems are perceived as lost souls, troubled and in need of loving attention like the self-cutters, bulimics, and anorexics.

Some girls with real problems avoid them through the short-term coping or self-injury of drug or alcohol use, but we believe these are problems for boys in equal measure. It is not about the reality of who uses drugs in the teen years as a form of escape but the different ways that drug use is glamorized for girls compared to boys. Teen magazines have regular stories of girls who've been addicted and who are now returning to the right path, but it's not just moral education. In a YM article by Linda Barth, "I Survived Crystal Meth," hear the excitement portrayed in these lines: "The last time she used, she was watching *Requiem for a Dream*, a movie with some intense drug scenes. 'It made me crave,' Julia says. 'I'd vowed not to, but I had a tiny bit left. . . .'" These are intensely emotional and glamorous stories. The girls are princesses of sorts, treated badly, the world turned against them, emerging in the end clean, pure, and healthy.

We think parents who try to prevent drug use may be taking too narrow an approach when they address only the issue of the experience of being high rather than the harm it can do. Not all kids do drugs for the experience; they do it for the image and the social involvement it provides. If parents began talking "image" from day one, critiquing cultural messages with their daughters from Disney to Destiny's Child, then they can take on the images of teens bonding over drug use and the particularly insidious image of the party girl who is constantly represented on MTV videos. If she still chooses to do drugs, and we hope she doesn't, she may avoid some of the other difficulties associated with the image. There's a little hope in that.

NEW SEX ACTS AND THE MEDIA

Journalists love stories about teens and sex. Always looking for a new trend, they are constantly recycling old stories in new packages. Every few years a major newsmagazine has a story about teen sex, and we are shocked by the "new" information. Whenever anything comes up in a grade school or middle school that makes it to the papers—a grade school boy suspended for kissing a girl; a middle school in which oral sex in the hallway was discovered—journalists can create a story by asking, "Is this a new trend?" The answer is usually no, it's an isolated incident. But statistics can always be trotted out to boost the argument that results in telling parents to be more attentive to their kids. These "new trend" stories are about girls and sex or girls and some disturbing behavior but are rarely about girls taking calculus (which is a bit of a new trend and exciting).

Media stories about acts such as bulimia far outnumber stories about high school girls who must babysit younger siblings because their single mothers work fourteen hours a day and have no access to affordable day care ("family responsibilities" are the primary reason girls drop out of school). Media attention to cutting (formally called self-mutilation) far outnumber articles about sexual harassment of girls in middle and high school (high school girls are the group at the highest risk for violence from partners). Girls who have sex too early and have learned their lesson are much more likely to make the news than the Radical Cheerleaders (political groups like these increase in the teen years—that would be a story!). Harassment, violence, and overburdened family responsibilities are actual problems but are more common and not as glamorous as the angst-ridden psychological problems of girls. Solutions to social problems that bring girls together don't play as well as the image of an isolated girl with her knife and her arm in the upstairs bathroom. With so much attention and the glamorous buildup around these kinds of problems, girls come to see them as alternative ways of coping with social problems in their environment.

More than any of these problems in girls' lives, journalists love to write about middle school girls and sex. Any related random event about the new world of sex that middle schoolers are about to enter is treated as a new trend, and parents are urged to increase their monitoring.

Take, for example, the stories about sex bracelets. Megan Stecher, eleven, was expelled from school for selling sex bracelets. Each color represented some different sex act: black was for intercourse and various other colors were for lap dances, using sex toys, having sex outdoors, having a "homosexual kiss," and oral sex. Megan said, on MSNTV (one of her many interviews): "I don't do this stuff. I just wear the colors." The eager male interviewer asked her, "Don't girls wear this to tell boys what they will or won't do?" She explained, in middle school fashion, that if a girl is also wearing color rings on her fingers and a boy snaps her bracelet, she doesn't actually have to do what the bracelet means. Aha! So a girl wears the bracelet to show that she knows what all those sophisticated sex acts are, but she protects herself by wearing the rings that say she doesn't have to act. Now who's at fault here? A savvy girl who's conscious of the sex-saturated culture she lives in or the journalists who have successfully reached her and now exploit this success? Sounds like bait and switch to us.

Two experts on the show commented on this as if it actually were a trend. Dr. Drew Pinsky argued that because we've looked at sexual freedom as some joyous celebration, our children haven't learned moderation. Sexual freedom? Joyous celebration? *Sex and the City* notwithstanding, there is still much anxiety about STDs and AIDS while abstinence-only sex education is the norm in schools. The editor of *Stepping Out* in New York, Chaunce Hayden (who is not an expert on the sexual behavior of middle school girls but on the media), criticized the *New York Post* for making this a story and sensibly added, "What a kid says and what a kid does are two different things." Sure, the sex talk has changed. Middle school girls have more information than they did thirty years ago, but how many are actually acting on this information? Most of the articles about oral sex in the junior high schools feature a female spokesperson saying that she knows girls who have done it but that she herself hasn't. In one article on metroactive.com, none of the thirteen-year-olds interviewed had had oral sex, but they all said they knew of girls who did and described it in detail. Wait a minute. When boys are caught keeping score of how many girls they have had sex with, parents defend them, but girls *knowing* about sex is cause for a media blitz?

The trouble with all this is, of course, the sole focus on girls *as a problem*. Whether it's cutting, disordered eating, or sex, there's a larger social context in which these actions make sense to girls and provide some respite or sense of power. The real story is this context, and the real focus ought to be on how girls and boys can experience the power that comes with mutual respect, choice, and safety. But we won't hear much about that in the media because it's not sexy enough.

REAL SEX

Sex in the teen years is everything the media say it is, except a little less and a little less frequently. Journalists seem to relish the idea that oral sex is more common than ever before, and keep asking experts why. Isn't the answer obvious? Boys purportedly like blow jobs (whether confused about sex or not), and girls want to please boys.

Another reason is that it's kind of a status thing. The teenage girl feels she is being daring when performing this illicit sex act. She may also feel she is playing an active and not a passive role as a sexual creature without having to think about or address her own body and sexual feelings. Perhaps her body may still be a source of embarrassment and shame or her feelings are confused. Perhaps when performing a sex act that gives someone else pleasure and that doesn't take much bodily investment by her, she can begin to feel like a sexual agent in a world that has taught her she is only an object. The irony is that this sex act exists in a world of sexual double standards, and she'll probably pay a price with her reputation.

Gail Dines argues that this is not necessarily so. She claims her students come to college proud to call themselves sluts. As *Sex and the City* girls, they feel they have the power to screw around, and, Dines states, culture is becoming "branded through pornography." Ariel Levy, author of *Female Chauvinist Pigs: Women and the Rise of Raunch Culture*, agrees. She writes that hotness has become "our cultural currency," and while it can mean popular, it really implies "fuckable."

Girls are giving blow jobs because it isn't sex, as they heard from

President Clinton. It is safer than having intercourse. While a girl can get an STD by performing oral sex, she won't get pregnant. And they don't have to think about their own sexual pleasure. Believe it or not, many girls still say "ewwww" when you ask about female masturbation or cunnilingus.

Most girls want boys' approval and were taught very early to orient their own sexuality, particularly their sexual image, toward pleasing boys. Because of this it is rarer for them to get as much pleasure from the sex act itself as it is from looking sexy or becoming a sexual object. While girls are taught by Victoria's Secret and the Lingerie Model of the Year Award to buy all sorts of sexy lingerie in order to present themselves as sexual packages to their boyfriends, they are less likely to find information on TV or in the mall about their bodies and sex in general.

Are boys returning the favor? Sometimes. The girls who spoke to us about the sex lives of their "friends" stated that boys do it to girls, too. But the girls we spoke to admitted (and a recent survey confirmed) that girls do it more often to boys. Are boys forcing girls to perform fellatio? It doesn't sound as if that's the case, though sometimes public displays take place at drunken parties. Sometimes girls may take the lead. It's a way to show sexual bravery without committing to the ultimate, more intimate, more physically invested act of intercourse.

Remember, parents, that although oral sex may seem like an epidemic and we have the statistics that show it's part of the teen sex routine of those teens who are sexually active, we don't have really good data on the meaning of it. We do know that more and more girls think it's an acceptable part of a sexual relationship with their boyfriends—but 99.99 percent are not going to "do" the men's basketball team. An older girl in a sexual relationship is probably going to include blow jobs as part of the repertoire, whether it's the new third base (a system still based on a boy's pleasure, not a girl's) or the last thing she does if she is committed to staying a virgin until college or marriage. A girl who is not in a relationship but going to lots of parties and perhaps "hooking up" with different guys at these parties, usually in a drunken or high state, will probably be performing oral sex.

The latter girl is the one to worry about because that sort of sleeping around is not going to benefit her. She also puts herself at risk for date rape, sexual acts she doesn't give permission for, and bad feelings. Girls in the habit of hooking up regularly with different guys generally feel bad about their bodies and don't get much pleasure. They feel a powerful sensation of being wanted and being sexual, but it's about partying, not about pleasure. They may talk a good game about being sexually free, but, as they told us, they actually feel a lot of shame and worry when they engage in acts with boys they are not attached to.

Then there are "friends with benefits." Occasionally—and not as often as the media fuss about it—girls and boys will experiment and have casual sex in small, intimate friendship groups, no strings attached. They might even plan what they are going to do and decide on the boundaries. The casualness of it doesn't work. Friends get jealous, feel new longing aroused for a more intimate relationship, and over time want exclusivity—particularly girls, who so much want to be special. On the other hand, to have a friend whom you trust to practice the intimacies of a relationship with and on doesn't sound quite so bad.

Ask a lesbian teenager who often does have the benefit of a friend who is a beginning lover. While the media runs amok with stories of teen girls having sex with male friends (we suppose they don't think it's a problem for girls to have sex with boys they hardly know), they don't touch the story of lesbian longing in the high school years. If girls learn anything about same-sex sexual interest, they hear over and over again that it's exciting to boys. Why is it okay to present two girls kissing to impress boys but not girls kissing to show sexual interest in each other? Ask who is running the media, writing the scripts, and creating the visual images. And *he* will tell you what is interesting to *teenagers* (read *male* teens).

Doing and Being: It's a Girl's Life

If teen sex stories worry you, take heart. There are a lot of activities out there to occupy a teenager besides dating and sex. The teen years may seem too late to take up an instrument or learn to play basketball, but they're not, and there are many other activities for girls that involve physical and intellectual skill that have nothing to do with shopping, fashion, or crushes. And when they face that eternal adolescent question "Who am I?" you like so many others can safely tell her:

"To do is to be."—Descartes

"To be is to do."—Sartre

"Dobedobedobedo."—attributed to Frank Sinatra, but Ella Fitzgerald sang it better

CHAPTER 6

Rebel, Resist, Refuse: Sample Conversations with Our Daughters

Your daughter's world is changing every second, but as you've seen, the more things change, the more they stay the same. Are there paths through the forest of sexy diva princess pink shopping hotties? Of course. As parents, however, given our age, our biases, and our disinclination to listen to and watch everything that is currently trendy, we're going to stumble and make mistakes that reveal our ignorance when talking with our daughters. Nevertheless, we need to be in the thick of it. This means knowing how marketers and the media work to capture girls' interests and then using what we have to counteract their power: our relationship with our daughter and our knowledge of what makes her uniquely her own person.

As we say in the introduction, when you talk with your daughter, we encourage you to follow three principles:

Principle 1: Do your own work.

Principle 2: Listen to what your daughter likes and why she likes it.

Principle 3: Bring your daughter the world on your terms, through your broader view.

In the following conversations we show some ways of talking and bringing up important topics at different ages. We've chosen topics that we think are essential, but your daughter may be pulled by different marketing strategies and drawn to different images than the ones we discuss. Even so, the strategies for talking will stay the same. Again, do your own work, listen, and bring her the world on your terms. If you are fully open to her world, you have a way of talking about it and a way of teaching her how to challenge it, too. These conversations start young and then move you through issues important to preteens and then teenagers. Feel free to skip around.

Conversations with Your Little Ones

INTRODUCING THE S WORD

With the youngest girls it's important to start by building a common vocabulary. What better way to introduce the S word, stereotype, with your daughter than by walking through the girls' department of any clothing store. As we noted earlier, as a parent you have so much power at this age to bring her a reality that competes with the limited fantasy of cheering bunnies and little girl versions of sexy. Take advantage of it. From about four years of age and on, give her the concepts that will set the stage for conversations for years to come. When she is older, you can talk with her about the "they" who make the decisions regarding the clothing that is put in the girl and boy aisles. But for ages four to seven, stay with the image and forget the producers and marketers. This means modeling a way of seeing and talking about the different choices presented to her and helping her notice when her world is becoming smaller and more limited so she can step back and say, "That's silly. That's a stereotype. Girls aren't really only like that."

Engage: It's easy to become involved in the world of your young daughter. Simply spend time with her and talk about the advertisements she observes on billboards, on the sides of buildings and buses, in subway stations, or at the mall. Parents with very young children might use distraction as a way to prevent them from seeing unacceptable images, but that's pretty much impossible when a girl reaches a certain age. Gender stereotypes are everywhere, and she doesn't have to be reading to get the messages loud and clear. The best way to provide her with a healthy resistance to the images is to help her name them and experience a little distance from what she sees.

Question: Stereotypes are oversimplified images repeated so often that we begin to see them as true or normal. At age four and five, though, your daughter doesn't need the repetition because she takes things at face value and believes what she sees. Your job is to question the images and remind her that the world is much richer than what she's being sold. If you question, she'll question. A great way to begin is to ask her about things so that she'll notice the repetition. Referring to clothing ads, you might ask, "Why are the girls always in pink? Where is the bright orange you love so much?" or "Why do the girls sit or pose and the boys run and do things? You and your friends love to run hard and play with action figures like the boys in this ad, so where are the girls?"

Listen: When she is very young, your daughter probably won't argue or take the side of mainstream media moguls, but because she has already been exposed to many stereotypes she might answer your "Why is she in pink?" with "Because she's a girl." And to "Why do the girls sit while the boys skate?" she may say, "Maybe they didn't feel like skating that day."

Don't argue: You can agree in part: "Yeah, it sure seems from what we're seeing that pink and shopping are girl things." Or "That could be. Maybe she and her friends skated all morning, but it would be nice to see them skate with the boys." This provides an opening for a discussion of stereotypes.

Reflect, share discomfort, and provide counterexamples: Begin the discussion with a definition: Stereotypes are things we think or we're told are true about all girls or most girls, but they aren't really true or are only true for some. You see them so often that sometimes you come to believe they're true when they're not. One stereotype is that only boys play sports, and a lot of what you see in movies and on TV is boys playing sports. But do only boys play sports? She'll say no proudly. You can then ask, "Who do you know who plays sports?" She may point to an older cousin or a neighborhood girl or her babysitter if she's a girl. And you can add, "You, too! You may not be on a team yet, but you swim and have such a good arm when we toss the ball. You'll probably be on some sports teams. TV should show that girls can be as good at sports as boys!"

Make a game of it: Create some activity that shows little girls what you're talking about. Even "girls wear pink" can be turned into a game. While you're walking through the mall or shopping in town, she can point out to you when she sees girls dressed in pink—or the reverse: girls dressed in other than pink. The same with certain sports or activities that defy type. The point will always be to follow up each stereotype spotted with a disclaimer: Girls can choose any color they like. My favorite color is green. Your grandmother's was yellow. Or, girls do adventurous things, too: Remember Aunt Theresa when she went to climb Mount Everest? And so on. They're not too young. We've tried this with little girls, and they love it. And it doesn't ruin pink for them at all. Being educated about a healthy diet doesn't ruin that piece of chocolate cake. You just may choose not to eat it every day after you've been educated about nutrition and balance.

BUY ME THAT!

Kids generally want things, and after a Saturday morning of TV cartoons they generally want the things advertisers tell them to want. Barbie looks like fun to dress up and play with. My L'il Cash Register looks like fun to work with friends. It's not a problem that kids want toys, just as it's not a problem that they want candy. The problem is that it's very difficult for parents to compete with the high-power advertisements that marketers use that include real kids making orgasmic sounds and using ecstatic expressions of joy while playing with a hunk of plastic. It's easy for your daughter to identify with these kids. That is why you have to invest the things you think are good for her with that kind of energy and excitement.

But not too much excitement. That's what marketers and the media do; they overstimulate. Kids who watch too much overly exciting TV aren't going to find reality fun and exciting. Like a drug, your daughter may require more and more to keep that overstimulated high going. Reality can't compete. The sheer number of those commercials teach your child that a certain high level of excitement is the only kind of fun.

But your daughter is young, and your relationship means a lot to her. Her identification with you will be much stronger than her identification with phony kids on the screen. Even so, you need to compete with emotional expression, repetition, and sharing. If you share the walk in the woods and ooh and ahh over the leaf printing activities you do together, it will be enough. If you emotionally invest in her block building and her car pushing, she'll come back for more.

Is it phony? A little. But don't parents do that all the time? "Hey, kids. We're going to have cauliflower soufflé for dinner. I looove cauliflower." We're not asking you to pretend to like things you don't. We're suggesting that when you have to compete with million-dollar marketers, it's okay to turn up your volume and ratchet up the excitement level. You don't have the resources and money to do promotions and contests, co-branding, viral marketing, advergaming, or program-length commercials, but you do have your relationship and your voice.

Engage: Let's say you've seen a commercial for Barbies and feel a whine coming about getting Barbie's glamorous Rock Star Diva outfit and guitar. You may be surprised to hear that we're not against your buying your daughters Barbies, although we don't advocate it. Barbie makes for super conversations. Barbie evokes a lot of thinking and fantasizing about what it means to grow up, albeit in a narrow sort of way. It's your job to understand these fantasies and see if you can turn them into goals and accomplishments for your daughter.

Question: While watching a Barbie commercial, you might ask, "Do you think the doll can really move like that? Oh, look. At the bottom of the screen it said something that you'll be able to read when you're older. It said that Barbie can't really perform like a rock star, that when you play with her, you dress her up and make her perform. I guess that's true for Barbie the president and Barbie the pilot, too. [These no longer exist, but it's good to throw these images in anyway!] Do you think it would be fun to dress up Barbie like that and play rock stars? Maybe if they have a Barbie astronaut you can take her to the moon."

Listen: This is really important at this age because what you'll hear from your daughter are really wishes and fantasies about herself. You may hear "She's so pretty." You might add, "It's nice to have a few pretty things to look at, but I love to see you play with things that aren't just pretty and are interesting to you in other ways." You may hear "I like the guitar," and to this you might add, "Oh, do you think you might like to play guitar when you grow up?"

Be honest: You don't have to be afraid to agree that Barbie is pretty and that her guitar is cool. There's no harm in that. It won't work to put down the blond diva idol look, but you might open the doors wider to "pretty" by saying, "I wish they made a Barbie who looks like Aunt Michelle."

Invest elsewhere: We don't ask you to roll your eyes or put down the toys she loves. We do suggest that you compete with the commercial by doing the following:

- Take the focus off Barbie by talking up guitar playing and saying how glad you are that they gave Barbie something to do besides changing clothes and looking pretty. Comment on how great guitar solos are and how much work it takes to play the guitar well. You might also mention her playing an instrument in the future, or, if she's already taking piano lessons, you might say her piano work is going to help her learn guitar or drums. The important part of this conversation is reinforcing her dreams and turning the opportunity into something more than being pretty or sexy-pretty.

- Invest in alternatives by introducing criticism. Whenever you see a Lego commercial, for example, with its motors, gears, and such, you can say, "Hey, where are the girls? Why do they let boys have all the fun on commercials?" Or you can ratchet up the excitement for such toys by saying, "Oh, wow! Those Legos look like so much fun. We have to get some of those sometime. I wonder how hard it is to make a vehicle that moves. They're showing a boy your age doing it, so you could surely make something like that!"

These conversations can take place before you go shopping. Before looking for a bicycle, for instance, you can talk about zooming and being free and having wings or blasting off. You can also talk loud and excitedly about other colors besides pink: "Look at that blue! I love blue."

Remember that the object of the conversation is to help your daughter invest energy and excitement in a range of alternatives to pretty and sweet. That's all. It's tough to do, but it is probably easier than getting her to eat cauliflower. After all, cauliflower isn't all that delicious, but building a car that moves or buying a new bicycle? That's really cool, every bit as cool, if not more so, than dressing Barbie up, don't you think?

GIRLS VERSUS BOYS

This conversation can happen whenever a girls-versus-boys situation arises. It may occur on a cartoon or in a book, or your daughter may hear a friend say, "Boys are better at x" or "Girls are better at y." This is an incredibly important conversation to have when girls are young be-cause they will be confronted all their lives with people telling them that girls are totally different from boys and women are completely dif-ferent from men. Unlike discussions about diversity, where she'll be told that people are all alike on the inside, she'll be bombarded with gender messages that tell her girls and boys look, act, feel, and think differently. If you don't start undermining this concept now, she'll join the rest of the culture who are convinced that biologically women and men are po-lar opposites. What girls and boys have in common—everything from a capacity for compassion to a potential love of science—will be gender coded. What almost always happens next is that difference turns into better or worse. Girls and women tend to fare badly in this game.

Engage: Here a mom might want to declare, "Oh, no! Another girls-versus-boys show" or "I see your friend thinks that girls and boys are total opposites. I wonder where she got that idea!" You might even bring it up in a conversation: "Isn't it funny that just because there are boys and girls, everyone seems to think they're opposite."

Question: "Do you think that girls and boys are opposites?" you might ask. Or "Why do you think they make girls and boys fight so much or put them on opposite sides on these shows. Surely your teachers don't do that in kindergarten, do they?" Many girls this age have friends who are boys, so you could also lead by example: "You and Tommy always find something you both like to play, and you laugh together. Are you oppo-sites?" "Are Mommy and Daddy total opposites when they cook dinner together or go to the movies or tuck you in at night?"

Listen: Your daughter may say that girls and boys *are* opposites and point out that boys play with trucks and girls play with dolls, and boys are rough and girls are gentle.

Don't argue: At this point you've elicited stereotypes from her that the world has taught her. Arguing may actually reinforce these stereo-types. The truth is within her, however, and is not something you need to educate her about. So you can agree to some extent:
"I see what you mean. On most of the cartoons we do see the boys playing rough and the girls being sweet." Or "A lot of people think that's absolutely true!"

Reflect, share discomfort, and provide counterexamples: It's important to provide a reality check with counterexamples whenever you can: "But we love to wrestle on the floor" or "You can be much louder than Tommy sometimes, so that doesn't quite hold true, does it?" Open up space for her to be more than a stereotype by affirming her complexity: "You like to be sweet sometimes and to play rough other times." Reflect on the narrow choices and share your discomfort: "It makes me sad when people say girls can only be some things and boys can only be others when kids want to do it all. I loved it when people told me I could do anything. I think you can do anything, too."

Conversations with Your Preteen

SHOPPING AND CONSUMERISM

The S word can go from the more general *stereotype* to the more specific *shopping* as your daughter moves into the preteen years. Shopping itself isn't a problem. It's that girls and women are almost exclusively defined by consumption and material belongings and that a multibillion-dollar beauty industry depends on girls and women feeling bad enough about how they look, dress, smell, and act to buy products to improve themselves. Built into the message that shopping is fun and freeing, a sign of a passion for color or romance or independence, is a message about what a girl or woman needs to match up to a marketer's vision of what it means to be female. There are also messages about the superficiality of girls, their competition with other girls over appearance, and that girls can resolve emotional problems by buying something to make them feel better. Messages such as "Shop 'til you drop" and "When the going gets tough, the tough go shopping" ignore realities like the poverty here in the U.S. and around the world and the impact of mass consumerism on the environment. Conversations with your daughter about shopping can therefore move in many different directions.

Since almost every aspect of girl culture promotes or reflects "a passion for fashion" and shopping, this conversation can happen almost anytime and anyplace. Your daughter may be playing with a Bratz doll or Shopping Avenger Kim Possible, reading an *American Girl* catalog or *Discovery Girl* magazine. She might be watching *Lizzie McGuire* or laughing at Trixie in *The Fairly OddParents*. Or you may actually be out shopping together.

Engage: The wonderful thing about preteen girls is their curiosity. Lyn and psychologist Carol Gilligan refer to girls this age as naturalists in the social world. Like a botanist observing a forest, girls notice the details in the social environments they frequent, so a mom can begin a dialogue with the very next image or message about shopping. The idea is really to identify the larger pattern so your daughter will begin thinking about it. It's always best to engage her in a conversation about something she has noticed first.

Question: If she has noticed a cute T-shirt with two teens going shopping or that awful Kim Possible shopping doll, one way into a conversation is to wonder why girls and women are almost always shown buying things or why people expect girls to be so excited about shopping. You might ask her what she thinks about that, adding that So-and-so hates to shop. If she hasn't noticed this, you don't have to address the issue at that moment but can suggest that the two of you make a game of it, such as the "punch buggy" game of playful punches when you see a VW Beetle ("Punch buggy red, no-punch-back" can become "Girl into shopping," no punch back).

Listen: If she has noticed, you can also ask her what she thinks about it or how she feels about shopping. You might be surprised by her answer. She may like shopping because it means spending time with you, away from her siblings. She might like it because she always gets something she wants. She may not like it but thinks she should. You might also wonder aloud about a specific product. You could, for example, ask her why they made a Kim Possible Shopping Avenger doll when she's a heroine and action figure who is supposed to be saving the world or rescuing her friend Ron.

Images of girls and women shopping are so common, she may assume it is just a normal part of what it means to be female. But she may also not register the images in the way you do and may not even call the same things shopping ("She's just being with her friends, and that's what her friends want to do"), in which case she may argue with you. She may respond to your questions by saying, "What's the big deal? Girls just love shopping," or "You love to go shopping, don't you? You always want me to go with you."

Be honest: If what she says about you and shopping is true, it's okay to say so. In fact, you might tell her what you love about shopping and let her in on what's going through your mind when you need to purchase something, such as decisions about budgeting, weighing options, thinking about what other people in the family need, quality versus junk, your frustration with the skinny mannequins in store windows, fads versus items with staying power, and gifts you plan to give friends for special occasions. Part of what you love might be comparison shopping for the best deal or finding secondhand treasures at yard sales. This opens the door for a conversation about saving money, recycling, and making thoughtful choices rather than knee-jerk reactions to the latest product. But don't go overboard about the power in making smart decisions when shopping. This is traditionally how women were first given power at the turn of the century (before they were given the vote). Promoters of big department stores promised women they'd have a certain kind of power through shopping—looking over fabric, comparing brands, and making important decisions about what to purchase (even if they were unable to make the more important decision of who to vote for). We see many ads these days with this same basic message!

You might love malls and going shopping because it's the only place in a rural area to people-watch and be where there's a lot of stimulation and excitement. If so, you might relate what it's like in bigger cities where you can sit on benches by a fountain or in a park and people-watch, feeling part of a big, exciting place. Malls have replaced public squares, and there are few places to feel the excitement of a downtown—the lights, the people, and the busyness.

Reflect, share discomfort, and provide counterexamples: Going to the mall with your daughter can be a bonding experience. Buying her first bra, negotiating clothing, and eventually placing limits on the wearing of makeup all provide opportunities for bigger discussions. These are moments when mothers relay important information to daughters about the joys and perils of growing up as a girl in a fast-paced world. But if shopping is really for spending time together, you might talk with her about other things you two can do. Mention how fathers are shown by the media, bonding with sons over sports, fishing, fixing things, and the natural world. Here is where counterexamples help. Talk about the girls you know who love these and many other activities, too. Remind her how much you've enjoyed going to the movies with her or exploring the bookstore and looking over books. You might even ask if she thinks she'd enjoy tackling a climbing wall together, playing a board game, taking a canoe trip, learning to snowboard, or going to a museum.

Continue conversations in a more reflective way: Your daughter may respond to your question about the Kim Possible Shopping Avenger doll with an astute observation such as, "They make Kim shop for the same reason they make her a cheerleader—so she seems more like someone girls want to be like." Or "She's cool, so she has to have the latest cool stuff." Or the coup de grâce: "Mom, it's just a toy."

You can agree here and point out how perceptive she is. Depending on her openness at the moment, you might still raise questions that encourage her to think a little more deeply about this toy: "Yes, it's just a toy, and you're probably right about the coolness thing. But I wonder how they know what girls your age think is cool." Don't forget to listen here and see if she really does think it's cool. You may hear that cool means feeling grownup, and she feels that it might be grownup or teenage-ish to be left in a mall with her friends, making decisions about what to spend her money on. If this is what you hear, you can remind her that the "grown-up" part of Kim Possible isn't so much that she shops like other girls but that she's so responsible and independent in that superhero kind of way.

The object of the conversation is not to make your daughter hate shopping but to help her see that the overwhelming number of images that associate shopping with girls makes them seem kind of dumb and superficial, like the giddy girls in *Rugrats: All Grown Up* who rush to buy the latest invention of little Dil. She may not even be "into shopping" yet if she's eight, or nine, or ten, but it's important to have this conversation in this age range, before the age when you'd let her be at a mall or at a downtown shopping street with her friends. It's part of broadening the way that she looks at how girls are represented. You will also be broadening the way she sees all people.

MEDIA AND IMAGE

Begin this conversation with an activity such as watching the special features sections on a favorite DVD where they discuss how they made the film, including behind-the-scenes looks. This opens the door to a particular kind of conversation about the choices made in a film and establishes a *they* to talk about.

Engage: Here you might want to talk about what she liked and didn't like about a film. Preteens tend to like certain characters or funny parts of the film and dislike the mean kids or the villains. They also might be watching for what a film changes or leaves out of a favorite book such as *Harry Potter* or *A Series of Unfortunate Events*.

Question: You can pick any aspects of the film that are girl-unfriendly, based on some of the things we described in our section on what girls watch. Here are examples: "Why do you think *they* chose to have the prince rescue [girl's name] three times?" "Why do you think *they* chose a girl who was so pretty and skinny to play the role?" "Why do you think *they* decided to make the sidekick or the creatures that accompany her all boys?" "Why do you think *they* don't include her best friend in the journey?"

Listen: Your daughter may say, "That's the way these movies go. All the girls in movies are pretty and skinny. You have to be that way to be in the movies." She may even say, "Princesses are supposed to be pretty" or "Because boys are funnier than girls" or "Because girls during that time weren't allowed to do that kind of stuff." "Because boys burp a lot" and "Because her best friend wasn't an important part of the story" are also possibilities.

Don't argue: It's unlikely you'll have a conversation if you argue with your daughter about how she perceives the world. Do remember that her perceptions come from somewhere, and this is your main concern.

Don't be afraid to agree: "You're right. That *is* the way these movies go. I've noticed that, too." Here a mom could even share something she watched as a child. "Most of the girls in movies always seem to be pretty and skinny—even when I was your age."

Reflect, share discomfort, and provide counterexamples: If she's noticed that once again a boy has rescued a girl, you can say. "I've noticed that too. And it's bothered me because girls can rescue boys, and the girls I know, like you, probably wouldn't wait for someone to rescue them."

She may argue and say, "But she couldn't move, so someone had to rescue her."

Then you might say, "This is true. I wonder why *they* made it so she couldn't move when the prince was there, so she had to rely on him. *They* could have changed the story there. Do you have any ideas?"

After listening to your daughter's ideas uncritically, you can share some counterexamples: "Maybe they could have shown her quick thinking about how to get out of a jam even though she couldn't move. Remember Elisa in *The Wild Thornberrys* movie? She saved the day when it seemed impossible." Or you can say, "I've noticed they seem to show girls like that in books more than movies. Remember *The Trouble with Trolls*? You loved that book when you were younger. And remember Matilda? She was so smart and a quick thinker." Or say, "Maybe they could have her best friend come by. I like it when they show how girls help each other." You can also share examples from TV or movies where they show a boy getting himself out of a jam when it seemed as if there was no possible solution.

You might prefer to take the discussion in a somewhat different direction: "You're right. Most of the girls in the movies do seem to be pretty and skinny. And I've also noticed that most of them tend to be white and rich."

We advise you to acknowledge the counterexamples. Your daughter may bring up the new Raven movie, and your role would be to compliment her on noticing that sort of thing and saying that you "like it when *they* include on TV and in the movies for girls who seem more like girls we know."

But let's say she doesn't counter your point when you talk about a movie that is full of stereotypes. Your questions may yield responses like "That's just the way it is" or "They pick actresses that everyone thinks is pretty." You then have an opportunity to say, "I wonder what would happen if they picked a girl who looked like the girls we know to star in a film like that. They're all so beautiful in their own way. Do you think the girls watching the movie wouldn't like them as much because they don't look like the typical actresses?"

Depending on how the conversation goes, a parent could even suggest going to the video store and looking for a movie about a girl where it seems *they* didn't think looks were the most important thing when they cast the part.

A parent has to make a judgment about where to stop. The goal is getting a girl to think outside the box. You don't need to have her think the way you do, and you don't have to come to an agreement. You just need to raise the questions. What you're doing is encouraging her to ask her own questions and not take things at face value. It doesn't really matter if your daughter just defends the general worldview of girls. If you bring up a series of questions, they will linger in her mind no matter what she is comfortable voicing at this time.

CHOOSING ACTIVITIES SHE LOVES

This conversation can happen during the school year when choices come up, but we suggest starting it in the summer before school begins or even at the end of the school year when the summer and all that free time loom ahead. A parent can anticipate activities for the coming year and look for summer ones that promote experimentation with a wide variety of choices. The best way to start conversations is with examples of girls doing things that are exciting, adventurous, athletic, and fun. You would begin by presenting counterexamples as naturally as possible whenever you see them. Keep your eyes open for these kinds of examples and even find articles in papers or magazines.

Engage: To engage, you might simply talk about all the different choices a girl has: the kinds of sports she can play, the types of activities she can participate in, and the various musical instruments she can learn. Holding up a magazine article you might say, "Look at this girl who's steering her own sailboat here. That looks like fun." Or "Hey, stay up late and watch this cool band I saw the other night on *Jay Leno*. It's only a guy and a girl. The guy plays the guitar, and the girl plays the drums. They wear only black and white. Weird, but they have an interesting sound." Or "Let's watch the U Conn women's basketball game. Those women are amazing. Do you see how they don't let up?"

Engage her through qualities of her own: Girls have heard thousands of compliments about their feminine qualities all their lives, but you can turn these to her advantage. "You're so graceful, Tatiana. I bet you'd be an excellent climber." Hear the unexpected? It's not ballet dancer but climber. We associate grace with an outdoor adventurous activity, not necessarily with dance. "You're so good with animals, Katori. I bet you'd be able to take a horse over some really high jumps someday if you took up horseback riding." Girls who like animals have been told they'd make good veterinarians, because they nurture, but they haven't been told they'd make good dog trainers, an activity that would ask them to take control. "You're such a good singer, Mallory. I bet you could make one of those big brass instruments really sound good." And try those other qualities that you don't hear attributed to girls very often, such as "You're a born leader" and "You have such a good head for business."

Question: Pushing girls is okay, but push them by asking questions and showing your curiosity. For example, moms and dads can push their girls to be more present and aggressive when they play sports. They can push them to try activities different from the ones they're used to through one-week summer camps or by taking a class with them. How about a surprise gift of ten rock-and-roll guitar lessons from a grandmother or a surprise weekend trying to learn how to snowboard with Dad?

Talking about gender is tricky and should be approached with an attitude of curiosity and questioning. That way you let your daughter know that you want to see it through her eyes. "I'm wondering why so few of the girls in your class chose the drums in band and so many chose the flute." "I noticed when I was watching soccer today that the boys were trying for the goals and the girls were passing to the boys. I was kind of surprised by that because there are so many good players among the girls on your team." Again, when you see TV commercials, cartoons, and movies, these "I wonder why" questions or "did you notice" remarks hang in there long after they're spoken. "Why did they have the boy make the goal in the commercial?" "Did you notice how they made the lead character on that show play the flute while her brother played the drums?"

Listen: Your daughter may say, "Girls don't like to play the drums," or "The boys all want to go for the goal. They're not very good at passing." Referring to your remark about her school, she may say, "That's not true. Julie's going to be playing the drums," thereby giving you an exception to the rule. She might instead get defensive and say, "I got a goal last week. Don't you remember?"

Don't argue: Again, it's unlikely you'll have a conversation if you argue with your daughter about how she perceives the world. In fact, if she feels you're criticizing her, you should try to turn the conversation into complimenting her on her participation and talents, and expressing curiosity about girls in general. You are trying to teach her and step back and reflect before she decides what it means personally to her.

Don't be afraid to agree: "You're right. Julie is going to make a great drummer! I think that was bold of her to step up when so many girls were saying how nice the flute is." Or "You did get a goal last week. I love to see you push through the crowd of kids. You were amazing." Then you can say, "I didn't mean you today. I was noticing that some girls are afraid to get aggressive and be the ones to take the ball."

Reflect, share discomfort, and provide counterexamples: Let's say the conversation continues about Julie. "Julie is going to make a great drummer. It bothers me when I see that girls don't want to try to make a big sound. Sometimes I think they're afraid to be 'out there' and that they choose a flute because they are more concerned with looking sweet and pretty." If she argues that the other instruments are too big for girls, you might add, "It's a good way to build up your muscles. People get used to their instruments. I've seen some rather small boys playing them."

Let's say the conversation continues about soccer. You say, "You're right. You were amazing. I love it when you take the field. I didn't mean you. I just felt sad when it seemed that some of the girls thought it was the boys' job to get the goals. And I saw a boy not pass to a girl on the same team but take it down the field himself. She was in such a good position. I hope the coach said something to that boy afterward. Next time I hope she screams at the top of her lungs 'I'm open!' "

Parents are in a position to ask "I wonder why" because they're not in the world of their daughters and have a right to their curiosity. If they truly listen to their daughter's musings and support her in doing that kind of musing, then they've set the stage for sharing their discomfort and their hopes for all girls.

A parent may end up with a daughter digging her feet in and saying, "I really want to play the flute because I like it." Okay. Let it go. There is nothing wrong with the flute per se. What we're aiming for are well-rounded girls, not girls who give up everything and anything that has been blessed with the fairy dust of pretty pink girlhood. Some of that stuff is fun!

Again, a parent always has to make a judgment about where to stop. Our children have sometimes looked at us and said, "Do you have to analyze everything?" To which we answer, "Well, yes. But we don't have to share it all the time. We'll be quiet and let you just enjoy this." What you've conveyed to your daughter is that it's a choice to consume and take it all in, and it's also a choice to step back and evaluate, and ask questions about the world.

Again, we want to reassure parents that it doesn't matter if your daughter defends her choices as being about her rather than about her being a girl. If you reflect on all the things she is and bring up questions about the world around her instead of her choices, these questions will linger in her mind. We guarantee she will voice them to her friends even if she can't yet to you.

Conversations with Your Middle Schoolers

MEDIA, IMAGE, AND GIRL TYPING

From stereotypes to shopping to, well, stereotypes again. We constantly return to them and hope you will, too. A more advanced clothing or shopping discussion involves not just pointing out stereotypical images but helping your daughter recognize how narrow a set of options are presented by marketers and the media for girls. This conversation is about the way marketers and the media "type" girls. You might recall your earlier conversations about stereotypes and say to your daughter: "It seems as if marketers have gotten around this problem by creating a variety of girl types and pretending you have a choice about which one to be." The message of this conversation will be: "Defy type!"

Engage: The time to engage your daughter is when you hear her referring to another girl as a type—a rocker, a goth, a prep, a skater girl, a girly girl. Let's say your daughter has referred to someone as a goth or that you just read a fashion section on Hilary Duff and how she's such a girly girl.

Question: A mom or dad can pick up on this immediately and ask, "What's a goth?" or "What's a girly girl?" Most likely your daughter will say something about what the person wears and what she does. You might ask the more sophisticated middle schoolers, "Isn't it funny that everyone wants to be an individual but keeps returning to the same old types? I wonder why that's so." Or if you're feeling feisty you can say, "Is everyone a type? Do you know any truly original people?"

Listen: You've learned something from your daughter and acknowledge that. Thank her for sharing what she knows because you really don't know her world. You may even want to share with her the types that were around in your middle school when you were growing up.

Don't argue or criticize: The problem is not that she's labeling other girls and it's bad to label. The problem isn't even that she's name-calling or that she may be wrong about these girls. The problem is not with her, it's with the marketers and the media. And for all you know these girls she's talking about identify themselves as goths or girly girls. That's not the point in this conversation.

Don't be afraid to agree: You can say, "I see what you mean. Caroline does seem to wear pink a lot, and she did try out for cheerleading, didn't she? Those *do* go together sometimes." Or "I see what you mean. So Dana is wearing black all the time and hanging out with some kids who might be smoking pot. Does she like to listen to really dark music, too?"

Reflect, share discomfort, and provide counterexamples: A parent should first be concerned with acknowledging that this is a time of life when kids want to be somebody, so the end point is not that you and your daughter call these girls *posers* (a word for a kid who is fake, just imitating a type, rather than being authentically so). Acknowledge the dilemma and say, "I guess everybody wants to be somebody. It's easy to fall into seeing yourself as a type of kid instead of just you!" Then try your best to show that this focus on types really constrains a girl. We thought of the recent example of seeing Hilary Duff on the Ellen DeGeneres show. You could say to your daughter, "Even though she plays those sweet, pretty, girly girl types in movies and is now trying to make herself into a sexy rock star, she showed that she had other qualities that didn't fit with that type at all! Did you know she was a gymnast? On the TV show she did some stunts on a trampoline and looked almost like a pro." You can probably find information about other stars that goes against their types. You're encouraging her to think outside the boxes provided for her. And you can also raise her awareness about the whole phrase "girly girl," which is a put-down: "First they sell you pink pink pink and dolls dolls dolls, and then when you turn thirteen they make fun of you for being a girly girl? Jeeesh!"

Another time to bring awareness and a critical eye to looking at types is when looking through magazines. You could share by saying, "Look at all the accessories they want to sell you to fit a certain type" and "They never say 'just be yourself' without giving you a product to make you more of 'yourself.' "

Again, decide when enough's enough. The point is to get your daughter to think outside the box. It will be good for her to feel uncomfortable when she hears someone type a girl, just as she gets uncomfortable when she hears a racial or ethnic slur. You don't need to have her think the way you do, and you don't have to come to an agreement. You just need to raise the questions.

MEAN GIRLS

One kind of typing that you have to have a conversation about early concerns the typing of a girl as a "mean girl." ("Snob" and "slut" are two other variations.) Competition among girls, dirty looks, gossip, and exclusion reach a crescendo in middle school, and the problem is enabled by labeling a behavior or a girl mean or snobby.

Engage: You can say, "There's a lot of talk about mean girls lately." If your daughter has been hurt, you can say, "I see you've been treated badly, and that's just wrong." If she's talking about another girl with her friends, say, "I see you are not hanging out with LaShandra anymore."

Question: Wonder aloud why people in the media are so interested in girls being mean to each other. You might say, "They focus on all the problems and leave out how great friends girls can be!" If your daughter has been hurt by another girl, ask, "What got in the way of this girl being a friend?" She may answer, "She's just mean." After hearing her put down another girl: "What got in the way of *you* being a friend?" The presumption in all of these questions is that the norm is friendship and solidarity rather than competition, envy, and gossip, and that some*thing* got in the way, not someone. That your daughter hears this presumption from you is so important. She may hear it from no one else.

Listen: You'll hear from your daughter a lot of what she hears on television, in school, and in movies—that girls just can't get along, girls can be meaner than boys, or there's one particular girl who is meaner than the others. You need to hear her ideas about this. If she's perceptive, she may even talk about the environment at school that pits girls against one another. If you've been helping her name stereotypes over the years, this will be a familiar one. Her ability to see the behavior as part of a larger pattern and not just about her might not take away the immediate sting, but it will help her feel less alone and more in control.

Be honest: Don't be afraid to agree. When you agree, you can agree without being in total agreement. Enter the conversation each time by partially agreeing. You may be tempted to disagree and say "not all girls" or "boys can be mean, too." You may be tempted to make some general statements about girls because you've been hearing these statements your whole life: "Girls can be so mean," or "Girls are meaner than boys." But try to be sympathetic and specific: "Yes, what Shannon did was mean and hurtful." Even share your own story if you've been there: "I remember when my best friend in eighth grade suddenly turned on me."

How do you react to the accusation that a particular girl is a mean girl? Depending on the situation, you might say, "It sounds like Donna is getting a lot of encouragement to be mean to other girls" (which might point the finger at her friends or at the boys). Also, "It sounds like Donna is in a pretty powerful position when she starts acting like that to you. I wish there were other ways Donna could feel powerful instead of taking her anger out on kids like you." Or "Wow, that does sound very mean," which focuses on what Donna did and not the predilection of her entire gender.

Reflect, share discomfort, and provide counterexamples: In this conversation you don't want to give counterexamples immediately about how girls can be nice, too. A comment such as "We're all mean sometimes" is not going to relieve the pain. You want to affirm her feelings and acknowledge how hard these situations are, and then you want her to experience a sense of control in the situation.

We like the approach of looking at the social context or the wider environment to see what was contributing to a girl's mean act and the lack of support your daughter felt at the time. This rescues her from being the victim and also recognizes that the mean girl is acting with some encouragement and that her meanness is a bid for power: "Usually when someone hurts others in the way Donna is hurting you, it's because she's afraid or because she needs power and attention. I know it probably doesn't help much, but we all have to deal with the Donnas of the world—people who take out their anger and insecurities on others. We can't control them, but we can control how we react to them. Let's work on that part." You might tell a story of someone you've encountered who sounds like Donna and how you reacted. It's okay to share your past feelings of fear, humiliation, or anger. It's important to share what you learned from that situation.

As for her sense of control, brainstorm some possible solutions and scenarios. Encourage her to speak up for herself but only when she feels safe and ready. Help her practice what she wants to say. It's important that you affirm the role of other friends she can count on. Here again, underscore the power and possibility of coalition. Nothing works better than standing firm and having your friends at your back. If she feels all alone, you may also need to seek activities and programs in your community that offer her a sense of power and place, such as a drama troupe, a martial arts course, or a technology course. This doesn't represent running away but supporting her right to choose places and people that are affirming. "They are out there," tell her, "and you deserve to be with people who are good to you."

SEX IN SONG

This next conversation can happen during the ride to school when she's fiddling with the radio dials. Music can be a great jumping-off point for talks about a number of middle school topics, the number one topic being sex. Use lyrics to talk to your daughter about sex. With a middle schooler you'll feel the most discomfort at the horrible degrading things said about women and the sometimes graphic sex and violence described in lyrics even though you may not hear these on the radio. If your teen has an MP3 player, you'll need to find the gadget to play it through the car radio. You need to be there, listening to the same lyrics she is. And when you hear a song that is demeaning to women, full of curse words, or talking about sex acts you'd rather she didn't know about yet, don't dismiss it out of hand. Instead, talk about it.

Engage: Sing along (though most kids hate this). Say "I like that beat." (They'll tolerate that.) Ask if they know who the drummer is. Play some songs that were risqué in your time and let them guess what the lyrics were. You can even dance with them in your living room.

Question: "Where are the girls?" This is an important question to ask if your daughter listens to rock or rap. Or you can say, "I wonder if it's more difficult for girls and girls' groups to get their songs out there in the world of rock or rap." And when it comes to the rap lyrics that insult women say, "I wonder if he really hates women or if he's just posing that way for the song." Ask her, "Do you tune it out or sing along with some of those lyrics?" When a female artist is doing her sexy thing: "Why does it seem that every girl with a good voice has to sex it up a bit to sell records now? Doesn't she trust her voice alone?" You can wonder who's next: "I wonder if Avril's going to do a sexy video in a year or two. Do you think that's the only alternative for girl singers or might she become an awesome guitarist and start a new band?" The point you want to make is not that sexy is bad but that it seems to be the only alternative for girl singers.

Listen: This refers to both the lyrics and your daughter. Also listen to the music. So many regrettable lyrics are put to fun music. In spite of the exaggerated sexuality in the lyrics, the music is often great to dance to.

Don't argue: Your daughter might say about the lyrics, "They're not bad," and you may want to avoid terms like *good* and *bad*. "No, they're not bad," you can say. She might even get defensive and talk about how it's not bad that girls have to be sexy to be in videos and make music. Don't get caught in the "sexy is bad" discussion. You won't win that one. It's best to just wonder if there are some other things that might be expressed about a girl or a girl's life in song that is not about being sexy or having a boyfriend. Far too many people have demeaning sexist thoughts about girls and women. Some of the more shocking lyrics show your daughter what she will learn about in high school or perhaps later—that girls are pieces of ass and that their main worth is in their sexuality. You need to express your thoughts about these lyrics.

Don't be afraid to agree. She may defend Eminem as someone who is trying to be bad and to shock people, even admiring him for his struggles in life. Ask her, "Why do you think what he says is shocking?" Let her explain that. She may argue that Eminem has the courage to express sentiments that a lot of people have. What a perceptive point that would be. You can agree with your daughter there.

Reflect, share discomfort, and provide counterexamples: If you detach from the lyrics, you can express a kind of boredom with the same old–same old, not a sense of shock and outrage that she might expect. If you think of it, it is sad that these lyricists are expressing a way of looking at girls and women that is not new. It can also be funny. Perhaps you can do an over-the-top parody of a song that will cause your daughter to scream with laughter! A little well-placed humor doesn't hurt.

Do some research. Listen to the radio and repeat the lyrics you hear that seem to be communicating something unusual or even supportive. We almost cried when we first heard "Video," the fantastic song by India.Arie. It has a great beat and great vocals. The lyrics explain that she's not built like a supermodel, her worth is not determined by her clothing, and she actually likes her looks: "My feet my thighs my lips my eyes, I'm lovin' what I see." What a sentiment for a fourteen-year-old girl to sing!

If you love music, let *your* music do the talking. It can't be just "no, stop, don't" when you talk to your daughter. It has to be "listen, hear, love," which means you're going to need to find songs like "Video" and artists like India.Arie. Read to your daughter from the credits of the album; she dedicates her album to Gramma Louise, her friend Amira, and her designer, co-writer, vocal coach, confidante, friend, and business partner—her mother.

And face it: Your daughter is going to listen to lyrics that are kind of shocking. She just is. When it's all about girls "blowing" guys, having a "more of that again?" expression is more likely to get through than a shocked "you're too young to hear that" response. If you're truly disgusted, explain what disgusts you—for example, that you're afraid she will get a mental image of cool, hip, sexy, grownup women living their lives to impress men with their bodies and their sex acts rather than taking pleasure in their wit or talents. You don't have to hide your worries from her, but don't parent from a position of anxiety. Parent from a position of maturity and critique.

Conversations with Your Teen

CHOOSING AND REFUSING AN IDENTITY

In middle school your daughter's fascination with goths, preps, princesses, nerds, stoners, and other groups in her school has to do with her anxiety about how much she knows or doesn't know and where she fits in. In high school she is still experimenting but more likely has settled into a group that has a certain way of dressing and being in the world. Sometimes girls stake out identities with a clarity and intensity that can be unsettling.

Now more than ever it is important to have done your homework; you should know the types available to her and what they signify—not to others but *to you!* The conversation is about identity, about how well her insides match her outsides; that is, how real, whole, and authentic she feels as she presents herself to the world. This requires a different kind of conversation, one in which you think aloud with her about all the ways to dress and how her choices express those parts of her that are important. At the same time you will offer observations about how the alternatives available to girls are limited.

Even teenagers who have been raised to resist don't want their *parents* to be the ones to point out that they've been manipulated, fooled, or made to conform by marketing and the media. In fact, never say, "Oh, you just want to buy that because you saw that commercial on TV." That's an incredible insult, and it makes your daughter feel as if she is the problem rather than the messages that bombard her. Teens want to believe that every choice they make comes from their unique, original, independent selves. Your daughter may very well be doing what she's doing to conform, but she feels that she has made a decision as an independent actor. The best way to work with teen daughters, therefore, is to be with them in their world, share observations, point to the culture and not directly at her fishnets, her music, or her slang.

The trickiest conversation to have is the one about being and looking sexy because everywhere she goes there are marketers promoting girls' *right* to look sexy and the power they get when they look sexy. It is difficult to talk about because the same culture that overvalues girls' sexiness disconnects it from the sexual violence we live with every day. Looking sexy doesn't get a female raped, but the same culture that overvalues looking sexy does not educate about or protect girls from rape drugs, date rape, harassment, and unfair legal practices that blame women for the violence perpetrated on them.

Engage: There are so many images of sexy women used to sell clothing and just about everything from cars to cleaning supplies that you have quite a canvas to work with. You might engage simply by saying something about the way some piece of clothing you see in a store, in a magazine, or on a friend looks sexy.

Question: The word *sexy* is everywhere, so you can ask her what it means. Does it mean something new, interesting, or trendy? What exactly is "hott"? You can also ask your daughter what she sees as hot and why. Is it important to look a little sexy? What does she see as the line between a little and a lot. This could lead to a question about the possibilities available to girls, such as what makes a teen girl look and feel powerful besides looking sexy.

Listen: Learn her thoughts on power and sexiness and image. In our experience girls love to talk about image, and if they're not being criticized but being consulted, they're more than willing to talk about themselves and their friends.

Don't argue or criticize. She may sense an argument or a criticism and become defensive. She might ask, "What about all the women *your* age getting plastic surgery or Botox?" Or she might say people your age are into looks and looking younger just as much or even more so than young people are into looking sexy.

Don't be afraid to agree. She is astute if she makes the point about older women because in many ways it *is* the same thing. This tells you something about her definition of sexy, so listen. It may mean that she connects sexy to improving one's appearance; it may also mean she holds some anxiety about the idea. If she doesn't make this connection, you might. You can use as examples people you know who worry too much about image even though they have wonderful characteristics and lives that aren't reflected in their attempts to look younger and sexier. You might add that young people may not appreciate that some older people they know, because they're older or overweight or don't look like models, are really very sexual people. It's okay if she says, "Ew, gross." And point out the number of people in romantic relationships around her, many of them not "hott" at all. You don't have to look sexy to find love.

Reflect, share discomfort, and provide counterexamples. Ultimately this is a conversation about image and what's inside, and the lesson is that image can go only so far to express a person. It's also important to convey how there's something genuinely sexy about being real to yourself and others. Think together about girls and women you know who have that something special that attracts people to them. It's not just how they look but something deeper, like a vibe they give off, an inner something that's hard to name or pin down. This can lead to a conversation about looking sexy versus being sexual in the sense of being embodied, owning, and expressing all of yourself. You can admit there are benefits or rewards for looking sexy in a world that gives power to the sexy. But don't be afraid to talk about your own hopes that she'll grow up to know herself as a sexual woman and that this is a joy you want her to have that goes beyond being looked at.

NEGATIVE IDENTITY: CUTTING, VOMITING, PIERCING, AND MORE

Pain in adolescence is difficult for parents to bear. We were there once and remember the awful loneliness that came at times, the weirdness that arose with friends, a sense of alienation, the wanting to reach out but the inability sometimes to do so, the appearance of hypocrisy in the world around us, the fierce loyalty to causes and sometimes lost causes in our friends. Yet there is something in the media that makes us parents forget these feelings and focus on the symptoms. If you see your daughter going over to what seems like the dark side of adolescent angst and self-destruction, it's good to clue into these feelings rather than to the media alarms about the rising percentages of self-cutting in the schools.

Your daughter has been hearing this hype, too. We call it hype because there's an element of marketing these acts as coping strategies to kids, and this hype takes place in books, movies, and song. Truth be told, negative coping is glamorized, and girls may choose this mode of expression.

Engage: Engaging any of these issues is tricky, and if you approach your daughter with worries about self-cutting, bulimia, not eating, or more minor expressions of difference or alienation such as piercing or hair dying, she's likely to feel your engagement as a criticism. You might connect on the level of pain. If you have a great relationship with your daughter, you can be direct: "You seem to be feeling awful lately. I wish I could help." But if you think the direct approach won't work, try talking about pop artists and friends who struggle with self-cutting, bulimia, and piercings in this way. You might say something like, "She's dealing with a lot of outside pressures in her life. I wonder if that has an impact."

Question: Here is where you might ask your daughter to consider this with you. "What do you and your friends do with all that sorrow or anger about the world around you when you really feel it?" Or "I wonder if anyone is listening to what this girl is saying about herself and the world she lives in."

Listen: You want to hear her thoughts on pain and sadness and anger in adolescence. That's exactly what the conversation should be about, not about the cutting, vomiting, or piercing. Everything we've heard from teens who've tried it and done it for some time indicates that they are in pain and are looking for a way that works for them to express it and relieve it.

Don't argue or criticize: She may sense an argument or a criticism and shut you out by saying things like "That's sick" about certain behaviors or "It's not about anything" to avoid analyzing.

Don't be afraid to agree: You'll want to agree if she labels these behaviors as unhealthy. You'll want to change words like *sick* and *disgusting* to *unhealthy* and agree that sometimes kids try these negative behaviors and acts just to try them. We know one girl who self-injures, and after confessing this to all her friends at a slumber party, each and every one of them tried it. For one or two it worked in some way. When it serves a purpose, then it's expressing something about the girl. If your daughter describes another girl doing anything "just for attention," you can agree and add that as girls develop there is a deep craving for attention, for being seen and heard. Don't make her feel ashamed for wanting attention; talk about positive ways to achieve it.

Reflect, share discomfort, and provide counterexamples. Ultimately this is a conversation about feelings. You want to provide your daughter with alternative ways of expressing pain, and she is dealing with negative emotions in one of the best ways: talking to you about them.

Remember that many of these acts are not only about expressing pain but about coping with that pain, getting rid of the feeling, numbing oneself, and in the end feeling nothing. The more a parent can bring feelings into a conversation, the better tolerance a girl will have for discussing her feelings and dealing with them. She will not need to numb herself.

You can share your discomfort with your daughter when she and her friends make choices that numb them to the world. You can share your own experience of doing the same when you veg out in front of the TV or isolate yourself in your bedroom after a hard day at work. If your stated goal is to help her become strong enough to tolerate these feelings and talk about them, then together you can think of people whom she can reach out to, people who express pain through song, art, writing, or dance, or who cope through work or meditation or jogging. You can also offer to help her find these modes for herself.

Most important, share your concern that the world around her presents her constantly with unhealthy solutions because the world of marketers doesn't care if she chooses to meditate or throw up. In fact, when drug companies that made laxatives started marketing their products to teenagers and young girls, therapists who worked with eating-disordered clients protested!

In short, if she's feeling pain, there may be good reasons—a boyfriend, a breakup, a fight with a best friend, a divorce, a bad relationship with a parent, no money, a faltering sense of direction, a fear of the unknown. But the means of coping have been molded by *Seventeen*, Gossip Girl books, movies, and TV shows. Point these out to her and then add some healthy ways of your own.

SEX ED: WHO ME?

Daughters are aching to talk about sex with someone mature and not just their friends. So why not their mothers or fathers? Because they think that sex is about what someone is doing with someone else, and they don't want their parents to know what they or their friends are doing. Because they think their mothers and fathers are asexual people who don't want to hear about their daughter's desires or sex life. Because sexual feelings are kind of private, and they don't want to talk about some of those feelings with anyone. Most important, because they think that their parents will judge them.

It is incredibly important to have done your homework on this one. If there is any place where you don't want to come at her with a "no, don't, stop" sign it's at the railway tracks of sexuality. That train is coming!

So think first, where are you as a sexual person? You may have to confront your wishes and fears about yourself when it comes to this issue. And think hard, not about what your daughter is doing or going to do, but about what kind of sexual person you want her to be. Far too often parents concentrate on what their daughter might, could, or will do and not on how they want her to be.

We take a strong stand on sex education. Knowing there are faulty abstinence education programs all over, you can't depend on the schools to give your daughter the correct information in the right way. And given the limited amount of time spent on sex education and the emphasis on the mechanics, STDs, and pregnancy prevention, there is little talk about her feelings and impressions about being a sexual person in the world today.

Sex is part of human development. Your best bet is to talk with your daughter about who you want her to be as a person, what kinds of relationships you want her to be involved in, and how sex fits into that picture. This is not a conversation about prohibitions and expectations; it is a conversation about how the media would like her to be sexual versus how you would like her to be sexual. And if you've done your homework and gotten over your worries and fears and the unrealistic desire that she never becomes sexual, you can approach her openhearted with good wishes for her future as a sexual being in this world.

Engage: You've talked to her about all the images that tell her to be sexy. Now what about everything that she has read, heard, and seen about sex? You might point out to her the over-the-top kissing that you and she saw in a particular movie. Or you might comment that sex in books is always so smooth and represented as the best—it never has any of the initial pain, awkwardness, or even the cute little intimacies.

Question: You might begin by asking her if she and her friends think about sex as an athletic event, given how much TV talk there is about Viagra and performance. Or even ask her if she thinks that all the TV shows showing swimsuit model competitions and hot-tubbing bachelorettes affect the way kids think sex really is or should be.

Listen: Listen to her thoughts on sex in general—what she has seen, read, or heard. Make it so that you can talk about sex without its having to be about her experiences. If she can feel that she is being consulted about her world, she won't feel criticized or intruded upon.

Don't judge. Assume that she's part of a sexual world out there, in talk if not in action, no matter how engaged or disengaged from it she is at the moment. If she thinks you are nosing around in her life, she might brush you off, but if you present yourself as curious about the world she lives in and the messages that stores, TV, and movies are giving her about so-called real sex, she may be interested.

Don't be afraid to agree: Give her the opportunity to tell you that she and her friends don't believe in that world of TV supermodel sex. She very likely thinks she and her friends are well informed about sex and what goes on. Acknowledge her knowledge and, well, expertise of a kind, and add that it's great she has friends she can talk to about all the sexual messages that invade our existence every day.

Reflect, share discomfort, and provide counterexamples: Reflecting on sex can be embarrassing for your daughter unless you have a sense of humor about it. If she knows that you want her to enjoy sex at some point, to know her body, and to be able to be intimate with someone she cares about, she may be open to discussing the sexual messages that the two of you see together.

Reflecting may be simply self-reflecting on your own experience. No, we don't mean your actual sex life over the past year but the way things were. What about this whole "friends with benefits" phenomenon? A mom or a dad could say, "Is this so new? I don't think it was unusual in my day for girls to hook up with guys they liked in hopes of their becoming more than friends, and boys might do the same with a girl they were friends with. I'm not sure why the media is making such a big deal of it! They're always trying to show that teens are doing horribly racy things that no one ever thought of!"

Reflecting may be commenting on those embarrassing sex scenes you watch together in a movie: "Boy, they always make these women look as if they're in total ecstasy. And they're always propping themselves up for the camera, aren't they? It's so interesting that they show a kind of porn sex for the camera, but rarely do they show sex that's a little fun, cute, loving, and, well, intimate." Imagine your daughter hearing you say that sex can be fun, cute, loving, and intimate. After all the sex she's read about that describes it as if it is an extreme sport, why not present an alternative?

We're *not* saying that that's the only sex that's "good" in the moral sense of the word. Parents may not want their daughters to have any sexual activity, or they may think it's fine for their daughter to experiment in a healthy way with nonrelationship sex (to name another extreme). We *are* saying that girls need to be presented with a version of what sex looks like, feels like, and sounds like that is different from the screaming, ecstatic, smooth, beautiful, lingerie-clad athletes seen in the movies and read about in books. Even if just the thought of talking about sex with your daughter is making you sweat, your mission is to name it as you see it—on TV, in the movies, in magazines, and in books. Use the words and phrases *porn, athletic, performance-oriented, camera-oriented, always hetero-sexual, overly ecstatic, too smooth, supposed male fantasy sex*, and so on. And after naming it, name something else—something real and less marketed that you know about sex. Your daughter is dying to hear this from you. She wants reality, and you can give it to her. You have to compete with the hypersexualized information she is getting because her feelings of self-worth and enjoyment as a sexual person are bound up with this very important aspect of her life.

What has become clear to us while doing this research is that what a girl is sold when she is younger comes back to affect her as a teen, and that the cute, sexy, boy-crazy shopper image in everything from Bratz dolls to board games, from beginning readers to cheerleading, will emerge in the "free choice" of teen girls to become a daring *Sex and the City* girl. You can believe that those Aldo shoes are in the My Scene Barbie Shopping Spree game set *because* marketers are counting on girls "freely" choosing Aldo shoes when they're old enough to wear them. Will it work? Sometimes. Is it more likely to work than not if the "girls love shopping" image is reinforced through other activities? Absolutely.

The identity that a girl seems to choose freely as a teen is the identity she practiced throughout her childhood. Any physics teacher will tell you that the best students are those who have had past experiences with toys that taught them motion, velocity, and trajectory. Those who put their minds to it can learn physics, but some will feel that physics is natural, something they are just good at. Those are the kids who have had lots of fun experiences with what is most elemental to physics. The same goes for "natural" tendencies to be good at decorating, shopping, or nurturing. While all children should be encouraged to pretend and engage in fantasy, we need to remember that such play is the stuff of identity.

While you can't keep your daughter away from all marketers reaching out to possess her or the media influences that rehash and resell stereotypes as she watches, listens, and reads, narrowing her choices for development whenever she tries to conform, you can help her observe this world and criticize it. If you're the parent of a teenager, you're getting used to your daughter's critical edge. We're asking you to celebrate it and put it to good use to help her see the difference between a marketer's dream image and reality. If you're a parent of a younger girl, all our conversations that teach her to be a bit more critical may make you sad. It may feel as if by teaching her to have a critical eye when seeing this junk, she will lose her sense of innocence, wonder, and appreciation. Remember that you are not the one taking it away from her. It's the media. It's the marketers. Their purposeful manipulation of your daughter leaves you no choice but to teach her to distance herself and take a critical look—and dare we say a moral look?—as early as possible.

There can still be wonder. As she develops her critical sense, you can wonder at her intelligence and her skills of observation. As she grows into a young woman with interests, opinions, and talents, you can wonder at the infinite resources and abilities she has found within. And when you and she direct your gaze outwards at the world of nature and even the world of material things, you can still wonder at the possibilities. Surely you and your daughter can appreciate the Mars landing for the science and the accomplishment once you've pushed past the literature and media photos showing boys and their fathers looking through telescopes. And surely you can wonder and appreciate the symphony after noting how few girls seem to play the trombone. The point isn't to make your daughter skeptical about the world, but about the people who are presenting a narrow view of it to her and thereby limiting her opportunities.

The bottom line is that you are the arbiter, the middleman or -woman between the media and your daughter. We urge you to take this position seriously. When you and your daughter have developed a relationship in which you both can reflect on the world around her, you've given her a voice she can internalize when she's out there in the world alone, a critical and reflective voice. Turning off the world is not the answer. Giving her the means to reflect on it and your company when doing so is.

Notes

INTRODUCTION

page 4 When Susan Linn: Linn, 2004, pp. 11–40.

1: PRETTY IN PINK: WHAT GIRLS WEAR

page 14 She writes that girls need to feel their bodies: Young, 1979, p. 152.
page 17 Proctor & Gamble set up a sweepstakes with Limited Too: AdAge.com, April 28, 2005.
page 26 On the other hand, manufacturers are buying: Bell, 2005.

2: SEE NO EVIL? WHAT GIRLS WATCH

page 58 . . . according to Children Now: www.mediawatch.com/word press, October 9, 2004, "Television Statistics."
page 65 Larson concluded that there are a "wealth of models": Larson, 2003, pp. 73–74.
page 71 So big, claimed Ann Globe, head of marketing: Schiller, 2004.
page 72 In fact, the inventors of Dora: Anderson, 2006.
page 73 More than one-fourth of the videos: www.mediawatch.com/word press, October 9, 2004, "Television Statistics."
page 75 Studies tell us that children who watch a great amount of TV: Ward and Harrison, 2005, p. 5.
page 75 It's also not surprising that a study of the cartoon action show Pokémon: Ogletree, et al., 2004, pp. 857–58.
page 76 Psychologist Norma Feshbach thinks so: Feshbach, 2005, p. 161.
page 80 Only 8 percent portrayed female scientists: Fort and Varney, 1989.
page 80 Of the 117 fifth graders: Barman, et al., 1997.
page 81 . . . fewer than one fourth of the scientists in the United States: National Science Foundation, 1999.
page 81 According to a more recent study, science fields: Lupart, Cannon, and Telfer, 2004. See also, Watson, Quatman, and Edler, 2002.
page 92 Children Now reports that 71 percent of lawyers: Children Now, 2003–2004, p. 10.
page 93 When a program has at least one woman writer: Lauzen, 2001.
page 95 "Stoned butterflies": Devine, 2005.
page 98 When 90210 ended its long run: Justin, 2002.
page 100 Women of color fare badly in these shows: Brown, 2005, p. 80.
page 107 Among the top twenty most watched shows by teens: Kaiser Family Foundation, "Sex on TV #4," 2005, p. 4.
page 107 By the way, a recent report to Congress: Connolly, 2004.
page 114 Parents who watch and listen to media with their daughters: Donnerstein and Smith, 2001, p. 298; Singer and Singer, 1986; Bryant and Rockwell, 1994.
page 115 She'll need to talk with you: Brown, Halpern, and L'Engle, 2005.

3: DO YOU HEAR WHAT I HEAR? WHAT GIRLS LISTEN TO

page 118 Anthropologist Mimi Nichter defines the "I'm so fat" language: Nichter, 2000, p. 4.
page 147 Amy Lee of Evanescence, began writing her songs: Moss, 2004.
page 148 "Swept away," as Carol Cassell wrote: Cassell, 1989.

5: WANNA PLAY? WHAT GIRLS DO

page 228 Colette Dowling, author of The Frailty Myth: Dowling, 2000; pp. 76–83 has a summary of this research. Or see the Women's Sports Foundation Web site, www.womenssportsfoundation.org.

page 229 Young girls are twice as likely to be sedentary: U.S. Surgeon General's Report on Physical Activity and Health, 1996.

page 229 Even when journalists such as Cathy Booth Thomas: Thomas, 2005, p. 59.

page 234 Between middle school and high school, girls experience: U.S. Secretary of Health and Human Services and U.S. Secretary of Education, 2000.

page 234 One study of girls ages ten through nineteen: Kimm, et al., 2002.

page 235 Research suggests that girls' attrition in sports: Shakib, 2003.

page 238 In one study, 96 percent of eight- and nine-year-olds said: Pickering and Repacholi, 2001.

page 238 In another study of kindergarteners to fifth graders: Abeles and Porter, 1978.

page 238 In still another, 77 percent of eight- and nine-year-old girls preferred "feminine" instruments: Harrison, 2003.

page 238 In one study where girls and boys heard an orchestra: Bruce and Kemp, 1993.

page 239 research shows that girls do play some games: Greenspan, 2003.

page 241 According to a UCLA study: Kafai, 1998.

page 242 A Pew Survey shows that only: Lenhart, Madden, and Hitlin, 2005.

page 242 Roberta Furger, author of Does Jane Compute?, *found in her research:* Furger, 1998.

page 242 Roberta Furger talked to the executives: Furger, 1998.

page 243 In 1994, the Wall Street Journal published an article: Pereira, 1994.

page 245 For the 2003 holiday season alone: Linn, 2004, p. 8.

page 248 It may not be great for her: Weintraub, 2001.

page 254 While many parents are worried that their child: Kornblum, 2005.

page 256 Twenty-something Vini Nair, co-creator of Platform Shoes: Nair, 2006.

page 259 In one article on metroactive.com: Lanzendorfer, 2002.

page 260 Gail Dines argues that this is not necessarily so: Dines, November 4, 2005, "Personal Communication."

page 260 Ariel Levy, author of Female Chauvinist Pigs: Levy, 2005, p. 31.

page 261 But the girls we spoke to admitted (and a recent survey confirmed): National Survey of Family Growth, Centers for Disease Control of Prevention, 2002, p. 15.

page 261 Remember, parents, that although this may seem like an epidemic: National Survey of Family Growth, Centers for Disease Control of Prevention, 2002.

page 262 Then there are "friends with benefits": Denizet-Lewis, 2004.

page 262 "To do is to be": Vonnegut, 1982.

6: REBEL, RESIST, REFUSE: SAMPLE CONVERSATIONS WITH OUR DAUGHTERS

page 293 While all children should be encouraged to pretend and engage in fantasy: See Penuel and Wertsch, 1995, and Tappan, 2005, for a more detailed discussion of how material life and social experiences impact identity formation.

Bibliography

Abeles, H. F., and Porter, S. Y. 1978. "The Sex-Stereotyping of Musical Instruments." *Journal of Research in Music Education* 26:65–75.

American Association of University Women. 1992. *How Schools Shortchange Girls.* Washington, D.C.: AAUW Educational Foundation.

———. 1998. *Gender Gaps: Where Schools Still Fail Our Children.* Washington, D.C.: AAUW Educational Foundation.

Anderson, D. 2006 "Does Watching TV Make Children Stupid?" Talk given at St. Michael's College, Colchester, VT, April 3.

Barman, C. R., et al. 1997. "Fifth Grade Students' Perceptions About Scientists and How They Study and Use Science." Paper presented at the Annual International Conference of the Association for the Education of Teachers in Science, Cincinnati, Ohio.

Barth, L. July 2004. "I Survived Crystal Meth." YM, 94–97.

Bartky, S. 1990. *Femininity and Domination.* New York: Routledge.

Bell, R. August 15, 2005. "It's Porn, Innit?" *The Guardian.*

Bordo, S. 2004. *Unbearable Weight: Feminism, Western Culture, and the Body.* Berkeley: University of California Press.

Brown, J., Halpern, C., and L'Engle, K. 2005. "Mass Media as a Sexual Super Peer for Early Maturing Girls." *Journal of Adolescent Health* 36 (5):420–27.

Brown, L. 2005. Outwit, Outlast, Out-flirt? The Women of Reality TV." In E. Cole and J. Henderson Daniel, eds., *Featuring Females: Feminist Analysis of Media.* Washington, D.C.: American Psychological Association, pp. 71–83.

Brown, L. M. 2003. *Girlfighting: Betrayal and Rejection Among Girls.* New York: New York University Press.

Brown, L. M., and Gilligan, C. 1992. *Meeting at the Crossroads: Women's Psychology and Girls' Development.* Cambridge, Mass.: Harvard University Press.

Bruce, R., and Kemp, A. 1993. "Sex-Stereotyping in Children's Preferences for Musical Instruments." *British Journal of Music Education* 10:213–17.

Bryant, J., and Rockwell, S. 1994. "Effects of Massive Exposure to Sexually Oriented Prime-Time Television on Adolescents' Moral Judgment." In D. Zillmann, J. Bryant, & A. Huston, eds., *Media, Children, and the Family.* Hillsdale, N.J.: Lawrence.

Cassell, C. 1984. *Swept Away: Why Women Confuse Love and Sex.* New York: Simon & Schuster.

Children Now. 2005. Fall Colors: 2003–2004 "Prime-Time Diversity Report."

Cole, E., and Henderson Daniel, J., eds., 2005. *Featuring Females: Feminist Analyses of Media.* Washington D.C.: American Psychological Association.

Connolly, C. December 2, 2004. "Some Abstinence Programs Mislead Teens, Report Says." *Washington Post.*

Denizet-Lewis, B. May 30, 2004. "Friends, Friends with Benefits, and the Benefits of the Local Mall." *New York Times Magazine.*

Devine. J. P. November 19, 2005. "Latest 'Harry Potter' Film Offers Fast-Moving Study in Dark Glory." *Waterville Morning Sentinel.*

Dines, G., and Humez, J., eds. 2003. *Gender, Race, and Class in Media.* Thousand Oaks, Calif.: Sage.

Donnerstein, E., and Smith, S. 2001. "Sex in the Media: Theory, Influences, and Solutions." In D.G. Singer and J.L. Singer, eds., *Handbook of Children and the Media,* pp. 289–307. Thousand Oaks, Calif.: Sage.

Dowling, C. 2000. *The Frailty Myth: Women Approaching Physical Equality.* New York: Random House.

Fagot, B. 1985. "Beyond the Reinforcement Principle: Another Step Toward Understanding Sex Role Development." *Developmental Psychology* 21:1097–1104.

Feshbach, N. 2005. "Gender and the Portrayal of Direct and Indirect Aggression on Television." In E. Cole and J. Henderson Daniel, eds., *Featuring Females: Feminist Analyses of Media* Washington, D.C.: American Psychological Association, pp. 155–65.

Fort, D., and Varney, H. 1989. "How Students See Scientists: Mostly Male, Mostly White, and Mostly Benevolent." *Science and Children* 26(8): 8–13.

Furger, R. 1998. *Does Jane Compute? Preserving Our Daughters' Place in the Cyber Revolution.* New York: Warner Books.

Greenspan, R. 2003. Girl Gamers Go Online. Internetnews.com. www.internetnews.com/stats/article.php/2232941. Accessed on January 11, 2006.

Harrison, A. C., and O'Neil, S. A. 2003. "Preferences and Children's Use of Gender-Stereotyped Knowledge About Musical Instruments: Making Judgments About Other Children's Preferences." *Sex Roles,* 49:389–400.

Johnson, S. 2005. *Everything Bad Is Good for You: How Today's Popular Culture Is Actually Making Us Smarter.* New York: Riverhead Books.

Justin, N. September 12, 2002. "Industry Offers Zip to '90210' Stars." Minneapolis–St. Paul *Star Tribune,* B6.

Kafai, Y. 1998. *From Barbie to Mortal Kombat: Gender and Computer Games.* Cambridge, Mass.: MIT Press.

Kaiser Family Foundation. November 9, 2005. "Sex on TV 4," (no. 7399).

Kilbourne, J. 2000. *Can't Buy My Love: How Advertising Changes the Way We Think and Feel.* New York: Free Press.

Kimm, S., et al. 2000. "Longitudinal Changes in Physical Activity in a Biracial Cohort During Adolescence." *Medicine & Science in Sports & Exercise* 32(8):1445–54.

Kimm, S., et al. 2002. "Decline in Physical Activity in Black Girls and White Girls During Adolescence. *New England Journal of Medicine* 347:709–15.

Kornblum, J. January 8, 2005. "Adults Question MySpace's Safety." *USA Today.* www.usatoday.com/tech/news/2006-01-08-myspace-sidebar_x.htm. Accessed on January 12, 2005.

Lamb, S. 2001. *The Secret Lives of Girls: What Girls Really Do—Sex Play, Aggression, and Their Guilt.* New York: Free Press.

Lanzendorfer, J. October 17–23, 2002. "It's 10 p.m. Do You Know?" www.metroactive.com/papers/sonoma/10.17.02/sex-0242.html.

Larson, M. S. 2003. "Gender, Race, and Aggression in Television Commercials That Feature Children," *Sex Roles,* 48:67–75.

Lauzen, M. 2001. "The Celluloid Ceiling: Behind-the-Scenes Employment of Women in the Top 250 Films of 2001." School of Communication, San Diego State University, San Diego, Calif.

Lenhart, A., Madden, M., and Hitlin, P. 2005. Pew/Internet, Teens and Technology. See Pew/Internet Web site for report: www.pewinternet.org/PPF/r/162/report_display.asp.

Levy, A. 2006. *Female Chauvinist Pigs: Women and the Rise of Raunch Culture.* New York: Free Press.

Linn, S. 2004. *Consuming Kids: The Hostile Takeover of Childhood.* New York: The New Press.

Lupart, J. Cannon, E., and Telfer, J. 2004. "SCIberMENTOR: Quantitative and Qualitative Mentee Research Results." Calgary, AB: University of Calgary.

Lynch, D. 2001. "Love and Boredom: Online, Teenagers Delve in Risqué Areas." abcnew.go.com/sections/scitech/Wired Women/wiredwomen010711.html. Accessed June 24, 2004.

Mosher, W., Chandra, A., and Jones, J. 2005. *Sexual Behavior and Selected Health Measures: Men and Women 15–44 Years of Age, United States, 2002.* Advance Data from Vital and Health Statistics; no. 362. Hyattsville, Md.: National Center for Health Statistics.

Moss, C. June 10, 2004. "Evanescence's Amy Lee Hopes to Get into Film, Rages Against Cheesy Female Idols." MTV News, MTV.com.

MSNTV 2004. Scarborough Country for May 25. www.msnbc.msn.com/id/5067191/.

Nair, V. April 8, 2006. *Personal Communication.*

National Science Foundation. 1999. *Women, Minorities, and Persons with Disabilities in Science and Engineering: 1998.* Arlington, Va. (NSF 99-338).

Nichter, M. 2000. *Fat Talk: What Girls and Parents Say About Dieting.* Cambridge, Mass.: Harvard University Press.

Odean, K. 1997. *Great books for Girls.* New York: Ballantine.

Ogletree, S. M., et al. 2004. "Pokémon: Exploring the Role of Gender." *Sex Roles* 50:851–59.

Penuel, W., and Wertsch, J. 1995. "Vygotsky and Identity Formation: A Sociocultural Approach." *Educational Psychologist* 30:83–92.

Pereira, J. March 16, 1994. "Computers: The Gender Divide: A Tool for Women, A Toy for Men: Video Games Help Boys Get a Head Start." *Wall Street Journal,* B1.

Pickering, S., and Repacholi, B. 2001. "Modifying Children's Gender-Typed Musical Instrument Preferences: The Effects of Gender and Age." *Sex Roles*, 45 (9/10): 623–43.

Phillips, L. 2000. *Flirting with Danger: Young Women's Reflections on Sexuality and Domination.* New York: New York University Press.

Quart, A. 2003. *Branded: The Buying and Selling of Teenagers.* Cambridge, Mass.: Perseus.

Sadker, M., and Sadker, D. 1994. *Failing at Fairness: How America's Schools Cheat Girls.* New York: Charles Scribner's Sons.

Schiller, G. May 19, 2004. "Shrek 2" to Swamp Retailers. *The Hollywood Reporter.* www.hollywoodreporter.com/thr/marketing/article_display.jsp?vnu_content_id=1000513274.

Schor, J. 2004. *Born to Buy: The Commercialized Child and the New Consumer Culture.* New York: Charles Scribner's Sons.

Tanenbaum, L. 2000. *Slut! Growing Up Female with a Bad Reputation.* New York: Perennial.

Tappan, M. 2005. "Domination, Subordination, and the Dialogical Self: Identity Development and the Politics of 'Ideological Becoming.'" *Culture and Psychology* 11(1):47–75.

Tolman, D. L., et al. 2006. "Looking Good, Sounding Good: Femininity Is Bad for Girls' Mental Health." Unpublished Manuscript.

U.S. Secretary of Health and Human Services and U.S. Secretary of Education. 2000. "Promoting Better Health for Young People Through Physical Activity and Sports: A Report to the President." Atlanta, Ga.: Centers for Disease Control and Prevention.

U.S. Surgeon General. 1996. "Physical Activity and Health, U.S. Surgeon General's Report." www.fitness.gov/adoles.html.

Vonnegut, K. 1982. *Deadeye Dick.* New York: Delta.

Vygotsky, L. S. 1978. *Mind in Society: The Development of Higher Psychological Processes,* ed. by M. Cole, V. John-Steiner, S. Scribner, and E. Souberman. Cambridge, Mass.: Harvard University Press.

Ward, L. M., and Harrison, K. 2005. "The Impact of Media Use on Girls' Beliefs about Gender Roles, Their Bodies, and Sexual Relationships: A Research Synthesis." In E. Cole and J. Henderson Daniel, eds., *Featuring Females: Feminist Analyses of Media.* Washington, D.C.: American Psychological Association, pp. 3–23.

Young, I. M. September 1979. "Is There a Woman's World? Some Reflections on the Struggle for Our Bodies." Lecture presented to The Second Sex—Thirty Years Later: A Commemorative Conference on Feminist Theory. New York Institute for the Humanities, New York University.

———. 1980. "Throwing Like a Girl: A Phenomenology of Feminine Body Comportment Motility and Spatiality." *Human Studies* 3:137–56.

Online Resources

Some are for girls, some for teens, and some for parents. Check them out first!

MEDIA LITERACY

www.media-awareness.ca
www.commonsensemedia.org
www.mediaandwomen.org
www.mediawatch.com
www.mediachannel.org
www.allianceforchildren.org
www.acmecoalition.org
www.childrennow.org/issues/media
www.911media.org
www.medialit.org
www.about-face.org
www.mindonthemedia.org
www.kff.org/entmedia/1260-gendr.cfm (Kaiser Family Foundation report)

ADVOCACY FOR GIRLS AND PARENTS AROUND COMMERCIALISM

www.commercialfreechildhood.org
www.pbskids.org/dontbuyit/
www.adaware.org
www.genderads.com
www.stayfreemagazine.org
www.phatgnat.com

GENERAL ONLINE COMMUNITIES AND RESOURCES FOR GIRLS AND THEIR PARENTS

www.hardygirlshealthywomen.org (Lyn's organization)
www.daughters.com
www.girlsallowed.org
www.girlscoalition.org
www.girlsinc.org
www.girlpower.gov/girlarea
www.newmoon.org
www.girlzone.com
www.smartgirl.com
www.blackgirlmagazine.com
www.agirlsworld.com
www.girlscouts.org
www.roshhodesh.org
www.sistagirls.org
www.withitgirl.com
www.dadsanddaughters.org

www.4girls.gov
www.latinitas.org
www.understandme.org
www.empowered.org
www.adiosbarbie.com
www.coloursofana.com
www.loveyourbody.nowfoundation.org
www.beaconstreetgirls.com
www.bidstrup.com/cool.htm (The Cool Place for Queer Teens)
www.allmadeup.net
www.smartgirl.org

SPECIFIC TO COMPUTERS, SCIENCE, AND MATHEMATICS

www.braincake.org
www.engineergirl.org
www.girlgeeks.org
www.mentornet.net
www.genderequity.org
www.womenswork.org
www.thinkquest.org
www.webgrrls.com
www.fragdolls.com (for girl gamers)
www.hhmi.org/dream (science and African American girls)
www.zoeysroom.com
www.coolcareersforgirls.com
www.binarygirl.com

SPECIFIC TO ATHLETICS

www.aahperd.org/nagws (National Association of Girls & Women in Sport)
www.girlsontherun.org
www.melpomene.org
www.womenssportsfoundation.org
www.gogirlgo.com
www.prettytough.com
www.caaws.ca/girlsatplay

SPECIFIC TO THE ARTS

www.nurturethroughnature.tripod.com
www.mediagirl.org
www.wmm.com/catalog/girlsproject.htm
www.guerillagirls.com
www.thattakesovaries.org
www.friendsoflulu.org
www.youngwomendrum.org
www.nawanet.org (National Association of Women Artists)
www.eamusic.dartmouth.edu/~wowem (Wow Em, electronic media, and the arts)
www.freshfilms.com
www.teenink.com
www.teenlit.com
www.indiegrrl.com
www.gogirlsmusic.com

www.positive.org
www.advocatesforyouth.org
www.goaskalice.columbia.edu
www.youthembassy.com
www.teenwire.com (Run by Planned Parenthood; info on sex, sexuality, and relationships)
www.coolnurse.com
www.wordscanwork.org

NEWS AND ACTIVISM

www.upcmkids.org (Eight to eighteen news bureau)
www.culturalenergy.org (World news with youth reporters)
www.pbs.org/merrow/listenup (Youth media network)
www.teenworldnews.com
www.pinchmefilms.org
www.scenariosusa.org (Kids creating social change)
www.mirrorproject.org (Social change and awareness)
www.eecom.net (Environment and youth)
www.girlspipeline.org
www.girlsforachange.org
www.girlsite.org
www.feminist.org
www.alternet.org/wiretapmag
www.girlsonthemove.org.uk
www.greatwomen.org
www.now.org
www.thirdwavefoundation.org
www.justiceforgirls.org
www.feministing.com
www.thewhitehouseproject.org
www.uswc.org (U.S. women connect to global issues)

BOOKS (MOST RECENT AND RELEVANT)

Consumer Culture and Marketing
Audrey Brashich, *All Made Up: A Girl's Guide to Seeing Through Celebrity Hype . . . And Celebrating Real Beauty*
Jean Kilbourne, *Can't Buy My Love*
Susan Linn, *Consuming Kids*
Alissa Quart, *Branded: The Buying and Selling of Teenagers*
Juliet B. Schor, *Born to Buy*

Girls
Lyn Mikel Brown, *Meeting at the Crossroads, Girlfighting, and Raising Their Voices*
Sharon Lamb, *Sex, Therapy and Kids* and *The Secret Lives of Girls*
Peggy Orenstein, *Schoolgirls*
Lynn Phillips, *Flirting with Danger*
Rivka Solomon, *That Takes Ovaries*
Deborah Tolman, *Dilemmas of Desire*
Janie Ward, *The Skin We're In*

Sexualization of Girls
Ariel Levy, *Female Chauvinist Pigs*
Diane Levin, "So Sexy So Soon," a chapter in *Childhood Lost*

And look for an upcoming report by the American Psychological Association, to be published in 2007 or 2008 by the Task Force on the Sexualization of Girls (www.apa.org)

Acknowlegments

We owe so much to the girls who let us into their world and shared their views and their enthusiasm for shops and books and movies and songs and artists and TV shows and more. Their opinions counted.

We also owe so much to colleagues, friends, family members, and students. The following students and girls we know did research, found examples, shared tales from their lives, and gave us advice along the way: Megan Williams, Ryan Woods, Emily Brostek, Anna Taupier, Emily Anstadt, Jennifer Kemp, Erin Cole, Vera Simon-Nobes, Jessica Torani, Rebecca Alpert, Sarah Koestner, Taina Lyons, Tristram Levine, and Ellen and Olivia Waxler. Our students at Saint Michael's College, Colby College, and Dartmouth College have presented papers over the years that have stimulated our thinking on cultural products, and they have answered crucial questions for us. They keep us informed and on our toes, and lend practical help when we ask. Larry Blum helped us identify great movies. Thanks to Alison Remillard and Jared Jewett for their gift of music. And thanks to Denise Brault who was especially helpful as well as the wonderful staff at Saint Michael's College library for their expert assistance with all things large and small.

We are very grateful to GirlZone.com, M. J. Real, Edith the webmaster, and Shari Levine who helped us create a survey to gather information from more than six hundred girls. We hope parents will turn to Shari's column on the GirlZone Web site for the excellent advice she gives to girls. Anastasia Goodstein's blog, called YPulse, kept us abreast of new media and marketing changes as soon as they arose. And occasionally the blog Adrants sent us to a wonderful example.

The academic work that has led us to our research has been amazing. Personally, we've been deeply influenced by former teachers. For thirty years Rachel Hare-Mustin has been writing and teaching young women how to look at the world systemically. She sees behind surfaces, labels inequalities presented as equalities, and contextualizes everything that seems at first to be an individual attribute. Twenty-five years ago Carol

Gilligan taught us to listen to girls' voices and how to follow the complicated psychological, social, and political pathways. Our friends and colleagues Jeanne Marecek, Deborah Tolman, Michael Kimmel, Bill Pollack, Lynn Phillips, Jessica Henderson Daniel, and Peggy Orenstein influence our work. And the insights of comrades Susan Linn, Juliet Schor, Alexa Quart, Ariel Levy, Sut Jhally, Jackson Katz, Polly Young Eisendrath, Tomi-Ann Roberts, Monique Ward, Rebecca Collins, Eileen Zurbriggen, Janet Hyde, Gwen Keita, Leslie Cameron, and Joe Kelly—all of whom have taken up the cause of marketing to kids—have inspired us. We owe a lot to Jean Kilbourne, who began this kind of cultural analysis with her look at advertising and bodies, and who continues to inspire our students through her documentary films. Gail Dines and Diane Levin have extended and deepened the analysis of gender, race, and class in the media's sexualized representations of girls and women. We thank them for their important research.

Many guidance counselors, parents, librarians, and teachers offered their insights, completed surveys, and helped us find girls to talk to and complete our surveys. Thank you to Penny Linn, Hannah Osborne, Angela Frame, Cindy Woodard, Amy Hornblas, Martha Olbrych, Mary Beiter, Lisa Ericson, Karen Thompson, Ru Freeman, and Michele Polacsek. Elise Whittemore-Hill read the entire manuscript and gave us incredibly insightful comments. We are indebted to her in particular for her suggestions for Chapter 5 on the arts. Doris Orgel and Laura Orgel also read chapters and gave excellent advice. Thanks also to the wonderful girls and women at Hardy Girls/Healthy Women for their support, and especially Jackie Dupont for her help with our resource section.

Our agent, Carol Mann, was persistent, upbeat, and encouraging throughout the lengthy process of looking for a publisher. She eventually found us the perfect editor, Sheila Oakes, mother of a four-year-old girl, who sensed how important this issue was and helped us envision the book differently. Carol's warm presence and Sheila's enthusiasm carried us through the many months of writing, rewriting, and editing.

Lyn thanks her partner, Mark Tappan, for his love and support, and her daughter, Maya, for her keen eyes and ears. She also thanks her friends Betty Sasaki, Sarah Willie, and Connie Coleman for listening and offering some wonderful examples. Sharon thanks her husband, Paul, for his support; her son, Julian, for pointing out moments on TV or in the movies that his so-called superfeminist mom might want to analyze and for leading her through MySpace; and her older son, Willy, for reading

sections and providing a stream of teenage girls to the house for questioning. Sharon's friends Sarah Sappington, Kate Schenck, Bev Colston,
Janet Marcus, and Diane Anstadt are always a huge support.

Finally, we are delighted to have worked with each other—for the
company along the journey, the chats and the arguments, the encouragement in the low phases, and the moments of inspiration and solidarity
while writing. We developed a trust while rewriting each other's sections
so that now we can hardly recall who first said what and tend to attribute
the best points to the other. Together we both thank Anne Lamott for
keeping us writing "bird by bird." When you love your work, love to write,
love to think through these issues, what could be better than to have a
friend to do it with you.

Index

About the Authors

Sharon Lamb is professor of psychology at Saint Michael's College in Vermont and the author of four books, including *The Secret Lives of Girls*. Her research on girls' development, teenagers and sex, and abuse and victimization is widely cited. As a clinical psychologist, she often works with girls, listening to their struggles and hearing their strengths, in her private practice in Shelburne, Vermont.

Lyn Mikel Brown, professor of education and human development at Colby College in Maine, is the author of three books on girls' development, including *Meeting at the Crossroads: Women's Psychology and Girls' Development* (with Carol Gilligan). She creates programs for girls at her nonprofit organization, Hardy Girls Healthy Women (www.hardygirls healthywomen.org).